Design Your Future

An Inspiring Major and Extraordinary Career

ASU: Major and Career Exploration

Customized version of
**College and Career Success,
Sixth Edition** by Marsha Fralick

Kendall Hunt
publishing company

Cover image © ASU

Kendall Hunt
publishing company

www.kendallhunt.com
Send all inquiries to:
4050 Westmark Drive
Dubuque, IA 52004-1840

Copyright © 2015 by ASU: Major and Career Exploration

ISBN 978-1-4652-8100-5

Printed in the United States of America

CONTENTS

PART I

College Success

CHAPTER 1

Understanding Motivation

Learning Objectives

Read to answer these key questions:

- What do I want from college?

- What is the value of a college education?

- How do I choose my major and career?

- How can I motivate myself to be successful?

- How can I begin habits that lead to success?

- How can I be persistent in achieving my goal of a college education?

Most students attend college with dreams of making their lives better. Some students are there to explore interests and possibilities, and others have more defined career goals. Being successful in college and attaining your dreams begin with motivation. It provides the energy or drive to find your direction and to reach your goals. Without motivation, it is difficult to accomplish anything.

Not everyone is successful in college. Unfortunately, about one-third of college students drop out in the first year. Forty percent of students who start college do not finish their degrees. Having a good understanding of your gifts and talents, reasons for attending college, career goals, and how to motivate yourself will help you to reach your dreams.

What Do I Want from College?

Succeeding in college requires time and effort. You will have to give up some of your time spent on leisure activities and working. You will give up some time spent with your friends and families. Making sacrifices and working hard are easier if you know what you want to achieve through your efforts. One of the first steps in motivating yourself to be successful in college is to have a clear and specific understanding of your reasons for attending college. Are you attending college as a way to obtain a satisfying career? Is financial security one of your goals? Will you feel more satisfied if you are living up to your potential? What are your hopes and dreams, and how will college help you to achieve your goals?

When you are having difficulties or doubts about your ability to finish your college education, remember your hopes and dreams and your plans for the future. It is a good idea to write these ideas down, think about them, and revise them from time to time.

What Is the Value of a College Education?

Many college students say that getting a satisfying job that pays well and achieving financial security are important reasons for attending college. By going to college you can get a job that pays more per hour. You can work fewer hours to earn a living and have more time for leisure activities. You can spend your time at work doing something that you like to do. A report issued by the Census Bureau in 2012 listed the following education and income statistics for all races and both genders throughout the United States.[1] Lifetime income assumes that a person works thirty years before retirement.

Average Earnings Based on Education Level

Education	Yearly Income	Lifetime Income
High school graduate	$33,904	$1,017,120
Some college, no degree	$37,804	$1,134,120
Associate degree	$40,820	$1,224,600
Bachelor's degree	$55,432	$1,662,960
Master's degree	$67,600	$2,028,000
Professional degree	$90,220	$2,706,600

Notice that income rises with educational level. Over a lifetime, a person with a bachelor's degree earns 66% more than a high school graduate. Of course these are average figures across the nation and some individuals earn higher or lower salaries. People fantasize about winning the lottery. The reality is that the probability of winning the lottery is very low. In the long run, you have a better chance of improving your financial status by going to college.

© 2014, sergign. Used under license with Shutterstock, Inc.

Let's do some further comparisons. A high school graduate earns an average of $1,017,120 over a lifetime. A college graduate with a bachelor's degree earns $1,662,960 over a lifetime. A college graduate earns $645,840 more than a high school graduate does over a lifetime. So how much is a college degree worth? It is worth $645,840 over a lifetime. Would you go to college if someone offered to pay you $645,840? Here are some more interesting figures we can derive from the above table:

Completing one college course is worth $16,146.
($645,840 divided by 40 courses in a bachelor's degree)

Going to class for one hour is worth $336.
($16,146 divided by 48 hours in a semester class)

Would you take a college class if someone offered to pay you $16,146? Would you go to class today for one hour if someone offered to pay you $336? Of course, if this sounds too good to be true, remember that you will receive these "payments" over a working lifetime of thirty years.

While college graduation does not guarantee employment, it increases your chances of finding a job. In 2012, high school graduates had an unemployment rate of 12.4% as compared to college graduates who had an unemployment rate of 4.5%.[2] Increase your chances of employment by continuing your education.

Employment and earning are only some of the values of going to college. Can you think of other reasons to attend college? Here are some less tangible reasons.

- College helps you to develop your potential.
- College opens the door to many satisfying careers.
- College prepares you to be an informed citizen and fully participate in the democratic process.
- College increases your understanding and widens your view of the world.
- College allows you to participate in a conversation with the great minds of all times and places. For example, reading the work of Plato is like having a conversation with that famous philosopher. You can continue great conversations with your faculty and fellow students.
- College helps to increase your confidence, self-esteem, and self-respect.

© 2014, iQoncept. Used under license with Shutterstock, Inc.

Choosing a Major and Career

Having a definite major and career choice is a good motivation for completing your college education. It is difficult to put in the work necessary to be successful if you do not have a clear picture of your future career; however, three out of four college students are undecided about their major. For students who have chosen a major, 30 to 75 percent of a graduating class will change that major two or more times.[3] Unclear or indefinite career goals are some of the most significant factors that identify students at risk of dropping out of college.[4] Students often drop out or extend their stay in college because they are uncertain about their major or want to change their major. Choosing an appropriate college major is one of the most difficult and important decisions that college students can make.

How can you choose the major that is best for you? The best way is to first understand yourself: become aware of your personality traits, learning style, interests, preferred lifestyle, values, gifts, and talents. The next step is to do career research to determine the career that best matches your personal characteristics. Then, plan your education to prepare for your career. Here are some questions to answer to help you understand yourself and what career and major would be best for you.

To learn about yourself, explore these areas:

- **What is my personality type?** Assessing your personality type will help you to become more aware of your individual gifts and talents and some careers that will give you satisfaction.
- **What is my learning style?** Being aware of your learning style will help you identify learning strategies that work best for you and increase your productivity in college, on the job, and in your personal life.
- **What are my aptitudes?** Focus on your strengths by identifying your multiple intelligences.
- **What are my interests?** Knowing about your interests is important in choosing a satisfying career.
- **What kind of lifestyle do I prefer?** Think about how you want to balance work, leisure, and family.
- **What are my values?** Knowing what you value (what is most important to you) will help you make good decisions about your life.

To learn about career possibilities, research the following:

- **What careers match my personality, learning style, aptitudes, interests, lifestyle, and values?** Learn how to do career research to find the best career for you. Find a career that has a good outlook for the future.
- **How can I plan my education to get the career I want?** Once you have identified a career that matches your personal strengths and interests, consult your college catalog or advisor to make an educational plan that matches your career goals.

By following the above steps, you can find the major that is best for you and minimize the time you spend in college.

How to Be Motivated

There are many ways to be motivated.

> "The purpose of our lives is to give birth to the best which is within us."
> Marianne Williamson

- You can **think positively about the future** and take the steps necessary to accomplish your goals.
- You can begin your studies by **looking for what is interesting** to you.
- You can **improve your concentration** and motivation for studying by managing your external and internal distractions.
- You can be motivated by internal or external factors called **intrinsic or extrinsic motivation.**
- You can become aware of your **locus of control,** or where you place the responsibility for control over your life. If you are in control, you are more likely to be motivated to succeed.
- You can join a club, organization, or athletic team. **Affiliation motivation** involves taking part in school activities that increase your motivation to stay in college.
- **Achievement** and competition are motivating to some students.
- You can **use rewards** as a motivation to establish desirable behaviors.

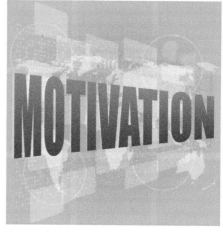

© 2014, fotoscool. Used under license with Shutterstock, Inc.

Let's examine each type of motivation in more detail and see if some of these ideas can be useful to you.

Thinking Positively about the Future

You can motivate yourself to complete your education by thinking positively about the future. If you believe that your chances of graduating from college are good, you can be motivated to take the steps necessary to achieve your goals. Conversely, if you think that your chances of graduating are poor, it is difficult to motivate yourself to continue. The degree of optimism that you possess is greatly influenced by past experiences. For example, if you were a good student in the past, you are likely to be optimistic about the future. If you struggled with your education, you may have some negative experiences that you will need to overcome. Negative thoughts can often become a self-fulfilling prophecy: what we think becomes true.

How can you train yourself to think more optimistically? First, become aware of your thought patterns. Are they mostly negative or positive? If they are negative, rewind the tape and make them more positive. Here is an example.

Pessimism

I failed the test. I guess I am just not college material. I feel really stupid. I just can't do this. College is too hard for me. My (teacher, father, mother, friend, boss) told me I would never make it. Maybe I should just drop out of college and do something else.

Optimism

I failed the test. Let's take a look at what went wrong, so I can do better next time. Did I study enough? Did I study the right material? Maybe I should take this a little slower. How can I get help so that I can understand? I plan to do better next time.

© 2014, kentoh. Used under license with Shutterstock, Inc.

Can a person be too optimistic? In some circumstances, this is true. There is a difference between optimism and wishful thinking, for example. Wishful thinking does not include plans for accomplishing goals and can be a distraction from achieving them. Working toward unattainable goals can be exhausting and demoralizing, especially when the resources for attaining them are lacking. Goals must be realistic and achievable. Psychologists recommend that "people should be optimistic when the future can be changed by positive thinking, but not otherwise."[4] Using optimism requires some judgment about possible outcomes in the future.

There are some good reasons to think more positively. Psychologists have done long-term studies showing that people who use positive thinking have many benefits over a lifetime, including good health, longevity, happiness, perseverance, improved problem solving, and enhanced ability to learn. Optimism is also related to goal achievement. If you are optimistic and believe a goal is achievable, you are more likely to take the steps necessary to accomplish the goal. If you do not believe that a goal is achievable, you are likely to give up trying to achieve it. Being optimistic is closely related to being hopeful about the future. If you are hopeful about the future, you are likely to be more determined to reach your goals and to make plans for reaching them. Be optimistic about graduating from college, find the resources necessary to accomplish your goal, and start taking the steps to create your success.

ACTIVITY

Are you generally an optimist or pessimist about the future? Read the following items and rate your level of agreement or disagreement:

Rate the following items using this scale:

5   I definitely agree
4   I agree
3   I neither agree or disagree (neutral)
2   I disagree
1   I strongly disagree

_____   My chances of graduating from college are good.

_____   I am confident that I can overcome any obstacles to my success.

_____   Things generally turn out well for me.

_____   I believe that positive results will eventually come from most problem situations.

_____   If I work hard enough, I will eventually achieve my goals.

_____   Although I have faced some problems in the past, the future will be better.

_____   I expect that most things will go as planned.

_____   Good things will happen to me in the future.

_____   I am generally persistent in reaching my goals.

_____   I am good at finding solutions to the problems I face in life.

Add up your total points and multiply by two. My total points (× 2) are _____.

90–100	You are an excellent positive thinker.
80–89	You are a good positive thinker.
70–79	Sometimes you think positively, and sometimes not. Can you re-evaluate your thinking?
60 and below	Work on positive thinking.

Journal Entry #3

Write five positive statements about your college education and your future.

Find Something Interesting in Your Studies

If you can think positively about what you are studying, it makes the job easier and more satisfying. Begin your studies by finding something interesting in the course and your textbook. Contrast these two ideas:

I have to take economics. It is going to be difficult and boring. What do I need economics for anyway? I'll just need to get through it so I can get my degree.

I have to take economics. I wonder about the course content. I often hear about it on the news. How can I use this information in my future? What can I find that is interesting?

> "No pessimist ever discovered the secrets of the stars, or sailed to an uncharted land, or opened a new doorway for the human spirit."
> Helen Keller

Make sure to attend the first class meeting. Remember that the professor is very knowledgeable about the subject and finds the content interesting and exciting. At the first class meeting, the professor will give you an overview of the course and should provide some motivation for studying the material in the course. Look at the course syllabus to find what the course is about and to begin to look for something that could be interesting or useful to you.

Skimming a textbook before you begin a course is a good way to find something interesting and to prepare for learning. Skimming will give you an organized preview of what's ahead. Here are the steps to skimming a new text:

1. **Quickly read the preface or introduction.** Read as if you were having a conversation with the author of the text. In the preface or introduction, you will find out how the author has organized the material, the key ideas, and his or her purpose in writing the text.

2. **Look at the major topics in the table of contents.** You can use the table of contents as a window into the book. It gives a quick outline of every topic in the text. As you read the table of contents, look for topics of special interest to you.

3. **Spend five to 15 minutes quickly looking over the book.** Turn the pages quickly, noticing boldfaced topics, pictures, and anything else that catches your attention. Again, look for important or interesting topics. Do not spend too much time on this step. If your textbook is online, skim through the website.

4. **What resources are included?** Is there an index, glossary of terms, answers to quiz questions, or solutions to math problems? These sections will be of use to you as you read. If your book is online, explore the website to find useful features and content.

Skimming a text or website before you begin to read has several important benefits. The first benefit is that it gets you started in the learning process. It is an easy and quick step that can help you avoid procrastination. It increases motivation by helping you notice items that have appeal to you. Previewing the content will help you to relax as you study and remember the information. Early in the course, this step will help you verify that you have chosen the correct course and that you have the prerequisites to be successful in the class.

Improving Your Concentration

Have you ever watched lion tamers concentrate? If their attention wanders, they are likely to become the lion's dinner. Skilled athletes, musicians, and artists don't have any trouble concentrating. They are motivated to concentrate. Think about a time when you were totally focused on what you were doing. You were motivated to continue. You can improve your concentration and motivation for studying by managing your external and internal distractions.

Manage your external environment. Your environment will either help you to study or distract you from studying. We are all creatures of habit. If you try to study in front of the TV, you will watch TV because that is what you are accustomed to doing in front of the TV. If you study in bed, you will fall asleep because your body associates the bed with sleeping. If you study in the kitchen, you will eat. Find an environment that minimizes distractions. One idea is to study in the library. In the library, there are many cues that tell you to study. There are books and learning resources and other people studying. It will be easier to concentrate in that environment. You may be able to set up a learning environment in your home. Find a place where you can place a desk or table, your computer, and your materials for learning. When you are in this place, use it for learning and studying only.

Increase your concentration and motivation as well as your retention by varying the places where you study and the content of what you are studying. Study at home, in the

> "A pessimist sees the difficulty in every opportunity; an optimist sees the opportunity in every difficulty."
> Winston Churchill

Managing Internal Distractions

1. Be here now
2. Spider technique
3. Worry time
4. Checkmark technique
5. Increase activity
6. Find an incentive
7. Change topics

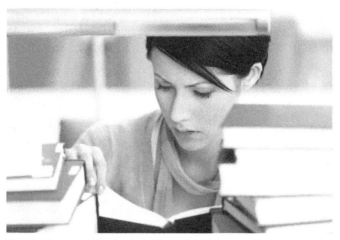

© 2014, Karramba Production. Used under license with Shutterstock, Inc.

library, outside, in a coffee shop or any place where you can focus your attention on your studies. You can also increase learning effectiveness by varying the content and subjects that you are studying. Athletes maintain concentration and motivation by including strength, speed and skill practice in each workout. Musicians practice scales, different musical pieces and rhythm exercises in one practice session. In your studies you can do the same. For example, when studying a foreign language, spend some time on reading, some time on learning vocabulary and some practice in speaking the language. Then do some problems for your math class.

Manage your internal distractions. Many of our distractions come from within. Here are some techniques for managing these internal distractions:

1. **Be here now.** Choose where you will place your attention. As I'm sure you have experienced, your body can be attending a lecture or at the desk reading, but your mind can be in lots of different and exciting places. You can tell yourself, "Be here now." You cannot force yourself to pay attention. When your mind wanders, notice that you have drifted off and gently return your attention to your lecture or reading. This will take some practice, since attention tends to wander often.

2. **The spider technique.** If you hold a tuning fork to a spider web, the web vibrates and the spider senses that it has caught a tasty morsel and goes seeking the food. After a while, the spider discovers that there is no food and learns to ignore the vibrations caused by the tuning fork. When you are sitting in the library studying and someone walks in talking and laughing, you can choose to pay attention either to the distraction or to studying. Decide to continue to pay attention to studying.

3. **Set up a worry time.** Many times worries interfere with concentration. Some people have been successful in setting up a worry time. Here's how it works:

   a. Set a specific time each day for worrying.

   b. When worries distract you from your studies, remind yourself that you have set aside time for worrying.

   c. Tell yourself, "Be here now."

   d. Keep your worry appointment.

   e. During your worry time, try to find some solutions or take some steps to resolve the things that cause you to worry.

4. **Take steps to solve personal problems.** If you are bothered by personal problems, take steps to solve them. See your college counselor for assistance. Another strategy is to make a plan to deal with the problem later so that you can study now.

5. **Use the checkmark technique.** When you find yourself distracted from a lecture or from studying, place a checkmark on a piece of paper and refocus your attention on the task at hand. You will find that your checkmarks decrease over time.

6. **Increase your activity.** Take a break. Stretch and move. Read and listen actively by asking questions about the material and answering them as you read or listen.

7. **Find an incentive or reward.** Tell yourself that when you finish, you will do something enjoyable.

8. **Change topics.** Changing study topics may help you to concentrate and avoid fatigue.

Intrinsic or Extrinsic Motivation

Intrinsic motivation comes from within. It means that you do an activity because you enjoy it or find personal meaning in it. With intrinsic motivation, the nature of the activity itself or the consequences of the activity motivate you. For example, let's say that I am interested in learning to play the piano. I am motivated to practice playing the piano because I like the sound of the piano and feel very satisfied when I can play music that I enjoy. I practice because I like to practice, not because I have to practice. When I get tired or frustrated, I work through it or put it aside and come back to it because I want to learn to play the piano well.

You can be intrinsically motivated to continue in college because you enjoy learning and find the college experience satisfying. Look for ways to enjoy college and to find some personal satisfaction in it. If you enjoy college, it becomes easier to do the work required to be successful. Think about what you say to yourself about college. If you are saying negative things such as "I don't want to be here," it will be difficult to continue.

Extrinsic motivation comes as a result of an external reward from someone else. Examples of extrinsic rewards are certificates, bonuses, money, praise, and recognition. Taking the piano example again, let's say that I want my child to play the piano. The child does not know if he or she would like to play the piano. I give the child a reward for practicing the piano. I could pay the child for practicing or give praise for doing a good job. There are two possible outcomes of the extrinsic reward. After a while, the child may gain skills and confidence and come to enjoy playing the piano. The extrinsic reward is no longer necessary because the child is now intrinsically motivated. Or the child may decide that he or she does not like to play the piano. The extrinsic reward is no longer effective in motivating the child to play the piano.

You can use extrinsic rewards to motivate yourself to be successful in college. Remind yourself of the payoff for getting a college degree: earning more money, having a satisfying career, being able to purchase a car and a house. Extrinsic rewards can be a first step in motivating yourself to attend college. With experience and achievement, you may come to like going to college and may become intrinsically motivated to continue your college education.

If you use intrinsic motivation to achieve your goal, you will be happier and more successful. If you do something like playing the piano because you enjoy it, you are more likely to spend the time necessary to practice to achieve your goal. If you view college as something that you enjoy and as valuable to you, it is easier to spend the time to do the required studying. When you get tired or frustrated, tell yourself that you are doing a good job (praise yourself) and think of the positive reasons that you want to get a college education.

© 2014, Anson0618. Used under license with Shutterstock, Inc.

Locus of Control

Being aware of the concept of locus of control is another way of understanding motivation. The word **locus** means place. The locus of control is where you place the responsibility for control over your life. In other words, who is in charge? If you place the responsibility on yourself and believe that you have control over your life, you have an internal locus of control. If you place the responsibility on others and think that luck or fate determines your future, you have an external locus of control. Some people use the internal and external locus of control in combination or favor one type in certain situations. If you favor an internal locus of control, you believe that to a great extent your actions determine your future. Studies have shown that students who use an internal locus of control are likely to have higher achievement in college.[5] The characteristics of students with internal and external loci of control are listed below.

Students with an internal locus of control:

- Believe that they are in control of their lives.
- Understand that grades are directly related to the amount of study invested.
- Are self-motivated.
- Learn from their mistakes by figuring out what went wrong and how to fix the problem.
- Think positively and try to make the best of each situation.
- Rely on themselves to find something interesting in the class and learn the material.

Students with an external locus of control:

- Believe that their lives are largely a result of luck, fate, or chance.
- Think that teachers give grades rather than students earning grades.
- Rely on external motivation from teachers or others.
- Look for someone to blame when they make a mistake.
- Think negatively and believe they are victims of circumstance.
- Rely on the teacher to make the class interesting and to teach the material.

> "Ability is what you're capable of doing. Motivation determines what you do. Attitude determines how well you do it."
>
> Lou Holtz

Internal or External Locus of Control

Decide whether the statement represents an internal or external locus of control and put a checkmark in the appropriate column.

Internal	External	
_____	_____	1. Much of what happens to us is due to fate, chance, or luck.
_____	_____	2. Grades depend on how much work you put into it.
_____	_____	3. If I do badly on the test, it is usually because the teacher is unfair.
_____	_____	4. If I do badly on the test, it is because I didn't study or didn't understand the material.
_____	_____	5. I often get blamed for things that are not my fault.
_____	_____	6. I try to make the best of the situation.
_____	_____	7. It is impossible to get a good grade if you have a bad instructor.
_____	_____	8. I can be successful through hard work.
_____	_____	9. If the teacher is not there telling me what to do, I have a hard time doing my work.
_____	_____	10. I can motivate myself to study.
_____	_____	11. If the teacher is boring, I probably won't do well in class.
_____	_____	12. I can find something interesting about each class.
_____	_____	13. When bad things are going to happen, there is not much you can do about it.
_____	_____	14. I create my own destiny.
_____	_____	15. Teachers should motivate the students to study.
_____	_____	16. I have a lot of choice about what happens in my life.

As you probably noticed, the even-numbered statements represent internal locus of control. The odd-numbered statements represent external locus of control. Remember that students with an internal locus of control have a greater chance of success in college. It is important to see yourself as responsible for your own success and achievement and to believe that with effort you can achieve your goals.

> "I am a great believer in luck, and I find that the harder I work, the more I have of it."
> Thomas Jefferson

Affiliation

Human beings are social creatures who generally feel the need to be part of a group. This tendency is called affiliation motivation. People like to be part of a community, family, organization, or culture. You can apply this motivation technique in college by participating in student activities on campus. Join an athletic team, participate in a club, or join the student government. In this way, you will feel like you are part of a group and will have a sense of belonging. College is more than going to class: it is participating in social activities, making new friends, and sharing new ideas. Twenty years after you graduate from college, you are more likely to remember the conversations held with college friends than the detailed content of classes. College provides the opportunity to become part of a new group and to start lifelong friendships.

Achievement

Some students are motivated by achievement. Individuals who are achievement-motivated have a need for success in school, sports, careers, and other competitive situations. These individuals enjoy getting recognition for their success. They are often known as the best student, the outstanding athlete, or the employee of the year. These people are attracted to careers that provide rewards for individual achievement, such as sales, law, architecture, engineering, and business. They work hard in order to enjoy the rewards of their efforts. In college, some students work very hard to achieve high grades and then take pride in their accomplishments. One disadvantage of using this type of motivation is that it can lead to excess stress. These students often need to remember to balance their time between work, school, family, and leisure so that they do not become too stressed by the need to achieve.

Using a Reward

You can use rewards to manage your own behavior. If you want to increase your studying behavior, follow it by a positive consequence or a reward. Think about what is rewarding to you (watching TV, playing sports, enjoying your favorite music). You could study (your behavior) and then watch a TV program (the reward). The timing of your reward is important. To be effective, it must immediately follow the behavior. If you watch TV and then study, you may not get around to studying. If you watch the TV program tomorrow or next week, it is not a strong reinforcement because it is not an immediate reward.

Be careful about the kinds of rewards you use so that you do not get into habits that are detrimental to your health. If you use food as a reward for studying, you may increase your studying behavior, but you may also gain a few pounds. Using alcohol or drugs as a reward can start an addiction. Buying yourself a reward can ruin your budget. Good rewards do not involve too many calories, cost too much money, or involve alcohol or drugs.

You can also use a negative consequence to decrease a behavior. If you touch a hot stove and get burned, you quickly learn not to do it again. You could decide to miss your favorite television program if you do not complete your studying. However, this is not fun and you may feel deprived. You might even rebel and watch your favorite TV show anyway. See if you can find a way to use positive reinforcement (a reward) for increasing a behavior that is beneficial to you rather than using a negative consequence.

When we are young, our attitudes toward education are largely shaped by positive or negative rewards. If you were praised for being a good reader as a child, it is likely that you enjoyed reading and developed good reading skills. Maybe a teacher embarrassed you because of your math skills and you learned to be anxious about math. Think about areas of your education in which you excel, and see if you can recall someone praising or otherwise reinforcing that behavior. If you are a good athlete, did someone praise your athletic ability when you were younger? How was it rewarded? If you are not good at math, what were some early messages about your math performance? These early messages have a powerful influence on later behavior. You may need to put in some effort to learn new and more beneficial behaviors.

As a college student, you can use a reward as a powerful motivator. Praise yourself and think positively about your achievements in college even if the achievements come in small steps.

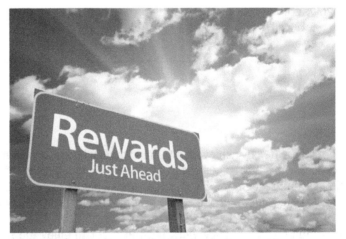

© 2014, Andy Dean Photography. Used under license with Shutterstock, Inc.

Success Is a Habit

We establish habits by taking small actions each day. Through repetition, these individual actions become habits. I once visited the Golden Gate Bridge in San Francisco and saw a cross section of the cable used to support the bridge. It was made of small metal strands twisted with other strands; then those cables were twisted together to make a stronger cable. Habits are a lot like cables. We start with one small action, and each successive action makes the habit stronger. Have you ever stopped to think that success can be a habit? We all have learned patterns of behavior that either help us to be successful or interfere with our success. With some effort and some basic understanding of behavior modification, you can choose to establish some new behaviors that lead to success or to get rid of behaviors that interfere with it.

> "Habits are first cobwebs, then cables."
> Spanish Proverb

> "We are what we repeatedly do. Excellence, then, is not an act but a habit."
> Aristotle

Seven Steps to Change a Habit

You can establish new habits that lead to your success. Once a habit is established, it can become a pattern of behavior that you do not need to think about very much. For example, new students often need to get into the habit of studying. Following is an outline of steps that can be helpful to establish new behaviors.

1. **State the problem.** What new habit would you like to start? What are your roadblocks or obstacles? What bad habit would you like to change? Be truthful about it. This is sometimes the most difficult step. Here are two different examples:

   - I need to study to be successful in college. I am not in the habit of studying. I easily get distracted by work, family, friends, and other things I need to do. At the end of the day, I am too tired to study.

   - I need to improve my diet. I am overweight. I eat too much fast food and am not careful about what I eat. I have no time for exercise.

2. **Change one small behavior at a time.** If you think about climbing a mountain, the task can seem overwhelming. However, you can take the first step. If you can change one small behavior, you can gain the confidence to change another. For example:

   - I plan to study at least one hour each day on Mondays through Fridays.

   - I plan to eat more fruits and vegetables each day.

Seven Steps to
Change a Habit

1. State the problem
2. Change one small
   behavior at a time
3. Be positive
4. Count the behavior
5. Picture the change
6. Practice the behavior
7. Reward yourself

"The difference in winning
and losing is most often . . .
not quitting."
Walt Disney

"It's not that I'm so smart;
it's just that I stay with
problems longer."
Albert Einstein

State the behavior you would like to change. Make it small.

3. **State in a positive way the behavior you wish to establish.** For example, instead of the negative statements "I will not waste my time" or "I will not eat junk food," say, "I plan to study each day" or "I plan to eat fruits and vegetables each day."

4. **Count the behavior.** How often do you do this behavior? If you are trying to establish a pattern of studying, write down how much time you spend studying each day. If you are trying to improve your diet, write down everything that you eat each day. Sometimes just getting an awareness of your habit is enough to begin to make some changes.

5. **Picture in your mind the actions you might take.** For example:

   - I picture myself finding time to study in the library. I see myself walking to the library. I can see myself in the library studying.

   - I see myself in the grocery store buying fruits and vegetables. I see myself packing these fruits and vegetables in my lunch. I see myself putting these foods in a place where I will notice them.

6. **Practice the behavior for 10 days.** In 10 days, you can get started on a new pattern of behavior. Once you have started, keep practicing the behavior for about a month to firmly establish your new pattern of behavior. The first three days are the most difficult. If you fail, don't give up. Just realize that you are human and keep trying for 10 days. Think positively that you can be successful. Write a journal entry or note on your calendar about what you have accomplished each day.

7. **Find a reward for your behavior.** Remember that we tend to repeat behaviors that are rewarded. Find rewards that do not involve too many calories, don't cost too much money, and don't involve alcohol or drugs. Also, rewards are most effective if they directly follow the behavior you wish to reinforce.

Ten Habits of Successful College Students

Starting your college education will require you to establish some new habits to be successful.

1. Attend class.

College lectures supplement the material in the text, so it is important to attend class. Many college instructors will drop you if you miss three hours of class. After three absences, most students do not return to class. If your class is online, log in frequently.

2. Read the textbook.

Start early and read a little at a time. If you have a text with 400 pages, read 25 pages a week rather than trying to read it all at once.

3. Have an educational plan.

Counselors or advisors can assist you in making an educational plan so that you take the right classes and accomplish your educational goal as soon as possible.

4. Use college services.

Colleges offer valuable free services that help you to be successful. Take advantage of tutoring, counseling, health services, financial aid, the learning resources center (library) and many other services.

5. Get to know the faculty.

You can get to know the faculty by asking questions in class or meeting with your instructors during office hours. Your instructors can provide extra assistance and write letters of recommendation for scholarships, future employment, or graduate school.

6. Don't work too much.

Research has shown that full-time students should have no more than 20 hours of outside employment a week to be successful in college. If you have to work more than 20 hours a week, reduce your college load. If you are working 40 hours a week or more, take only one or two classes.

7. Take one step at a time.

If you are anxious about going to college, remember that each class you attend takes you another step toward your goal. If you take too many classes, especially in the beginning, you may become overwhelmed.

8. Have a goal for the future.

Know why you are in college and what you hope to accomplish. What career will you have in the future? Imagine your future lifestyle.

9. Visualize your success.

See yourself walking across the stage and receiving your college diploma. See yourself working at a job you enjoy.

10. Ask questions if you don't understand.

Asking questions not only helps you to find the answers, but it shows you are motivated to be successful. Starting your college education will require you to establish some new habits to be successful.

QUIZ

Motivation, Part II

1. When you participate in student activities in campus such as athletics, student government, or a club, you will be

   a. distracted from your studies.
   b. using affiliation motivation.
   c. decreasing your chances of success in college.

2. If the behavior is followed by a reward

   a. it is likely to be increased.
   b. it is likely to be decreased.
   c. there will probably be no effect.

3. For rewards to be effective, they must occur

   a. before the behavior.
   b. immediately after the behavior.
   c. either before or after the behavior.

4. If you plan to increase time spent studying, the following statement is most likely to help you to achieve your goal.

   a. I will increase the time I spend studying.
   b. I plan to study for at least one hour each day on Mondays through Fridays.
   c. I will study for five hours on Monday to prepare for the test on Tuesday.

5. To change a habit,

   a. set high goals.
   b. focus on negative behavior.
   c. begin with a concrete behavior that can be counted.

How did you do on the quiz? Check your answers: 1. b, 2. a, 3. b, 4. b, 5. c

Persistence

There is an old saying that persistence will get you almost anything eventually. This saying applies to your success in life as well as in college. The first two to six weeks of college are a critical time in which many students drop out. Realize that college is a new experience and that you will face new challenges and growth experiences. Make plans to persist, especially in the first few weeks. Get to know a college counselor or advisor. These professionals can help you to get started in the right classes and answer any questions you might have. It is important to make a connection with a counselor or faculty member so that you feel comfortable in college and have the resources to obtain needed help. Plan to enroll on time so that you do not have to register late. It is crucial to attend the first class. In the first class, the professor explains the class requirements and expectations and sets the tone for the class. You may even get dropped from the class if you are not there on the first day. Get into the habit of studying right away. Make studying a habit that you start immediately at the beginning of the semester or quarter. If you can make it through the first six weeks, it is likely that you can finish the semester and complete your college education.

It has been said that 90 percent of success is just showing up. Any faculty member will tell you that the number one reason for students dropping out of college is lack of attendance. They know that when students miss three classes in a row, they are not likely to return. Even very capable students who miss class may find that they are lost when they come back. Many students are simply afraid to return. Classes such as math and foreign languages are sequential, and it is very difficult to make up work after an absence. One of the most important ways you can be successful is to make a habit of consistently showing up for class.

You will also need commitment to be successful. Commitment is a promise to yourself to follow through with something. In athletics, it is not necessarily the one with the best physical skills who makes the best athlete. Commitment and practice make a great athlete. Commitment means doing whatever is necessary to succeed. Like the good athlete, make a commitment to accomplishing your goals. Spend the time necessary to be successful in your studies.

When you face difficulties, persistence and commitment are especially important. History is full of famous people who contributed to society through persistence and commitment. Consider the following facts about Abraham Lincoln, for example.

- Failed in business at age 21.
- Was defeated in a legislative race at age 22.
- Failed again in business at age 24.
- Overcame the death of his sweetheart at age 26.
- Had a nervous breakdown at age 27.
- Lost a congressional race at age 34.
- Lost a congressional race at age 36.
- Lost a senatorial race at age 45.
- Failed in an effort to become vice president at age 47.
- Lost a senatorial race at age 49.
- Was elected president of the United States at age 52.[6]

You will face difficulties along the way in any worthwhile venture. The successful person keeps on trying. There are some precautions about persistence, however. Make sure that the goal you are trying to reach is attainable and valuable to you. As you learn more about yourself, you may want to change your goals. Also, persistence can be misguided if it involves other people. For example, if you decide that you want to marry someone and this someone does not want to marry you, it is better to focus your energy and attention on a different goal.

One of the best ways to be persistent is to accomplish your goals one step at a time. If you look at a mountain, it may seem too high to climb, but you can do it one step at a time. Araceli Segarra became the first Spanish woman to climb Mount Everest. At 29,028 feet, Mount Everest is the highest mountain in the world. It is so high that you need an oxygen tank to breathe at the top. So how did Araceli climb the mountain? She says that it took strength and concentration. She put one foot in front of the other. When she was near the top of the mountain, she was more tired than she had ever been in her life. She told herself that she would take 10 more steps. When she had taken 10 steps, she said, "I'm OK. I made it." Then she took 10 more steps until she reached the top of the mountain.

The goal of getting a college education may seem like a mountain that is difficult to climb. Break it into smaller steps that you can accomplish. See your college counselor or advisor, register for classes, attend the first class, read the first chapter, do the first assignment, and you will be on the road to your success. Then continue to break tasks into small, achievable steps and continue from one step to the next. And remember, persistence will get you almost anything eventually.

Journal Entry #5

What will you do if you are tempted to drop out of college? What steps can you take to be persistent in achieving your college goals? Are there times when it is best to change goals rather than to be persistent if your efforts are not working? Write a paragraph about how you will be persistent in reaching your college goals.

JOURNAL ENTRIES

Understanding Motivation

Go to http://www.collegesuccess1.com/JournalEntries.htm for Word files of the Journal Entries

Success over the Internet

Visit the *College Success Website* at http://www.collegesuccess1.com/

The *College Success Website* is continually updated with new topics and links to the material presented in this chapter. Topics include:

- How to improve concentration
- Motivation
- Positive attitude
- Balancing work, school, and social life
- Success factors for new college students
- How to change a habit
- Dealing with cravings and urges

Contact your instructor if you have any problems accessing the *College Success Website.*

Notes

1. U.S. Census Bureau, "Earnings and Unemployment by Educational Attainment 2012" retrieved from http://www.bls.gov/emp/ep_chart_001.htm

2. Ibid

3. W. Lewallen, "The Impact of Being Undecided on College Persistence," *Journal of College Student Development* 34 (1993): 103–12.

4. Marsha Fralick, "College Success: A Study of Positive and Negative Attrition," *Community College Review* 20 (1993): 29–36.

5. Christopher Peterson, *A Primer in Positive Psychology* (New York: Oxford University Press, 2006), 127.

6. M. J. Findlay and H. M. Cooper, "Locus of Control and Academic Achievement: A Literature Review," *Journal of Personality and Social Psychology* 44 (1983): 419–27.

7. Anthony Robbins, *Unlimited Power* (New York: Ballantine Books, 1986), 73.

CHAPTER 2

Managing Time

Learning Objectives

Read to answer these key questions:

- What are my lifetime goals?

- How can I manage my time to accomplish my goals?

- How much time do I need for study and work?

- How can I make an effective schedule?

- What are some time management tricks?

- How can I deal with procrastination?

Success in college requires that you manage both time and money. You will need time to study and money to pay for your education. The first step in managing time and money is to think about the goals that you wish to accomplish in your life. Having goals that are important to you provides a reason and motivation for managing time and money. This chapter provides some useful techniques for managing time and money so that you can accomplish the goals you have set for yourself.

What Are My Lifetime Goals?

Setting goals helps you to establish what is important and provides direction for your life. Goals help you to focus your energy on what you want to accomplish. Goals are a promise to yourself to improve your life. Setting goals can help you turn your dreams into reality. Steven Scott, in his book *A Millionaire's Notebook,* lays out five steps in this process:

1. Dream or visualize.

2. Convert the dream into goals.

3. Convert your goals into tasks.

4. Convert your task into steps.

5. Take your first step, and then the next.[1]

As you begin to think about your personal goals in life, make your goals specific and concrete. Rather than saying, "I want to be rich," make your goal something that you can break into specific steps. You might want to start learning about money management or begin a savings plan. Rather than setting a goal for happiness, think about what brings you happiness. If you want to live a long and healthy life, think about the health habits that will help you to accomplish your goal. You will need to break your goals down into specific tasks to be able to accomplish them.

GOAL SETTING

Specific
Measurable
Achievable
Realistic
Timely

© 2014, winui. Used under license with Shutterstock, Inc.

Here are some criteria for successful goal setting:

1. **Is it achievable?** Do you have the skills, abilities, and resources to accomplish this goal? If not, are you willing to spend the time to develop the skills, abilities, and resources needed to achieve this goal?

2. **Is it realistic?** Do you believe you can achieve it? Are you positive and optimistic about this goal?

3. **Is it specific and measurable?** Can it be counted or observed? The most common goal mentioned by students is happiness in life. What is happiness, and how will you know when you have achieved it? Is happiness a career you enjoy, owning your own home, or a travel destination?

4. **Do you want to do it?** Is this a goal you are choosing because it gives you personal satisfaction, rather than meeting a requirement or an expectation of someone else?

5. **Are you motivated to achieve it?** What are your rewards for achieving it?

6. **Does the goal match your values?** Is it important to you?

7. **What steps do you need to take to begin?** Are you willing to take action to start working on it?

8. **When will you finish this goal?** Set a date to accomplish your goal.

> "A goal is a dream with a deadline."
>
> Napoleon Hill

Journal Entry #1

Write a paragraph about your lifetime goals. Use any of these questions to guide your thinking:

- What is your career goal? If you do not know what your career goal is, describe your preferred work environment. Would your ideal career require a college degree?

- What are your family goals? Are you interested in marriage and family? What would be your important family values?

- What are your social goals (friends, community, and recreation)?

- When you are older and look back on your life, what are the three most important life goals that you want to have accomplished?

A Goal or a Fantasy?

One of the best questions ever asked in my class was, "What is the difference between a goal and a fantasy?" As you look at your list of lifetime goals, are some of these items goals or fantasies? Think about this question as you read the following scenario:

When Linda was a college student, she was walking through the parking lot, noticed a beautiful red sports car, and decided that it would become a lifetime goal for her to own a similar car one day. However, with college expenses and her part-time job, it was not possible to buy the car. She would have to be content with the used car that her dad had given her so that she could drive to college. Years passed by, and Linda now has a good job, a home, and a family. She is reading a magazine and sees a picture of a similar red sports car. She cuts out this picture and tapes it to the refrigerator. After it has been on the refrigerator for several months, her children ask her why the picture is on the refrigerator. Linda replies, "I just like to dream about owning this car." One day, as Linda is driving past a car dealership, she sees the red sports car on display and stops in for a test drive. To her surprise, she decides that she does not like driving the car. It doesn't fit her lifestyle, either. She enjoys outdoor activities that would require a larger car. Buying a second car would be costly and reduce the amount of money that the family could spend on vacations. She decides that vacations are more important than owning the sports car. Linda goes home and removes the picture of the red sports car from the refrigerator.

© 2014, Natursports. Used under license with Shutterstock, Inc.

There are many differences between a goal and a fantasy. A fantasy is a dream that may or may not become a reality. A goal is something that we actually plan to achieve. Sometimes we begin with a fantasy and later it becomes a goal. A fantasy can become a goal if steps are taken to achieve it. In the preceding example, the sports car is a fantasy until Linda actually takes the car for a test drive. After driving the car, she decides that she really does not want it. The fantasy is sometimes better than the reality. Goals and fantasies change over a lifetime. We set goals, try them out, and change them as we grow and mature and find out what is most important in life. Knowing what we think is important, and what we value most, helps us make good decisions about lifetime goals.

What is the difference between a goal and a fantasy? A goal is something that requires action. Ask yourself if you are willing to take action on the goals you have set for yourself. Begin to take action by thinking about the steps needed to accomplish the goal. Then take the first step and continue. Change your goals if they are no longer important to you.

Journal Entry #2

Write a paragraph about how you will accomplish one of your important lifetime goals. Start your paragraph by stating an important goal from the previous journal entry. What is the first step in accomplishing this goal? Next, list some additional steps needed to accomplish it. How can you motivate yourself to begin taking these steps?

For example:

One of my important lifetime goals is _____. The first step in accomplishing this goal is . . . Some additional steps are . . . I can motivate myself to accomplish this goal by . . .

The ABCs of Time Management

Using the **ABCs of time management** is a way of thinking about priorities. Priorities are what you think is important. An **A priority** is a task that relates to your lifetime goal. For example, if my goal is to earn a college degree, studying becomes an A priority. This activity would become one of the most important tasks that I could accomplish today. If my goal is to be healthy, an A priority would be to exercise and plan a healthy diet. If my goal is to have a good family life, an A priority would be to spend time with family members. Knowing about your lifetime goals and spending time on those items that are most important to you will help you to accomplish the goals that you have set for yourself. If you do not spend time on your goals, you may want to look at them again and decide which ones are fantasies that you do not really value or want to accomplish.

A **B priority** is an activity that you have to do, but that is not directly related to your lifetime goal. Examples of B priorities might be getting out of bed, taking a shower, buying groceries, paying bills, or getting gas for the car. These activities are less important, but still are necessary for survival. If I do not put gas in the car, I cannot even get to school or work. If I do not pay the bills, I will soon have financial difficulties. While we often cannot postpone these activities in order to accomplish lifetime goals, we can learn efficient time management techniques to accomplish these tasks quickly.

A **C priority** is something that I can postpone until tomorrow with no harmful effect. For example, I could wait until tomorrow or another day to wash my car, do the laundry, buy groceries, or organize my desk. As these items are postponed, however, they can move up the list to a B priority. If I cannot see out of my car window or have no clean clothes to wear, it is time to move these tasks up on my list of priorities.

Have you ever been a victim of "**C fever**"? This is an illness in which we do the C activities first and do not get around to doing the A activities that are connected to lifetime goals. Tasks required to accomplish lifetime goals are often ones that are more difficult, challenge our abilities, and take some time to accomplish. These tasks are often more difficult than the B or C activities. The C activities can fill our time and exhaust the energy we need to accomplish the A activities. An example of C fever is the student who cleans the desk or organizes the CD collection instead of studying. C fever is doing the endless tasks that keep us from accomplishing goals that are really important to us. Why do we fall victim to C fever? C activities are often easy to do and give us a sense of accomplishment. We can see immediate progress without too much effort. I can wash my car and get a sense of accomplishment and satisfaction in my shiny clean car. The task is easy and does not challenge my intellectual capabilities.

© 2014, iQoncept. Used under license
with Shutterstock, Inc.

Setting Priorities

To see how the ABCs of time management work, read the profile of Justin, a typical college student, below.

Justin is a 19-year-old college student who plans to major in physical therapy. He is athletic and values his good health. He cares about people and likes helping others. He has a part-time job working as an assistant in the gym, where he monitors proper use of the weightlifting machines. Justin is also a member of the soccer team and practices with the team every afternoon.

Here is a list of activities that Justin would like to do today. Label each task as follows:

A if it relates to Justin's lifetime goals

B if it is something necessary to do

C if it is something that could be done tomorrow or later

_____ Get up, shower, get dressed	_____ Study for biology test that is tomorrow
_____ Eat breakfast	_____ Meet friends for pizza at lunch
_____ Go to work	_____ Call girlfriend
_____ Go to class	_____ Eat dinner
_____ Visit with friends between classes	_____ Unpack gear from weekend camping trip
_____ Buy a new battery for his watch	_____ Watch football game on TV
_____ Go shopping for new gym shoes	_____ Play video games
_____ Attend soccer practice	_____ Do math homework
_____ Do weightlifting exercises	

While Justin is the only one who can decide how to spend his time, he can take some steps toward accomplishing his lifetime goal of being healthy by eating properly, exercising, and going to soccer practice. He can become a physical therapist by studying for the biology test and doing his math homework. He can gain valuable experience related to physical therapy by working in the gym. He cares about people and likes to maintain good relationships with others. Any tasks related to these goals are high-priority A activities.

What other activities are necessary B activities? He certainly needs to get up, shower, and get dressed. What are the C activities that could be postponed until tomorrow or later? Again, Justin needs to decide. Maybe he could postpone shopping for a new watch battery and gym shoes until the weekend. He would have to decide how much time to spend visiting with friends, watching TV, or playing video games. Since he likes these activities, he could use them as rewards for studying for the biology test and doing his math homework.

How to Estimate Study and Work Time

Students are often surprised at the amount of time necessary for study to be successful in college. A general rule is that you need to study two hours for every hour spent in a college class. A typical weekly schedule of a full-time student would look like this:

Typical College Schedule

> 15 hours of attending class
> +30 hours of reading, studying, and preparation
> 45 hours total

A full-time job involves working 40 hours a week. A full-time college student spends 45 hours or more attending classes and studying. Some students will need more than 45 hours a week if they are taking lab classes, need help with study and learning skills, or are taking a heavy course load.

Some students try to work full-time and go to school full-time. While some are successful, this schedule is extremely difficult.

The Nearly Impossible Schedule

> 15 hours attending class
> 30 hours studying
> +40 hours working
> 85 hours total

This schedule is the equivalent of having two full-time jobs! Working full-time makes it very difficult to find the time necessary to study for classes. Lack of study causes students to do poorly on exams and to doubt their abilities. Such a schedule causes stress and fatigue that make studying difficult. Increased stress can also lead to problems with personal relationships and emotional problems. These are all things that lead to dropping out of college.

Many students today work and go to college. Working during college can provide some valuable experience that will help you to find a job when you finish college. Working can teach you to manage your time efficiently and give you a feeling of independence and control over your own future. Many people need to work to pay for their education. A general guideline is to work no more than 20 hours a week if you plan to attend college full-time. Here is a workable schedule.

Part-Time Work Schedule

> 12 hours attending class
> 24 hours studying
> +20 hours working
> 56 hours total

A commitment of 56 hours a week is like having a full-time job and a part-time job. While this schedule takes extra energy and commitment, many students are successful with it. Notice that the course load is reduced to 12 hours. This schedule involves taking one less class per semester. The class missed can be made up in summer school, or the time needed to graduate can be extended. Many students take five years to earn the bachelor's degree because they work part-time. It is better to take longer to graduate than to drop out of college or to give up because of frustration. If you must work full-time, consider reducing your course load to one or two courses. You will gradually reach your goal of a college degree.

> "The key is not to prioritize what's on the schedule, but to schedule your priorities."
> Stephen Covey

> "When you do the things you have to do when you have to do them, the day will come when you can do the things you want to do when you want to do them."
> Zig Ziglar

Part-Time Student Schedule

6 hours attending class
12 hours studying
+40 hours working
58 hours total

Add up the number of hours you are attending classes, double this figure for study time, and add to it your work time, as in the above examples. How many hours of commitment do you have? Can you be successful with your current level of commitment to school, work, and study?

To begin managing your schedule, use the weekly calendar located at the end of this chapter to write in your scheduled activities such as work, class times, and athletics.

Schedule Your Success

If you have not used a schedule in the past, consider trying a schedule for a couple of weeks to see if it is helpful in completing tasks and working toward your lifetime goals. There are several advantages to using a schedule:

- It gets you started on your work.
- It helps you avoid procrastination.
- It relieves pressure because you have things under control.
- It frees the mind of details.
- It helps you find time to study.
- It eliminates the panic caused by doing things at the last minute.
- It helps you find time for recreation and exercise.

Once you have made a master schedule that includes classes, work, and other activities, you will see that you have some blanks that provide opportunities for using your time productively. Here are some ideas for making the most of your schedule:

1. Fill in your study times. Use the time immediately before class for previewing and the time immediately after class for reviewing. Remember that you need to study two hours or more for each hour spent in a college class.

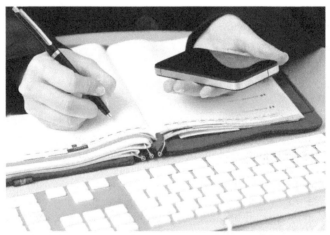

© 2014, Caroline Eibl. Used under license with Shutterstock, Inc.

2. Break large projects such as a term paper or studying for a test into small tasks and begin early. Double your time estimates for completion of the project. Larger projects often take longer than you think. If you finish early, use the extra time for something fun.

3. Use the daylight hours when you are most alert for studying. It may take you longer to study if you wait until late in the day when you're tired.

4. Think about your day and see if you can determine when you are most alert and awake. Prime time differs with individuals, but it is generally earlier in the day. Use the prime time when you are most alert to accomplish your most challenging tasks. For example, do your math homework during prime time. Wash your clothes during nonprime time, when you are likely to be less alert.

5. Set priorities. Make sure you include activities related to your lifetime goals.

6. Allow time for sleep and meals. It is easier to study if you are well rested and have good eating habits.

7. Schedule your time in manageable blocks of an hour or two. Having every moment scheduled leads to frustration when plans change.

8. Leave some time unscheduled to use as a shock absorber. You will need unscheduled time to relax and to deal with unexpected events.

9. Leave time for recreation, exercise, and fun.

Return to the schedule at the end of this chapter. After you have written in classes, work times, and other scheduled activities, use the scheduling ideas listed earlier to write in your study times and other activities related to your lifetime goals. Leave some unscheduled time to provide flexibility in the schedule.

> "The only thing even in this world is the number of hours in a day. The difference in winning or losing is what you do with these hours."
> Woody Hayes

If You Dislike Schedules

Some personality types like more freedom and do not like the structure that a schedule provides. There are alternatives for those who do not like to use a schedule. Here are some additional ideas.

1. A simple and fast way to organize your time is to use a to-do list. Take an index card or small piece of paper and simply write a list of what you need to do during the day. You can prioritize the list by putting an A or star by the most important items. Cross items off the list as you accomplish them. A list helps you focus on what is important and serves as a reminder not to forget certain tasks.

2. Another idea is to use monthly or yearly calendars to write down important events, tasks, and deadlines. Use these calendars to note the first day of school, when important assignments are due, vacations, and final exams. Place the calendars in a place where they are easily seen.

© 2014, iQoncept. Used under license with Shutterstock, Inc.

3. Alan Lakein, who wrote a book titled *How to Get Control of Your Time and Your Life,* suggests a simple question to keep you on track.[2] Lakein's question is, "What is the best use of my time right now?" This question works well if you keep in mind your goals and priorities.

4. Use reminders and sticky notes to keep on track and to remind yourself of what needs to be done each day. Place the notes in a place where you will see them, such as your computer, the bathroom mirror, or the dashboard of your car.

5. Some families use their refrigerators as time management devices. Use the refrigerator to post your calendars, reminders, goals, tasks, and to-do lists. You will see these reminders every time you open the refrigerator.

6. Invent your own unique ideas for managing time. Anything will work if it helps to accomplish your goals.

Manage Your Time with a Web Application

There are thousands of new web applications available to organize your life. You can use a web application on your phone, laptop, computer, or other mobile device to:

- Create a to-do list or schedule.
- Send reminders when assignments are due.
- Organize your calendar and plan your tasks.
- Organize your study time and plan assignments.
- Avoid procrastination.
- Create a virtual assistant to keep you organized.

QUIZ

Time Management, Part I

Test what you have learned by selecting the correct answers to the following questions.

1. The most important difference between a goal and a fantasy is
   a. imagination.
   b. procrastination.
   c. action.

2. An A priority is
   a. related to your lifetime goals.
   b. something important.
   c. something you have to do.

3. A general rule for college success is that you must spend ___ hours studying for every hour spent in a college class.
   a. one
   b. four
   c. two

4. For a workable study schedule,
   a. fill in all the blank time slots.
   b. leave some unscheduled time to deal with the unexpected.
   c. plan to study late at night.

5. To complete a large project such as a term paper,
   a. break the project into small tasks and begin early.
   b. schedule large blocks of time the day before the paper is due.
   c. leave time for exercise, recreation, and fun before beginning on the project.

How did you do on the quiz? Check your answers: 1. c, 2. a, 3. c, 4. b, 5. a

Time Management Tricks

Life is full of demands for work, study, family, friends, and recreation. Time management tricks can help you get started on the important tasks and make the most of your time. Try the following techniques when you are feeling frustrated and overwhelmed.

Divide and Conquer

When large tasks seem overwhelming, think of the small tasks needed to complete the project and start on the first step. For example, suppose you have to write a term paper. You have to take out a paper and pencil, log onto your computer, brainstorm some ideas, go to the library to find information, think about your main ideas, and write the first sentence. Each of these steps is manageable. It's looking at the entire project that can be intimidating.

I once set out hiking on a mountain trail. When I got to the top of the mountain and looked down, I enjoyed a spectacular view and was amazed at how high I had climbed. If I had thought about how high the mountain was, I might not have attempted the hike. I climbed the mountain by taking it one step at a time. That's the secret to completing any large project: break it into small, manageable parts, then take the first step and keep going.

Learning a small part at a time is also easy and helps with motivation for learning. While in college, carry around some material that you need to study. Take advantage of five or ten minutes of time to study a small part of your material. In this way you make good use of your time and enhance memory by using distributed practice. Don't wait until you have large blocks of uninterrupted study time to begin your studies. You may not have the luxury of large blocks of time, or you may want to spend that time in other ways.

Time Management Tricks

- Divide and conquer
- Do the first small step
- 80/20 rule
- Aim for excellence, not perfection
- Make learning fun
- Take a break
- Study in the library
- Learn to say no

Do the First Small Step

The most difficult step in completing any project is the first step. If you have a challenging project to do, think of a small first step and complete that small step. Make the first step something that you can accomplish easily and in a short amount of time. Give yourself permission to stop after the first step. However, you may find that you are motivated to continue with the project. If you have a term paper to write, think about some small step you can take to get started. Log onto your computer and look at the blank screen. Start writing some ideas. Type the topic into a computer search engine and see what information is available. Go to the library and see what is available on your topic. If you can find some interesting ideas, you can motivate yourself to begin the project. Once you have started the project, it is easier to continue.

© 2014, iQoncept. Used under license with Shutterstock, Inc.

The 80/20 Rule

Alan Lakein is noted for many useful time management techniques. One that I have used over the years is the 80/20 rule. Lakein says, "If all items are arranged in order of value, 80 percent of the value would come from only 20 percent of the items, while the remaining 20 percent of the value would come from 80 percent of the items."[3] For example, if you have a list of ten items to do, two of the items on the list are more important than the others. If you were to do only the two most important items, you would have accomplished 80 percent of the value. If you are short on time, see if you can choose the 20 percent of the tasks that are the most valuable. Lakein noted that the 80/20 rule applies to many situations in life:

- 80 percent of file usage is in 20 percent of the files.
- 80 percent of dinners repeat 20 percent of the recipes.
- 80 percent of the washing is done on the 20 percent of the clothes worn most frequently.
- 80 percent of the dirt is on the 20 percent of the floor used most often.

Think about how the 80/20 rule applies in your life. It is another way of thinking about priorities and figuring out which of the tasks are C priorities. This prioritizing is especially important if you are short on time. The 80/20 rule helps you to focus on what is most important.

Aim for Excellence, Not Perfection

Are you satisfied with your work only if it is done perfectly? Do you put off a project because you cannot do it perfectly? Aiming for perfection in all tasks causes anxiety and procrastination. There are times when perfection is not necessary. Dave Ellis calls this time management technique "It Ain't No Piano."[4] If a construction worker bends a nail in the framing of a house, it does not matter. The construction worker simply puts in another nail. After all, "it ain't no piano." It is another matter if you are building a fine cabinet or finishing a piano. Perfection is more important in these circumstances. We need to ask: Is the task important enough to invest the time needed for perfection? A final term paper needs to be as perfect as we can make it. A rough draft is like the frame of a house that does not need to be perfect.

In aiming for excellence rather than perfection, challenge yourself to use perspective to see the big picture. How important is the project and how perfect does it need to be? Could your time be better invested accomplishing other tasks? This technique requires flexibility and the ability to change with different situations. Do not give up if you cannot complete a project perfectly. Do the best that you can in the time available. In some situations, if life is too hectic, you may need to settle for completing the project and getting it in on time rather than doing it perfectly. With this idea in mind, you may be able to relax and still achieve excellence.

Make Learning Fun by Finding a Reward

Time management is not about restriction, self-control, and deprivation. If it is done correctly, time can be managed to get more out of life and to have fun while doing it. Remember that behavior is likely to increase if followed by a reward. Think about activities that you find rewarding. In our time management example with Justin who wants to be a physical therapist, he could use many tasks as rewards for completing his studies. He could meet friends for pizza, call his girlfriend, play video games, or watch TV. The key idea is to do the studying first and then reward the behavior. Maybe Justin will not be able to do all of the activities we have mentioned as possible rewards, but he could choose what he enjoys most.

Studying first and then rewarding yourself leads to peace of mind and the ability to focus on tasks at hand. While Justin is out having pizza with his friends, he does not have to worry about work that he has not done. While Justin is studying, he does not have to feel that he is being deprived of having pizza with friends. In this way, he can focus on studying while he is studying and focus on having a good time while relaxing with his friends. It is not a good idea to think about having pizza with friends while studying or to think about studying while having pizza with friends. When you work, focus on your work and get it done. When you play, enjoy playing without having to think about work.

"Don't say you don't have enough time. You have exactly the same number of hours per day that were given to Helen Keller, Pasteur, Michelangelo, Mother Teresa, Leonardo da Vinci, Thomas Jefferson, and Albert Einstein."

H. Jackson Browne

Take a Break

If you are overwhelmed with the task at hand, sometimes it is best to just take a break. If you're stuck on a computer program or a math problem, take a break and do something else. As a general rule, take a break of 10 minutes for each hour of study. During the break, do something totally different. It is a good idea to get up and move around. Get up and pet your cat or dog, observe your goldfish, or shoot a few baskets. If time is really at a premium, use your break time to accomplish other important tasks. Put your clothes in the dryer, empty the dishwasher, or pay a bill.

Study in the Library

If you are having difficulty with studying, try studying at school in the library. Libraries are designed for studying, and other people are studying there as well. It is hard to do something else in the library without annoying the librarian or other students. If you can complete your studying at school, you can go home and relax. This may be especially important if family, friends, or roommates at home easily distract you.

Learn to Say No Sometimes

Learn to say no to tasks that you do not have time to do. Follow your statement with the reasons for saying no: you are going to college and need time to study. Most people will understand this answer and respect it. You may need to say no to yourself as well. Maybe you cannot go out on Wednesday night if you have a class early on Thursday morning. Maybe the best use of your time right now is to turn off the TV or get off the Internet and study for tomorrow's test. You are investing your time in your future.

© 2014, NorGal. Used under license with Shutterstock, Inc.

Dealing with Time Bandits

Time bandits are the many things that keep us from spending time on the things we think are important. Another word for a time bandit is a time waster. In college, it is tempting to do many things other than studying. We are all victims of different kinds of bandits.

ACTIVITY

Put a checkmark next to the items that waste your time. Add your own personal time wasters at the end of the list.

_____ TV

_____ Other electronic devices

_____ Daydreaming

_____ Social networking

_____ Saying yes when you mean no

_____ Friends

_____ Internet

_____ Social time

_____ Family

_____ Phone

_____ Household chores

_____ Roommates

_____ Video games

_____ Partying

_____ Children

_____ iPod

_____ Waiting time

_____ Girlfriend, boyfriend, spouse

_____ Sleeping in

_____ Shopping

_____ Being easily distracted

_____ Studying at a bad time

_____ Reading magazines

_____ Studying in a distracting place

_____ Movies

_____ Commuting time (travel)

List some of your personal time bandits here.

_____

_____

Here are some ideas for keeping time bandits under control:

- **Schedule time for other people.** Friends and family are important, so we do not want to get rid of them! Discuss your goal of a college education with your friends and family. People who care about you will respect your goals. You may need to use a Do Not Disturb sign at times. If you are a parent, remember that you are a role model for your children. If they see you studying, they are more likely to value their own education. Plan to spend quality time with your children and the people who are important to you. Make sure they understand that you care about them.

- **Remember the rewards.** Many of the time bandits listed above make good rewards for completing your work. Put the time bandits to work for you by studying first and then enjoying a reward. Enjoy the TV, Internet, iPod, video games, or phone conversations after you have finished your studies. Aim for a balance of work, study, and leisure time.

- **Use your prime time wisely.** Prime time is when you are most awake and alert. Use this time for studying. Use non-prime time for the time bandits. When you are tired, do household chores and shopping. If you have little time for household chores, you might find faster ways to do them. If you don't have time for shopping, you will notice that you spend less and have a better chance of following your budget.

- **Remind yourself about your priorities.** When time bandits attack, remind yourself of why you are in college. Think about your personal goals for the future. Remember that college is not forever. By doing well in college, you will finish in the shortest time possible.

- **Use a schedule.** Using a schedule or a to-do list is helpful in keeping you on track. Make sure you have some slack time in your schedule to handle unexpected phone calls and deal with the unplanned events that happen in life. If you cannot stick to your schedule, just get back on track as soon as you can.

Journal Entry #3

Write a paragraph about how you will manage your time to accomplish your goal of a college education. Use any of these questions to guide your thinking:

- What are your priorities?
- How will you balance school, work, and family/friends?
- What are some time management tools you plan to use?
- How can you deal with time bandits?

Dealing with Procrastination

Procrastination means putting off things until later. We all use delaying tactics at times. Procrastination that is habitual, however, can be self-destructive. Understanding some possible reasons for procrastination can help you use time more effectively and be more successful in accomplishing goals.

Why Do We Procrastinate?

There are many psychological reasons for procrastinating. Just becoming aware of these may help you deal with procrastination. If you have serious difficulty managing your time for psychological reasons, visit the counseling center at your college or university. Do you recognize any of these reasons for procrastination in yourself or others?

- **Fear of failure.** Sometimes we procrastinate because we are afraid of failing. We see our performance as related to how much ability we have and how worthwhile we are as human beings. We may procrastinate in our college studies because of doubts about our ability to do the work. Success, however, comes from trying and learning from mistakes. There is a popular saying: falling down is not failure, but failing to get up or not even trying is failure.

- **Fear of success.** Most students are surprised to find out that one of the reasons for procrastination is fear of success. Success in college means moving on with your life, getting a job, leaving a familiar situation, accepting increased responsibility, and sometimes leaving friends behind. None of these tasks is easy. An example of fear of success is not taking the last step required to be successful. Students sometimes do not take the last class needed to graduate. Some good students do not show up for the final exam or do not turn in a major project. If you ever find yourself procrastinating on an important last step, ask yourself if you are afraid of success and what lies ahead in your future.

© 2014, bloomua. Used under license with Shutterstock, Inc.

- **Perfectionism.** Some people who procrastinate do not realize that they are perfectionists. Perfectionists expect more from themselves than is realistic and more than others expect of themselves. There is often no other choice than to procrastinate because perfectionism is usually unattainable. Perfectionism generates anxiety that further hinders performance. Perfectionists need to understand that perfection is seldom possible. They need to set time limits on projects and do their best within those time limits.

- **Need for excitement.** Some students can only be motivated by waiting until the last minute to begin a project. These students are excited and motivated by playing a game of "Beat the Clock." They like living on the edge and the adrenaline rush of responding to a crisis. Playing this game provides motivation, but it does not leave enough time to achieve the best results. Inevitably, things happen at the last minute to make the game even more exciting and dangerous: the printer breaks, the computer crashes, the student gets ill, the car breaks down, or the dog eats the homework. These students need to start projects earlier to improve their chances of success. It is best to seek excitement elsewhere, in sports or other competitive activities.

- **Excellence without effort.** In this scenario, students believe that they are truly outstanding and can achieve success without effort. These students think that they can go to college without attending classes or reading the text. They believe that they can pass the test without studying. They often do not succeed in college the first semester, which puts them at risk of dropping out of school. They often return to college later and improve their performance by putting in the effort required.

- **Loss of control.** Some students fear loss of control over their lives and procrastinate to gain control. An example is students who attend college because others (such as parents) want them to attend. Procrastination becomes a way of gaining control over the situation by saying, "You can't make me do this." They attend college but accomplish nothing. Parents can support and encourage education, but students need to choose their own goals in life and attend college because it is an important personal goal.

Tips for Dealing with Procrastination

When you find yourself procrastinating on a certain task, think about the consequences. Will the procrastination lead to failing an exam or getting a low grade? Think about the rewards of doing the task. If you do well, you can take pride in yourself and celebrate your success. How will you feel when the task is completed? Will you be able to enjoy your leisure time without guilt about not doing your work? How does the task help you to achieve your lifetime goals?

Maybe the procrastination is a warning sign that you need to reconsider lifetime goals and change them to better suit your needs.

Procrastination Scenario

George is a college student who is on academic probation for having low grades. He is required to make a plan for improving his grades in order to remain in college. George tells the counselor that he is making poor grades because of his procrastination. He is an accounting major and puts off doing homework because he dislikes it and does not find it interesting. The counselor asks George why he had chosen accounting as a major. He replies that accounting is a major that is in demand and has a good salary. The counselor suggests that George consider a major that he would enjoy more. After some consideration, George changes his major to psychology. He becomes more interested in college studies and is able to raise his grades to stay in college.

Most of the time, you will reap benefits by avoiding procrastination and completing the task at hand. Jane Burka and Lenora Yuen suggest the following steps to deal with procrastination:

1. Select a goal.

2. Visualize your progress.

3. Be careful not to sabotage yourself.

4. Stick to a time limit.

5. Don't wait until you feel like it.

6. Follow through. Watch out for excuses and focus on one step at a time.

7. Reward yourself after you have made some progress.

8. Be flexible about your goal.

9. Remember that it does not have to be perfect.[5]

Notes

1. Steven K. Scott, A Millionaire's Notebook, *quoted In Rob Gilbert, Editor, Bits & Pieces*, November 4, 1999, 15.

2. Alan Lakein, *How to Get Control of Your Time and Your Life* (New York: Peter H. Wyden, 1973).

3. Ibid., 70–71.

4. Dave Ellis, *Becoming a Master Student* (Boston: Houghton Mifflin, 1998).

5. Jane Burka and Lenora Yuen, *Procrastination* (Reading, MA: Addison-Wesley, 1983).

CHAPTER 3

Thinking Critically and Creatively

Learning Objectives

Read to answer these key questions:

- What is critical thinking?

- What are fallacies in reasoning?

- What is moral reasoning?

- What are some techniques for critical thinking?

- What is creativity?

- How can I improve my creativity?

- How is laughter a key to success?

Your college experience will help you to develop critical thinking, moral reasoning, and creative thinking skills. Critical thinking involves analyzing data, generating alternatives, and solving problems. Moral reasoning guides thought and action to help you live an ethical life. Creative thinking helps you to find new ideas to solve problems in your personal and professional life.

Critical Thinking

Critical thinking involves questioning established ideas, creating new ideas, and using information to solve problems. In critical thinking, reasoning is used in the pursuit of truth. Part of obtaining a college education is learning to think critically. Understanding the concepts of critical thinking will help you succeed in college courses in which critical thinking is used.

Beyond college, critical thinking is helpful in being a good citizen and a productive member of society. Throughout history, critical thinkers have helped to advance civilization. Thoughts that were once widely accepted were questioned, and newer and more useful ideas were introduced. For example, it was once assumed that bloodsucking leeches were helpful in curing diseases. Some critical thinkers questioned this practice, and the science of medicine was advanced. It was not so long ago that women were not allowed to vote. Critical thinkers questioned this practice so that women could participate in a democratic society.

A lack of critical thinking can lead to great tragedy. In his memoirs, Adolf Eichmann, who played a central role in the Nazis' killing of six million Jews during World War II, wrote:

"From my childhood, obedience was something I could not get out of my system. When I entered the armed services at the age of 27, I found being obedient not a bit more difficult than it had been during my life at that point. It was unthinkable that I would not follow orders. Now that I look back, I realize that a life predicated on being obedient and taking orders is a very comfortable life indeed. Living in such a way reduces to a minimum one's own need to think."[1]

Critical and creative thinking are closely related. If you can think critically, you have the freedom to be creative and generate new ideas. The great American jurist and philosopher Oliver Wendell Holmes noted:

"There are one-story intellects, two-story intellects, and three-story intellects with skylights. All fact-collectors who have no aim beyond their facts are one-story men. Two-story men compare, reason, generalize, using the labor of the fact-collectors as their own. Three-story men idealize, imagine, predict—their best illumination comes from above through skylights."

Use the information in this chapter to become a three-story intellect with skylights. And by the way, even though Oliver Wendell Holmes talked about men, women can be three-story intellects too.

"A person's mind stretched to a new idea never goes back to its original dimensions."
Oliver Wendell Holmes

"I think, therefore I am (Cogito, ergo sum)."
Descartes

Fallacies in Reasoning

To think critically, you need to be able to recognize fallacies in reasoning.[2] Fallacies are patterns of incorrect reasoning. Recognizing these fallacies can help you to avoid them in your thinking and writing. You can also become aware of when others are using these fallacies to persuade you. They may use these fallacies for their own purpose, such as power or financial gain. As you read through these fallacies in reasoning, think about examples you have experienced in your personal life.

- **Appeal to authority.** It is best to make decisions by reviewing the information and arguments and reaching our own conclusions. Sometimes we are encouraged to rely on experts for a recommendation because they have specialized information. Obviously, we need to have trust in the experts to accept their conclusions. However, when we cite some person as an authority in a certain area when they are not, we make an appeal to a questionable authority. For example, when a company uses famous sports figures to endorse a product, a particular brand of athletic shoes or breakfast cereal, they are appealing to a questionable authority. Just because the athletes are famous does not mean they are experts on the product they are endorsing. They are endorsing the product to earn money. Many commercials you see on TV use appeals to a questionable authority.

- **Jumping to conclusions.** When we jump to conclusions, we make hasty generalizations. For example, if a college student borrows money from a bank and does not pay it back, the manager of the bank might conclude that all college students are poor risks and refuse to give loans to other college students.

- **Making generalizations.** We make generalizations when we say that all members of a group are the same, as in:

  All lawyers are greedy.
  All blondes are airheads.

Of course, your occupation does not determine whether or not you are greedy, and the color of your hair does not determine your intelligence. Such thinking leads to harmful stereotypes and fallacies in reasoning. Instead of generalizing, think of people as unique individuals.

- **Attacking the person rather than discussing the issues.** To distract attention from the issues, we often attack the person. Political candidates today are routinely asked about personal issues such as extramarital affairs and drug use. Of course personal integrity in politicians is important, but attacking the person can serve as a smokescreen to direct attention away from important political issues. Critical thinkers avoid reacting emotionally to personalities and use logical thinking to analyze the issues.

- **Appeal to common belief.** Just because something is a common belief does not mean that it is true. At one time people believed that the world was flat and that when you got to the edge of the earth, you would fall off. If you were to survey the people who lived in that period in history, the majority would have agreed that the earth was flat. A survey just tells us what people believe. The survey does not tell us what is true and accurate.

- **Appeal to common practice.** Appealing to common practice is the "everyone else is doing it" argument. Just because everyone else does it doesn't mean that it is right. Here are some common examples of this fallacy:

  It is okay to cheat in school. Everyone else does it.
  It is okay to speed on the freeway. Everyone else does it.
  It is okay to cheat on your taxes. Everyone else does it.

- **Appeal to tradition.** Appeal to tradition is a variation of the "everyone else is doing it" argument. The appeal to tradition is "we've always done it that way." Just because that is the way it has always been done doesn't mean it is the best way to do it. With this attitude, it is very difficult to make changes and improve our ways of doing things. While tradition is very important, it is open to question. For example, construction and automotive technology have traditionally been career choices for men, but not for women. When women tried to enter or work in these careers, there was resistance from those who did not want to change traditions. This resistance limited options for women.

> "The function of education is to teach one to think intensively and to think critically. Intelligence plus character—that is the goal of true education."
> Martin Luther King, Jr.

Fallacies in Reasoning

- Appeal to authority
- Jumping to conclusions
- Making generalizations
- Attacking the person
- Appeal to common belief
- Appeal to common practice
- Appeal to tradition
- Two wrongs
- Domino theory
- Wishful thinking
- Scare tactics
- Appeal to pity
- Appeal to loyalty
- Appeal to prejudice
- Appeal to vanity
- False causes
- Straw man/woman
- Cult behavior

- **Two wrongs.** In this fallacy, it is assumed that it is acceptable to do something because other people are doing something just as bad. For example, if someone cuts you off on the freeway, you may assume that it is acceptable to zoom ahead and cut in front of his or her car. The "two wrongs" fallacy has an element of retribution, or getting back at the other person. The old saying, "Two wrongs do not make a right," applies in this situation.
- **The slippery slope or domino theory.** The slippery slope or domino theory is best explained with an example. A student might think: If I fail the test, I will fail this class. If I fail this class, I will drop out of college. My parents will disown me and I will lose the respect of my friends. I will not be able to get a good job. I will start drinking and end up homeless. In this fallacy, the negative consequences of our actions are only remotely possible, but are assumed to be certain. These dire consequences influence people's decisions and change behavior. In this situation, it is important to evaluate these consequences. One does not necessarily lead to the other. If you fail the test, you could study and pass the next test. As a child you were probably cautioned about many slippery slopes in life:

> Brush your teeth or your teeth will fall out.
> Do your homework or you will never get into college and get a good job.

ACTIVITY

Practice Matching Fallacies in Reasoning, Part I

The column on the left contains examples of fallacies in reasoning. Match each example with the name of the fallacy on the right.

Example:

_____ 1. Women should not be automotive mechanics.

_____ 2. The best sports shoes are those endorsed by famous athletes.

_____ 3. It is OK for athletes to take drugs to enhance their performance. They all do it.

_____ 4. All women with red hair get angry easily.

_____ 5. If you fail the test, you are a failure for life.

_____ 6. To defeat a politician, research his personal background and let the public know of any past mistakes.

_____ 7. Since some children steal, children should not be allowed into the store without their parents.

_____ 8. All sharks are dangerous and should be killed.

_____ 9. If someone insults you, you should insult them back.

Fallacy:

A. Appeal to authority

B. Appeal to tradition

C. Common practice

D. Two wrongs

E. Attack the person

F. Making generalizations

G. Appeal to a common belief

H. Slippery slope

I. Jumping to conclusions

Answers: 1. B, 2. A, 3. C, 4. F, 5. H, 6. E, 7. I, 8. G, 9. D

- **Wishful thinking.** In wishful thinking, an extremely positive outcome, however remote, is proposed as a distraction from logical thinking. For example, a new sports stadium may be proposed. Extremely positive outcomes may be presented, such as downtown redevelopment, the attraction of professional sports teams, increased revenue, and the creation of jobs. Opponents, on the other hand, might foresee increased taxes, lack of parking, and neglect of other important social priorities such as education and shelter for the homeless. Neither position is correct if we assume that the outcomes are certain and automatic. Outcomes need to be evaluated realistically.

  Wishful thinking is often used in commercials to sell products. Here are a few examples:

  > Eat what you want and lose weight.
  > Use this cream and look younger.
  > Use this cologne and women will be attracted to you.
  > Invest your money and get rich quick.

- **Appeal to fear or scare tactics.** Sometimes people appeal to fear as a way of blocking rational thinking. I once saw a political commercial that showed wolves chasing a person through the forest. It was clearly designed to evoke fear. The message was to vote against a proposition to limit lawyers' fees. The idea was that if lawyers' fees were limited, the poor client would be a victim of limited legal services.

  This commercial used scare tactics to interfere with rational thinking about the issue.

- **Appeal to pity.** In an appeal to pity, emotion is used to replace logic. It is what is known as a "sob story." Appeals to pity may be legitimate when used to foster charity and empathy. However, the sob story uses emotion in place of reason to persuade and is often exaggerated. College faculties often hear sob stories from students having academic difficulties:

  > Please don't disqualify me from college. I failed all my classes because I was emotionally upset when my grandmother died.

  > Please don't fail me in this class. If you fail me, my parents will kick me out of the house and I will not be able to get health insurance.

  > If you fail me in this class, I won't be eligible to play football and my future as a professional will be ruined.

- **Appeal to loyalty.** Human beings are social creatures who enjoy being attached to a group. We feel loyalty to our friends, families, schools, communities, teams, and favorite musicians. Appeals to loyalty ask you to act according to a group's best interests without considering whether the actions are right or wrong. Critical thinkers, however, do not support an idea just to show support for a group with which they identify.

  Peer pressure is related to the loyalty fallacy. With peer pressure, members of a group may feel obliged to act in a certain way because they think members of the group act that way. Another variation of the loyalty fallacy is called the bandwagon argument. It involves supporting a certain idea just to be part of the group. This tendency is powerful when the group is perceived to be powerful or "cool." In elections, people often vote for the candidate that is perceived to be the most popular. If everyone else is voting for the candidate, they assume the candidate must be the best. This is not necessarily true.

- **Appeal to prejudice.** A prejudice is judging a group of people or things positively or negatively, even if the facts do not agree with the judgment. A prejudice is based on a stereotype in which all members of a group are judged to be the same. Speakers sometimes appeal to prejudice to gain support for their causes. Listen for the appeal to prejudice in hate speeches or literature directed against different ethnicities, genders, or sexual orientations.

- **Appeal to vanity.** The appeal to vanity is also known as "apple polishing." The goal of this strategy is to get agreement by paying compliments. Students who pay compliments to teachers and then ask for special treatment are engaging in apple polishing.

- **Post hoc reasoning, or false causes.** Post hoc reasoning has to do with cause and effect. It explains many superstitions. If I play a good game of golf whenever I wear a certain hat, I might conclude that the hat causes me to play a good golf game. The hat, however, is a false cause of playing a good game of golf. I may feel more comfortable wearing my lucky hat, but it is a secondary reason for playing well. I play well because I practice my golf skills and develop my self-confidence. In scientific research, care is taken to test for false causes. Just because an event regularly follows another event does not mean that the first event caused the second event. For example, when the barometer falls, it rains. The falling barometer does not cause the rain; a drop in atmospheric pressure causes the rain. If falling barometers caused the rain, we could all be rainmakers by adjusting our barometers.

- **Straw man or woman.** Watch for this fallacy during election time. Using this strategy, a politician creates a misleading image of someone else's statements, ideas, or beliefs to make them easy to attack. For example, politicians might accuse their opponents of raising taxes. That may only be part of the story, however. Maybe their opponents also voted for many tax-saving measures. When politicians or anyone else use the straw man fallacy, they are falsifying or oversimplifying. Use your critical thinking to identify the straw man or woman (political opponent) in the next election. Of course you don't have to be a politician to use this strategy. People use this strategy when they spread gossip or rumors about someone they want to discredit.

- **Cult behavior.** Cults and doomsday forecasters spread unorthodox and sometimes harmful beliefs with great fervor. These thoughts are perpetuated through mind-control techniques. With mind control, members of a group are taught to suppress natural emotions and accept the ideas of the group in exchange for a sense of belonging. These groups do not allow members to think critically or question the belief system. Mind control is the opposite of critical thinking. It is important to use critical thinking when you encounter beliefs for which there is no hard evidence. An example is the Heaven's Gate cult:

  > It all seems perfectly ludicrous: 39 people don their new sneakers, pack their flight bags and poison themselves in the solemn belief that a passing UFO will whisk them off to Wonderland.

Practice Matching Fallacies in Reasoning, Part II

The column on the left contains examples of fallacies in reasoning. Match each example with the name of the fallacy on the right.

Example:

_____1. You look really nice today. Can I ask you a favor?

_____2. I'll vote for a woman because I am a woman.

_____3. Earn $10,000 a month by working part time at home.

_____4. If you fail me on this test, the coach will not let me play next week.

_____5. I'm more likely to win if I wear my lucky socks.

_____6. If you vote for this politician, she will raise taxes.

_____7. If you don't buy this car, you are putting your family at risk.

_____8. All large dogs are dangerous.

_____9. The leader knows what is best for me.

Fallacy:

A. Wishful thinking

B. Scare tactics

C. Appeal to pity

D. Appeal to loyalty

E. Appeal to prejudice

F. Appeal to vanity

G. Post hoc reasoning

H. Straw man or woman

I. Cult behavior

Answers: 1. F, 2. D, 3. A, 4. C, 5. G, 6. H, 7. B, 8. E, 9. I

Journal Entry #1

Fallacies in reasoning are frequently used in advertisements and politics. From your personal experience, describe an example of a fallacy in reasoning.

How to Become a Critical Thinker

The Critical Thinking Process

When thinking about a complex problem, use these steps in the critical thinking process:

1. **State the problem in a clear and simple way.** Sometimes the message is unclear or obscured by appeals to emotion. Stating the problem clearly brings it into focus so that you can identify the issue and begin to work on it.

2. **Identify the alternative views.** In looking at different views, you open your mind to a wider range of options. The diagram entitled "Alternative Views" below gives a perspective on point of view. For every issue, there are many points of view.

The larger circle represents these many points of view. The individual point of view is represented by a dot on the larger circle. Experience, values, beliefs, culture, and knowledge influence an individual's point of view.

3. **Watch for fallacies** in reasoning when looking at alternative views.

4. **Find at least three different answers.** In searching for these different answers, you force yourself to look at all the possibilities before you decide on the best answer.

5. **Construct your own reasonable view.** After looking at the alternatives and considering different answers to the problem, construct your own reasonable view. Practice this process using the critical thinking exercises at the end of this chapter.

Figure 11.1 Alternative Views

Tips for Critical Thinking

1. **Be aware of your mindset.** A mindset is a pattern of thought that you use out of habit. You develop patterns of thinking based on your personal experiences, culture, and environment. When the situation changes, your old mindset may need to change as well.

2. **Be willing to say, "I don't know."** With this attitude you are open to exploring new ideas. In today's rapidly changing world, it is not possible to know everything. Rather than trying to know everything, it is more important to be able to find the information you need.

3. **Practice tolerance for other people's ideas.** We all have different views of the world based on our own experiences and can benefit from an open exchange of information.

4. **Try to look for several answers and understand many points of view.** The world is not either-or or black-and-white. Looking at all the possibilities is the first step in finding a creative solution.

5. **Understand before criticizing.** Life is not about justifying your point of view. It is important to understand and then offer your suggestions.

6. **Realize that your emotions can get in the way of clear thinking.** We all have beliefs that are important to us. It is difficult to listen to a different point of view when someone questions your personal beliefs. Open your mind to see all the alternatives. Then construct your reasonable view.

7. **Notice the source of the information you are analyzing.** Political announcements are required to include information about the person or organization paying for the ad. Knowing who paid for an advertisement can help you understand and evaluate the point of view that is being promoted.

8. **Ask the question, "What makes the author think so?"** In this way, you can discover what premises the author is using to justify his or her position.

9. **Ask the question, "So what?"** Ask this question to determine what is important and how the author reached the conclusion.

Figure 11.2
Adapted from the Foundation for Critical Thinking[3]

Critical Thinking over the Internet

The Internet is revolutionizing the way we access and retrieve information today. Through the use of search engines, websites, electronic periodicals, and online reference materials, it is possible to find just about any information you need. The Internet is also full of scams, rumors, gossip, hoaxes, exaggerations, and illegal activity. Anyone can put anything on the Internet. You will need to apply critical thinking to the information that you find on the Internet. Author Reid Goldsborough offers these suggestions for thinking critically about material on the Internet:

- **Don't be fooled by appearances.** It is easy to create a flashy and professional-looking website. Some products and services are legitimate, but some are scams.

- **Find out about the person or organization providing the information.** There should be links to a home page that lists the author's background and credentials. You need to be skeptical if the author is not identified. If you cannot identify the person who authored the website, find out what organization sponsored the site. Most of the Internet resources cited in this text are provided by educational or government sources. It is the goal of these organizations to provide the public with information.

Critical Thinking Tips

- Be aware of your mindset.
- Say "I don't know."
- Be tolerant.
- Look for several answers.
- Understand.
- Recognize emotions.
- Examine the source.
- Ask, "Why?"
- Ask, "So what?"

- **Look for the reason the information was posted.** What is the agenda? Keep this in mind when evaluating the information. Many websites exist to sell a product or influence public opinion.
- **Look for the date that the information was created or revised.** A good website posts the date of creation or revision.
- **Try to verify the information elsewhere,** especially if the information is at odds with common sense or what you believe to be true. Verify the information through other websites or your local library.[4]

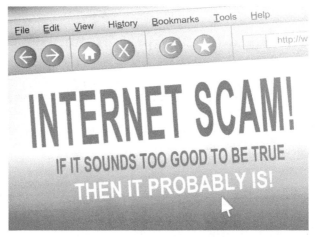

© 2014, Sam72. Used under license with Shutterstock, Inc.

How to Recognize a Scam

Use your critical thinking skills to recognize a scam or hoax. How can you recognize a scam? Here are some signs to watch for:

- **Be aware of big promises.** If something sounds too good to be true, it probably is a hoax. If you are promised $5,000 a month for working part time out of your home, be careful. If you are offered a new TV in a box for $50, the box may contain stolen goods or even rocks!
- **The word "free" is often used to catch your attention to make a sale.** Few things in life are free.
- **A similar tactic is to offer money or a prize.** The scam goes like this: "Congratulations! You have just won a . . ." Be especially careful if you have to pay money to claim your prize.
- **Beware of high-pressure tactics.** A common scam is to ask you to pay money now or the price will go up. Take your time to think carefully about your expenditures. If the deal is legitimate, it will be there tomorrow.
- **To avoid identity theft, be careful about disclosing personal information** such as Social Security numbers and credit card numbers. Disclose this information only to people and organizations you know and trust.
- **If you suspect a scam, research the offer on the Internet.** Use a search engine such as yahoo.com or google.com and type in the word "scam." You can find descriptions of many different types of scams. You can also find information on the latest scams or file a complaint at the Federal Trade Commission website at www.ftc.gov.

Critical Thinking

Test what you have learned by selecting the correct answers to the following questions.

1. Critical thinking involves

   a. being critical of others' opinions.
   b. identifying alternative views.
   c. finding only one correct answer.

2. To be a critical thinker it is important to

   a. understand before criticizing.
   b. justify your point of view.
   c. tell yourself that you know the answer.

3. Construct your reasonable view by

   a. advocating for your point of view.
   b. always defending your mindset.
   c. first considering different answers.

4. An Internet site is legitimate if it

   a. looks professional.
   b. has useful information.
   c. has an identifiable and reputable source.

5. If you are offered something that is too good to be true,

   a. be thankful for your good fortune.
   b. suspect that it could be a scam.
   c. it could be a good investment.

How did you do on the quiz? Check your answers: 1. b, 2. a, 3. c, 4. c, 5. b

---

Journal Entry #2

How can you apply critical thinking in your college courses?

Critical Thinking and Moral Reasoning

Beyond recognizing fallacies in reasoning, critical thinking involves rationally deciding what to believe, how to act, and what is right or wrong. It involves assessing personal views and the views of others in order to make good decisions about living your life in an ethical manner. Psychologist Lawrence Kohlberg studied stages of moral reasoning by investigating the reactions of individuals to moral dilemmas. Here is an example of Kohlberg's most famous dilemma:

Heinz Steals the Drug

In Europe, a woman was near death from a special kind of cancer. There was one drug that the doctors thought might save her. It was a form of radium that a druggist in the same town had recently discovered. The drug was expensive to make, but the druggist was charging 10 times what the drug cost him to make. He paid $200 for the radium and charged $2,000 for a small dose of the drug.

"It is the mark of an educated mind to be able to entertain a thought without accepting it."
Aristotle

"Education's purpose is to replace an empty mind with an open one."
Malcolm Forbes

© 2014, Lorelyn Medina. Used under license with Shutterstock, Inc.

The sick woman's husband, Heinz, went to everyone he knew to borrow the money, but he could only get together about $1,000 which was half of what it cost. He told the druggist that his wife was dying and asked him to sell it cheaper or let him pay later. But the druggist said, "No, I discovered the drug and I'm going to make money from it." So Heinz got desperate and broke into the man's store to steal the drug for his wife. Should the husband have done that?[5]

Journal Entry #3

What would you do in the Heinz dilemma? Would you steal the drug? Why?

Kohlberg was not interested in the question of whether what Heinz did what was right or wrong, but the reasoning used in reaching a decision. He found that children moved through different levels and stages of moral reasoning, from an egocentric view of the world in which they made decisions based on what was good for the individual, to a more socially responsible view of the world in which decisions were made based on what was good for society, and finally to decisions based on the universal principles of fairness and justice. Individuals progress through these stages as they gain experience thinking about moral problems.

Level 1. Pre-Conventional Morality

This stage of reasoning is common in children, but is sometimes used by adults. At this level, morality is determined by consequences to the individual involved.

Stage 1: Obedience and Punishment

At this stage, children obey the rules to avoid punishment. In the case of the Heinz dilemma, here are possible actions:

- Heinz should not steal the drug because it is against the law.
- Heinz should steal the drug because the pharmacist is asking too much money for it.

Stage 2: Individualism and Exchange

At this stage, children make decisions based on how it will best serve their needs as an individual: "How will it affect me?"

- Heinz should not steal the drug because he will be unhappy if he goes to prison.
- Heinz should steal the drug because he will be happier if he can save his wife.

© 2014, Ivelin Radkov. Used under license with Shutterstock, Inc.

Level 2. Conventional Morality

Conventional morality is more typical of adolescents and adults. People take into consideration society's views and expectations in making decisions about moral behavior. The individual follows society's conventions about what is right or wrong without questioning the fairness or appropriateness of the rule.

Stage 3: Interpersonal Relationships

At this stage, individuals attempt to live up to societal expectations and are concerned about others. The child attempts to be a "good boy" or a "good girl." Adults attempt to "be nice" or conform to the rules of society.

- Heinz should not steal the drug because stealing is bad and he is not a criminal.
- Heinz should steal the drug because he is a good husband and wants to take care of his wife.

Stage 4: Maintaining Social Order

At this stage it is important to do one's duty, respect authority, and follow the rules to maintain law and order. If one person violates a law, others will do it also and society will cease to function in an orderly way.

- Heinz should not steal the drug because the law prohibits stealing. If everyone broke the law, there would be no order in society.
- Heinz should steal the drug, but be prepared to accept the punishment for his actions and to repay the druggist.

Level 3. Post-Conventional Morality

In this level of morality, individuals are seen as separate entities from society and live by the highest principles based on basic human rights such as life, liberty, and justice. Rules are viewed as useful, but changeable in order to protect human rights and maintain social order. Rules and laws are not absolute dictates that must be obeyed without question. A totalitarian society where everyone followed the rules would be well organized, but unjust.

Stage 5: Social Contract and Individual Rights

Rules are important for maintaining a society, but there are differing values, opinions, and beliefs about what is right and wrong. Laws are regarded as social contracts, and individuals should agree on them. If laws do not promote the general welfare, they should be changed to promote what is best for most people. It is important to protect human rights and resolve differences through democratic processes.

- Heinz should not steal the drug because a scientist has a right to fair compensation for the discovery. Fair compensation encourages further drug development.
- Heinz should steal the drug because everyone has the right to life, regardless of the law.

Stage 6: Universal Principles

Democratic processes do not always work as when the majority votes for laws that harm the minority. Laws are only valid if they result in justice and respect for all people; people should disobey unjust laws. The individual acts because it is right, not because is expected, legal, or agreed upon by the majority. Examples of individuals who operated at this level include Gandhi, Martin Luther King, and Cesar Chavez, who all used civil disobedience to achieve just laws. Kohlberg found it difficult to find people who consistently operated at this level.

- Heinz should not steal the drug because others may need the drug just as badly and all lives are equally important.
- Heinz should steal the drug because saving a human life is more important than property rights.

At this stage, Kohlberg suggests that we reach decisions by taking an impartial look at the situation through one another's eyes. When the druggist looks at the situation from Heinz's perspective, he might realize that human life is more important than property rights and agree to give the drug to the wife. When Heinz looks at the situation from the druggist's perspective, he might agree to make payments for the drug. This would be a fair and just solution in which everyone is given full and equal respect.

© 2014, Hermin. Used under license with Shutterstock, Inc.

What Is Creativity?

To see creativity in action, all we need to do is to look at young children. Movie producer Steven Spielberg describes their creativity:

> *"The greatest quality that we can possess is curiosity, a genuine interest in the world around us. The most used word—and I have five kids, so I know what I'm talking about—the most used word in a child's vocabulary is 'why.' A child doesn't blindly accept things as they are, doesn't blindly believe in limits, doesn't blindly believe in the words spoken by some authority figure like me."[6]*

Creativity involves both divergent and convergent thinking. **Divergent thinking** is the ability to discover many alternatives. The creative individual looks for problems, asks why, and comes up with many different answers. J. P. Guilford, a researcher on creativity, said that "the person who is capable of producing a large number of ideas per unit of time, other things being equal, has a greater chance of having significant ideas."[7] After many ideas are created, **convergent thinking** is used to combine the ideas to find new and creative solutions. These creative ideas are used to make a new plan of action.

Creative thinking is useful in fields such as the arts, science, and business. Creativity helps in the enjoyment of outside activities, such as hobbies, that help us to lead satisfying lives. Creativity is important in generating alternatives necessary for effective problem solving and coming up with creative solutions to the challenges we all face in life. Creative individuals are motivated, engaged, and open to new ideas. Guilford defines creative behavior as follows:

> *"The individual who behaves creatively is oriented toward selecting and solving meaningful problems, using an inner drive to recombine his or her storehouse of experiences in new ways. In attacking problems, he or she does not act as a conformist; instead, he or she pioneers often, is not afraid to fail frequently, but is productive in the long run."[8]*

The Three S's of Creativity: Sensitivity, Synergy, and Serendipity

The creative process involves sensitivity, synergy, and serendipity. Creative persons use their **sensitivity** to discover the world and spot problems, deficiencies, and incongruities. A person who is sensitive asks, "Why does this happen?" Sensitive persons are also inventive and ask the question, "How can I do this?" They are problem finders as well as problem solvers.

Synergy occurs when two or more elements are associated in a new way and the result is greater than the sum of the parts. For example, imagine a machine that combines the telephone, the computer, the television, and a music player. The combining of these familiar devices into one machine is changing the way we live. Another example of synergy is the old saying, "Two heads are better than one." When two or more people work together and share ideas, the result is often greater than what one person could produce alone. This is the essence of creativity.

"Questions are the creative acts of intelligence."
Frank Kingdon

"Happiness lies in the joy of achievement and the thrill of creative effort."
Franklin Roosevelt

"The real voyage of discovery consists not in making new landscapes but in having new eyes."
Marcel Proust

The word **serendipity** is attributed to Horace Walpole, who wrote a story about the Persian princes of Serendip. The princes made unexpected discoveries while they were looking for something else. Serendipity is finding something by a lucky accident. You can only take advantage of a lucky accident if you look around and find new meaning and opportunity in the event. An example of serendipity comes from a story about the famous musician Duke Ellington. He was playing at an outdoor concert when a noisy plane flew over the stage. He changed the tempo of the music to go with the sounds of the airplane and directed the plane along with the orchestra. Another example of serendipity is Alexander Fleming's discovery of penicillin. He was growing bacteria in his lab when a spore of *penicillium notatum* blew in the window, landed on the bacteria, and killed it. Instead of throwing away a ruined experiment, he discovered the antibiotic penicillin, one of the most important medical discoveries ever made. Serendipitous people are flexible and open to possibilities as well as fearless in trying something new. They learn to seize the opportunities that just happen in life.

Figure 11.3 Sensitivity, synergy, and serendipity are the three S's of creativity.

Creative Thinking Techniques

- **Brainstorming.** One of the most important components of creativity is the ability to use divergent thinking to generate many ideas or alternatives. Brainstorming is one of the most frequently used techniques to develop divergent thinking. The key to brainstorming is to delay critical judgment to allow for the spontaneous flow of ideas. Critical judgment about the merit of ideas can hinder the creative process if it is applied too early. Here are the rules of brainstorming:

© 2014, VLADGRIN. Used under license with
Shutterstock, Inc.

- Generate a large quantity of ideas without regard to quality. This increases the likelihood that some of the ideas will be good or useful.
- Set a time limit to encourage quick thinking. The time limit is generally short, from three to five minutes.
- Set a goal or quota for the number of ideas you want to generate. The goal serves as a motivator.
- The wilder and more unusual the ideas, the better. It is easier to tame down crazy ideas than to think up new ideas.
- Use synergy by brainstorming with a group of people. Build on other people's ideas. Sometimes two ideas combined can make one better idea.
- Select the best ideas from the list.

- **Relaxed attention.** Can you imagine being relaxed and paying attention at the same time? Robert McKim describes this as the paradox of the Ho-hum and the Aha![8] To be creative, it is first necessary to relax. The brain works better when it is relaxed. By relaxing, the individual releases full energy and attention to the task at hand. Athletes and entertainers must master the art of relaxation before they can excel in athletics or entertainment. If the muscles are too tense, blood flow is restricted and energy is wasted. However, totally relaxed individuals cannot think at all. They might even be asleep!

Some tension, but not too much, is needed to think and be creative; hence the term "relaxed attention." In the creative process, the person first thinks about a task, problem, or creation and then relaxes to let the ideas incubate. During this incubation period, the person often gets a flash of insight or feeling of "Aha!" Famous artist Pablo Picasso described this process:

> "For me creation first starts with contemplation, and I need long, idle hours of meditation. It is then that I work most. I look at flies, at flowers, at leaves and trees around me. I let my mind drift at ease, just like a boat in the current. Sooner or later, it is caught by something. It gets precise. It takes shape . . . my next painting motif is decided."[9]

As a student you can apply the principle of relaxed attention to improve your creativity. If you are thinking about a problem and get stuck, relax and come back to it later. Take a break, do something else, or even sleep on it. You are likely to come up with creative inspiration while you are relaxing. Then get back to solving the problem and pay attention to it.

"The best way to have a good idea is to have lots of ideas."

Linus Pauling

Creative Thinking Techniques

- Brainstorming
- Relaxed attention
- Idea files
- Visualization and imagination
- Read
- Keep a journal
- Think critically

- **Use idea files.** Keep files of ideas that you find interesting. People in advertising call these "swipe files." No one creates in a vacuum. Some of the best creative ideas involve recombining or building on the ideas of others or looking at them from a different perspective. This is different from copying other people's ideas; it is using them as the fertilizer for creative thinking.

  As a college student, you might keep files of the following:

  - Interesting ideas and their sources for use in writing term papers
  - Information about careers
  - Information for your resume
  - Information that you can use to apply for scholarships
  - Ideas related to your hobbies
  - Ideas for having fun
  - Ideas for saving money

- **Practice using visualization and imagination.** Visualizing and imagining are important in the creative process. Young children are naturally good at these two skills. What happens as we grow older? As we grow older, we learn to follow the rules and color between the lines. We need rules to have an orderly society, yet we need visualization and imagination to move forward and create new ideas. Don't forget to use and practice visualization and imagination.

  Visualization and imagination can be fun and interesting activities to help you relax. We have often been told not to daydream, but daydreams can be a tool for relaxation as well as creativity. It is important to come back to reality once we are finished daydreaming. The last step in the creative process is doing something with the best of our creative ideas.

- **Read.** One of the best ways to trigger your creativity is to read a wide variety of materials, including newspapers, magazines, novels, nonfiction books, and articles on the Internet. The ideas that you discover will provide background information, helping you gain perspective on the world, and give you ideas for making your own contributions. When you read, you expose your mind to the greatest people who have ever lived. Make reading a habit.

- **Keep a journal.** Keep a journal of your creative ideas, thoughts, and problems. Writing often will help you think clearly. When you write about your problems, it is almost like having your own private therapist. In college, your journal can be a source of creative ideas for writing term papers and completing assignments.

- **Think critically.** Approach learning with a sense of awe, excitement, and skepticism. Here is another paradox! Creative and critical thinkers have much in common. Both ask questions, look at the world from different perspectives, and generate new alternatives.

"To dream anything that you want to dream, that is the beauty of the human mind. To do anything that you want to do, that is the strength of the human will. To trust yourself to test the limits, that is the courage to succeed."
Bernard Edmonds

"Creativity is allowing yourself to make mistakes. Art is knowing which ones to keep."
Scott Adams

"Imagination is everything. It is the preview of life's coming attractions."
Albert Einstein

Creative Thinking

Test what you have learned by selecting the correct answers to the following questions.

1. Divergent thinking is a creative thinking technique that involves:

   a. defending the correct answer.
   b. selecting the one best alternative.
   c. the ability to discover many different alternatives.

2. The following saying is a good definition for synergy:

   a. Seeing is believing.
   b. Two heads are better than one.
   c. Practice makes perfect.

3. Serendipity is:

   a. finding something by a lucky accident.
   b. finding something humorous in the situation.
   c. improvising while playing music.

4. When using relaxed attention as a creative process,

   a. the creative person is totally relaxed.
   b. the creative person is focusing attention.
   c. the creative person first thinks about the problem and then relaxes.

5. For brainstorming, it is important to:

   a. select the best ideas as a last step.
   b. consider only the good ideas.
   c. consider only the workable ideas.

How did you do on the quiz? Check your answers: 1. c, 2. b, 3. a, 4. c, 5. a

---

"Laugh at yourself first, before anyone else can."
Elsa Maxwell

"If we couldn't laugh, we would all go insane."
Jimmy Buffett

Journal Entry #4

Describe at least two creativity techniques that you use or are willing to try. Creativity techniques include brainstorming, using relaxed attention, idea files, visualization, imagination, reading, keeping a journal, and thinking critically.

KEYS TO SUCCESS

Learn to Laugh at Life

"Have a laugh at life and look around you for happiness instead of sadness. Laughter has always brought me out of unhappy situations. Even in your darkest moment, you usually can find something to laugh about if you try hard enough." Red Skelton

All of us face difficult times in life; but if we can learn the gift of laughter and have a good sense of humor, it is easier to deal with the difficulties.

Laughter has important physical as well as emotional benefits. Laughter relaxes the body, boosts the immune system, and even improves the function of blood vessels and increases blood flow, which can protect the heart. It adds joy and zest to life, reduces anxiety, relieves stress, improves mood, and enhances resilience. Being more relaxed can help you to shift perspective, solve problems, and be more creative.

Just putting a smile on your face can help. German psychologist Fritz Strack had his subjects watch a cartoon with a pencil in their mouths. Half of his subjects held the pencil between their teeth, which made them smile. The other half of his subjects held the pencil between their lips, which made them frown. The smiling group thought that the cartoon was funnier. It seems that there is a connection between our physical responses and our internal feelings. The physical act of smiling actually makes you feel happier.[10]

If you do not feel happy, smile and pretend to feel happy. Neurophysicist Richard Hamilton says that if you pretend to be happy, you actually feel better because positive thoughts and behavior impact the biochemistry of the brain. Positive thinking helps the brain produce serotonin, a neurotransmitter linked with feelings of happiness.[11]

Humor has several components. Humor involves looking at the incongruities of life and laughing at them. It is looking at adversity and finding the humor in the situation. It is a playful attitude and the ability to make other people smile. Most children are playful, but socialization reduces their playfulness. You can develop your sense of humor by taking yourself less seriously and being grateful for the good things in your life. Learn to laugh at yourself by sharing your embarrassing moments and laughing at them. Be careful not to use humor that puts down other people or groups. Surround yourself with people who enjoy humor and laughter. Look for the humor in difficult situations. Life is full of irony and absurdity, and laughing about it unites people during difficult times. By laughing at the situation, you will be in a better position to deal with it. Keep a positive perspective by focusing on the good things that are happening in your life rather than dwelling on the negatives.

The author Mark Twain was a good example of using humor in life. Mark Twain said that he had never worked a day in his life. He said, "What I have done I have done because it has been play. If it had been work, I shouldn't have done it." He used humor throughout his life despite facing many adversities. His father died when he was 11 years old and he started work at age 12 as a printer's apprentice. He was constantly in trouble and spent some time in jail. He served in the Civil War. His wife died at an early age, and three out of four of his children died before he did.

As a child, Twain enjoyed playing pranks on his mother, and she responded with a sense of humor. After he played a prank on his mother, she told him that he gave her more trouble than all the other children. He replied, "I suppose you were afraid I wouldn't live," and she responded, "No, afraid you would." When Mark Train almost drowned in the river, she pulled him out and said, "I guess there wasn't much danger. People born to be hanged are safe in water." Mark Twain's children described him as "a very good man, and a very funny one . . . He does tell perfectly delightful stories." He started every day by making jokes at the breakfast table, and his humor is reflected in his famous books, including *Huckleberry Finn* and *Tom Sawyer.* He wrote that "humor is a great thing . . . the saving thing after all. The minute it crops up, all our hardnesses yield, all our irritations, and resentments flit away, and a sunny spirit takes their place."[12]

The path to achieving your goals is much smoother if you choose to be happy. So relax, smile, and be happy. Then work on making positive changes in your life.

How can you learn to relax and laugh at life a little more?

JOURNAL ENTRIES

Thinking Critically and Creatively

Go to http://www.collegesuccess1.com/JournalEntries.htm for Word files of the Journal Entries

Success over the Internet

Visit the *College Success Website* at http://www.collegesuccess1.com/

The *College Success Website* is continually updated with new topics and links to the material presented in this chapter. Topics include:

- Critical thinking in college-level courses
- Techniques for thinking excellently
- The core concepts of critical thinking
- Avoiding scams

Contact your instructor if you have any problems accessing the *College Success Website*.

Notes

1. Roger Cohen, "Nazi Leader's Notes Cite 'Obedience' as Reason for His Genocidal Actions," *San Diego Union Tribune*, 13 August 1999.

2. Information in this section is adapted from the Institute for Teaching and Learning website Mission Critical, http://www.sjsu.edu/depts/itl/index.html.

3. Richard Paul and Linda Elder, "The Miniature Guide to Critical Thinking," The Foundation for Critical Thinking, http://www.criticalthinking.org.

4. Reid Goldsborough, "Teaching Healthy Skepticism about Information on the Internet," *Technology and Learning,* January 1998.

5. W.C. Crain, *Theories of Development* (New York: Prentice-Hall, 1985), 118–136, http://faculty.plts.edu/gpence/html/kohlberg.htm.

6. Steven Spielberg, commencement address at the University of Southern California, 1994.

7. Sidney Parnes, Ruth Noller, and Angelo Biondi, *Guide to Creative Action* (New York: Charles Scribner's Sons, 1977), 52.

8. Ibid., 9.

9. Robert McKim, *Experiences in Visual Thinking* (Monterey, CA: Brooks/Cole, 1972).

10. Joan Smith, "Nineteen Habits of Happy Women," *Redbook Magazine,* August 1999, 68.

11. Ibid.

12. Christopher Peterson and Martin Seligman, *Character Strengths and Virtues: A Handbook and Classification* (Oxford: University Press, 2004), 583–584.

Crime and Punishment

Name _____   Date _____

In 1974, at the age of 19, Doris Drugdealer was arrested for selling $200 worth of heroin to an undercover police officer in Michigan. She received a 10- to 20-year prison sentence for this crime. After serving about eight months of her sentence, she decided that she could not tolerate prison, and with the help of her grandfather, plotted an escape. She used a work pass to walk away from prison. In May 2008, after 34 years, Doris was captured again by detectives who matched fingerprints from her driver's license to her prison records.

Doris said that in 1974, she was a "stupid little . . . hippie-ish girl . . . a pothead." During the 34 years that Doris evaded prison, she worried every day that she would be caught. While looking at a sunset, she would marvel at her freedom and wonder if the past would catch up with her. She was very careful to lead the life of a model citizen and even volunteered for Common Cause, an organization that promotes government ethics and accountability. She married an executive and had three children and lived a comfortable life in an upper-middle-class neighborhood in California. She never told her family about her past. Her husband of 23 years stated that he loved his wife as much as he had the day they were married and that she was a "person of the highest integrity and compassion" and had dedicated her life to raising her children. She taught her children to be responsible citizens and to avoid drugs. Her husband said that the arrest "was the next worst thing to having a death in the family." Doris worried about the effect of her arrest on her son, who had just graduated from high school and her older daughters. A neighbor commented that it would not be useful to society to send Doris back to prison.

Undercover drug officers believed that Doris had connections to "higher-ups" in the drug world and was a teenage leader in a 1970s drug ring. They had found $600, paraphernalia for cutting heroin, and pictures of her with other drug dealers in her apartment. Doris described herself as a recent high school graduate who was strapped for cash, working at a minimum-wage job, and driving a $400 car. She said that every day of her life she regretted getting herself into this situation. She was extradited back to Michigan to serve her original prison term. Her family and friends submitted a plea for clemency to the governor of Michigan. Should the governor grant her clemency?

Use your critical thinking to analyze this situation. Your professor may use this exercise as a group discussion. Use the Critical Thinking Worksheet that follows for your analysis.

This exercise is based on excerpts from "Former Fugitive Drawing Sympathy" and "Captured Fugitive Now Waiting for Extradition, and to Learn Fate" from the *San Diego Union Tribune*, May 1 and 2, 2008. From *CollegeScope/College and Career Success* by Dr. Marsha Fralick.

CHAPTER 4

Maintaining a Healthy Lifestyle

Learning Objectives

Read to answer these key questions:

- How long can I expect to live in the new millennium?

- What are the best ideas on nutrition for maintaining optimum health?

- What are the dangers of smoking, alcohol abuse, and other drugs?

- How can I protect others and myself from HIV/AIDS and other sexually transmitted diseases?

- Why is it important to get enough sleep?

- What is stress and how can I deal with it?

- What are some relaxation techniques?

- How can I make positive changes in my life?

etting a college education is an investment in the quality of your life in the future. Enjoying this increased quality of life depends on maintaining your good health. What you do every day affects your future health. The ordinary choices you make, such as what you eat and how much you exercise, avoiding harmful substances, protecting the body, relaxing, getting enough sleep, and thinking positively, will have a big effect on how long you will enjoy good health and reap the benefits of your education.

Life Expectancy

How long can you expect to live in the new millennium? Since life expectancy is increasing, it is possible that you might live to be 100 years old or older. Life expectancy depends on heredity, environment, and lifestyle. Heredity cannot be changed, but environment and lifestyle depend on personal choice. The choices made at a young age can have a major impact on health in later life.

U.S. Life Expectancy

Year	Male	Female
1900	48.2	51.1
1940	60.8	65.2
1950	65.6	71.1
1960	66.6	73.3
1970	67.1	74.7
1980	70.0	77.4
1990	71.8	78.8
2000	74.1	79.5
2011	76.3	81.1

Source: National Center for Health Statistics[1]

Scientists have been studying centenarians around the world to identify the secrets of longevity.[2] It has been found that 90 percent of centenarians remain functionally independent until age 92. From studies of identical twins that were separated at birth and reared apart, it has been determined that 20 to 30 percent of longevity is genetically determined. The most important factor in longevity is lifestyle. One group that has been studied is the Seventh-Day Adventists in Utah. They avoid alcohol, caffeine, and tobacco and live an average of eight years longer than the average American.

Another group that has been studied is centenarians who live in Okinawa, Japan. These centenarians get plenty of physical and mental exercise. Their diet is rich in fruits and vegetables containing fiber and antioxidants that protect against cancer, heart disease, and stroke. Their diets are low in fat and salt, and they eat more soy than any other population on earth. Soy contains flavonoids that protect against cancer. They practice a dietary philosophy called hara hachi bu, which means eating until 80 percent full. Seiryu Toguchi of Okinawa was a centenarian who lived to be 105 years old. Here is a description of a typical day for him:[3]

. . . He wakes at 6 A.M., in the house in which he was born, and opens the shutters. "It's a sign to my neighbors," he says, "that I am still alive." He does stretching exercises along with a radio broadcast, then eats breakfast: whole-grain rice and miso soup with vegetables. He puts in two hours of picking weeds in his 1,000 sq. ft. field. . . . A fellow has to make a living, so Toguchi buys rice and meat with the profits from his produce. At 12:30 Toguchi eats lunch: goya stir fry with egg and tofu. He naps for an hour or so, then spends two more hours in his field. After dinner he plays traditional songs—a favorite is Spring When I Was 19—on the three-stringed sanchin and makes an entry in his diary as he has done every night for the past decade. "This way," he says, "I won't forget my Chinese characters. It's fun. It keeps my mind sharp."

There are almost 100,000 centenarians in the United States and the population is increasing rapidly. Daisy McFadden of the Bronx in New York is a good example of a centenarian who eats sensibly, exercises, and stays mentally active. For breakfast she has oatmeal, cranberry juice, and a banana. For lunch she has a salad with beets, cucumbers, tomatoes, and either chicken or fish. Dinner is a plate of steamed vegetables and lean meat. She does not drink soda, but occasionally indulges in chocolate chip cookies. McFadden enjoys regular exercise walking to the senior center at least three times a week to use a treadmill, bicycle, or rowing machine. To stay mentally active, she reads the newspaper daily and does the crossword puzzles.[4]

The best advice for living a long and healthy life is to eat sensibly, exercise, and find activities that keep you mentally alert.

> "Life expectancy would grow by leaps and bounds if green vegetables smelled as good as bacon."
> Doug Larson

Can You Cheat Death?

YEARS		YEARS
You have a blood relative who has lived to be 95 or older. +10		You drink more than 5 cups of coffee a day. -.5
		You get less than 6 to 8 hours of sleep a night. -1
You regularly play puzzles like Scrabble or Sudoku. +5		You have a family history of diabetes. -1
You are a married man. +5		You don't wear sunscreen and are outdoors a lot. -2.5
		You are slowly putting on weight. -5
You eat five servings of fruits/vegetables a day. +3		You frequently feel stressed out. -5
		You eat red meat more than twice a week. -5
You floss your teeth daily. +2		You have less than

© 2014, ruigsantos. Used under license with Shutterstock, Inc.

Balance Nutrition and Exercise for Good Health

Balancing good nutrition with exercise contributes to a long and healthy life. A good diet helps you to enjoy life and feel your best. Being informed about the basic principles of nutrition can help you to make healthful choices. The federal government has proposed dietary guidelines that take into account age, gender, and level of exercise.[5]

> "We don't stop playing because we grow old, we grow old because we stop playing."
> George Bernard Shaw

Aim for a healthy weight. Maintaining a healthy weight is one of the keys to a long and healthy life. Being overweight increases the risk of high blood pressure, high blood cholesterol, heart disease, stroke, diabetes, cancer, arthritis, and breathing problems. The problem of overweight children and adults is a major health concern today. The best way to lose weight is by establishing patterns of healthy eating and exercise.

Americans are struggling with how to maintain a healthy weight. Some are turning to crash diets that severely restrict calories and food choices. Crash diets are not recommended because the weight loss is temporary and the body can be deprived of important nutrients. Another serious problem is eating disorders such as anorexia, which can lead to serious health problems and even death in severe cases. Symptoms of an eating disorder include a preoccupation with food or body weight, dramatic weight loss, excessive exercise, self-induced vomiting, and abuse of laxatives. Anyone with these symptoms should consult a health care provider.

Body Mass Index

The Body Mass Index (BMI) is a commonly used method of evaluating a person's weight. It is based on the ratio of weight to height. To calculate your BMI, first answer these two questions:

1. What is your height in inches? _____

2. What is your weight in pounds?_____

Calculate your BMI using the following formula:

$$BMI = (705 \times body\ weight) \div (height \times height)$$

Example: A person who is 66 inches tall and weighs 155 pounds:

$$BMI = (705 \times 155) \div (66 \times 66) = 25$$

Calculate your BMI here. To evaluate your weight, locate your BMI in the chart below.

My BMI = (705 × my weight ____) ÷ (my height in inches____ × my height in inches _____) = _____

Body Mass Index Categories[6]

BMI	Weight
Less than 18.5	Underweight
18.5–24.9	Normal weight
25–29.9	Overweight
30 and above	Obese

There are some exceptions to consider when using BMI to evaluate weight:

- Bodybuilders and other athletes may have a higher BMI because muscle weighs more than fat.
- For the elderly, a BMI between 25 and 27 may be healthier and protect against osteoporosis.
- The BMI is not designed to be used with children.

Another way to evaluate your weight is to simply measure around your waist. A measurement of over 35 inches for women or 40 inches for men places a person at greater risk of health problems. If your BMI is over 25 or your waist measurement increases, reduce calories and increase activity.

Journal Entry #1

Calculate your BMI. Based on your BMI, do you need to maintain, lose, or gain weight?

My BMI is . . .

Based on my BMI, I need to . . .

Here are some suggestions for managing your weight:

- Be physically active.
- Choose healthy foods.
- Choose foods low in fat and sugars.
- Eat sensible portions.
- Lose weight slowly.

Be physically active each day. There are many benefits to regular physical activity:

- Increases your fitness, endurance, and strength
- Maintains healthy bones, muscles, and joints
- Helps in managing weight
- Lowers risk of cardiovascular disease, colon cancer, and Type 2 diabetes
- Promotes psychological well-being
- Reduces depression and anxiety

© 2014, Monkey Business Images. Used under license with Shutterstock, Inc.

> "Walking is the best possible exercise. Habituate yourself to walk very far."
>
> Thomas Jefferson

Two kinds of physical activity are recommended. Aerobic activity speeds up your heart rate and breathing and increases cardiovascular fitness. Strength and flexibility exercises such as lifting weights and stretching help to maintain strong bones. Choose activities that you enjoy and include them in your daily routine. It is important to remain active throughout your life.

New federal guidelines suggest the need for 30 to 60 minutes of moderately intense physical activity each day. These activities could include an hour of walking, slow swimming, leisurely bicycle riding, or golfing without a cart. More intense exercise such as jogging can provide needed exercise in a shorter time.[7]

Eat healthy. A good diet helps you to enjoy life and feel your best. Use the government dietary guidelines at http://www.choosemyplate.gov/ to make good nutritional choices. At this site you can enter your personal information for a customized recommendation of the types and amounts of food to eat for optimal health. The plate icon on the previous page provides a visual of the five different food groups with half of the plate filled with fruits and vegetables and the other half filled with whole grains and proteins.

Here are some examples of recommended food consumption based on age, gender, and activity levels. In these examples, 30 to 60 minutes of physical activity are assumed:

	Female Age 6	Female Age 18	Male Age 18	Male Age 50
Grains	5 oz	6 oz	10 oz	8 oz
Vegetables	1.5 cups	2.5 cups	3.5 cups	3 cups
Fruits	1.5 cups	2 cups	2.5 cups	2 cups
Oils	4 tsp	6 tsp	8 tsp	7 tsp
Milk	2 cups	3 cups	3 cups	3 cups
Meat/Beans	4 oz	5.5 oz	7 oz	6.5 oz
Extra Calories from Fat and Sugar	170	265	425	360
Total Calories	1400	2000	2800	2400

Here are some suggestions for making healthy food choices:

- In establishing a pattern of healthy eating, it is recommended that plant foods form the foundation of a good diet. Two-thirds of the dinner plate should be covered with fruits, vegetables, whole grains, and beans. Use meats and dairy products in moderation and use fats and sweets sparingly. This type of diet is helpful in controlling weight as well as reducing your risk of cancer.[8]

- Eat a variety of grains daily, especially whole grains. Whole grains include brown rice, cracked wheat, graham flour, whole-grain corn, oatmeal, popcorn, barley, whole rye, and whole wheat. Whole grains provide vitamins, minerals, and fiber, which helps you to feel full with fewer calories.

- Eat a variety of fruits and vegetables daily. Eating many kinds and colors of fruits and vegetables provides important vitamins and minerals. Enjoy five servings of fruits and vegetables each day with at least two servings of fruit and three servings of vegetables.

- Limit the use of solid fats such as butter, lard, margarines, and partially hydrogenated shortenings. Solid fats raise blood cholesterol and increase your chances of coronary heart disease. Use vegetable oils instead. Aim for a fat intake of no more that 30 percent of your calories.

- Moderate your intake of sugar. Foods containing added sugars have added calories and little nutritional value. The number one source of added sugar is soft drinks. Drink water instead of or in addition to soft drinks. Sweets, candies, pies, cakes, cookies, and fruit drinks are also major sources of added sugars. Eating too many foods with added sugar contributes to weight gain or eating less of the nutritious foods. Added sugar also contributes to tooth decay.

- Choose and prepare foods with less salt. Eating too much salt can increase your chances of having high blood pressure. High salt intake causes the body to secrete calcium, which is necessary for healthy bones. Only small amounts of salt occur naturally in foods. Most salt is added during food processing. Eat fresh fruits and vegetables to avoid eating too much salt.

How to Lose Weight

If you need to lose weight, you are not alone! Increasing numbers of adults in the United States are struggling with being overweight or obese. The Centers for Disease Control report that approximately 33 percent of adults are overweight and another 33 percent are obese.[9] Being overweight is defined as having a BMI between 25 and 29.9. Obesity is defined as having a BMI of 30 or above. For example, a woman who is five feet four inches tall and weighs 180 pounds is considered obese. Maintaining your ideal weight is a matter of balancing calories in from food and beverages with calories expended through physical activity.

CALORIES IN
Food
Beverages

CALORIES OUT
Body functions
Physical activity

Source: From the U.S. Center for Disease Control, 2010.

Here are some practical suggestions for losing weight if your BMI is over 25 and you are not an athlete:

- Stop drinking sodas. One out of every five calories consumed in the United States is from sodas, and they are the biggest contributors to obesity.[10] Instead of drinking sodas, substitute water or unsweetened tea. Flavor your water with lemons, oranges, limes, strawberries, or mint. Be careful not to substitute sugary fruit juice, coffee, or tea for the sodas, since these drinks are often higher in calories.

- Exercise at least an hour to an hour and a half daily. Exercise is needed to burn the excess calories.

- Use the information at www.choosemyplate.gov/ to determine the number of calories needed to maintain your ideal weight. For example, the average 18-year-old female needs 2,000 calories a day. To lose weight, subtract 300 to 500 calories a day from this total.

- Eat five servings of fruits and vegetables a day. Use these fruits and vegetables as snacks.

- To control hunger, eat several small meals of 300 to 400 calories each.

- Make sure to eat breakfast. Eating breakfast helps to provide energy and avoid hunger, which leads to overeating.

- Eat smaller portions. Use a salad plate instead of a dinner plate. When you eat out, save half of your food for another meal.

- Minimize eating out at fast-food restaurants, since it is difficult to make good food choices there.

- If you are sad or anxious, try exercise instead of eating to relieve these symptoms. Practice stress reduction techniques.

"Acorns or chocolate cake?"

QUIZ

Longevity and Nutrition

Test what you have learned by selecting the correct answer to the following questions.

1. Longevity is mostly determined by

   a. heredity.
   b. lifestyle choices.
   c. being lucky.

2. If you are not an athlete and your BMI is over 25, it is probably a good idea to

   a. severely limit caloric intake.
   b. go on a diet that limits food choices.
   c. reduce calories and increase activities.

3. The Choose My Plate Plan suggests that we need to balance

   a. our eating habits and our lifestyle.
   b. our desserts and vegetables.
   c. what we eat with our physical activity.

4. It is suggested that two-thirds of the dinner plate be covered with

   a. potatoes.
   b. plant foods such as fruits, vegetables, whole grains, and beans.
   c. meats, fish, or poultry.

5. The biggest contributor to obesity in the United States is

   a. fried food.
   b. sodas.
   c. candy.

How did you do on the quiz? Check your answers: 1. b, 2. c, 3. c, 4. b, 5. b

"It's never too late to be what you might have been."

George Elliot

"The greatest wealth is health."

Virgil

Avoiding Addictions to Smoking, Alcohol, and Other Drugs

Smoking, abusing alcohol, or using illegal drugs can interfere with your success in college, on the job, and in life. These addictions can cause illness and a shortened life expectancy. Knowledge in these areas will help you make the best choices to maintain your quality of life.

Smoking Tobacco: A Leading Cause of Preventable Illness and Death

Smoking is widespread in our society. Despite a gradual decrease in the rate of smoking, one out of every 5 high school seniors and adults are still smoking. Tobacco use is the leading cause of preventable illness and death in the United States.[11] One out of every

© 2014, ra2studio. Used under license with Shutterstock, Inc.

five deaths in the United States is related to smoking. Each year, over 443,000 Americans die too young as a result of smoking-related illnesses.[12] Imagine that three jumbo jets carrying 400 people each crashed every day of the year. This would be similar to the number of people who die each year from smoking-related illnesses.

Smoking is related to a variety of illnesses:

- Smoking damages and irritates the respiratory system. Smoking a package of cigarettes a day is like smearing a cup of tar over the respiratory tract. Smoking causes lung cancer, emphysema, and chronic bronchitis.
- Smoking affects the heart and circulatory system. Smoking causes premature coronary heart disease and several types of blood-vessel diseases.
- Smoking increases the probability of having strokes, which damage the brain and often leave a person with permanent disabilities.
- Smoking affects the eyes and vision. It is speculated that smoking causes vision loss by restricting blood flow to the eyes. Recent studies have connected smoking with macular degeneration, an irreversible form of blindness. Cataracts, or clouding of the lenses of the eyes, are also associated with smoking.
- Smoking irritates the eyes, nose, throat, and gums and can lead to cancer of the mouth, throat, or esophagus.
- Smoking is associated with osteoporosis, the thinning of bones due to mineral loss.
- During pregnancy, smoking damages the developing fetus, causing miscarriages, low birth weight, developmental problems, and impaired lung function at birth.
- Smoking causes premature facial wrinkling due to vasoconstriction of the capillaries of the face.[13]

Why is smoking such a major health problem? It is because smoking is an addiction that is difficult to overcome. Only 20 percent of smokers who decide to quit smoking are successful on a long-term basis.[14] For those who are successful in quitting, tobacco-related health risks are improved over time. Although smoking cessation is difficult, it is worth the investment in improved healthy living. Refraining from smoking, along with a healthy diet and exercise, can increase your life span by as much as 10 years.[15] For help with smoking cessation, visit your physician or college health office. The resources on the College Success1 website provide helpful hints for giving up smoking.

Alcohol

Each year, many college students die as a result of excessive drinking. Some students drink and drive and die in car accidents. Others die from alcohol poisoning or alcohol-related accidents. Excessive drinking is a factor in poor college performance and high dropout rates. Studies have shown that heavy drinking causes brain damage and interferes with memory.[16] Having some knowledge about alcohol use can help you to make choices to ensure your future quality of life.

Alcohol Abuse Quiz

Read each statement and decide if it is true or false. Place a checkmark in the appropriate column.

True	False	
		Alcohol abuse is the third leading health problem in the United States, behind heart disease and cancer.
		Thirteen percent of people in the United States have a problem with alcohol dependency.
		Alcohol is the most abused drug worldwide.
		Alcohol use or dependency reduces one's lifespan by 10 years.
		Alcohol is involved in 50 percent of all traffic fatalities and homicides.
		Alcohol is involved in two-thirds of college student suicides.
		Alcohol is a major factor in HIV infection.
		Alcohol is involved in 90 percent of college rapes.
		Women are at higher risk than men of serious medical conditions related to alcohol use.
		The age span 18 to 21 is the period of heaviest alcohol consumption for most drinkers in the United States.
		Each year college students spend about $5.5 billion on alcohol, mostly beer.
		College students drink enough beer each year to fill an Olympic-size swimming pool on every campus in the United States.
		Students spend more money on beer than they do on books, soda, coffee, juice, and milk combined.
		Excessive alcohol use leads to memory loss and neurological problems.
		More students drink than use cocaine, marijuana, or cigarettes combined.

How did you do on the quiz? All of the above statements are true. The fact that all of the above statements are true points to the serious nature of alcohol abuse on college campuses and in society in general.[17]

Binge Drinking

Heavy drinking causes students to miss class and fall behind in schoolwork. College students who are considered binge drinkers are at risk of many alcohol-related problems. Binge drinking is simply drinking too much alcohol at one time. In men, binge drinking is defined by researchers as drinking five or more drinks in a row. In women, it is drinking four or more drinks in a row.[18] It takes about one hour to metabolize one drink, so it would take five hours to metabolize five drinks. Researchers estimate that two out of five college students (44 percent) are binge drinkers.[19] Students who are binge drinkers are 21 times more likely to:

- Be hurt or injured
- Drive a car after drinking
- Get in trouble with campus or local police
- Engage in unprotected sex
- Engage in unplanned sexual activity
- Damage property
- Fall behind in schoolwork
- Miss class[20]

© 2014, advent. Used under license with Shutterstock, Inc.

It is particularly significant that there is a connection between binge drinking and driving. Among frequent binge drinkers, 62 percent of men and 49 percent of women said that they had driven a car after drinking. About half of the students in this study reported being a passenger in a car in which the driver was high or drunk.[21] A drink is defined as:

- A 12-ounce beer
- A four-ounce glass of wine
- A shot of liquor (1.5 ounces of 80-proof distilled spirits) straight or in a mixed drink

National studies on alcohol consumption in colleges find that students are less likely to participate in binge drinking when they put a high priority on studying, have special interests or hobbies, and participate in volunteer activities. The majority of college students (56 percent nationally) either abstain from drinking or drink in moderation. Students least likely to be binge drinkers are African American, Asian, 24 years or older, or married. Students at highest risk for binge drinking include intercollegiate athletes and members of fraternities and sororities. Students most likely to be binge drinkers are white, male, and under 24 years of age.[22]

Blood Alcohol Content (BAC)

The amount of alcohol in your blood is referred to as blood alcohol content (BAC). It is recorded in milligrams of alcohol per 100 milliliters of blood. For example, a BAC of .10 means that 1/10 of 1 percent or 1/1,000 of your total blood is alcohol. BAC depends on the amount of blood in your body, which varies with your weight, and the amount of alcohol consumed over time. The liver can only process one drink per hour. The rest builds up in the bloodstream. Below are listed the effects of increasing BAC:

.02 Mellow feeling, slight body warmth, less inhibited

.05 Noticeable relaxation, less alert, less self-focused, coordination impairment begins, most people reach this level with one or two drinks

.08 Drunk driving limit, definite impairment in coordination and judgment

.10 Noisy, possible embarrassing behavior, mood swings, reduction in reaction times

.15 Impaired balance and movement, clearly drunk

.30 Many lose consciousness

.40 Most lose consciousness, some die

.50 Breathing stops, many die[23]

The above figures point out some important facts for college students. It does not take many drinks to reach the drunk driving limit. Most people reach the drunk driving limit if they have one to three drinks, depending on weight and time since the last drink. BAC increases if you are lighter weight or if you have just had a drink. As the BAC increases, more serious effects occur. Tragically, each year college students die from alcohol poisoning, which occurs when large quantities of alcohol are consumed in a short period of time. This sometimes occurs during the hazing periods in college fraternities and sororities. Colleges are taking steps to stop hazing on college campuses nationwide.

Increased Risks for Women

Because women absorb and metabolize alcohol differently than men do, they are at greater risk of alcohol-related problems. Women have less body water than men and achieve a higher concentration of alcohol in the blood after drinking the same amount as men. Women are more likely to develop liver damage, brain damage, and heart damage. Some research has suggested that women who are moderate to heavy drinkers are at higher risk for breast cancer.[24]

Besides considering health effects, women need to be concerned about personal safety when alcohol is being used. When alcohol is being consumed, women are at higher risk of becoming the victims of violent crime. Among frequent binge drinkers, women report higher rates of rape and nonconsensual sex.[25]

What Is Moderate Drinking?

If adults choose to drink alcohol, it is recommended that they drink in moderation.[26] Moderation is defined as no more than one drink per day for women or two drinks per day for men. Drinking more than this can increase the risks for car accidents, high blood pressure, stroke, violence, suicide, and certain types of cancer. Women who drink during pregnancy increase the risk of birth defects. Too much alcohol causes social and psychological problems, cirrhosis of the liver, inflammation of the pancreas, and damage to the brain and heart. Heavy drinkers are also at risk for malnutrition, since alcohol contains calories that may be substituted for more nutritional foods.

It has been found that drinking in moderation may lower the risk of coronary heart disease in men over the age of 45 and women over the age of 55. However, there are other factors contributing to a healthy heart, including a healthy diet, exercise, avoidance of smoking, and maintaining a healthy weight.

There are certain people who should not drink:

- Children and adolescents
- Individuals of any age who cannot restrict their drinking to moderate levels
- Women who are pregnant or who are likely to become pregnant
- Individuals who drive or operate machinery that requires skill, attention, or coordination
- Individuals taking over-the-counter or prescription drugs that interact with alcohol

Warning Signs of Alcoholism

Alcoholics Anonymous has published 12 questions to determine if alcohol is a problem in your life. Answer these questions honestly:

1. Have you ever decided to stop drinking for a week or so but could only stop for a couple of days?

2. Do you wish people would mind their own business about your drinking and stop telling you what to do?

3. Have you ever switched from one kind of drink to another in the hope that this would keep you from getting drunk?

4. Have you ever had to have a drink upon awakening during the past year? Do you need a drink to get started or to stop shaking?

5. Do you envy people who can drink without getting into trouble?

6. Have you had problems connected with drinking during the past year?

7. Has your drinking caused problems at home?

8. Do you ever try to get extra drinks at a party because you do not get enough?

9. Do you tell yourself you can stop drinking any time you want to, even though you keep getting drunk when you don't mean to?

10. Have you missed days of work or school because of drinking?

11. Do you ever have blackouts from drinking, when you cannot remember what happened?

12. Have you ever felt that your life would be better if you did not drink?

If you answered yes to four of the above questions, it is likely that you have a problem with alcohol.

© 2014, iQoncept. Used under license with Shutterstock, Inc.

Other Drugs

While alcohol is the most commonly used drug, street drugs such as marijuana, cocaine, LSD, methamphetamines, rohypnol (the "date rape drug"), ecstasy, ketamine (a PCP-like anesthetic), and heroin interfere with the accomplishment of life goals. Clark Carr, President of Narconon, describes the following impact of illegal drug usage:

> *"One of the worst impacts of street drugs is their impact on ambition. Drugs have insidious yet devastating effects upon children and their ability to envision hopes and dreams. Ambition enables a person to learn to enjoy life and to pursue happiness without drugs, but it can be destroyed through drug use. When a person is intoxicated by drugs, important functions are adversely affected, including concentration, recording, and recalling. These tools are essential to learning, and without them education is impaired. Addiction becomes the all-consuming focus of activities aimed at procuring more drugs. Education, careers, relationships, and life itself take a back seat."[27]*

People take drugs in order to feel better. However the high from taking drugs is followed by a low that is relieved by taking more drugs, leading to addiction. With increased drug use, the lows get lower and it becomes more difficult to reach a high. Drugs have varying levels of toxicity, but they all stress the body's nervous, digestive, respiratory, circulatory, and reproductive systems. The problem is that drugs can become life-destroying. Anyone contemplating taking drugs should ask these four questions:

1. Are the benefits going to outweigh the liabilities?

2. Will I experience more pleasure than pain, or more pain than pleasure?

3. Will the pleasure be temporary? How will I feel tomorrow?

4. Will the drug do more harm than good?

Answering these questions honestly can help you to make the right choices. An addiction to smoking, alcohol, or illegal drugs can be difficult to control. If you need help with problems caused by drug or alcohol addiction, see your physician or contact your college health office. The *College Success1 Website* contains useful links to help you to cope with addictive behavior and make some positive changes in your life.

QUIZ

Avoiding Addictions

Test what you have learned by selecting the correct answers to the following questions.

1. The leading cause of preventable death in the United States is

   a. car accidents.
   b. smoking-related illnesses.
   c. obesity.

2. The most abused drug worldwide is

   a. marijuana.
   b. cocaine.
   c. alcohol.

3. Binge drinking for men is defined as

   a. five drinks in a row.
   b. seven drinks in a row.
   c. 10 drinks in a row.

4. Depending on weight and time of last drink, a person generally reaches the drunk driving limit of .08 with

   a. one to three drinks.
   b. three to five drinks.
   c. five to nine drinks.

5. Moderate drinking for women is defined as

   a. one drink per day.
   b. two drinks per day.
   c. three drinks per day.

How did you do on the quiz? Check your answers: 1. b, 2. c, 3. a, 4. a, 5. a

Protecting Yourself from HIV/AIDS and Other Sexually Transmitted Infections

Human immunodeficiency virus (HIV) and acquired immune deficiency syndrome (AIDS) have been described as the worst plague in modern history. AIDS is the fourth leading cause of death in the world. It is estimated that by 2020, the number of people dying from AIDS will be approximately equal to all people killed in wars in the 20th century.[28] New drugs have been developed that inhibit the growth of the virus that leads to AIDS, but there is still no cure for AIDS. These new medications are extending the healthy life of infected patients.[29] Since AIDS continues to be a leading cause of death among Americans ages 25 to 44, knowing how to protect yourself from HIV/AIDS and other sexually transmitted diseases is an important survival skill.[30] The U.S. Centers for Disease Control and Prevention provide some helpful information to minimize your risk of infection.[31]

What is HIV? HIV is the human immunodeficiency virus that causes AIDS. The virus kills the "CD4" cells that help your body fight off infection.

What is AIDS? AIDS is the acquired immunodeficiency syndrome. It is the disease you get when HIV destroys the body's immune system. Normally your immune system helps to fight off illness. When the immune system is destroyed, you can become very sick and die.

© 2014, Amir Ridhwan. Used under license with Shutterstock, Inc.

How is HIV acquired? HIV is acquired in the following ways:

- It is acquired by having unprotected sex (sex without a condom) with someone who has HIV. The virus can be in an infected person's blood, semen, or vaginal secretions. It can enter the body through tiny cuts or sores on the skin, or the lining of the vagina, penis, rectum, or mouth.
- It is acquired by sharing a needle and syringe to inject drugs or by sharing equipment used to prepare drugs for injection with someone who has HIV.
- HIV can be acquired from a blood transfusion received before 1985. Since 1985, blood is tested for HIV.
- Babies born to women who are HIV-positive can become infected during pregnancy, birth, or breastfeeding.

You cannot get HIV from the following:

- Working with or being around someone who has HIV
- Sweat, tears, spit, clothes, drinking fountains, phones, or toilet seats
- Insect bites or stings
- Donating blood
- A closed-mouth kiss

© 2014, Alev Bagater. Used under license with Shutterstock, Inc.

What are the best ways to protect yourself? Here are some guidelines:

- Don't share needles or syringes for injecting drugs, steroids, or vitamins, or for tattooing or body piercing. Germs from an infected person can stay in the needle and then be injected into the next person using the needle.
- Don't have sex. This is truly "safe sex."
- If you choose to have sex, have sex with only one partner that you know doesn't have HIV and is only having sex with you.
- Use a latex condom every time you have sex. This is referred to as "safer sex."
- Don't share razors or toothbrushes because of the possibility of contact with blood.
- If you are pregnant, get tested for HIV. Drug treatments are available to reduce the chances of your baby being infected with HIV.

How do I know if I have HIV or AIDS? A person can have HIV or AIDS and feel perfectly healthy. The only way to know is to get tested. Most college health offices and your local health department offer confidential testing.

What other infections are spread through sexual activity? There are more than 25 different infections spread through sexual activity. There are 19 million new cases of sexually transmitted infections (STIs) each year, half of them in young people ages 15–24.[32] According to the Centers for Disease Control and Prevention, these infections can "result in severe health consequences, cancer, impaired fertility, premature birth, infant death and disability."[33] The increase in STIs has paralleled the AIDS epidemic. The guidelines for protecting against HIV apply to other STIs as well.

The most common STIs in the United States include chlamydia, gonorrhea, syphilis, genital herpes, human papillomavirus (HPV), hepatitis B, trichomoniasis, and bacterial vaginosis. Bacterial infections such as gonorrhea, syphilis, and chlamydia can be cured with antibiotics. Viral infections such as herpes, hepatitis, and genital warts can be treated but not cured. New vaccines are now available to prevent hepatitis B which can cause serious liver damage and for HPV that causes genital warts and can lead to cancer. It is recommended that college students (both men and women) keep their immunizations up to date and include these newer vaccinations.

Women suffer the most from STIs because they have more frequent and serious complications from them than men do. Many STIs can be passed to the fetus, newborn, or infant before, during, or after birth. Chlamydia and gonorrhea can lead to pelvic inflammatory disease (PID), which can cause chronic pelvic pain, infertility, or potentially fatal ectopic pregnancies. The human papilloma virus (HPV) can increase the risk of cervical cancer in women.

> "Sleep is a golden chain that ties our health and our bodies together."
> Thomas Dekker

> "A good laugh and a long sleep are the best cures in the doctor's book."
> Irish Proverb

Getting Enough Sleep

College students often miss out on sleep while cramming for exams, enjoying an active social life, and trying to balance work and school. However, getting enough sleep is important for learning. Without enough sleep, long-term memory is impaired and concentration is difficult.[34] If you are sleep-deprived, it is more difficult to read, study and store information in long-term memory.

Getting enough sleep is important for optimal brain function. Nobel Laureate Francis Crick, who studies the brain at the Salk Institute in California, has proposed that the purpose of sleep is to allow the brain to "take out the trash."[35] Sleep gives the brain time to process the day's events, store what is needed, and delete irrelevant material. Sleep is necessary to properly store the experiences of each day in the brain. It is believed that sleeping helps the brain to replenish its energy supplies.[36]

© 2014, Andrey_Kuzmin. Used under license with Shutterstock, Inc.

Not getting enough sleep results in a decline in mental performance. Colonel Gregory Belenky of the Walter Reed Army Institute of Research studied the effects of sleeplessness on military personnel.[37] He found that mental performance declined by 25 percent in every 24-hour sleepless period. Another researcher found that being awake for 24 hours causes the same mental impairment as being drunk.[38] After 24 hours of continuous simulated combat, artillery teams lost track of where they were and what they were firing at. During the Persian Gulf War, sleep-deprived soldiers lost a sense of where they were and began firing on their own tanks, destroying two of them. Lack of sleep impairs higher cognitive functions such as critical thinking. It becomes more difficult to make decisions, pay attention to detail, and react to new information. College students who stay up all night studying for exams suffer from the same declines in mental performance.

Depriving yourself of sleep also has negative impacts on your health.[39] Lack of sleep can make you less energetic, increase your irritability, cause depression, and make you accident-prone. It is estimated that sleepy drivers cause about 100,000 car accidents each year. Lack of sleep can harm brain cells, weaken the immune system, and decrease muscle-building growth hormones. Blood levels of the stress hormone cortisol are increased. Sleep deprivation can cause increased stress, memory impairment, risk of illness, and the growth of fat instead of muscle. Researchers are now finding evidence that lack of sleep hastens the aging process.[40]

So, how much sleep do you need? Everyone has different needs for sleep. One way to determine your personal need for sleep is to think about how much sleep you get at the end of a long vacation when you do not have to get up at a certain time. At first you may sleep longer to make up for any sleep deficits. Toward the end of the vacation, you will probably be getting the amount of sleep your body needs for optimum performance. Gregory Belenky recommends, "If you simply want to put one foot in front of the other, five hours will do. But if you want to be doing things where you're required to think, plan, or anticipate, then you probably need eight or eight and a half hours of sleep."[41] It is interesting to note that current research shows that it is not healthy to sleep more than eight hours because too much sleep can alter sleep patterns and lead to sluggishness, fatigue, and other health problems.[42]

Journal Entry #3

Are you getting enough sleep for optimum performance in school and to maintain good health? If not, what is your plan to get more sleep?

Can You Cheat Death?

YEARS		YEARS
You have a blood relative who has lived to be 95 or older................. +10	You drink more than 5 cups of coffee a day. .... -.5	
You regularly play puzzles like Scrabble or Sudoku. .... +5	You get less than 6 to 8 hours of sleep a night.................... -1	
	You have a family history of diabetes. .... -1	
You are a married man. .... +5	You don't wear sunscreen and are outdoors a lot.................... -2.5	
	You are slowly putting on weight. .... -5	
You eat five servings of fruits/vegetables a day................... +3	You frequently feel stressed out............................... -5	
	You eat red meat more than twice a week.......................... -5	
You floss your teeth daily. .... +2	You have less than 12 years of education...................... -5	
You regularly snack on nuts. .... +2	You engage in unprotected sex with multiple partners............ -7	
	You smoke. .... -15	
You are a married woman. .... +0	You use IV drugs. .... -15	

Figure 12.1 Steps to increase longevity.

Stress and Relaxation

One of the major challenges in life is dealing with stress and being able to relax. For college students, it is important to realize that too much stress interferes with memory, concentration, and learning. After graduation, it is important to be able to deal with stress on the job.

What Is Stress?

Imagine that you are a caveman or cavewoman. You come out of your cave and notice that the sun is up and the birds are chirping. You are feeling good and your heart rate is normal. All of a sudden you hear a twig snap. You look to your right and notice a large saber-toothed tiger. You have two choices. You can either fight the tiger or take flight. This is called the "fight or flight" reaction to stress.

The body produces some powerful hormones to help give you the strength to fight or to run away. These hormones increase your heart rate and metabolism to give you quick energy. During the fighting or fleeing, the stress hormones are used up and the body returns to normal. The problem today is that the stresses we face are not saber-toothed tigers and we do little physical fighting or running away. The stress hormones still accumulate, but we no longer use them up.

Is all stress bad? Imagine a world where there is absolutely no stress. While the thought is intriguing, it would probably be very boring. Some stress is positive and essential for well-being. For example, when we run a race, play a game of football, or act in a play, we experience stress, but it provides excitement and motivation. When a teacher announces a test, a little stress can cause the student to study for the test. Hans Selye, a famous researcher on stress, called this positive type of stress "eustress." He even went so far as to suggest, "Without stress, there could be no life."[43]

Hans Selye described negative stress as "distress." Distress has several physical symptoms that are uncomfortable and detract from good health. These symptoms can range from headaches, stomachaches, and sleeplessness to serious health problems such as high blood pressure, heart disease, and stroke. It is helpful to know some relaxation techniques to deal with the distress.

> "Slow down and everything you are chasing will come around and catch you."
> John De Paola

> "Tension is who you think you should be. Relaxation is who you are."
> Chinese Proverb

Get Aerobic Exercise

Aerobic exercise is simply exercise that raises your heart rate and exercises your heart. It includes activities such as walking, running, swimming, dancing, and playing sports. It is recommended that people do some type of aerobic exercise three to five times a week. In addition to strengthening the heart, aerobic exercise burns up stress hormones and allows us to relax.

One of the best relaxation techniques is to find some physical activities that you enjoy and participate in them often. It often requires some planning to fit these activities into our busy schedules. It is important to see these activities as a priority and to take time to enjoy them.

Practice Stress-Reducing Thoughts

Much of the stress we experience is a result of the thoughts we have in our heads, specifically, negative self-talk. We experience a situation, we say negative things to ourselves about it, and the result is an emotional reaction that causes stress. This sequence of events is referred to as the ABCs of emotions:

Situation (A) $\longrightarrow$ Self-statement (B) $\longrightarrow$ Emotion (C)

For example, Nicole is caught in rush hour traffic. She wonders why traffic is not moving. She watches the light, hoping that she can make it through the intersection before the light changes to red. She gets angry when the car in front of her stops just as the light changes to yellow. She has to wait for another light. She glances at her watch and watches the time go by as she sits in traffic. She thinks about all the things she needs to do at home. She realizes that she needs to stop at the grocery store to get something for dinner. She thinks about getting fast food on the way home but remembers that she has spent too much money this month. Besides, she realizes that the fast food is not good for her diet. Finally she arrives home at 6:04 p.m. She has a headache and feels stressed out.

Here is an analysis of this situation using the ABCs of emotion:

Situation (A) $\longrightarrow$ Self-statement (B) $\longrightarrow$ Emotion (C)
Traffic jam (A) $\longrightarrow$ Negative self-statement (B) $\longrightarrow$ Angry, stressed (C)

Negative self-statements run through Nicole's head as she deals with the traffic jam:

- Why does this always happen to me?
- Why are the cars ahead so slow?
- Stupid drivers! Can't they move any faster?
- I'm always broke.
- I'll never lose weight.

As a result of these statements, Nicole feels angry and stressed out and even has a headache. Let's look at a different way of handling this situation. Diane is also caught in rush hour traffic. She thinks to herself, "Rush hour traffic. Oh, well. Can't do anything about that." She decides to relax. She turns on her favorite radio station and enjoys the music. She notices the trees and plants along the side of the road and notices that spring is coming. She notices a new restaurant along the way and decides to try it out next Saturday night. She starts to think about spring break and how she will spend her vacation time. She anticipates the warm greetings of her family when she arrives home. She arrives home at 6:04 p.m. with a smile on her face. Let's analyze this situation:

Situation (A) $\longrightarrow$ Self-statement (B) $\longrightarrow$ Emotion (C)

Traffic jam (A) $\longrightarrow$ Positive self-statements (B) $\longrightarrow$ Happy (C)

When you are trying to deal with a stressful situation, listen to your self-statements. What are you saying to yourself? If these statements are negative, you will have negative emotions and will be stressed out. Think of some positive, stress-reducing thoughts that you can use in stressful situations. Here are some examples, but you will be better off to think up some of your own:

- That's the way it goes. No use getting upset.
- It's not the end of the world.
- Keep cool.
- It's no big deal.
- Relax.
- Life's too short to let this bother me.
- It's their problem.
- Life's like that.
- Be happy.
- I'll just do the best I can.
- No need to worry.

Take Action to Resolve Your Problems

If you have problems that are causing stress, take action to resolve them. Here are some steps you can take to solve problems and reduce stress:

- Concentrate your efforts on doing something about the problem.
- Seek information on how to solve the problem. This step may involve doing research or speaking to others.
- Make a plan of action.
- Make it a priority to solve the problem.
- Do what needs to be done to solve the problem, one step at a time.

Psychological Hardiness

Psychologists have studied people who are psychologically hardy.[44] These individuals are able to deal with stress in a positive way and avoid the negative consequences of stress. How do they stay healthy in spite of high-powered jobs and constant challenges? People who are stress-resistant have a positive attitude toward life and the challenges it presents. Psychologically hardy individuals have the following qualities:

- They are open to change. They view change as a challenge rather than a threat.
- They have a feeling of involvement in whatever they are doing. They are committed to their occupations and endeavors.

- They have a sense of control over events rather than a feeling of powerlessness. Having a sense of control is essential to good mental health.

Some of the hardiest individuals were those who survived the concentration camps during World War II. In spite of enduring extreme hardships, some found the strength to survive their ordeal and to live well-adapted lives. Scientists studying these survivors discovered that they used several resources for survival. Knowledge and intelligence was one resource. With knowledge and intelligence, these people could see many ways of dealing with the situation and were able to choose the best alternative. These survivors also had a strong sense of identity. They were confident and powerful individuals. Another important resource was a strong social network that gave people the collective strength to survive.

© 2014, Tatiana Popova. Used under license with Shutterstock, Inc.

Other Relaxation Techniques

Another way to deal with stress is to practice some physical and mental relaxation techniques. Here are a few suggestions:

- Listen to soothing music. Choose music that has a beat that is slower than your heart rate. Classical or New Age music can be very relaxing.
- Take a few deep breaths.
- Focus on your breathing. If you are thinking about breathing, it is difficult to think about your worries.
- Lie down in a comfortable place and tense and relax your muscles. Start with the muscles in your head and work your way down to your toes. Tense each muscle for five to 10 seconds and then release the tension completely.
- Imagine yourself in a pleasant place. When you are actually in a beautiful place, take the time to make a mental photograph. Memorize each detail and then close your eyes to see if you can still recall the scene. Return to this place in your mind when you feel stressed. Some people visualize the mountains, the beach, the ocean, a mountain stream, waterfalls, a tropical garden, or a desert scene. Choose a scene that works for you.
- Use positive thinking. Look for the good things in life and take the time to appreciate them.
- Maintain a healthy diet and get enough exercise.
- Practice yoga or tai chi.

- Keep things in perspective. Ask yourself, "Will it be important in 10 years?" If so, do something about it. If not, just relax.
- Focus on the positives. What have you learned from dealing with this problem? Has the problem provided an opportunity for personal growth?
- Discuss your feelings with a friend who is a good listener or get professional counseling.
- Keep your sense of humor. Laughter actually reduces the stress hormones.
- Maintain a support network of friends and loved ones.
- Practice meditation. It is a way of calming the mind.
- Get a massage or give one to someone else.

Journal Entry # 4

Comment on your level of stress. What stress management techniques work best for you?

Making Positive Changes in Your Life

You are probably aware of the importance of implementing many of the ideas in this chapter. However, actually making some positive changes is difficult. Dr. James Prochaska has studied the process of change and identifies the six stages:[45]

1. **Precontemplation.** In this stage, a person denies that there is a problem and is not ready to change. If the habit causes difficulties, the person may blame the problems on others, especially those who are pressuring for change. There are two ways to move out of this stage. One way is through an increasing awareness or knowledge of the problem. Another way is through emotional arousal. For example, a person may see another dying of lung cancer and decide that it is time to quit smoking.

2. **Contemplation.** In this stage, a person begins to be aware of a problem and thinks seriously about taking some action. He or she weighs the pros and cons, the benefits and sacrifices, and thinks about the difficulty of change. People can only move to the next stage when they develop the self-confidence to believe that they can make a change. In the example of smoking cessation, at this stage a person would begin to look at the negative consequences of smoking but would consider change difficult.

3. **Preparation.** During this stage, people develop a strategy for change. They realize that change is necessary and desire to make the change. They discuss the change with friends and find the needed resources to make the change. They set an actual date to take action. In our smoking example, a person would start talking with friends and family members about quitting smoking and would set a time to stop smoking.

4. **Action.** This is the "just do it" stage. Without action, the goal cannot be accomplished. This stage requires some commitment. A person trying to quit smoking might just stop smoking "cold turkey" or cut down on daily smoking by a specific amount.

5. **Maintenance.** Once you have reached your goal, maintenance is the next step. This stage is the most difficult one as people struggle with the impulse to return to old patterns. Once a person has stopped smoking, the real test is maintaining the behavior.

6. **Termination.** This is permanent change. It is a time when temptations stop. Many people find it difficult to reach this stage.

What is important to realize about Prochaska's model is that change is a process and that there will be slip-ups along the way. His research shows that successful changers experience some failures along the way. However, he suggests that action that fails is better than no action at all. His research shows that those who tried to act and failed were more likely to succeed in the future. In one study of 200 people who made New Year's resolutions and were still keeping them two years later, the subjects had an average of 14 lapses before they were successful in keeping their resolutions.

Setbacks in the process of change are natural, and it is important not to give up. The process of change is difficult, but rewarding when you can follow through. When you are successful, you enjoy better health and gain confidence in your ability to make positive changes.

> ### Six Stages of Change
>
> 1. Precontemplation
> 2. Contemplation
> 3. Preparation
> 4. Action
> 5. Maintenance
> 6. Termination

KEYS TO SUCCESS

Live to Be 100

It is possible that you could live to be 100 years old. Of course, if you live to be 100, you will want to be healthy and capable of enjoying your life. Many people are doing this already.

John Glenn, the world's oldest astronaut at age 77, returned from space in 1998. Dr. John Charles joked that "he did pretty good for a 40-year-old guy."[46] He suffered no more bone or muscle loss than the younger astronauts on the mission, and his heart rate was slightly better than those of the younger astronauts. Doctors were so impressed with John Glenn's physical condition that they decided to take better care of their own health. How does John Glenn stay fit? He has taken care of himself over his lifetime. He walks several miles a day, does some light weight training, and eats a balanced diet. He challenges the notion that seniors are frail individuals. Glenn enjoyed the ride and is encouraging NASA to send more senior citizens into orbit.

Sarah "Sadie" Delaney wrote a bestselling novel with her sister Bessie at age 104. It contained their reminiscences of a century of achievement of African American women. They shared memories of slavery, segregation, and racism that they had experienced during their lives. Sadie lived to be 109 years old and Bessie died at age 104. They were from a family of 10 children, all of whom went to college. Their mother was a teacher and taught the children self-discipline, compassion, and confidence. When Bessie and Sadie were asked how they had lived so long, Bessie said, "Honey, we never married; we never had husbands to worry us to death." Sadie added, "Don't get married just because he looks pretty. He's got to have good genes and have some sense."[47]

> "Nobody grows old by merely living a number of years. We grow old by deserting our ideals. Years may wrinkle the skin, but to give up enthusiasm wrinkles the soul."
>
> Samuel Ullman
>
> "Wrinkles should merely indicate where smiles have been."
>
> Mark Twain
>
> "Anyone who stops learning is old, whether at twenty or eighty."
>
> Henry Ford

Mae Laborde became an actress at age 93. She has played the role of Vanna White (40 years in the future), appeared on *MADtv*, and faced down the Grim Reaper in a commercial about the elderly without health insurance. She is always smiling, has a positive attitude, and is ready to take on the world. She says it is never too late to follow your dreams.

Jerry Bloch at age 81 became the oldest man to climb El Capitan Mountain in Yosemite National Park. He chose the toughest and most challenging route up the mountain because he felt it might be his last mountain-climbing adventure because he was getting older.

Jeanne Calment passed away in 1997 at the age of 122. She was the oldest living person at that time. She was quite active into her old age. She took up fencing at age 85, rode a bicycle at

(Continued)

age 100, and produced a rap CD at age 121. During her younger life she engaged in activities such as playing the piano, tennis, roller-skating, bicycling, swimming, hunting, and going to the opera. She was never bored, and remained spirited and mentally sharp until the end. She became known for her wit and humor. One of her sayings was, "I've never had but one wrinkle, and I'm sitting on it."

Since you may live to be 100, take some advice from the experts: exercise to stay physically fit, be careful about whom you marry, stay active, have a positive attitude, and maintain your sense of humor.

© 2014, Tutti Fruitti. Used under license with Shutterstock, Inc.

Journal Entry #5

Write at least five intention statements about improving your health. Think about nutrition, exercise, avoiding addictions, preventing disease and relaxation, or other factors influencing your health. I intend to . . . .

JOURNAL ENTRIES

Maintaining a Healthy Lifestyle

Go to http://www.collegesuccess1.com/JournalEntries.htm for Word files of the Journal Entries

Success over the Internet

Visit the *College Success Website* at http://www.collegesuccess1.com/

The *College Success Website* is continually updated with new topics and links to the material presented in this chapter. Topics include:

- Health Topics A–Z
- Wellness
- Men and women's health topics
- Resources for smoking cessation
- Pregnancy
- Sexually transmitted diseases
- HIV/AIDS
- Planned Parenthood
- Nutrition
- Fitness
- Addictive behavior (drugs, alcohol, smoking)
- Resources for dealing with addiction to drugs, alcohol, or smoking
- Treatment centers for alcohol and drug problems
- Internet addictions
- Sleep problems
- Stress
- Panic attacks
- Anxiety
- Mental health

Contact your instructor if you have any problems in accessing the *College Success Website.*

Notes

1. U.S. Department of Health and Human Services, Centers for Disease Control and Prevention, National Center for Health Statistics, "Deaths, Preliminary Data for 2011," http://www.cdc.gov/nchs/data/nvsr/nvsr61/nvsr61_06.pdf

2. Richard Corliss and Michael Lemonick, "How to Live to be 100," *Time,* August 30, 2004.

3. Ibid.

4. Jenna Goudreau, "How to Live to Be 101," MSN Health and Fitness, accessed July 2010, http://health.msn.com.

5. U.S. Department of Agriculture, www.choosemyplate.gov/

6. U.S. Department of Agriculture, *Body Mass Index and Health*, March 2000.

7. U.S. Department of Agriculture, www.choosemyplate.gov/

8. Associated Press, "Proper Diet Urged to Fight Cancer, Not Supplements," *San Diego Union Tribune,* September 5, 2000.

9. U.S. Centers for Disease Control and Prevention, "Overweight and Obesity,"accessed August 3, 2010, http://www.cdc.gov/obesity/causes/index.html.

10. Marilyn Marchione, "Soda Causes Obesity, Researchers Report," *San Diego Union Tribune*, March 5, 2006.

11. U.S. Department of Health and Human Services, Centers for Disease Control and Prevention, Preventing Tobacco Use Among Youth and Young Adults, Executive Summary, http://www.cdc.gov/tobacco, 2012.

12. Ibid.

13. Ibid.

14. Ibid.

15. Gary Fraser and David Shavlik, "Ten Years of Life," *Archives of Internal Medicine* 161, no. 13 (9 July 2001).

16. "Binge Drinking Affects Brain, Memory," http://www.alcoholism.about.com.

17. Samuel Autman, "CSU Panel Urges Offensive against Alcohol Abuse," *San Diego Union Tribune,* May 8, 2001. Lewis Eigan, *Alcohol Practices, Policies and Potentials of American Colleges and Universities*, U.S. Department of Health and Human Services, 1991. National Institute on Alcohol Abuse and Alcoholism, U.S. Department of Health and Human Services, *Are Women More Vulnerable to Alcohol's Effects?,* 1999. Pacific Institute for Research and Evaluation, *Cost of Underage Drinking*, U.S. Department of Justice, 1999. Also from http://www.alcoholism.about.com and http://www.stop collegebinging.com.

18. Henry Wechsler and Toben Nelson, "Binge Drinking and the American College Student: What's Five Drinks?" *Psychology of Addictive Behaviors* 15, no. 4 (2001): 287–91.

19. Henry Wechsler, *Binge Drinking on America's College Campuses: Findings from the Harvard School of Public Health College Alcohol Study*, 2000.

20. Henry Wechsler, "College Binge Drinking in the 1990s: A Continuing Problem," *Journal of American College Health* 48 (2000): 199–210.

21. Ibid.

22. Henry Wechsler, *Findings from the Harvard School of Public Health College Alcohol Study,* 2000, http://www.hsph.harvard.edu/cas.

23. From http://www.habitsmart.com/bal.html.

24. National Institute on Alcohol Abuse and Alcoholism, U.S. Department of Health and Human Services, Alcohol Alert, No. 46, *Are Women More Vulnerable to Alcohol's Effects?,* 1999.

25. Henry Wechsler, Kuo Lee, and H. Lee, Harvard School of Public Health, 1999.

26. U.S. Department of Agriculture, *Dietary Guidelines for Americans*, 2000.

27. Clark Carr, "There is No Free Ride," *Freedom* (1998).

28. Lawrence Altman, "Peak of AIDS Epidemic Still to Come, U.N. Says," *San Diego Union Tribune*, July 3, 2002.

29. E. J. Mundell, "Hope for AIDS Cure Remains Alive," *WashingtonPost.com*, January 5, 2007.

30. U.S. Centers for Disease Control and Prevention, *Comprehensive HIV Prevention Messages for Young People*, 2002.

31. U.S. Centers for Disease Control and Prevention, National Center for HIV, STD, and TB Prevention, Divisions of HIV/AIDS Prevention, *HIV and AIDS: Are You at Risk?*, 2000.

32. U.S. Centers for Disease Control and Prevention, "Surveillance 2006: Trends in Sexually Transmitted Diseases in the United States 2006," http://cdc.gov/STD/trends2006.htm.

33. Cheryl Clark, "Sex Cops Help Find Those Who Spread Diseases," *San Diego Union Tribune,* March 11, 2002.

34. Darryl E. Owens, "Sleep's Impact on Learning A to Zzzzz," *San Diego Union Tribune,* October 2, 2000.

35. Scott LaFee, "A Chronic Lack of Sleep Can Lead to the Big Sleep," *San Diego Union Tribune,* October 8, 1997.

36. Ronald Kotulak, "Skimping on Sleep May Make You Fat, Clumsy and Haggard," *San Diego Union Tribune,* June 14, 1998.

37. Gregory Belenky, Walter Reed Army Institute of Research, *Sleep, Sleep Deprivation, and Human Performance in Continuous Operations*, 1997.

38. Lindsey Tanner, "AMA Backs 80-hour Workweek Limit for Doctors-in-Training," *San Diego Union Tribune*, June 21, 2002.

39. Ronald Kotulak, "Skimping on Sleep."

40. Nicole Ziegler Dizon, "Aging Men's Flab Tied to a Lack of Deep Sleep," *San Diego Union Tribune,* August 16, 2000.

41. From http://www.thirdage.com/cgi-bin/NewsPrint.cgi, 2002.

42. Francesco Cappuccio, Warwick Medical School, "Researchers Say Lack of Sleep Doubles Risk of Death . . . But So Can Too Much Sleep," http://www2warwick.ac.uk, 2008.

43. From http://www.stress.org, 2002.

44. Maya Pines, "Psychological Hardiness: The Role of Challenge in Health," *Psychology Today,* December 1980.

45. James Prochaska, "What It Takes to Change," *Health Net News,* Fall 1997.

46. Katherine Rizzo, "John Glenn, 77, Handled Space Like a Young Man," *San Diego Union Tribune,* January 29, 2000.

47. Chelsea Carter, "Sarah 'Sadie' Delaney, 109, Wrote Best Seller with her Sister at 104," *San Diego Union Tribune,* 1999.

CHAPTER 5

Appreciating Diversity

Learning Objectives

Read to answer these key questions:

- What is diversity and why is it important?

- How can an understanding and appreciation of diversity help me to be successful in school and in work?

- What is some vocabulary useful for understanding diversity?

- What are some ideas for communicating across cultures?

- What are some myths and facts about sexual orientation?

- How can I gain an appreciation of diversity?

Our schools, our workplaces, and our nation are becoming more diverse. Gaining an understanding and appreciation of this diversity will enhance your future success. Understanding yourself and having pride in your unique characteristics is the first step in the process. Self-knowledge includes information about your personality, interests, talents, and values. Earlier in this text you had the opportunity to begin this exploration. This chapter challenges you to examine some additional characteristics that make you a unique individual and to take pride in yourself while respecting the differences of others.

© 2014, RyFlip. Used under license with Shutterstock, Inc.

Diversity Is Increasing

Another word for diversity is differences. These differences do not make one group inferior or superior. Differences are not deficits: they are just differences. Look around your classroom, your place of employment, or where you do business. You will notice people of a variety of races, ethnic groups, cultures, genders, ages, socioeconomic levels, and sexual orientations. Other differences that add to our uniqueness include religious preference, political affiliation, personality, interests, and values. It is common to take pride in who we are and to look around and find people who share our view of the world. The challenge is to be able to look at the world from the point of view of those who are different from us. These differences provide an opportunity for learning.

Our schools and communities are becoming increasingly diverse. In the United States, one in every five students has a parent born in a foreign country. Nationwide, students who are non-Latiino whites make up only 56% of the population. The current school population includes 21% Latinos, 17% African Americans, 5% Asians and 1% Native Americans. There is also an increase in people who identify themselves as multi-racial. About seven million people or 2.4 percent of the population identify with at least two different racial groups. California, one of the most populous states, is leading the nation in student diversity. There is no single group in the majority: 49% are latinos, 30 percent are non-latino whites, 8 percent are African Americans, and 12 percent are Asians.[1] In New Mexico, Hawaii, and the District of Columbia, non-Latino whites are also in the minority.[2]

In our schools, places of work, and communities, we increasingly study, work, and socialize with people from different ethnic groups. This morning I talked with a student from Mexico and another from France. My classes have students from Mexico, Japan, Argentina, and Iraq. A colleague called on the phone and we spoke in Spanish. He invited me to a Greek café and deli where we ate Greek salad and purchased feta cheese and baklava. This diversity provides different perspectives, and products from other countries enrich our lives. It requires open-mindedness and respect for differences for it all to work.

We also live in a **global economy**. Increased international trade will result in new career opportunities that require and understanding and appreciation of cultural differences. The United States is in the center of the largest free-trade area in the world. In 1994, the North American Free Trade Agreement (NAFTA) created a free-trade area that includes Canada, the United States, and Mexico. This act resulted in a freer flow of goods among these countries and an increase in international business. The success of this international business depends on increased cooperation and problem solving among these nations. Free-trade agreements will probably be expanded to other countries in Latin America in the near future.

Another major step toward the global economy was the creation of a single currency in Europe, the euro, which was successfully launched on January 1, 2002. The purpose of this largest money changeover in history was to establish a system in which people, goods, services, and capital can move freely across national borders. The European countries using the euro have made their economies more competitive by facilitating trade, travel, and investment.

International trade accounts for a quarter of all economic activity in the United States.[3] All we have to do is look around us to see that many of the foods and products we use in our daily lives come from other countries.

Last night Jessica invited friends over for dinner and made stir-fried vegetables with chicken. She used ingredients from Vietnam, Thailand, Italy, Japan and Mexico. These foods were all purchased at her local grocery store. The guests ate dinner on plates made in Malaysia and drank wine from Australia. The next morning, she got up and dressed in a shirt made in the Dominican Republic and pants made in Mexico. She then put on her walking shoes, which were made in Thailand, and listened to Jamaican music on her iPod, which was made in China. For breakfast she ate a banana grown in Honduras and drank coffee from Colombia. She drove to school in a car that was made in Japan.

Global trade brings us many new and inexpensive products and is having a major impact on the economy and careers of the future.

Changes in technology have made an awareness and appreciation of diversity more important. The world is becoming an **electronic village** connected by an array of communication and information technologies: computers, the Internet, communications satellites, cell phones, fax machines, and the myriad of electronic devices that are an integral part of our lives today. These devices make rapid communication possible all over the world and are essential for international business and trade. The Internet is like a vast information superhighway, and each computer is an onramp to the highway. Those who do not have a computer or lack computer skills will be left off the highway and have limited access to information and opportunities.

The increased use of the Internet offers both great opportunities and challenges. The Internet can help to break down barriers between people. When communicating with someone over the Internet, differences such as race, age, religion, or economic status are not obvious. The flow of information and ideas is unrestricted, and people with similar interests can communicate easily with one another. There is great potential for use as well as misuse of the Internet. Chat groups can share information about medical conditions or treatments, but hate groups can also use the Internet to promote their political agendas.

Journal Entry #1

How will the global economy and the electronic village affect your future career and lifestyle?

© 2014, maxstockphoto. Used under license with Shutterstock, Inc.

Benefits of Diversity

- Gain critical thinking skills
- Pride in self and culture
- Learn from others
- Improve interpersonal skills
- Learn flexibility
- Develop cultural awareness

Why Is Diversity Important?

Our society, schools, and work environments are becoming more diverse. Having an understanding and appreciation of diversity can help you to be successful at school, at work, and in your personal life. Here are some benefits:

- **Gain skills in critical thinking.** Critical thinking requires identifying different viewpoints, finding possible answers, and then constructing your own reasonable view. Critical thinking skills are one of the expected outcomes of higher education. Many of your college assignments are designed to teach these skills. Whether you are writing an essay in an English class, participating in a discussion in a history class, or completing a laboratory experiment, critical thinking skills will help you to complete the task successfully. Critical thinking skills are also helpful in finding good solutions to problems or challenges you might find at work. For example, for a business manager, an important task is helping employees to work together as a team. The critical thinking process results in greater understanding of others and better problem-solving skills. To stay competitive, businesses need to find creative solutions for building better products and providing good customer service. Critical thinking skills help people work together to come up with good ideas to make a business a success.

- **Have pride in yourself and your culture.** Having pride in yourself is the foundation of good mental health and success in life. Sonia Nieto did research on a group of successful students. These students had good grades, enjoyed school, had plans for the future, and described themselves as successful. Nieto found that "one of the most consistent, and least expected, outcomes to emerge from these case studies has been a resoluteness with which young people maintain pride and satisfaction in their culture and the strength they derive from it."[4] Having pride in yourself and your culture is an important part of high self-esteem and can help you to become a better student and worker. Having good self-esteem provides the confidence to accept and care for others. The best schools and workplaces provide an environment where people can value their own culture as well as others. With respect between different cultures, ideas can be freely exchanged and the door is opened to creativity and innovation.

  The world is constantly changing and we must be ready to adapt to new situations. Sometimes it is difficult to balance "fitting in" and maintaining our own cultural identity. Researchers have described a process called **transculturation,** in which a person adapts to a different culture without sacrificing individual cultural identity. One study of Native Americans showed that retention of traditional cultural heritage was an important predictor of success. A Native American student described the process this way: "When we go to school, we live a non-Indian way but we still keep our values. . . . I could put my values aside just long enough to learn what it is I want to learn but that doesn't mean I'm going to forget them. I think that is how strong they are with me."[5] Cultural identity provides strength and empowerment to be successful.

- **Gain the ability to network and learn from others.** In college, you will have the opportunity to learn from your professors and other students who are different from yourself. You may have professors with very different personality styles and teaching styles. Your success will depend on being aware of the differences and finding a way to adapt to the situation. Each student in your classes will also come from a different perspective and have valuable ideas to add to the class.

It is through networking with other people that most people find jobs. You are likely to find a job through someone you know, such as a college professor, a student in one of your classes, a community member, or a previous employer. Once you have the job, you will gain proficiency by learning from others. The best managers are open to learning from others and help different people to work together as a team. No matter how educated or experienced you become, you can always learn from others. Bill Cosby once told a graduating class at Washington University, "Don't ever think you know more than the person mopping the floor."[6] Every person has a different view of the world and has important ideas to share.

- **Improve interpersonal skills.** A popular Native American proverb is that you cannot understand another person until you have walked a few miles in their moccasins. Being able to understand different perspectives on life will help you to improve your personal relationships. Good interpersonal skills bring joy to our personal relationships and are very valuable in the workplace. The Secretary of Labor's Commission on Achieving Necessary Skills (SCANS) identifies having good interpersonal skills as one of the five critical competencies needed in the workplace. Workers need to work effectively in teams, teach others, serve customers, exercise leadership, negotiate to arrive at a decision, and work well with cultural diversity.[7] Efficiency and profits in any industry depend on good interpersonal skills and how well workers can provide customer service.

- **Learn to be flexible and adapt to the situation.** These two qualities are necessary for dealing with the rapid change that is taking place in our society today. We learn these qualities by successfully facing personal challenges. If you are a single parent, you have learned to be flexible in managing time and resources. If you served in the military overseas, you have learned to adapt to a different culture. If you are a new college student, you are probably learning how to be independent and manage your own life. Flexibility is a valuable skill in the workplace. Today's employers want workers who can adapt, be flexible, and solve problems.

- **Develop cultural awareness.** Cultural awareness is valuable in your personal life and in the workplace. In your personal life, you can have a wider variety of satisfying personal relationships. You can enjoy people from different cultural backgrounds and travel to different countries.

In a global economy, cultural awareness is increasingly important. Tuning into cultural differences can open up business opportunities. For example, many companies are discovering that the buying power of minorities is significant. They are developing ad campaigns to sell products to Asians, Latinos, African Americans, and other groups.

Companies now understand that cultural awareness is important in international trade. American car manufacturers could not understand why the Chevy Nova was not selling well in Latin America. In Spanish, "No va" means "It doesn't go" or "It doesn't run." Kentucky Fried Chicken found out that "Finger-lickin' good" translates as "Eat your fingers off" in Chinese! Being familiar with the cultures and languages of different countries is necessary for successful international business.

Journal Entry #2

How will an understanding of diversity help you to be successful in school and work?

Vocabulary for Understanding Diversity

Knowing some basic terms will aid in your understanding of diversity.

- **Race.** Race refers to a group of people who are perceived to be physically different because of traits such as facial features, color of skin, and hair.
- **Ethnicity.** Ethnicity refers to a sense of belonging to a particular culture and sharing the group's beliefs, attitudes, skills, ceremonies, and traditions. An ethnic group usually descends from a common group of ancestors, usually from a particular country or geographic area.
- **Ethnocentrism.** Ethnocentrism is the belief that one's own ethnic, religious, or political group is superior to all others.
- **Culture.** Culture is the behavior, beliefs, and values shared by a group of people. It includes language, morals, and even food preferences. Culture includes everything that we learn from the people around us in our community.
- **Gender, sex.** Gender refers to cultural differences that distinguish males from females. Different cultures raise men and women to act in specified ways. Sex refers to anatomical differences.
- **Sexism.** Sexism is a negative attitude or perception based on sex.
- **Stereotype.** A stereotype is a generalization that expresses conventional or biased ideas about people in a certain group. Stereotypes can lead to discrimination based on these ideas. They cause us to view others in a limited way and reduce our ability to see people as individuals.
- **Prejudice.** A prejudice is a prejudgment of someone or something. Prejudices are often based on stereotypes and reflect a disrespect for others. Sometimes people who are prejudiced are insecure about their own identities.
- **Discrimination.** Discrimination happens when people are denied opportunities because of their differences. Prejudice and stereotype are often involved.
- **Racism.** Racism occurs when one race or ethnic group holds a negative attitude or perception of another group. It is prejudice based on race. Anthropologists generally accept that the human species can be categorized into races based on physical and genetic makeup. **These scientists accept the fact that there is no credible evidence that one race is superior to another**. People who believe that their own race is superior to another are called racists.
- **Cultural pluralism.** Each group celebrates the customs and traditions of their culture while participating in mainstream society.
- **Genocide.** Genocide is the deliberate and systematic destruction of a racial, political, or cultural group. It can include the destruction of the language, religion, or cultural practices of a group of people.

Understanding Diversity

There are 7.2 billion people in the world today. Statistics provided by the Population Reference Bureau and the United Nations can give us a better understanding of diversity in the world today. By geographic area, the world's population can be broken down into these percentages:[8]

- 60 Asians
- 16 Africans
- 10 Europeans
- 9 Central and South Americans
- 5 North Americans (Canada and the United States)

If visitors from outer space were to visit the earth and report back about the most common human being found, they would probably describe someone of Asian descent. Statistics also show that approximately 50 percent of the world population suffers from malnutrition and 80 percent live in substandard housing. Moreover, 6 percent of the population living in the United States, Japan, and Germany owns half of the wealth of the world. In addition, continuous wars and fighting among the people of the earth have contributed to human suffering and the flight of many refugees.

As children, we accept the values, assumptions, and stereotypes of our culture. We use our own culture as a filter to understand the world. Because of this limited perception, people often consider their culture to be superior and other cultures to be inferior.[9] The belief that one's own culture, religious, or political group is superior to others is called **ethnocentrism.** Native Americans have argued that the celebration of Columbus Day, commemorating the discovery of the New World by Christopher Columbus, is an example of ethnocentrism. In reality, the Native Americans lived here long before Christopher Columbus arrived in 1492.

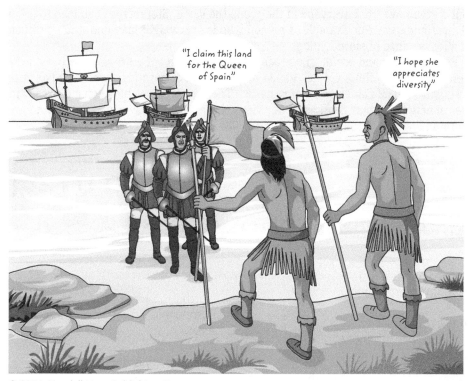

Ethnocentrism can lead to discrimination, interpersonal conflict, and even wars between different groups of people. In extreme cases, it can even lead to **genocide**, the deliberate and systematic destruction of a racial, political, or cultural group. History is full of examples of genocide. In the United States, Native Americans were massacred and their land was confiscated in violation of treaties. In Mexico and South America, the Spanish conquerors systematically destroyed native populations. During World War II, six million Jews were killed. Pol Pot and the Khmer Rouge killed millions of Cambodians. Unfortunately, genocide continues today in various conflicts around the world.

An understanding of the harmful effects of stereotypes is necessary to improve our understanding and appreciation of diversity. A **stereotype** is an assumption that all members of a group are alike. For example, a tall African American woman in one of my classes was constantly dealing with the assumption that she must be attending college to play basketball. Actually, she was very academically oriented and not athletic at all. It is important to remember that we all have individual differences within groups of the same ethnicity or cultural background.

All of us use stereotypes to understand people different from ourselves. Why does this happen? There are many different reasons:

- It is a fast way to make sense of the world. It requires little thought.
- We tend to look for patterns to help us understand the world.
- We are often unable or unwilling to obtain all the information we need to make fair judgments about other people.
- Stereotypes can result from fear of people who are different. We often learn these fears as children.
- The media promotes stereotypes. Movies, magazines, and advertisements often present stereotypes. These stereotypes are often used as the basis of humor. For example, the media often uses people who are overweight in comedy routines.

The problem with stereotypes is that we do not get to know people as individuals. All members of a culture, ethnic group, or gender are not alike. If we make assumptions about a group, we treat everyone in the group the same. Stereotypes can lead to prejudice and discrimination. For example, a person who is overweight may find it more difficult to find a job because of stereotyping.

Psychologists and sociologists today present the idea of **cultural relativity**, in which different cultures, ethnic groups, genders, and sexual orientations are viewed as different but equally valuable and worthy of respect.[10] These differences between cultures can help us learn new ideas that can enrich our view of the world. They can also promote greater understanding and better relationships among individuals and nations.

QUIZ

Understanding Diversity, Part I

Test what you have learned by selecting the correct answers to the following questions.

1. The belief that one's own ethnic, religious, or political group is superior to all others is called

   a. cultural pluralism.
   b. cultural relativity.
   c. ethnocentrism.

2. The assumption that all members of a group are alike is

   a. discrimination.
   b. stereotype.
   c. prejudice.

3. The deliberate destruction of a racial, cultural, or political group of people is called

   a. genocide.
   b. racism.
   c. ethnocentrism.

4. Most people on the earth are

   a. North Americans.
   b. Europeans.
   c. Asians.

5. Cultural relativity is defined as

   a. the belief that one's own ethnic group is superior.
   b. groups that are viewed as different, but equally valuable.
   c. an ethnic group that descends from a common group of ancestors.

How did you do on the quiz? Check your answers: 1. c, 2. b, 3. a, 4. c, 5. b

Journal Entry # 3

Describe an incidence in which you experienced discrimination. Consider discrimination in a broad context, including ethnicity, culture, language, gender, sexual orientation, weight, height, appearance, personality type, values, politics, religion, age, experience, socioeconomic background, academic skills, or any other factor which could cause discrimination.

© 2014, Sergey Nivens. Used under license with Shutterstock, Inc.

A New Look at Diversity:
The Human Genome Project

Although the people of the world represent many racial, ethnic, and cultural groups, biologists are taking a new look at diversity by learning about human genes. Genes are composed of segments of DNA that determine the transmission of hereditary traits by controlling the operation of cells. Cells are the basic building blocks of the human body.

The Human Genome Project, a multibillion-dollar and multinational government-sponsored research project to map all human genes has now been completed. This map is a catalog of all the genetic information contained in human cells. They have identified the genes and determined the sequence of the three billion chemical base pairs in human DNA. Although the project is completed, analysis of the data will continue for many years.[11] The human genome is considered a biological treasure chest that will allow scientists to discover how a body grows, ages, stays healthy, or becomes ill. This knowledge is invaluable in discovering new medications and improving health.

Results of the Human Genome Project show that we are all genetically similar while having unique individual differences. One of the interesting findings is that "as scientists have long suspected, though the world's people may look very different on the outside, genetically speaking humans are all 99.9 percent identical."[12] While we are genetically very similar, each individual can be identified by his or her genetic code. With the exception of identical twins, each individual human being is slightly different because of the unique combination of DNA letters inherited from one's parents.

Dr. Craig Venter, head of Celera Genomics Corporation, has stated that "race is a social concept, not a scientific one."[13] While it may be easy to look at people and describe them as Caucasian, African, or Asian, there is little genetic material to distinguish one race from another. Venter says, "We all evolved in the last 100,000 years from the same small number of tribes that migrated out of Africa and colonized the world."[14] Very few

"So let us not be blind to our differences, but let us also direct attention to our common interests and to the means by which those differences can be resolved."
John F. Kennedy

"We need to help students and parents cherish and preserve the ethnic and cultural diversity that nourishes and strengthens this community and this nation."
César Chavez

genes control traits that distinguish one race from another, such as skin color, eye color, and width of nose. These outward characteristics have been able to change quickly in response to environmental pressures. People who lived near the equator evolved dark skin to protect them from ultraviolet radiation. People who lived farther from the equator evolved pale skins to produce vitamin D from little sunlight. The genes responsible for these outward appearances are in the range of .01 percent of the total. Researchers on the Human Genome Project agree that **there is only one race: the human race**.

The Human Genome Project will be important for understanding the human body and will help us to find ways to prevent or cure illnesses. It may also provide new information for critical thinking about the idea of ethnocentrism and discover some basic ways in which all human beings are similar.

> "Our language is the reflection of ourselves. A language is an exact reflection of the character and growth of its speakers."
> César Chavez

Communicating across Cultures

Human beings communicate through the use of symbols. A symbol is a word that stands for something else. Problems in communication arise when we assume that a symbol has only one meaning and that everyone understands the symbol in the same way. For example, we use the word "dog" to stand for a four-legged animal that barks. However, if I say the word "dog," the picture in my mind probably doesn't match the picture in your mind because there are many varieties of dogs. I might be picturing a Chihuahua while you are picturing a German shepherd. Language becomes even more complex when we have multiple meanings for one symbol. Consider the ways we use the word "dog":

- She is a dog. (She is unattractive.)
- He is a dog. (He is promiscuous.)
- He is a lucky dog. (He is fortunate.)
- It's a dog. (It is worthless.)
- Just dog it. (Just do enough to get by.)
- He went to the dogs. (He was not doing well.)
- He was in the doghouse. (He was in trouble.)
- Let sleeping dogs lie. (Leave the situation alone.)
- My dogs hurt. (My feet hurt.)
- He put on the dog. (He assumed an attitude of wealth or importance.)
- These are the dog days of summer. (These are hot days when people feel lazy.)
- The book is dog-eared. (The corners of the pages are bent.)
- He led a dog's life. (He was not happy.)
- May I have a doggy bag? (May I have a bag for my leftovers?)
- Doggone it! (I am frustrated!)
- I am dog-tired. (I am very tired.)

© 2014, Erik Lam. Used under license with Shutterstock, Inc.

Imagine how a computer would translate the above sentences. The translations would be incomprehensible, since there are so many variations in meaning depending on the context. The problem of communication becomes even more difficult for those who are learning English. People who speak a different language might not understand the word "dog" at all because they use a different symbol for the object. Even after studying the language, it is easy to misinterpret the meaning of the word "dog." A recent immigrant was horrified when he was offered a hot dog at a ball game. He thought that this was a civilized country and was surprised that we ate dogs!

The symbols we use to stand for objects are arbitrary, complex, and dependent on our culture, language, and frame of reference. As a result, misunderstandings are common. When my son was very young, he was very frightened by noises on the roof of our house. He was afraid that aliens had landed. He said that he was certain there were aliens on the roof and that Dad said he had seen them too. I later found out that his father said that he had seen illegal aliens, or undocumented workers, in our neighborhood. It is strange that in the English language we use the word "alien" to refer to someone from outer space and someone from a different country. The "aliens" in my son's case turned out to be raccoons playing on the roof. The words that we use have a powerful influence on our lives and can make clear communication difficult.

Both verbal and nonverbal symbols have different meaning in different cultures. George Henderson, in his book *Cultural Diversity in the Workplace*,[15] gives the example of the common thumbs-up gesture, which we commonly interpret as "okay." In Japan the same gesture means money. In Ghana and Iran, it is a vulgar gesture similar to raising your middle finger in the United States. Another example is silence. In the United States, if a teacher asks a question and no one responds right away, the situation is uncomfortable. In Native American cultures, the person who remains silent is admired. Many Asian students listen more than they speak. According to a Zen proverb, "He who knows does not speak and he who speaks does not know." Think about how different our communications, especially business and sales techniques, would have to be in order to be effective in different cultures.

Here are some ideas to help improve your communications with people who are culturally different from you or speak a different language:

- Be sensitive to the fact that communication is difficult and that errors in understanding are likely.

- Remember that the message sent is not necessarily the message received.

- Give people time to think and respond. You do not have to fill in the silence right away.

- Check your understanding of the message. Rephrase or repeat the information to make sure it is correct. Ask questions.

- If you feel insulted by the message, remember that it is quite possible that you could be misinterpreting it. (Remember all the meanings for "dog" listed above.)

- If you are having problems communicating with someone who speaks a different language, speak slowly and clearly or use different words. Talking louder will not help.

- Remain calm and treat others with respect. Be patient.

- Find a translator if possible.

- Study a different language. This will help in understanding other cultures and the different ways that other cultures use symbols.

- Before traveling to a different country, read about the culture and learn some basic phrases in the language used. This will help you to enjoy your travel and learn about other cultures. Attempting to speak the language will show others that you care about and respect the culture.

- Sometimes nonverbal communication can help. If you are adventurous or desperate, smile and act out the message. Be aware that nonverbal communication can be misunderstood also.
- Don't forget your sense of humor.

Journal Entry # 4

What advice would you give to a person preparing to visit another country with a very different culture and language?

© 2014, David C. Rehner. Used under license with Shutterstock, Inc.

Understanding Sexual Orientation

Major causes of stereotyping and the resulting prejudice and discrimination are fear and lack of knowledge of those who are different. Prejudice and discrimination against gays and other minorities have sometimes led to hate crimes. For example, in 1998, Matthew Shepard, a gay student at the University of Wyoming, was lured from a bar, beaten, and tied to a log fence, where he was left during cold weather. He died five days later. His murderers received life sentences in prison. At Matthew's funeral, protesters held up signs saying, "God hates fags."[16] The term "faggot," which comes from the Latin word for a bundle of sticks, may refer to the time of the Inquisition when gays were actually burned at the stake along with witches.[17]

Stereotypes about sexual orientation and the resulting discrimination are common in society today and affect a great number of people. One out of four families has a gay family member and it is estimated that up to 10 percent of the population is gay or lesbian. In a class of 30 students, it is likely that three are gay men or lesbians. Many of these people are fearful of identifying themselves as gay because of potential discrimination and lack of acceptance by the general population. Think about these stereotypes as you read the following scenario:

My brother Jake was always a little different; he was not the "typical boy." Growing up he was my best friend. It was as if he were the sister I never had. He was kind and gentle and compassionate toward all creatures. He enjoyed cooking, taking care of children and growing flowers. I remember that my father tried to make a man of him by encouraging him to join in manly activities such as hunting. My father was frustrated because Jake could not kill a deer. Jake looked the deer in the eye and decided that he could not kill such a beautiful creature. I had to agree with him, but my father was disappointed. He was frustrated in all his attempts to make my brother a man and had frequent conflicts with him. At age 16, my brother ran away from home and was "adopted" by a female teacher at our high school. She encouraged my brother to go to college and he moved across the continent, eventually working his way through medical school and becoming a well-known and respected cardiologist and critical care specialist. I was happy for my brother because he could do what he loved best: helping other people. One day my father had a heart attack and Jake returned home and saved my father's life. At this point, my father was finally proud of the man he had become.

I remember having a conversation with my other brothers about whether Jake was gay or not. I acknowledged the possibility, but said that it would be awful if we asked him and it were not true, so we never asked him. He did not look or act gay; he was just different. In fact, my girlfriends were always trying to get a date with him. One day I received a call from my brother. He was saying good-bye because he was dying. He did not want the family to visit; he just wanted to say good-bye, and he died the next day at the age of 43. Against Jake's wishes, my mother and some of my brothers traveled to New York and were shocked to find that Jake was living with a man who was HIV-positive and that Jake had died of AIDS. My father told everyone that Jake died of cancer. I felt an overwhelming sense of sadness at losing my brother and that he never felt comfortable enough to tell us that he was gay. I will always wonder if I should have asked him about being gay and if I possibly could have been more a part of his life. Since I lost my opportunity to do this, I have resolved to gain a better understanding and appreciation of sexual orientation, which is sadly the only thing I can do at this point.

Becoming educated about sexual orientation can help to diminish anti-gay prejudice and help people who are struggling with their sexual identity. Here is a list of myths and facts about gay men and lesbians. The corrected information below is provided by the Parents, Families, and Friends of Lesbians and Gays (PFLAG). This organization provides information on its website, www.pflagla.org. An organization called Rainbow Bridge also provides educational materials on gays and lesbians. Most college campuses have organizations that support gay, lesbian, bisexual, and transgender students. It is common that people disagree with the following facts because of common stereotypes about sexual orientation.

Myths and Facts about Gays and Lesbians

Myth: Only one percent of the world's population is gay, lesbian, or bisexual.

Fact: It is estimated that about 10 percent of the world's population is gay, lesbian, or bisexual.

Myth: Effeminate men and masculine women are always gay.

Fact: Effeminate men and masculine women can be heterosexual. Some gay persons fit this stereotype, but most look and act like individuals from the heterosexual majority.

Myth: Homosexuality is a choice, a preference, or a learned behavior.

Fact: Homosexuality is not something that one chooses to be or learns to be. As children, gay men and lesbians are not taught or influenced by others to be homosexual. Most current research cites genetic or inborn hormonal factors in homosexuality.[18]

(Continued)

Myth: You can always tell from a person's appearance if he or she is gay.

Fact: Most gay men and lesbians look and act like individuals from the heterosexual majority.

Myth: Lesbians and gay men never make good parents.

Fact: Gay men and lesbians can make good parents. Children of gay and lesbian parents are no different in any aspects of psychological, social, or sexual development from children in heterosexual families. These children tend to be more tolerant of differences.

Myth: Gay men and lesbian women are often involved in child abuse.

Fact: Gay men and lesbians are rarely involved in child abuse. In the United States, heterosexual men commit 90 percent of all sexual child abuse. The molesters are most often fathers, stepfathers, grandfathers, uncles, or boyfriends of the mothers.

Myth: The word "homosexual" is preferred over "gay" or "lesbian."

Fact: The term "gay man" or "lesbian" is preferred over the term "homosexual."

Myth: The term "gay" refers only to men.

Fact: The term "gay" refers to both men and women.

Myth: Some cultures do not have gay men and lesbians.

Fact: All cultures have gay men and lesbians.

Myth: Only gay men get AIDS and it is a death sentence.

Fact: AIDS is increasingly a heterosexual disease. Advances in the early detection and treatment of AIDS make it a chronic, controllable disease for most patients.

Myth: Being gay is an emotional or mental disorder.

Fact: The American Psychological Association does not list being gay as an emotional or mental disorder.

Myth: Through psychotherapy, a gay person can be turned into a heterosexual.

Fact: Psychotherapy has not been successful in changing a person's sexual orientation. In some states, psychotherapy aimed at changing gay men and women into heterosexuals is now illegal.

Myth: A person is either completely heterosexual or completely homosexual.

Fact: Based on Dr. Alfred Kinsey's research, few people are predominantly heterosexual or homosexual. Most people fall on a continuum between the two extremes. A person on the middle of the continuum between heterosexual and homosexual would be a bisexual. Bisexuals are attracted to both sexes.[19]

Myth: Homosexuality does not exist in nature. It is dysfunctional.

Fact: Research suggests that homosexuality is "natural." It exists among all animals and is frequent among highly developed species.[20]

Myth: Gay people should not be teachers because they will try to convert their students.

Fact: Homosexual seduction is no more common than heterosexual seduction. Most gay teachers fear they will be fired if it is found out that they are gay.[21]

How to Appreciate Diversity

Having an appreciation for diversity enriches all of us. Poet Maya Angelou has described the world as a rich tapestry and stressed that understanding this concept can enrich and improve the world:

"It is time for us to teach young people early on that in diversity there is beauty and strength. We all should know that diversity makes for a rich tapestry, and we must understand that the threads of the tapestry are equal in value, no matter their color; equal in importance, no matter their texture."[22]

Here are some ways to appreciate diversity:

- Educate yourself about other cultures and people who are different from you. Read about or take courses on the literature or history of another culture, or learn another language.
- Explore your own heritage. Learn about the cultures that are part of your family history.
- Value diversity and accept the differences of others.
- View differences as an opportunity for learning.
- Realize that you will make mistakes when dealing with people from other cultural backgrounds. Learn from the mistakes and move on to better understanding.
- Work to understand differences of opinion. You do not have to agree, but respect different points of view.
- Travel to other countries to discover new ideas and cultures.
- Think critically to avoid stereotypes and misconceptions. Treat each person as an individual.
- Avoid judgments based on physical characteristics such as color of skin, age, gender, or weight.
- Put yourself in the other person's place. How would you feel? What barriers would you face?
- Make friends with people from different countries, races, and ethnic groups.
- Find some common ground. We all have basic needs for good health, safety, economic security, and education. We all face personal challenges and interests. We all think, feel, love, and have hope for the future.
- Be responsible for your own behavior. Do not participate in or encourage discrimination.
- Do good deeds. You will be repaid with good feelings.
- Learn from history so that you do not repeat it. Value your own freedom.
- Challenge racial or homophobic remarks or jokes.
- Teach children and young people to value diversity and respect others. It is through them that we can change the world.

Journal Entry #5

Frequently we learn discrimination through our parents, our community, the media, and our environment. What would you teach your children about diversity?

Stages of Ethical Development

After much study, Harvard University professor William Perry developed the theory that students move through stages of ethical development.[23] Students move through these patterns of thought and eventually achieve effective intercultural communication.

Stage 1: Dualism

In this stage we view the world in terms of black or white, good or bad, "we" versus "they." Role models and authorities determine what is right. The right answers exist for every problem. If we work hard, we can find the correct answers and all will be well. Decisions are often based on common stereotypes.

Stage 2: Multiplicity

At this stage we become aware that there are multiple possibilities and answers. We know that authorities can disagree on what is right and wrong. We defend our position, but acknowledge that on any given issue, everyone has a right to his or her own opinion.

Stage 3: Relativism

As we learn more about our environment and ourselves, we discover that what is right is based on our own values and culture. We weigh the evidence and try to support our opinions based on data and evidence.

Stage 4: Commitment in Relativism

At this stage, we look at our environment and ourselves and make choices. In an uncertain world, we make decisions about careers, politics, and personal relationships based on our individual values. We make certain commitments based on the way we wish to live our lives. We defend our own values but respect the values of others. There is openness to learning new information and changing one's personal point of view. This position allows for the peaceful coexistence of different points of views and perspectives. It is at this point that we become capable of communicating across cultures and appreciating diversity.

Understanding Diversity, Part II

Test what you have learned by selecting the correct answers to the following questions.

1. Results of the Human Genome Project show that humans are

    a. 80 percent identical.
    b. 50 percent identical.
    c. 99.9 percent identical.

2. Problems in communication occur when we assume that

    a. a symbol has only one meaning.
    b. words have many meanings.
    c. it is easy to match the picture in one person's mind to a picture in another person's mind.

3. The thumbs-up gesture

    a. means "okay" in Japan.
    b. is a vulgar gesture in Iran.
    c. is understood in the same way in all cultures.

4. The following statement about sexual orientation is generally accepted as true:

    a. sexual orientation is not something one chooses or can change.
    b. some cultures do not have gay men and lesbians.
    c. homosexuality is a learned behavior.

5. In the last stage of ethical development, commitment in relativism, we

    a. view the world in terms of "good" and "bad."
    b. become aware of multiple possibilities.
    c. defend our own values but respect the values of others.

How did you do on the quiz? Check your answers: 1. c, 2. a, 3. b, 4. a, 5. c

Student Perspectives on Diversity

The following are some student comments on the subject of diversity. Many students have faced incidents of discrimination and hope for a better future.

> I am always faced with problems because I'm black or my hair is long or because I am a large man. I wish people could be more sensitive and love me as a person and not judge me based on what I look like.
>
> I am frequently discriminated against because of my religion. I feel really bad when it happens and it hurts a lot.
>
> I have always faced discrimination because of my sexual orientation and will probably continue to experience discrimination in the future. If you are part of a minority, discrimination is inevitable. The key is to not let it drag you down so that you become a second-class citizen. That can be accomplished by taking pride in who you are and then working to fight against discrimination.
>
> I come from Japan. I noticed that people here think their culture is better than any other. I think it's not bad to love your culture, but it is important to be open to other cultures.

(Continued)

There is a story I tell my children about words being nails. When we speak, we pound our nails into the other person's spirit. We can go back and apologize for hurtful words and maybe that removes the nail, but it still leaves a hole in the spirit.

If you constantly hear people say that you are not as good as another, you eventually start to believe it.

I've been discriminated against because I am female and a blonde. When I hear blonde jokes, I've learned to laugh with people most of the time, but it still hurts my feelings.

Discrimination is passed on to the next generation because a child believes what a parent tells them. We need to teach our children tolerance for differences.

Discrimination hurts people's feelings and doesn't allow them to become successful in life because they lose confidence and self-esteem.

Because I am black, salespeople tend to follow me around in the store thinking I am going to steal something. People of different races call me "nigger."

When I was younger, I used to wear thick glasses. People would call me names such as "four eyes," "nerd," "dork," and "geek." I can look back and laugh at this now, but it made me feel inferior. Discrimination is based on ignorance and hate.

Black kids used to mistreat me because I was not as black as them.

Once when I was 10 years old, I was playing in the park. I noticed this Caucasian kid playing on the slide and he was about to fall off the slide. I went over to catch him and the mother ran over to me and told me to take my hands off of him and that she would rather have him fall than to have some "nigger" put her hands on him. I will never forget this incident!

When I was younger, my father frequently made negative comments about women. Because of his prejudice, I felt less worthy of getting equal treatment for equal education and work. Now my father is trying to overcome this mindset, and I plan to graduate from college to earn equal pay with men.

It is sad that humans can be so cruel to one another. I hope someday this will all end and we can live in peace with one another.

By celebrating diversity, all the people of the world could come together and have peace.

Diversity Is Valuable and People Are Important

In 1963, Dr. Martin Luther King, Jr., made a famous speech in which he said, "I have a dream that my four little children will one day live in a nation where they will not be judged by the color of their skin, but by the content of their character." Because of his message of brotherhood and understanding, his birthday is celebrated as a national holiday. Tragically, King was assassinated because of his strong stand against racism. We are still working toward his ideal of brotherly love.

When I ask students to describe what success means to them, they often talk about having a good career, financial stability, owning a home, and having a nice car. Some students mention family and friends and people who are important to them. Understanding diversity and appreciating other people can add to your personal success and enjoyment of life.

To gain perspective on what is important to your success, it is interesting to think about what people will say about you after you die. What will you think is important at the end of your life? If you can ponder this idea, you can gain some insight into how to live your life now. Go to the following website:

http://www.lindaellisonline.com/The_Dash_Poem_Copyright_Linda_Ellis.htm

Read "The Dash" by Linda Ellis.

Learn to understand, respect, and appreciate the different people in your life. Take time to love those who are important to you. Focus on cooperation and teamwork on the job. Don't forget about the people you meet on your road to success; they are important too. Having an understanding and appreciation of diversity will make the world a better place in which to live.

JOURNAL ENTRIES

Appreciating Diversity

Go to http://www.collegesuccess1.com/JournalEntries.htm for Word files of the Journal Entries

Success over the Internet

Visit the *College Success Website* at http://www.collegesuccess1.com/

The *College Success Website* is continually updated with new topics and links to the material presented in this chapter. Topics include:

- Tolerance
- Ways to fight hate
- Diversity and multicultural resources
- Asian-Pacific students
- Latinos
- Women
- Minorities

Contact your instructor if you have any problems accessing the *College Success Website*.

Notes

1. "Diversity in the Classroom," The New York Times, December 22, 2011 accessed at http://projects.nytimes.com/immigration/enrollment/california

2. Ibid.

3. David Broder, "Congress Wants to Shape Trade Debate," *San Diego Union Tribune*, November 7, 2001.

4. Sonia Nieto, *Affirming Diversity: The Sociopolitical Context of Multicultural Education* (New York: Longman, 1996), 283.

5. Terry Huffman, "The Transculturation of Native American College Students," in *American Mosaic: Selected Readings on America's Multicultural Heritage,* ed. Young Song and Eugene Kim (Englewood Cliffs, NJ: Prentice-Hall, 1993), 211–19.

6. Richard Bucher, *Diversity Consciousness* (Englewood Cliffs, NJ: Prentice-Hall, 2000), 119.

7. Secretary's Commission of Achieving Necessary Skills (SCANS), U.S. Department of Labor, *Learning a Living: A Blueprint for High Performance*, 1991.

8. "World Population Prospects, The 2012 Revision, Highlights and Advance Tables," United Nations, New York, 2013 accessed from http://esa.un.org/unpd/wpp/Documentation/pdf/WPP2012_HIGHLIGHTS.pdf

9. H. Triandis, "Training for Diversity," paper presented at the annual meeting of the American Psychological Association, San Francisco, 1991.

10. Benjamin Lahey, *Psychology: An Introduction* (Dubuque, IA: Brown and Benchmark, 1995), 20. "Human Genome Project Information," U.S. Department of Energy Office of Science, http://www.ornl.gov/sci/techresources/Human_Genome/home.shtml, 2008.

11. "Human Genome Project Information," U.S. Department of Energy, Office of Science.

12. Sue Goetinck Ambrose, "First Look at Genome Data Leaves Scientists in 'Awe'," *San Diego Union Tribune*, February 11, 2001.

13. Natalie Angier, "Do Races Differ? Not Really, Genes Show," *New York Times,* August 22, 2000.

14. Ibid.

15. George Henderson, *Cultural Diversity in the Workplace: Issues and Strategies* (Westport, CT: Praeger, 1994).

16. "Mourners Gather to Honor Gay Murdered in Wyoming," *Bellingham Herald,* October 17, 1998, A8.

17. California Rainbow Bridge pamphlet, 2000.

18. American Psychological Association, http://www.apa.org.pubinfo.html, 2001.

19. Ibid.

20. Ibid.

21. Ibid.

22. Maya Angelou, *Wouldn't Take Nothing for My Journey Now* (New York: Random House, 1993).

23. William G. Perry, "Cognitive and Ethical Growth: The Making of Meaning," in *The Modern American College* by Arthur Chickering and Associates (Hoboken, NJ: Jossey-Bass, 1981), 76–116.

CHAPTER 6

Managing Money

Learning Objectives

Read to answer these key questions:

- How can I manage my money to accomplish my financial goals?

- What are some ways to save money?

- How can I pay for my education?

- How can I use priorities to manage my time?

Managing Your Money

To be successful in college and in life, you will need to manage not only time, but money. One of the top reasons that students drop out of college is that they cannot pay for their education or that they have to work so much that they do not have time for school. Take a look at your lifetime goals. Most students have a goal related to money, such as becoming financially secure or becoming wealthy. If financial security or wealth is one of your goals, you will need to begin to take some action to accomplish that goal. If you don't take action on a goal, it is merely a fantasy.

© 2014, ARENA Creative. Used under license with Shutterstock, Inc.

How to Become a Millionaire

Save regularly. Frances Leonard, author of *Time Is Money*, cites some statistics on how much money you need to save to become a millionaire.[1] You can retire with a million dollars by age 68 by saving the following amounts of money at various ages. These figures assume a 10 percent return on your investment.

At age 22, save $87 per month
At age 26, save $130 per month
At age 30, save $194 per month
At age 35, save $324 a month

Notice that the younger you start saving, the less money is required to reach the million-dollar goal. (And keep in mind that even a million dollars may not be enough money to save for retirement.) How can you start saving money when you are a student struggling to pay for college? The answer is to practice money management techniques and to begin a savings habit, even if the money you save is a small amount to buy your books for next semester. When you get that first good job, save 10 percent of the money. If you are serious about becoming financially secure, learn about investments such as real estate, stocks and bonds, and mutual funds. Learning how to save and invest your money can pay big dividends in the future.

Think thrifty. Money management begins with looking at your attitude toward money. Pay attention to how you spend your money so that you can accomplish your financial goals such as getting a college education, buying a house or car, or saving for the future. The following example shows how one woman accomplished her financial goals through being thrifty. Amy Dacyczyn, author of *The Tightwad Gazette*, says, "A lot of people get a thrill out of buying things. Frugal people get a rush from the very act of saving. Saving can actually be fun—we think of it almost as a sport."[2] She noticed that people were working harder and harder for less and less. Amy Dacyczyn had the goals of marriage, children, and a New England farmhouse to live in. She wanted to stay home and take care of her six children instead of working. In seven years, she was able to accomplish her goals with her husband's income of $30,000 a year. During this time, she saved $49,000 for the down payment on a rural farmhouse costing $125,000. She also paid cash for $38,000 worth of car, appliance, and furniture purchases while staying at home with her children. How did she do this? She says that she just started paying attention to how she was spending her money.

To save money, Amy Dacyczyn made breakfast from scratch. She made oatmeal, pancakes, and muffins instead of purchasing breakfast cereals. She saved $440 a year in this way. She purchased the family clothing at yard sales. She thought of so many ideas to save money that she began publishing *The Tightwad Gazette* to share her money-saving ideas with others. At $12 per subscription, she grosses a million dollars a year!

Challenge yourself to pay attention to how you spend your money, and make a goal of being thrifty in order to accomplish your financial goals. With good money management, you can work less and have more time for college and recreational activities.

Managing Your Money

- Monitor your spending
- Prepare a budget
- Beware of credit and interest
- Watch spending leaks

Budgeting: The Key to Money Management

It is important to control your money, rather than letting your money control you. One of the most important things that you can do to manage your money and begin saving is to use a budget. A budget helps you become aware of how you spend your money and will help you make a plan for how you would like to spend your money.

Monitor how you spend your money. The first step in establishing a workable budget is to monitor how you are actually spending your money at the present time. For one month, keep a list of purchases with the date and amount of money spent for each. You can do this on a sheet of paper, on your calendar, on index cards, or on a money management application for your phone. If you write checks for items, include the checks written as part of your money monitor. At the end of the month, group your purchases in categories such as food, gas, entertainment, and credit card payments, and add them up. Doing this will yield some surprising results. For example, you may not be aware of just how much it costs to eat at a fast-food restaurant or to buy lunch or coffee every day.

© 2014, koya979. Used under license with Shutterstock, Inc.

Prepare a budget. One of the best tools for managing your money is a budget. At the end of this chapter, you will find a simple budget sheet that you can use as a college student. After you finish college, update your budget and continue to use it. Follow these three steps to make a budget:

1. Write down your income for the month.
2. List your expenses. Include tuition, books, supplies, rent, telephone, utilities (gas, electric, water, cable TV, internet), car payments, car insurance, car maintenance (oil, repairs), parking fees, food, personal grooming, clothes, entertainment, savings, credit card payments, loan payments, and other bills. Use your money monitor to discover how you are spending your money and include categories that are unique to you.
3. Subtract your total expenses from your total income. You cannot spend more than you have. Make adjustments as needed.

Beware of credit and interest. College students are often tempted to use credit cards to pay for college expenses. This type of borrowing is costly and difficult to repay. It is easy to pull out a plastic credit card and buy items that you need and want. Credit card companies earn a great deal of money from credit cards. Jane Bryant Quinn gives an example of the cost of credit cards.[3] She says that if you owe $3,000 at 18 percent interest and pay the minimum payment of $60 per month, it will take you 30 years and 10 months to get out of debt! Borrowing the $3,000 would cost about $22,320 over this time! If you use a credit card, make sure you can pay it off in one to three months. It is good to have a credit card in order to establish credit and to use in an emergency.

Watch those spending leaks. We all have spending problem areas. Often we spend small amounts of money each day that add up to large spending leaks over time. For example, if you spend $3 on coffee each weekday for a year, this adds up to $780 a year! If you eat lunch out each weekday and spend $8 for lunch, this adds up to $2,080 a year. Here are some common areas for spending leaks:

- Fast food and restaurants
- Entertainment and vacations
- Clothing
- Miscellaneous cash
- Gifts

© 2014, Andrey Armyagov. Used under license with Shutterstock, Inc.

To identify your spending problem areas, write down all of your expenditures for one month. Place a three-by-five card in your wallet or use your phone to monitor your cash expenditures. At the end of the month, organize your expenditures into categories and total them up. Then ask yourself if this is how you want to spend your money.

Need More Money?

You may be tempted to work more hours to balance your budget. Remember that to be a full-time college student, it is recommended that you work no more than 20 hours per week. If you work more than 20 hours per week, you will probably need to decrease your course load. Before increasing your work hours, see if there is a way you can decrease your monthly expenses. Can you make your lunch instead of eating out? Can you get by without a car? Is the item you are purchasing a necessity, or do you just want to have it? These choices are yours.

"Money is, in some respects, like fire; it is a very excellent servant, but a terrible master."
P. T. Barnum

"Empty pockets never held anyone back. Only empty heads and empty hearts can do that."
Norman Vincent Peale

1. **Check out financial aid.** All students can qualify for some type of financial aid. Visit the Financial Aid Office at your college for assistance. Depending on your income level, you may qualify for one or more of the following forms of aid.

   - **Loans.** A loan must be paid back. The interest rate and terms vary according to your financial need. With some loans, the federal government pays the interest while you are in school.

   - **Grants.** A grant does not need to be repaid. There are both state and federal grants based on need.

   - **Work/study.** You may qualify for a federally subsidized job depending on your financial need. These jobs are often on campus and provide valuable work experience for the future.

   The first step in applying for financial aid is to fill out the Free Application for Federal Student Aid (FAFSA). This form determines your eligibility for financial aid. You can obtain this form from your college's financial aid office or over the Internet at www.fafsa.ed.gov.

   Here are some other financial aid resources that you can obtain from your financial aid office or over the Internet.

   - **Student Guide.** The Student Guide, published by the U.S. Department of Education, describes in detail the kinds of financial aid available and eligibility requirements; it is available over the Internet at Student Guide: http://studentaid.ed.gov/resources.

   - **How to apply for financial aid.** Learn how to apply for federal financial aid and scholarships at www.finaid.org.

2. **Apply for a scholarship.** Applying for a scholarship is like having a part-time job, only the pay is often better, the hours are flexible, and you can be your own boss. For this part-time job, you will need to research scholarship opportunities and fill out applications. There are multitudes of scholarships available, and sometimes no one even applies for them. Some students do not apply for scholarships because they think that high grades and financial need are required. While many scholarships are based on grades and financial need, many are not. Any person or organization can offer a scholarship for any reason they want. For example, scholarships can be based on hobbies, parent's occupation, religious background, military service, and personal interests, to name a few.

   There are several ways to research a scholarship. As a first step, visit the financial aid office on your college campus. This office is staffed with persons knowledgeable about researching and applying for scholarships. Organizations or persons wishing to fund scholarships often contact this office to advertise opportunities.

   You can also research scholarships through your public or college library. Ask the reference librarian for assistance. You can use the Internet to research scholarships as well. Use any search engine such as Google.com and simply type in the keyword scholarships. The following websites index thousands of scholarships:

- The Federal Student Aid Scholarship site is located at http://studentaid.ed.gov/types/grants-scholarships/finding-scholarships
- fastweb.com
- college-scholarships.com
- http://www.scholarships.com/
- collegenet.com/mach25
- studentscholarshipsearch.com
- collegeboard.com/paying

To apply for scholarships, start a file of useful material usually included in scholarship applications. You can use this same information to apply for many scholarships.

- Three current letters of recommendation
- A statement of your personal goals
- A statement of your financial need
- Copies of your transcripts
- Copies of any scholarship applications you have filled out

Be aware of scholarship scams. You do not need to pay money to apply for a scholarship. No one can guarantee that you will receive a scholarship. Use your college scholarship office and your own resources to research and apply for scholarships.

© 2014, mangostock. Used under license with Shutterstock, Inc.

The Best Ideas for Becoming Financially Secure

Financial planners provide the following ideas as the best ways to build wealth and independence.[4] If you have financial security as your goal, plan to do the following:

1. **Use a simple budget to track income and expenses.** Do not spend more than you earn.

2. **Have a financial plan.** Include goals such as saving for retirement, purchasing a home, paying for college, or taking vacations.

3. **Save 10 percent of your income.** As a college student, you may not be able to save this much, but plan to do it as soon as you get your first good-paying job. If you cannot save 10 percent, save something to get in the habit of saving. Save to pay for your tuition and books.

4. **Don't take on too much debt.** Be especially careful about credit cards and consumer debt. Credit card companies often visit college campuses and offer high-interest credit cards to students. It is important to have a credit card, but pay off the balance each month. Consider student loans instead of paying college fees by credit card.

5. **Don't procrastinate.** The earlier you take these steps toward financial security, the better.

Tips for Managing Your Money

Keeping these guidelines in mind can help you to manage your money.

- Don't let friends pressure you into spending too much money. If you can't afford something, learn to say no.
- Keep your checking account balanced or use online banking so you will know how much money you have.
- Don't lend money to friends. If your friends cannot manage their money, your loan will not help them.
- Use comparison shopping to find the best prices on the products that you buy.
- Get a part-time job while in college. You will earn money and gain valuable job experience.
- Don't use shopping as a recreational activity. When you visit the mall, you will find things you never knew you needed and will wind up spending more money than intended.
- Make a budget and follow it. This is the best way to achieve your financial goals.

Do What Is Important First

The most important thing you can do to manage time and money is to spend it on what is most important. Manage time and money to help you live the life you want. How can you do this? Author Stephen Covey wrote a book titled *The Seven Habits of Highly Effective People.* One of the habits is "Put first things first." Covey suggests that in time management, the "challenge is not to manage our time but to manage ourselves."[5]

How can you manage yourself? Our first thoughts in answering this question often involve suggestions about willpower, restriction, and self-control. Schedules and budgets are seen as instruments for self-control. It seems that the human spirit resists attempts at control, even when we aim to control ourselves. Often the response to control is rebellion. With time and money management, we may not follow a schedule or budget. A better approach to begin managing yourself is to know your values. What is important in your life? Do you have a clear mental picture of what is important? Can you describe your values and make a list of what is important to you? With your values and goals in mind, you can begin to manage both your time and your money.

When you have given some thought to your values, you can begin to set goals. When you have established goals for your life, you can begin to think in terms of what is most important and establish your priorities. Knowing your values is essential in making decisions about how to invest your time and money. Schedules and budgets are merely tools for helping you accomplish what you have decided is important. Time and money management is not about restriction and control, but about making decisions regarding what is important in your life. If you know what is important, you can find the strength to say no to activities and expenditures that are less important.

As a counselor, I have the pleasure of working with many students who have recently explored and discovered their values and are highly motivated to succeed. They are willing to do what is important first. I recently worked with a young couple who came to enroll in college. They brought their young baby with them. The new father was interested in environmental engineering. He told me that in high school, he never saw a reason for school and did just the minimum needed to get by. He was working as a construction laborer and making a living, but did not see a future in the occupation. He had observed an environmental engineer who worked for the company and decided that was what he wanted for his future. As he looked at his new son, he told me that he needed to have a better future for himself and his family.

He and his wife decided to do what was important first. They were willing to make the sacrifice to attend school and invest the time needed to be successful. The father planned to work during the day and go to school at night. Later, he would go to school full-time and get a part-time job in the evening. His wife was willing to get a part-time job also, and they would share in taking care of the baby. They were willing to manage their money carefully to accomplish their goals. As they left, they added that their son would be going to college as well.

How do you get the energy to work all day, go to school at night, and raise a family? You can't do it by practicing self-control. You find the energy by having a clear idea of what you want in your life and focusing your time and resources on the goal. Finding what you want to do with your life is not easy either. Many times people find what they want to do when some significant event happens in their lives.

Begin to think about what you want out of life. Make a list of your important values and write down your lifetime goals. Don't forget about the people who are important to you, and include them in your priorities. Then you will be able to do what is important first.

> "Fathers send their sons to college either because they went to college or because they didn't."
>
> L. L. Henderson

Journal Entry #5

What is your plan for managing your money? Consider these ideas when thinking about your plan: monitoring how you spend your money, using a budget, applying for financial aid and scholarships, saving money, and spending money wisely.

JOURNAL ENTRIES

Managing Time and Money

Go to http://www.collegesuccess1.com/JournalEntries.htm for Word files of the Journal Entries

Success over the Internet

Visit the *College Success Website* at http://www.collegesuccess1.com/

The *College Success Website* is continually updated with new topics and links to the material presented in this chapter. Topics include:

- Suggestions for time management
- How to overcome procrastination
- How to deal with perfectionism
- Goal setting
- Goal setting in sports
- Goal setting and visualization
- Scholarship websites
- Recognizing scholarship scams
- Financial aid websites

Ask your instructor if you need any assistance in accessing the *College Success Website.*

Notes

1. Frances Leonard, *Time Is Money* (Addison-Wesley), cited in the *San Diego Union Tribune,* October 14, 1995.

2. Amy Dacyczyn, *The Tightwad Gazette II* (Villard Books), cited in the *San Diego Union Tribune,* February 20, 1995.

3. Jane Bryant Quinn, "Money Watch," *Good Housekeeping*, November 1996, 80.

4. Robert Hanley, "Breaking Bad Habits," *San Diego Union Tribune,* September 7, 1992.

5. Stephen R. Covey, *The Seven Habits of Highly Effective People* (New York: Simon and Schuster, 1990), 150.

PART II
Success in the Classroom

CHAPTER 7

Taking Notes, Writing, and Speaking

Learning Objectives

Read to answer these key questions:

- Why is it important to take notes?

- What are some good listening techniques?

- What are some tips for taking good lecture notes?

- What are some note-taking systems?

- What is the best way to review my notes for the test?

- What is power writing?

- How can I make a good speech?

Knowing how to listen and take good notes can make your college life easier and may help you in your future career as well. Professionals in many occupations take notes as a way of recording key ideas for later use. Whether you become a journalist, attorney, architect, engineer, or other professional, listening and taking good notes can help you to get ahead in your career.

Good writing and speaking skills are important to your success in college and in your career. In college, you will be asked to write term papers and complete other writing assignments. The writing skills you learn in college will be used later in jobs involving high responsibility and good pay; on the job, you will write reports, memos, and proposals. In college, you will probably take a speech class and give oral reports in other classes; on the job, you will present your ideas orally to your colleagues and business associates.

Why Take Notes?

The most important reason for taking notes is to remember important material for tests or for future use in your career. If you just attend class without taking notes, you will forget most of the material by the next day.

How does taking notes enhance memory?

- In college, the lecture is a way of supplementing the written material in the textbook. Without good notes, an important part of the course is missing. Note taking provides material to rehearse or recite, so that it can be stored in long-term memory.

- When you take notes and impose your own organization on them, the notes become more personally meaningful. If they are meaningful, they are easier to remember.

- Taking notes helps you to make new connections. New material is remembered by connecting it to what you already know.

- For kinesthetic and tactile learners, the physical act of writing the material is helpful in learning and remembering it.

- For visual learners, notes provide a visual map of the material to be learned.

- For auditory learners, taking notes is a way to listen carefully and record information to be stored in the memory.

- Note taking helps students to concentrate, maintain focus, and stay awake.

- Attending the lectures and taking notes helps you to understand what the professor thinks is important and to know what to study for the exam.

© 2014, Monkey Business Images. Used under license with Shutterstock, Inc.

The College Lecture

You will experience many different types of lectures while in college. At larger universities, many of the beginning-level courses are taught in large lecture halls with 300 people or more. More advanced courses tend to have fewer students. In large lecture situations, it is not always possible or appropriate to ask questions. Under these circumstances, the large lecture is often supplemented by smaller discussion sessions where you can ask questions and review the lecture material. Although attendance may not be checked, it is important to attend both the lectures and the discussion sessions.

A formal college lecture is divided into four parts. Understanding these parts will help you to be a good listener and take good notes.

1. **Introduction.** The professor uses the introduction to set the stage and to introduce the topic of the lecture. Often an overview or outline of the lecture is presented. Use the introduction as a way to begin thinking about the organization of your notes and the key ideas you will need to write down.

2. **Thesis.** The thesis is the key idea in the lecture. In a one-hour lecture, there is usually one thesis statement. Listen carefully for the thesis statement and write it down in your notes. Review the thesis statement and related ideas for the exam.

3. **Body.** The body of the lecture usually consists of five or six main ideas with discussion and clarification of each idea. As a note taker, your job is to identify the main ideas, write them in your notes, and put in enough of the explanation or examples to understand the key ideas.

4. **Conclusion.** In the conclusion, the professor summarizes the key points of the lecture and sometimes asks for questions. Use the conclusion as an opportunity to check your understanding of the lecture and to ask questions to clarify the key points.

How to Be a Good Listener

Effective note taking begins with good listening. What is good listening? Sometimes students confuse listening with hearing. Hearing is done with the ears. Listening is a more active process done with the ears and the brain engaged. Good listening requires attention and concentration. Practice these ideas for good listening:

*   **Be physically ready.** It is difficult to listen to a lecture if you are tired, hungry, or ill. Get enough sleep so that you can stay awake. Eat a balanced diet without too much caffeine or sugar. Take care of your health and participate in an exercise program so that you feel your best.

*   **Prepare a mental framework.** Look at the course syllabus to become familiar with the topic of the lecture. Use your textbook to read, or at least survey, the material to be covered in the lecture. If you are familiar with the key concepts from the textbook, you will be able to understand the lecture and know what to write down in your notes. If the material is in your book, there is no need to write it down in your notes.

    The more complex the topic, the more important it is for you to read the text first. If you go to the lecture and have no idea what is being discussed, you may be overwhelmed and find it difficult to take notes on material that is totally new to you. Remember that it is easier to remember material if you can connect it to material you already know.

*   **Find a good place to sit.** Arrive early to get a good seat. The best seats in the classroom are in the front and center of the room. If you were buying concert tickets, these would be the best and most expensive seats. Find a seat that will help

you to hear and focus on the speaker. You may need to find a seat away from your friends to avoid distractions.

- **Have a positive mental attitude.** Convince yourself that the speaker has something important to say and be open to new ideas. This may require you to focus on your goals and to look past some distractions. Maybe the lecturer doesn't have the best speaking voice or you don't like his or her appearance. Focus on what you can learn from the professor rather than outward appearances.

- **Listen actively to identify the main points.** As you are listening to the lecture, ask yourself, "What is the main idea?" In your own words, write the main points down in your notes. Do not try to write down everything the professor says. This will be impossible and unnecessary. Imagine that your mind is a filter and you are actively sorting through the material to find the key ideas and write them down in your notes. Try to identify the key points that will be on the test and write them in your notes.

- **Stay awake and engaged in learning.** The best way to stay awake and focused is to listen actively and take notes. Have a mental debate with the professor. Listen for the main points and the logical connection between ideas. The physical act of writing the notes will help to keep you awake.

Tips for Good Note Taking

Here are some suggestions for taking good notes:

1. Attend all of the lectures. Because many professors do not take attendance, students are often tempted to miss class. If you do not attend the lectures, however, you will not know what the professor thinks is important and what to study for the test. There will be important points covered in the lectures that are not in the book.

2. Have the proper materials. A three-ring notebook and notebook paper are recommended. Organize notes chronologically and include any handouts given in class. You can have a small notebook for each class or a single large notebook with dividers for each class. Just take the notebook paper to class and later file it in your notebook at home. Use your laptop as an alternative to a paper notebook.

3. Begin your notes by writing the date of the lecture, so you can keep your notes in order.

4. Write notes on the front side only of each piece of paper. This will allow you to spread the pages out and see the big picture or pattern in the lectures when you are reviewing.

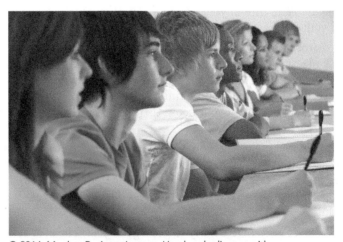

© 2014, Monkey Business Images. Used under license with Shutterstock, Inc.

5. Write notes neatly and legibly so you can read and review them easily.

6. Do not waste time recopying or typing your notes. Your time would be better spent reviewing your notes.

7. As a general rule, do not rely on a tape recorder for taking notes. With a tape recorder, you will have to listen to the lecture again on tape. For a semester course, this would be about 45 hours of tape! It is much faster to review carefully written notes.

8. Copy down everything written on the board and the main points from PowerPoint or other visual presentations. If it is important enough for the professor to write on the board, it is important enough to be on the test.

9. Use key words and phrases in your notes. Leave out unimportant words and don't worry about grammar.

10. Use abbreviations as long as you can read them. Entire sentences or paragraphs are not necessary and you may not have time to write them.

11. Don't loan your whole notebook to someone else because you may not get it back. If you want to share your notes, make copies.

12. If the professor talks too fast, listen carefully for the key ideas and write them down. Leave spaces in your notes to fill in later. You may be able to find the information in the text or get the information from another student.

13. Explore new uses of technology for note taking. Students are taking notes and sharing them on Facebook and GradeGuru, for example.

Journal Entry #1

Write one paragraph giving advice to a new student about taking notes in college. Use any of these questions to guide your thinking:

- Why is note taking necessary in college?
- How can you be a good listener?
- What are some tips for taking good notes?
- What are some ideas that don't work?

Note-Taking Systems

There are several systems for taking notes. How you take notes will depend on your learning style and the lecturer's speaking style. Experiment with these systems and use what works best for you.

Note-Taking Systems
- Cornell format
- Outline method
- Mind map

The Cornell Format

The Cornell format is an efficient method of taking notes and reviewing them. It appeals to students who are logical, orderly, and organized and have lectures that fit into this pattern. The Cornell format is especially helpful for thinking about key points as you review your notes.

Step 1: Prepare. To use the Cornell format, you will need a three-ring notebook with looseleaf paper. Draw or fold a vertical line 2½ inches from the left side of the paper. This is the recall column that can be used to write key ideas when reviewing. Use the

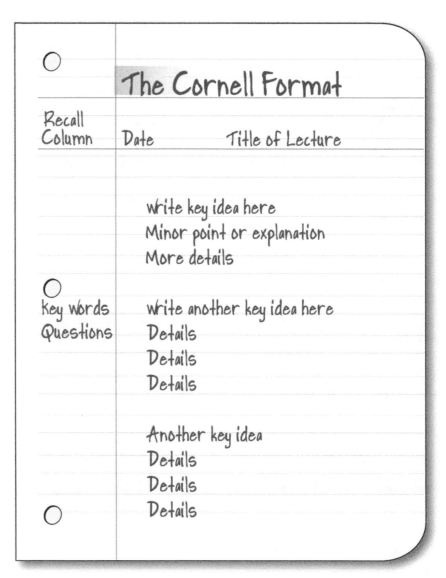

Figure 8.1 The Cornell format is an efficient way of organizing notes and reviewing them.

remaining section of the paper for your notes. Write the date and title of the lecture at the top of the page.

Step 2: Take notes. Use the large area to the right of the recall column to take notes. Listen for key ideas and write them just to the right of the recall column line, as in the diagram above. Indent your notes for minor points and illustrative details. Then skip a space and write the next key idea. Don't worry about using numbers or letters as in an outline format. Just use the indentations and spacing to highlight and separate key ideas. Use short phrases, key words, and abbreviations. Complete sentences are not necessary, but write legibly so you can read your notes later.

Step 3: Use the recall column for review. Read over your notes and write down key words or ideas from the lecture in the recall column. Ask yourself, "What is this about?" Cover up the notes on the right-hand side and recite the key ideas of the lecture. Another variation is to write questions in the margin. Find the key ideas and then write possible exam questions in the recall column. Cover your notes and see if you can answer the questions.

The Outline Method

If the lecture is well organized, some students just take notes in outline format. Sometimes lecturers will show their outline as they speak.

- Use Roman numerals to label main topics. Then use capital letters for main ideas and Arabic numerals for related details or examples.
- You can make a free-form outline using just indentation to separate main ideas and supporting details.
- Leave spaces to fill in material later.
- Use a highlighter to review your notes as soon as possible after the lecture.

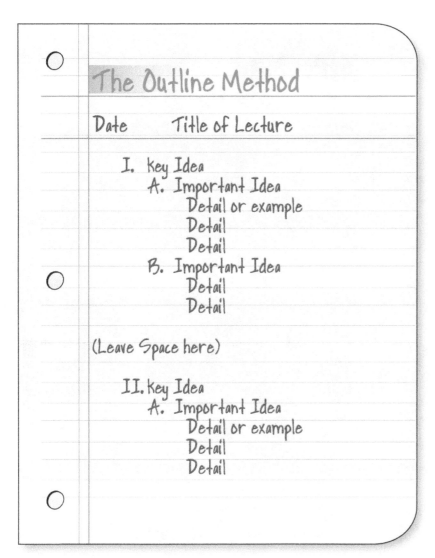

Figure 8.2 If a lecture is well organized, the outline format of taking notes works well.

The Mind Map

A mind map shows the relationship between ideas in a visual way. It is much easier to remember items that are organized and linked together in a personally meaningful way. As a result, recall and review is quicker and more effective. Mind maps have appeal to visual learners and those who do not want to be limited by a set structure, as in the outline formats. They can also be used for lectures that are not highly structured. Here are some suggestions for using the mind-mapping technique:

- Turn your paper sideways to give you more space. Use standard-size notebook paper or consider larger sheets if possible.
- Write the main idea in the center of the page and circle it.
- Arrange ideas so that more important ideas are closer to the center and less important ideas are farther out.
- Show the relationship of the minor points to the main ideas using lines, circles, boxes, charts, and other visual devices. Here is where you can use your creativity and imagination to make a visual picture of the key ideas in the lecture.

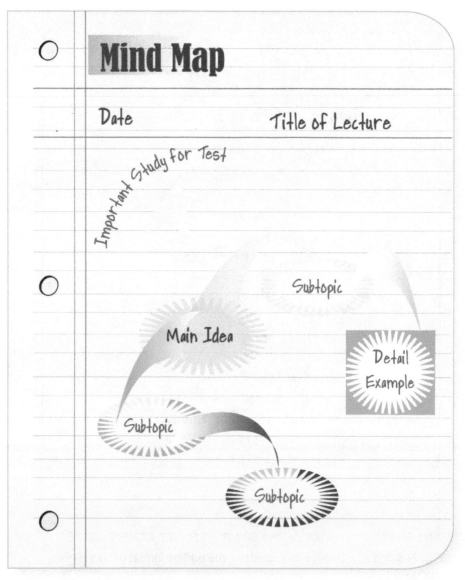

Figure 8.3 The mind map format of taking notes shows the relationship between ideas in a visual way.

- Use symbols and drawings.
- Use different colors to separate main ideas.
- When the lecturer moves to another main idea, start a new mind map.
- When you are done with the lecture, quickly review your mind maps. Add any written material that will be helpful in understanding the map later.
- A mind map can also be used as:
  - a review tool for remembering and relating the key ideas in the textbook;
  - a preparation tool for essay exams in which remembering main ideas and relationships is important; and
  - the first step in organizing ideas for a term paper.

Improving Note-Taking Efficiency

Improve note-taking efficiency by listening for key words that signal the main ideas and supporting details. Learn to write faster by using telegraphic sentences, abbreviations, and symbols.

Telegraphic Sentences

Telegraphic sentences are short, abbreviated sentences used in note taking. They are very similar to the text messages sent on a cell phone. There are four rules for telegraphic sentences:

1. Write key words only.
2. Omit unnecessary words (*a, an, the*).
3. Ignore rules of grammar.
4. Use abbreviations and symbols.

Here is an example of a small part of a lecture followed by a student's telegraphic notes:

Heavy drinking of alcoholic beverages causes students to miss class and to fall behind in schoolwork. College students who are considered binge drinkers are at risk for many alcohol-related problems. Binge drinking is simply drinking too much alcohol at one time. Binge drinking is defined by researchers as drinking five or more drinks in a row for men or four or more drinks in a row for women. Researchers estimate that two out of five college students (40 percent) are binge drinkers.

Binge drinking—too much alcohol at one time
    Men = 5 in row
    Women = 4
    2 out of 5 (40%) college students binge

Signal Words

Signal words are clues to understanding the structure and content of a lecture. Recognizing signal words can help you identify key ideas and organize them in your notes. The table on the following page lists some common signal words and their meaning.

Signal Words

Type	Examples	Meaning
Main idea words	And most important A major development The basic concept is Remember that The main idea is We will focus on The key is	Introduce the key points that need to be written in your notes.
Example words	To illustrate For example For instance	Clarify and illustrate the main ideas in the lecture. Write these examples in your notes after the main idea. If multiple examples are given, write down the ones you have time for or the ones that you understand the best.
Addition words	In addition Also Furthermore	Add more important information. Write these points down in your notes.
Enumeration words	The five steps First, second, third Next	Signal a list. Write down the list in your notes and number the items.
Time words	Before, after Formerly Subsequently Prior Meanwhile	Signal the order of events. Write down the events in the correct order in your notes.
Cause and effect words	Therefore As a result If . . ., then	Signal important concepts that might be on the exam. When you hear these words, label them "cause" and "effect" in your notes and review these ideas for the exam.
Definition words	In other words It simply means That is In essence	Provide the meanings of words or simplify complex ideas. Write these definitions or clarifications in your notes.
Swivel words	However Nevertheless Yes, but Still	Provide exceptions, qualifications, or further clarification. Write down qualifying comments in your notes.
Compare and contrast words	Similarly Likewise In contrast	Present similarities or differences. Write these similarities and differences in your notes and label them.
Summary words	In conclusion To sum up In a nutshell	Restate the important ideas of the lecture. Write the summaries in your notes.
Test words	This is important. Remember this. You'll see this again. You might want to study this for the test.	Provide a clue that the material will be on the test. Write these down in your notes and mark them in a way that stands out. Put a star or asterisk next to these items or highlight them. Each professor has his or her own test clue words.

Abbreviations

If you have time, write out words in their entirety for ease of reading. If you are short on time, use any abbreviation as long as you can read it. Here are some ideas:

1. Use the first syllable of the word.

democracy	dem
education	ed
politics	pol
different	diff
moderate	mod
characteristic	char
develop	dev

2. Use just enough of the word so that you can recognize it.

republican	repub
prescription	prescrip
introduction	intro
intelligence	intell
association	assoc

3. Abbreviate or write out the word the first time, then use an acronym. For example, for the United States Department of Agriculture, abbreviate it as "US Dept of Ag" and then write it as USDA in subsequent references. Other examples:

short-term memory	STM
as soon as possible	ASAP

4. Omit vowels.

background	bkgrnd
problem	prblm
government	gvt

5. Use g in place of ing.

checking	ckg
decreasing	decrg

6. Write your notes in text message format.

Symbols

Use common symbols or invent your own to speed up the note-taking process.

Common Symbols Used in Note Taking

Symbol	Meaning	Symbol	Meaning
&	and	B4	before
w	with	BC	because
wo	without	esp	especially
wi	within	diff	difference
<	less than	min	minimum
>	more than	gov	government

(Continued)

Symbol	Meaning	Symbol	Meaning
@	at	ex	example
/	per	↑	increasing
2	to, two, too	↓	decreasing
∴	therefore	=	equal
vs	versus, against	≠	not equal

How to Review Your Notes

© 2014, Terence. Used under license with Shutterstock, Inc.

Immediate review. Review your notes as soon as possible after the lecture. The most effective review is done immediately or at least within 20 minutes. If you wait until the next day to review, you may already have forgotten much of the information. During the immediate review, fill in any missing or incomplete information. Say the important points to yourself. This begins the process of rehearsal for storing the information in long-term memory.

There are various methods for review depending on your note-taking system:

- For the Cornell format, use the recall column to write in key words or questions. Cover your notes and see if you can recall the main ideas. Place checkmarks by the items you have mastered. Don't worry about mastering all the key points from the beginning. With each review, it will be easier to remember the information.
- For the outline format, use a highlighter to mark the key ideas as you repeat them silently to yourself.
- For mind maps, look over the information and think about the key ideas and their relationships. Fill in additional information or clarification. Highlight important points or relationships with color.

Intermediate review. Set up some time each week for short reviews of your notes and the key points in your textbook from previous weeks. Quickly look over the notes and recite the key points in your mind. These intermediate reviews will help you to master the material and avoid test anxiety.

Test review. Complete a major review as part of your test preparation strategy. As you look through your notes, turn the key ideas into possible test questions and answer them.

Final review. The final review occurs after you have received the results of your test. Ask yourself these questions:

- What percentage of the test questions came from the lecture notes?
- Were you prepared for the exam? If so, congratulate yourself on a job well done. If not, how can you improve next time?
- Were your notes adequate? If not, what needs to be added or changed?

"You have to get your education. Then nobody can control your destiny."
Charles Barkley

Listening and Note Taking

Test what you have learned by selecting the correct answer to the following questions.

1. When taking notes on a college lecture, it is most important to

    a. write down everything you hear.
    b. write down the main ideas and enough explanation to understand them.
    c. write down names, dates, places, and numbers.

2. To be a good listener,

    a. read or skim over the material before you attend the lecture.
    b. attend the lecture first and then read the text.
    c. remember that listening is more important than note taking.

3. To stay awake during the lecture,

    a. drink lots of coffee.
    b. sit near your friends so you can make some comments on the lecture.
    c. listen actively by taking notes.

4. Since attendance is not always checked in college classes,

    a. it is not necessary to attend class if you read the textbook.
    b. it is acceptable to miss lectures as long as you show up for the exams.
    c. it is up to you to attend every class.

5. The best time to review your notes is

    a. as soon as possible after the lecture.
    b. within 24 hours.
    c. within one week.

How did you do on the quiz? Check your answers: 1. b, 2. a, 3. c, 4. c, 5. a

Journal Entry #2

Write five intention statements about improving your note-taking skills. Consider your note-taking system, how to take notes more efficiently, and the best way to review your notes. I intend to . . .

> "The highest reward for a person's toil is not what they get for it, but what they become by it."
> John Ruskin

Power Writing

Effective writing will help you in school, on the job, and in your personal life. Good writing will help you to create quality term papers. The writing skills that you learn in college will be used later in jobs involving high responsibility and good pay. You can become an excellent writer by learning about the steps in POWER writing: prepare, organize, write, edit, and revise.

Power Writing
- Prepare
- Organize
- Write
- Edit
- Revise

Prepare

Plan your time. The first step in writing is to plan your time so that the project can be completed by the due date. Picture this scene: It is the day that the term paper is due. A few students proudly hand in their term papers and are ready to celebrate their accomplishments. Many of the students in the class are absent, and some will never return to the class. Some of the students look as though they haven't slept the night before. They look stressed and weary. At the front of the class is a line of students wanting to talk with the instructor. The instructor has heard it all before:

- I had my paper all completed and my printer jammed.
- My hard drive crashed and I lost my paper.
- I was driving to school and my paper flew off my motorcycle.
- I had the flu.
- My children were sick.
- I had to take my dog to the vet.
- My dog ate my paper.
- My car broke down and I could not get to the library.
- My grandmother died and I had to go to the funeral.
- My roommate accidentally took my backpack to school.
- I spilled salad dressing on my paper, so I put it in the microwave to dry it out and the writing disappeared!

© 2014, Benjamin Howell. Used under license with Shutterstock, Inc.

Prepare

- Plan your time
- Find space and time
- Choose general topic
- Gather information
- Write thesis statement

To avoid being in this uncomfortable and stressful situation, plan ahead. Plan to complete your project at least one week ahead of time so that you can deal with life's emergencies. Life does not always go as planned. You or your children may get sick, or your dog may do strange things to your homework. Your computer may malfunction, leading you to believe it senses stress and malfunctions just to frustrate you even more.

To avoid stress and do your best work, start with the date that the project is due and then think about the steps needed to finish. Write these dates on your calendar or on your list of things to do. Consider all these components:

Project due date:

To do	By when?
1. Brainstorm ideas.	_____
2. Choose a topic.	_____
3. Gather information.	_____
4. Write a thesis statement.	_____
5. Write an outline.	_____
6. Write the introduction.	_____
7. Write the first draft.	_____
8. Prepare the bibliography.	_____
9. Edit.	_____
10. Revise.	_____
11. Print and assemble.	_____

Find a space and time. Find a space where you can work. Gather the materials that you will need to write. Generally, writing is best done in longer blocks of time. Determine when you will work on your paper and write the time on your schedule. Start right away to avoid panic later.

Choose a general topic. This task will be easy if your topic is already clearly defined by your instructor or your boss at work. Make sure that you have a clear idea of what is required, such as length, format, purpose, and method of citing references and topic. Many times the choice of a topic is left to you. Begin by doing some brainstorming. Think about topics that interest you. Write them down. You may want to focus your attention on brainstorming ideas for five or 10 minutes, and then put the project aside and come back to it later. Once you have started the process of thinking about the ideas, your mind will continue to work and you may have some creative inspiration. If inspiration does not come, repeat the brainstorming process.

Gather information. Go to your college library and use the Internet to gather your information. As you begin, you can see what is available, what is interesting to you, and what the current thinking is on your topic. Note the major topics of interest that might be useful to you. Once you have found some interesting material, you will feel motivated to continue your project. As you find information relevant to your topic, make sure to write down the sources of your information to use in your bibliography. The bibliography contains information about where you found your material. Write down the author, the title of the publication, the publisher, and the place and date of publication. For Internet resources, list the address of the website and the date accessed.

Write the thesis statement. The thesis statement is the key idea in your paper. It provides a direction for you to follow. It is the first step in organizing your work. To write a thesis statement, review the material you have gathered and then ask these questions:

- What is the most important idea?
- What question would I like to ask about it?
- What is my answer?

© 2014, Elena Elisseeva. Used under license with Shutterstock, Inc.

For example, if I decide to write a paper for my health class on the harmful effects of smoking, I would look at current references on the topic. I might become interested in how the tobacco companies misled the public on the dangers of smoking. I would think about my thesis statement and answer the questions stated above.

- **What is the most important idea?** Smoking is harmful to your health.
- **What question would I like to ask about it?** Did the tobacco companies mislead the public about the health hazards of smoking?
- **What is my answer?** The tobacco companies misled the public about the hazards of smoking in order to protect their business interests.
- **My thesis statement:** Tobacco companies knew that smoking was hazardous to health, but to protect their business interests, they deliberately misled the public.

The thesis statement helps to narrow the topic and provide direction for the paper. I can now focus on reference material related to my topic: research on health effects of smoking, congressional testimony relating to regulation of the tobacco industry, and how advertising influences people to smoke.

Organize

Organize
- List related topics
- Arrange in logical order
- Have an organizational structure

At this point you have many ideas about what to include in your paper, and you have a central focus, your thesis statement. Start to organize your paper by listing the topics that are related to your thesis statement. Here is a list of topics related to my thesis statement about smoking:

- Tobacco companies' awareness that nicotine is addictive
- Minimizing health hazards in tobacco advertisements
- How advertisements encourage people to smoke
- Money earned by the tobacco industry
- Health problems caused by smoking
- Statistics on numbers of people who have health problems or die from smoking
- Regulation of the tobacco industry
- Advertisements aimed at children

Think about the topics and arrange them in logical order. Use an outline, a mind map, a flowchart, or a drawing to think about how you will organize the important topics. Keep in mind that you will need an introduction, a body, and a conclusion. Having an organizational structure will make it easier for you to write because you will not need to wonder what comes next.

Write

Write the First Sentence

Begin with the main idea.

Write the Introduction

This is the road map for the rest of the paper. The introduction includes your thesis statement and establishes the foundation of the paper. It introduces topics that will be discussed in the body of the paper. The introduction should include some interesting points that provide a "hook" to motivate the audience to read your paper. For example, for a paper on the hazards of smoking, you might begin with statistics on how many people suffer from smoking-related illnesses and premature death. Note the large profits earned by the tobacco industry. Then introduce other topics: deception, advertisements, and regulation. The introduction provides a guide or outline of what will follow in the paper.

Write

- First sentence
- Introduction
- Body
- Conclusion
- References

Write the Body of the Paper

The body of the paper is divided into paragraphs that discuss the topics that you have introduced. As you write each paragraph, include the main idea and then explain it and give examples. Here are some good tips for writing:

1. Good writing reflects clear thinking. Think about what you want to say and write about it so the reader can understand your point of view.

2. Use clear and concise language. Avoid using too many words or scholarly-sounding words that might get in the way of understanding.

3. Don't assume that the audience knows what you are writing about. Provide complete information.

4. Provide examples, stories, and quotes to support your main points. Include your own ideas and experiences.

5. Beware of plagiarism. Plagiarism is copying the work of others without giving them credit. It is illegal and can cause you to receive a failing grade on your project or even get you into legal trouble. Faculty regularly uses software programs that identify plagiarized material in student papers. You can avoid plagiarism by using quotation marks around an author's words and providing a reference indicating where you found the material. Another way to avoid plagiarism is by carefully reading your source material while using critical thinking to evaluate it. Then look away from the source and write about the ideas in your own words, including your critical thinking about the subject. Don't forget to include a reference for the source material in your bibliography.

Write the Conclusion

The conclusion summarizes the topics in the paper and presents your point of view. It makes reference to the introduction and answers the question posed in your thesis statement. It often makes the reader think about the significance of your point and the implications for the future. Make your conclusion interesting and powerful.

Include References

No college paper is complete without references. References may be given in footnotes, endnotes, a list of works cited, or a bibliography. You can use your computer to insert these references. There are various styles for citing references depending on your subject area. There are computer programs that put your information into the correct style.

Ask your instructor which style to use for your particular class or project. Three frequently used styles for citing references are APA, Chicago, and MLA.

1. The American Psychological Association (APA) style is used in psychology and other behavioral sciences. Consult the *Publication Manual of the American Psychological Association*, 6th ed. (Washington, DC: American Psychological Association, 2010). You can find this source online at www.apastyle.org.

2. Chicago style is used by many professional writers in a variety of fields. Consult the *Chicago Manual of Style*, 16th ed. (Chicago: University of Chicago Press, 2010). You can find this source online at www.chicagomanualofstyle.org/home.html.

3. The Modern Language Association (MLA) style is used in English, classical languages, and the humanities. Consult the *MLA Handbook for Writers of Research Papers*, 7th ed. (New York: Modern Language Association, 2009). This source is available online at www.mla.org/style.

Each of these styles uses a different format for listing sources, but all include the same information. Make sure you write down this information as you collect your reference material. If you forget this step, it is very time-consuming and difficult to find later.

- Author's name
- Title of the book or article
- Journal name
- Publisher
- City where book was published
- Publication date
- Page number (and volume and issue numbers, if available)

Here are some examples of citations in the APA style:

- **Book.** Include author, date of publication, title, city of publication, and publisher.

  Fralick, M. (2014). *College and career success* (6th ed.). Dubuque, IA: Kendall Hunt.

- **Journal article.** Include author, date, title, name of journal, volume and issue numbers, pages.

  Fralick, M. (1993). College success: A study of positive and negative attrition. *Community College Review, 20*(5), 29–36.

- **Website.** Include author, date listed or updated, document title or name of website, URL or website address, and date accessed. Include as many of the above items as possible. Methods of citing information from the Internet are still evolving.

  Fralick, M. (2014, October). Note taking. Retrieved October 2013 from College Success 1 at www.collegesuccess1.com/

Save Your Work

As soon as you have written the first paragraph, save it on your computer. If your computer is not backed up by a remote server such as iCloud or Carbonite, save another copy on a flash drive. When you are finished, print your work and save a paper copy. Then, if your hard drive crashes, you will still have your work at another location. If your file becomes corrupted, you will still have the paper copy. Following these procedures can save you a lot of headaches. Any writer can tell you stories of lost work because of computer problems, lightning storms, power outages, and other unpredictable events.

Put It Away for a While

The last step in writing the first draft is easy. Put it away for a while and come back to it later. In this way, you can relax and gain some perspective on your work. You will be able to take a more objective look at your work to begin the process of editing and revising.

Writer's Block

Many people who are anxious about writing experience "writer's block." You have writer's block if you find yourself staring at that blank piece of paper or computer screen not knowing how to begin or what to write. Here are some tips for avoiding writer's block.

- **Write freely.** Just write anything about your topic that comes to mind. Don't worry about organization or perfection at this point. Don't censure your ideas. You can always go back to organize and edit later. Free-writing helps you to overcome one of the main causes of writer's block: you think it has to be perfect from the beginning. This expectation of perfection causes anxiety. You freeze up and become unable to write. Perhaps you have past memories of writing where the teacher made many corrections on your paper. Maybe you lack confidence in your writing skills. The only way you will become a better writer is to keep writing and perfecting your writing skills, so to start the writing process, just write what comes to mind. Don't worry how great it is. You can fix it later. Just begin.

- **Use brainstorming if you get stuck.** For five minutes, focus your attention on the topic and write whatever comes to mind. You don't even need to write full sentences; just jot down ideas. If you are really stuck, try working on a different topic or take a break and come back to it later.

- **Realize that it is only the first draft.** It is not the finished product and it does not have to be perfect. Just write some ideas on paper; you can revise them later.

- **Read through your reference materials.** The ideas you find can get your mind working. Also, reading can make you a better writer.

- **Break the assignment up into small parts.** If you find writing difficult, write for five minutes at a time. Do this consistently and you can get used to writing and can complete your paper.

Tips to Overcome Writer's Block

1. Write freely
2. Use brainstorming
3. Realize it's a first draft
4. Read reference materials
5. Break up assignment
6. Find a good place to write
7. Beware of procrastination

© 2014, Creativa. Used under license with Shutterstock, Inc.

- **Find a good place for writing.** If you are an introvert, look for a quiet place for concentration. If you are an extrovert, go to a restaurant or coffee shop and start your writing.

- **Beware of procrastination.** The more you put off writing, the more anxious you will become and the more difficult the task will be. Make a schedule and stick to it.

Edit and Revise

The editing and revising stage allows you to take a critical look at what you have written. It takes some courage to do this step. Once people see their ideas in writing, they become attached to them. With careful editing and revising, you can turn in your best work and be proud of your accomplishments. Here are some tips for editing and revising:

1. **Read your paper as if you were the audience.** Pretend that you are the instructor or another person reading your paper. Does every sentence make sense? Did you say what you meant to say? Read what you have written, and the result will be a more effective paper.

2. **Read paragraph by paragraph.** Does each paragraph have a main idea and supporting details? Do the paragraphs fit logically together? Use the cut-and-paste feature on your computer to move sentences and paragraphs around if needed.

3. **Check your grammar and spelling.** Use the spell check and grammar check on your computer. These tools are helpful, but they are not thorough enough. The spell check will pick up only misspelled words. It will skip words that are spelled correctly but not the intended word—for example, if you use "of" instead of "on" or "their" instead of "there." To find such errors, you need to read your paper after doing a spell check.

4. **Check for language that is biased in terms of gender, disability, or ethnic group.** Use words that are gender neutral. If a book or paper uses only the pronoun "he" or "she," half of the population is left out. You can often avoid sexist language by using the plural forms of nouns:

   (singular) The successful student knows *his* values and sets goals for the future.

   (plural) Successful students know *their* values and set goals for the future.

   After all, we are trying to make the world a better place, with opportunity for all. Here are some examples of biased language and better alternatives.

Biased Language	*Better Alternatives*
policeman	police officer
chairman	chair
fireman	firefighter
postman	mail carrier
mankind	humanity
manmade	handcrafted
housewife	homemaker
crippled and disabled persons	persons with disabilities

5. **Have someone else read your paper.** Ask your reader to check for clarity and meaning. After you have read your paper many times, you do not really see it anymore. If you need assistance in writing, colleges offer tutoring or writing labs where you can get help with editing and revising.

6. **Review your introduction and conclusion.** They should be clear, interesting, and concise. The introduction and conclusion are the most powerful parts of your paper.

Tips for Editing and Revising

1. Read your paper objectively
2. Read paragraph by paragraph
3. Check grammar and spelling
4. Check for biased language
5. Have someone else read your paper
6. Review the introduction and conclusion
7. Prepare final copy
8. Prepare title page

7. **Prepare the final copy.** Check your instructor's instructions on the format required. If there are no instructions, use the following format:

- Use double-spacing.
- Use 10- or 12-point font.
- Use one-inch margins on all sides.
- Use a three-inch top margin on the first page.
- Single-space footnotes and endnotes.
- Number your pages.

8. **Prepare the title page.** Center the title of your paper and place it one third of the page from the top. On the bottom third of the page, center your name, the professor's name, the name of the class, and the date.

Final Steps

Make sure you follow instructions about using a folder or cover for your paper. Generally professors dislike bulky folders or notebooks because they are difficult to carry. Imagine your professor trying to carry 50 notebooks to his or her office! Unless asked to do so, do not use plastic page protectors. Professors like to write comments on papers, and it is extremely difficult to write on papers with page protectors.

Turning your paper in on time is very important. Some professors do not accept late papers. Others subtract points if your paper is late. Put your paper in the car or someplace where you will have to see it before you go to class. **Then reward yourself for a job well done!**

Journal Entry #3

Write five intention statements about improving your writing. While thinking about your statements, consider the steps of POWER writing: prepare, organize, write, edit, and revise. Do you need to work on problems such as writer's block or getting your writing done on time? I intend to . . .

Effective Public Speaking

You may need to take a speech class in order to graduate from college, and many of your classes will require oral presentations. Being a good speaker can contribute to your success on the job as well. A study done at Stanford University showed that one of the top predictors of success in professional positions was the ability to be a good public speaker.[1] You will need to present information to your boss, your colleagues, and your customers or clients.

"Let us think of education as the means of developing our greatest abilities, because in each of us there is a private hope and dream which, fulfilled, can be translated into greater benefit for everyone and greater strength for our nation."
John F. Kennedy

Learn to Relax

Whenever I tell students that they will need to take a speech class or make an oral presentation, I see a look of panic on their faces. Good preparation can help you to feel confident about your oral presentation. Professional speaker Lilly Walters believes that you can deal with 75 percent of your anxiety by being well prepared.[2] You can deal with the remaining 25 percent by using some relaxation techniques.

- If you are anxious, admit to yourself that you are anxious. If it is appropriate, as in a beginning speech class, you can even admit to the audience that you are anxious. Once you have admitted that you are anxious, visualize yourself confidently making the speech.
- You do not have to be perfect; it is okay to make mistakes. Making mistakes just shows you are human like the rest of us.
- If you are anxious before your speech, take three to five deep breaths. Breathe in slowly and hold your breath for five seconds, and then breathe out slowly. Focus your mind on your breathing rather than your speech.
- Use positive self-talk to help you to relax. Instead of saying to yourself, "I will look like a fool up there giving the speech," tell yourself, "I can do this" or "It will be okay."
- Once you start speaking, anxiety will generally decline.
- With experience, you will gain confidence in your speaking ability and will be able to relax more easily.

Preparing and Delivering Your Speech
Write the Beginning of the Speech

The beginning includes a statement of your objective and what your speech will be about. It should prepare the audience for what comes next. You can begin your speech with a personal experience, a quote, a news article, or a joke. Jokes can be effective, but they are risky. Try out your joke with your friends to make sure that it is funny. Do not tell jokes that put down other people or groups.

Write the Main Body of the Speech

The main body of the speech consists of four or five main points. Just as in your term paper, state your main points and then provide details, examples, or stories that illustrate them. As you present the main points of your speech, consider your audience. Your speech will be different depending on whether it is made to a group of high school students, your college classmates, or a group of professionals. You can add interest to your speech by using props, pictures, charts, PowerPoint, music, or video clips. College students today are increasingly using PowerPoint software to make classroom presentations. If you are planning to enter a professional career, learning how to make PowerPoint presentations will be an asset.

Write the Conclusion

In your conclusion, summarize and review the key points of your speech. The conclusion is like the icing on a cake. It should be strong, persuasive, and interesting. Invest some time in your ending statement. It can be a call to action, a recommendation for the future, a quote, or a story.

Practice Your Speech

Practice your speech until you feel comfortable with it. Prepare a memory system or notes to help you deliver your speech. You will want to make eye contact with your audience, which is difficult if you are trying to read your speech. A memory system useful for delivering speeches is the loci system. Visualize a house, for example: the entryway is the introduction, and each room represents a main point in the speech. Visualize walking into each room and what you will say in each room. Each room can have items that remind you of what you are going to say. At the conclusion, you say good-bye at the door. Another technique is to prepare brief notes or outlines on index cards or sheets of paper. When you are practicing your speech, time it to see how long it is. Keep your speech within the time allowed. Most people tend to speak longer than necessary.

Review the Setup

If you are using props, make sure that you have them ready. If you are using equipment, make sure it is available and in working condition. Make arrangements in advance for the equipment you need and, if possible, check to see that it is running properly right before your presentation.

Deliver the Speech

Wear clothes that make you feel comfortable, but not out of place. Remember to smile and make eye contact with members of the audience. Take a few deep breaths if you are nervous. You will probably be less nervous once you begin. If you make a mistake, keep your sense of humor. I recall the famous chef Julia Child doing a live television production on how to cook a turkey. As she took the turkey out of the oven, it slipped and landed on the floor right in front of the television cameras. She calmly picked it up and said, "And remember that you are the only one that really knows what goes on in the kitchen." It was one of the shows that made her famous.

Writing and Speaking

Test what you have learned by selecting the correct answers to the following questions.

1. To make sure to get your paper done on time,

   a. have someone remind you of the deadline.
   b. write the due date on your calendar and the date for completion of each step.
   c. write your paper just before the due date to increase motivation.

2. The thesis statement is the

   a. most important sentence in each paragraph.
   b. key idea in the paper.
   c. summary of the paper.

3. If you have writer's block, it is helpful to

   a. delay writing your paper until you feel relaxed.
   b. make sure that your writing is perfect from the beginning.
   c. begin with brainstorming or free writing.

4. No college paper is complete without

   a. the references.
   b. a professional-looking cover.
   c. printing on quality paper.

5. You can deal with most of your anxiety about public speaking by

   a. striving for perfection.
   b. visualizing your anxiety.
   c. being well prepared.

How did you do on the quiz? Check your answers: 1. b, 2. b, 3. c, 4. a, 5. c

Journal Entry #4

Write one paragraph giving advice to a new college student on how to make a speech. Use any of these questions to guide your thinking:

- What are some ways to deal with anxiety about public speaking?
- How can you make your speech interesting?
- What are some steps in preparing a speech?
- What are some ideas that don't work?

KEYS TO SUCCESS

Be Selective

Psychologist and philosopher William James said, "The essence of genius is knowing what to overlook."[3] This saying has a variety of meanings. In reading, note taking, marking a college textbook, and writing, it is important to be able to pick out the main points first and then identify the supporting details. Imagine you are trying to put together a jigsaw puzzle. You bought the puzzle at a garage sale and all the pieces are there, but the lid to the box with the picture of the puzzle is missing. It will be very difficult, if not impossible, to put this puzzle together. Reading, note taking, marking, and writing are very much like putting a puzzle together. First you will need an understanding of the main ideas (the big picture) and then you can focus on the details.

How can you get the overall picture? When reading, you can get the overall picture by skimming the text. As you skim the text, you get a general outline of what the chapter contains and what you will learn. In note taking, actively listen for the main ideas and write them down in your notes. In marking your text, try to pick out about 20 percent of the most important material and underline or highlight it. In writing, think about what is most important, write your thesis statement, and then provide the supporting details. To select what is most important, be courageous, think, and analyze.

Does this mean that you should forget about the details? No, you will need to know some details too. The supporting details help you to understand and assess the value of the main idea. They help you to understand the relationship between ideas. Being selective means getting the general idea first, and then the details will make sense to you and you will be able to remember them. The main ideas are like scaffolding or a net that holds the details in some kind of framework so you can remember them. If you focus on the details first, you will have no framework or point of reference for remembering them.

Experiment with the idea of being selective in your personal life. If your schedule is impossibly busy, be selective and choose to do the most important or most valuable activities. This takes some thinking and courage too. If your desk drawer is stuffed with odds and ends and you can never find what you are looking for, take everything out and only put back what you need. Recycle, give away, or throw away surplus items around the house. You can take steps toward being a genius by being selective and taking steps to simplify and organize your life and your work.

Journal Entry #5

How can being selective help you achieve success in college and in life? Use any of these questions to guide your thinking:

- How can being selective help you to be a better note taker, writer, or speaker?
- How can being selective help you to manage your time and your life?
- What is the meaning of this quote by William James: "The essence of genius is knowing what to overlook?"

JOURNAL ENTRIES

Taking Notes, Writing, and Speaking

Go to http://www.collegesuccess1.com/JournalEntries.htm for Word files of the Journal Entries

Success over the Internet

Visit the *College Success Website* at http://www.collegesuccess1.com/

The *College Success Website* is continually updated with new topics and links to the material presented in this chapter. Topics include:

- Note taking
- Mind maps
- Memory and note taking
- Telegraphic sentences
- Signal words
- Listening to lectures
- Grammar and style
- Quotes to use in speeches and papers
- The virtual public speaking assistant
- Researching, organizing, and delivering a speech
- Best speeches in history

Contact your instructor if you have any problems accessing the *College Success Website*.

Notes

1. T. Allesandra and P. Hunsaker, *Communicating at Work* (New York: Fireside, 1993), 169.

2. Lilly Walters, *Secrets of Successful Speakers: How You Can Motivate, Captivate, and Persuade* (New York: McGraw-Hill, 1993), 203.

3. Quoted in Rob Gilbert, ed., *Bits and Pieces*, August 12, 1999, 15.

CHAPTER 8

Improving Memory and Reading

Learning Objectives

Read to answer these key questions:

- How does the memory work?

- Why do we forget?

- How can I remember what I study?

- What are some memory tricks?

- How can I apply memory techniques to reading?

- What is a reading system for college texts?

- What are some ways to improve reading speed and comprehension?

- Why is positive thinking a key to remembering and reading?

Learning how to improve your memory and remember what you read will be a great asset in college, on the job, and in life in general. This chapter describes how memory works and provides some practical techniques for improving your memory. Once you understand how memory works, you can apply these techniques to remembering what you read. Positive thinking will help you be successful in remembering and reading effectively.

Improving Your Memory

How Does the Memory Work?

Understanding how the memory works provides the framework for effective study techniques. There are three stages of memory: **sensory register, short-term memory,** and **long-term memory**. Understanding these stages of memory will help you learn how to store information in your long-term memory, which lasts a lifetime.

- **Sensory register.** The first stage of memory is called sensory register. It is the initial moment of perception. This stage of memory lasts less than a second and is used to record sensory experience (what you see, hear, taste, touch, or do). It is like a quickly fading snapshot of what your senses perceive. The purpose of the sensory register is to allow the brain to process information and to focus on relevant information. To remember information for more than a second, it must be transferred to short-term memory.

- **Short-term memory (STM).** Paying attention to the information you have perceived in the sensory register transfers the information to STM. STM is temporary and limited, lasting only about half a minute. The information must be rehearsed or renewed for longer storage. STM records what we see, hear, feel, taste, or touch. Information is best stored in STM through recitation or mentally talking to ourselves. If the information is not repeated, it is very quickly lost. For example, when you meet a person for the first time, the person's name is often quickly forgotten because it is only stored in short-term memory. The purpose of STM is to ponder the significance of the stimuli we have received, detect patterns, and decide if the information is important enough to remember.

  Grouping together or chunking bits of information can increase the limited capacity of STM. George Miller of Harvard University found that the optimum number of chunks or bits of information that we can hold in STM is five to nine.[1] For example, we remember telephone numbers of seven digits by using a hyphen to separate the numbers into two more easily remembered chunks. We divide our Social Security numbers into three chunks for easier recall.

  According to George Miller's research, we often use the "Magical Number Seven" technique to remember material. It is much easier to remember material that is grouped in chunks of seven or less. You can find many examples of groups of seven used to enhance memory. There are seven days of the week and seven numbers in your driver's license and license plate. There are also seven dwarfs, seven deadly sins, and seven wonders of the world!

- **Long-term memory (LTM).** Long-term memory has a large capacity and is used to store information more permanently. You will want to use your LTM to store important information that you want to be able to recall at a later date. Most psychologists agree that once information is in LTM, it is there forever. Although the information is available, the problem becomes how to access it. Think of LTM as a library in which many available books are stored. If the books in the library are randomly stored, retrieval of information becomes extremely difficult. If the books are properly stored and indexed, we can find them more easily.

How are long-term memories formed? Short-term memories become long-term through repetition or meaningful association. Creating long-term memories takes some purposeful action. We are motivated to take some purposeful action to remember if the information has some survival value. When we touch a hot stove, this memory moves from sensory register to short-term memory and then is stored in long-term memory to avoid injury in the future. In an academic setting, we must convince ourselves of the survival value of what we are learning. Is the information needed to pass a test, to be successful in a career, or for personal reasons? If so, it is easier to take the action required to store information in long-term memory. Emotions such as fear, anger, or joy are also involved in the storing of memories. In the hot stove example, fear elevates the importance of the memory and helps us to store it in long-term memory. In the educational setting, an interest or joy in learning helps to store information in long-term memory.

In summary, when you are trying to store information in your memory, the first step is receiving information through the five senses to store in the sensory register, similar to entering data in a computer through the use of a keyboard. This takes less than a second. The next step involves paying attention to the sensory stimulus in order to transfer it to STM for the purpose of seeing patterns and judging significance or importance. Information only stays in STM for 30 seconds or less unless rehearsed or repeated. If you decide that the information is likely to be on a test and you need to remember it, you must organize the material in a meaningful way or repeat it to store the information in LTM. Information must be stored in LTM in order for you to remember it permanently. Effective techniques for storing information in LTM will be presented later in this chapter.

How Does the Memory Work?

Sensory Register	Initial moment of perception	Lasts less than a second
STM Short Term Memory	Temporary and limited	Lasts less than 30 seconds
LTM Long Term Memory	Permanent storage of information	Lasts forever, although you may lose access through disuse

Figure 7.1 Short-Term Memory and Long-Term Memory

Why Do We Forget?

Is it true that we never forget? Material that is stored in the sensory register is forgotten in less than one second. Material stored in STM is forgotten in 30 seconds unless rehearsed or repeated. We do not forget material stored in LTM, but we can lose access to the information, similar to when a book is filed incorrectly in the library. The book is in the library, but we cannot find it.

© 2014, Edyta Pawlowska. Used under license with Shutterstock, Inc.

Examining the following lists of items frequently forgotten or remembered can give us insight into why forgetting or losing access occurs.

We frequently forget these things:

- Unpleasant experiences
- Names of people, places, or things
- Numbers and dates
- What we have barely learned
- Material we do not fully understand
- What we try to remember when embarrassed, frustrated, tired, or ill
- Material we have learned by cramming
- Ideas or theories that conflict with our beliefs

We tend to remember these things:

- Pleasant experiences
- Material that is important to us
- What we have put an effort into learning
- What we have reviewed or thought about often
- Material that is interesting to us
- Muscular skills such as riding a bike
- What we had an important reason to remember
- Items we discuss with others
- Material that we understand
- Frequently used information

Theories of Forgetting

An understanding of theories of forgetting is also helpful in developing techniques for effective study and learning. There are many theories about why we forget or lose access to information stored in LTM.

1. **I forgot.** If you forget a name, number, or fact, you might just say, "I forgot." The information was stored in STM and never made it to LTM. Have you ever been introduced to a person and really not listened to his or her name? You didn't forget it. You never learned it.

2. **The mental blur.** If you are studying and don't understand the material, you will not remember it.

3. **The decay theory.** If you do not use information, you lose access to it, just as weeds grow over a path that is seldom used.

4. **Interference theory.** New memories interfere with old memories, and old memories interfere with new memories. Interference is especially likely when the memories are similar. For example, when I meet my students in the hallway, it is difficult to remember which class they are in because I have several similar classes.

5. **Reactive interference.** We tend not to remember ideas or subjects that we dislike.

6. **Reconstruction theory.** What we remember becomes distorted over time. Our personal biases affect what we remember.

7. **Motivated forgetting.** We choose to remember pleasant experiences and to forget unpleasant experiences.

Minimizing Forgetting

Herman Ebbinghaus (1850–1909), a German psychologist and pioneer in research on forgetting, described a curve of forgetting.[2] He invented nonsense syllables such as WUX, CAZ, BIJ, and ZOL. He chose these nonsense syllables so that there would be no meaning, associations, or organizations that could affect the memory of the words. He would learn these lists of words and measure forgetting over time. The following is a chart of time and forgetting of nonsense syllables.

Time	Percent Forgotten
After 20 minutes	47
After 1 day	62
After 2 days	69
After 15 days	75
After 31 days	78

We can draw three interesting conclusions from examining these figures. First, **most of the forgetting occurs within the first 20 minutes**. Immediate review, or at least review during the first 20 minutes, would prevent most of the forgetting. Second, forgetting slows down over time. The third conclusion is that forgetting is significant after 31 days. Fortunately, we do not need to memorize nonsense syllables. We can use meaning, associations, organization, and proper review to minimize forgetting.

Review is important in transferring information from short-term to long-term memory. You can also minimize forgetting over time through the proper use of review.[3] Let's assume that you spend 45 minutes studying and learning something new. The optimum schedule for review would look like this:

After 10 minutes	Review for 5 minutes
After 1 day	Review for 5 minutes
After 1 week	Review for 3 minutes
After 1 month	Review for 3 minutes
After 6 months	Review for 3 minutes

> "Just as iron rusts from disuse, even so does inaction spoil the intellect."
> Leonardo da Vinci

Memorization Tips

- Meaningful organization
- Visualization
- Recitation
- Develop an interest
- See the big picture first
- Intend to remember
- Learn small amounts frequently
- Basic background
- Relax

Improving Your Memory

Test what you have learned by circling the letters of the correct answers to the following questions.

1. Information is stored permanently in the
   a. sensory register.
   b. short-term memory (STM).
   c. long-term memory (LTM).

2. You never forget.
   a. False.
   b. True.
   c. This is true only if the information is stored properly in long-term memory.

3. According to Ebbinghaus, the greatest rate of forgetting occurs
   a. within the first 20 minutes.
   b. within the first day.
   c. within the first 15 days.

4. If you do not review information stored in long-term memory, you will
   a. still remember it because it is in long-term memory.
   b. probably lose access to the information.
   c. lose the information forever.

5. The best way to review is
   a. in a 45-minute study session.
   b. in a 20-minute study session.
   c. in three- to five-minute study sessions spaced out over time.

How did you do on the quiz? Check your answers: 1. c, 2. c, 3. a, 4. b, 5. c

By spending about 20 minutes in review time, you can remember 90 to 100 percent of the material. The short periods of review are much easier to accomplish than spending larger periods of review. Make good use of your time by having material for review immediately available. When you have three to five minutes available, review some material that you have learned previously. You will be improving access to material stored in long-term memory, and you will be able to easily recall the information for an exam or for future use in your career.

How Can I Remember What I Study?

Based on the above theories of memory and forgetting, here are some practical suggestions for storing information in LTM. Information stored in LTM can be retrieved for tests in college and for success in your career and personal life.

"Today I will do what others won't, so I can accomplish what others can't."

Jerry Rice

Meaningful Organization

There is no better method of memory improvement than imposing your own form of personal organization on the material you are trying to remember. Psychologists have even suggested that your intelligence quotient (IQ) may be related to how well you have organized material you learned in the past. When learning new material, cluster facts and ideas into categories that are meaningful to you.

Magical Number Seven

Remember George Miller's Magical Number Seven Theory? It is more efficient to limit the number of categories to seven or less, although you can have subcategories. Examine the following list of words.

goat	horse	cow
carrot	cat	lettuce
banana	tomato	pig
celery	orange	peas
cherry	apple	strawberry

Look at the list for one minute. Then look away from the list and write down all the words you can recall. Record the number of words you remembered: _____

Note that the following lists are divided into categories: animals, crops, and tropical fruits.

animals	crops	tropical fruits
lion	wheat	banana
giraffe	beans	kiwi
kangaroo	corn	mango
coyote	hay	guava
bear	oats	orange

Look at the above list for one minute. Then look away from the list and write down the words you recall. Record the number of words you remembered: _____

You probably remembered more from the second list because the list is organized into categories. Notice that there are only five words in each category. Remember that it is easier to remember lists with seven items or less. If these words have some meaning for you, it is easier to remember them. A farmer from the Midwest would probably have an easier time remembering the crops. A person from Hawaii would probably remember the list of tropical fruits. We also tend to remember unusual items and the first and last items on the list. If you need to memorize a list, pay more attention to the mundane items and the items in the middle of the list.

Visualization

Another very powerful memorization technique is visualization. The right side of the brain specializes in visual pictures and the left side in verbal functions. If you focus on the words only, you are using only half of your brain. If you can focus on the words and accompany them with pictures, you are using your brain in the most efficient way. Advertisers use pictures as powerful influences to motivate you to purchase their products. You can use the same power of visualization to enhance your studying. While you are studying history, picture what life would be like in that time period. In engineering, make pictures in your mind or on paper to illustrate scientific principles. Challenge yourself to see the pictures along with the words. Add movement to your pictures, as in a video. During a test, relax and recall the pictures.

© 2014, scyther5. Used under license with Shutterstock, Inc.

Recitation

Although scientists are still researching and learning how the memory works and how information is stored, we do know that recitation, rehearsal, and reviewing the ideas are powerful techniques for learning. Memories exist in the brain in the form of a chemical neural trace. Some researchers think that it takes about four or five seconds for this neural trace to be established in LTM. It is through recitation that we keep the ideas in our mind long enough to store them in LTM. Often students say they cannot remember the material that they have just read. The reason for this problem is not a lack of intelligence, but rather a simple lack of rehearsal. If information obtained through reading is stored in STM, it is very quickly forgotten. Say aloud or to yourself the material you want to remember. This process takes about five seconds.

Applying the recitation technique can help you remember names. When you are introduced to someone, first pay attention to make sure that you have heard the name correctly. Ask the person to repeat their name if necessary. Repeat the name out loud or in your mind. Say something like, "Glad to meet you, *Lydia*." Say the name silently to yourself five times to establish the neural trace. If possible, make a visual connection with the name. If the person's name is Frank, you might picture a hot dog, for example. Thinking about the name or reviewing it will help to access the name in the future.

Remember that most of the forgetting occurs in the first 20 minutes after learning something. Reviewing the material within 20 minutes is the fastest and most effective way to remember it. You will also need to review the information you have stored in LTM periodically so it is more accessible. This periodic review can be done effectively in three to five minutes.

Develop an Interest

"Knowledge is power, but enthusiasm pulls the switch."

Ivern Ball

"The secret of a good memory is attention, and attention to a subject depends on interest in it. We rarely forget what makes a deep impression on our mind."

Tyron Edwards

We tend to remember what interests us. People often have phenomenal memories when it comes to sports, automobiles, music, stamp collecting, or anything they consider fun or pursue as a hobby. Find something interesting in your college studies. If you are not interested in what you are studying, look for something interesting or even pretend that you are interested. Reward yourself for studying by doing something enjoyable.

Attitude has a significant impact on memory. Approaching your studies with a positive attitude will help you to find something interesting and make it easier to remember. In addition, the more you learn about a topic, the more interesting it becomes. Often we judge a subject as boring because we know nothing about it.

Another way to make something interesting is to look for personal meaning. How can I use this information in my future career? Does the information relate to my personal experience in some way? How can I use this information? What is the importance of this information? And finally, is this information likely to be on the test?

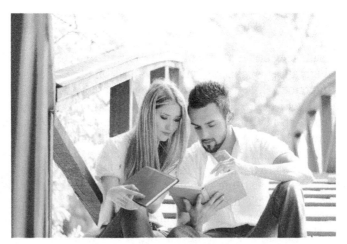

© 2014, Zurijeta. Used under license with Shutterstock, Inc.

See the Big Picture First

Imagine looking at a painting one inch at a time. It would be difficult to understand or appreciate a painting in this way. College students often approach reading a textbook in the same way. They focus on the small details without first getting an idea of the main points. By focusing on the details without looking at the main points, it is easy to get lost.

The first step in reading is to skim the chapter headings to form a mental outline of what you will be learning. Then read for detail. Think of the mind as a file cabinet or a computer. Major topics are like folders in which we file detailed information. When we need to find or access the information, we think of the major topic and look in the folder to find the details. If we put all of our papers into the file drawer without organization, it is difficult to find the information we need. Highlight or underline key ideas to focus on the main points and organize what you are learning.

Be selective and focus on key ideas to increase learning efficiency. Herman Ebbinghaus studied the length of time needed to remember series of six nonsense syllables and 12 nonsense syllables.[4] We might assume that it would take twice as long to remember 12 syllables as it would six syllables. Ebbinghaus found that it took 15 times longer to memorize 12 syllables. The Magic Number Seven Theory seems to apply to the number of items that can be memorized efficiently.

Does this mean that we should try to remember only seven or less ideas in studying a textbook chapter? No—it is most efficient to identify seven or fewer key ideas and then cluster less important ideas under major headings. In this way, you can remember the key ideas in the chapter you are studying. The critical thinking required by this process also helps in remembering ideas and information.

Intend to Remember

Tell yourself that you are going to remember. If you think you won't remember, you won't remember. This step also relates to positive thinking and self-confidence and will take some practice to apply. Once you have told yourself to remember, apply some of the above techniques such as organizing, visualizing, and reciting. If you intend to remember, you will pay attention, make an effort to understand, and use memory techniques to strengthen your memory.

One practical technique that involves intent to remember is the memory jogger. This involves doing something unusual to jog or trigger your memory. If you want to be sure to remember your books, place your car keys on the books. Since you cannot go anywhere without your keys, you will find them and remember the books too. Another application is putting your watch on your right hand to remember to do something. When you look at your left hand and notice that the watch is not there, the surprise will jog your memory for the item you wish to recall. You can be creative with this technique and come up with your own memory joggers.

Distribute the Practice

Learning small amounts of material and reviewing frequently are more effective than a marathon study session. One research study showed that a task that took 30 minutes to learn in one day could be learned in 22 minutes if spread over two days. This is almost a 30 percent increase in efficiency.[5]

If you have a list of vocabulary words or formulas to learn, break the material into small parts and frequently review each part for a short period of time. Consider putting these facts or figures on index cards to carry with you in your purse or pocket. Use small amounts of time to quickly review the cards. This technique works well because it prevents fatigue and helps to keep motivation high. One exception to the distributed practice rule is creative work such as writing a paper or doing an art project, where a longer time period is needed for creative inspiration and immediate follow-through.

A learning technique for distributed practice is summed up in the acronym **SAFMEDS**, which stands for Say All Fast for one Minute Each Day and Shuffle.[6] With this technique, you can easily and quickly learn 100 or more facts. To use this technique, prepare flash cards that contain the material to be learned (vocabulary, foreign language words, numbers, dates, places, names, formulas). For example, if you are learning Spanish, place the Spanish word on one side of the card and the English word on the other side. Just writing out the flash cards is an aid to learning and is often sufficient for learning the material. Once the cards are prepared, *say* the Spanish word and see if you can remember what it means in English. Look at the back of the card to see if your answer is correct. Do this with *all* of the cards as *fast* as you can for *one minute each day*. Then *shuffle* the cards and repeat the process the next day.

It is important that you do this activity quickly. Don't worry if you do not know the answer. Just flip each card over, quickly look at the answer, and put the cards that you missed into a separate pile. At the end of the minute, count the number of cards you answered correctly. You can learn even faster if you take the stack of cards you missed and practice them quickly one more time. Shuffling the cards helps you to remember the actual meanings of the words, instead of just the order in which they appear. In the case of the Spanish cards, turn the cards over and say each English word to see if you can remember the equivalent word in Spanish. Each day, the number of correct answers will increase, and you will have a concrete measure of your learning. Consider this activity as a fun and fast-moving game to challenge yourself.

Create a Basic Background

You remember information by connecting it to things you already know. The more you know, the easier it is to make connections that make remembering easier. You will even find that it is easier to remember material toward the end of a college class because you have established a basic background at the beginning of the semester. With this in mind, freshman-level courses will be the most difficult in college because they form the basic background for your college education. College does become easier as you establish this basic background and practice effective study techniques.

You can enhance your basic background by reading a variety of books. Making reading a habit also enhances vocabulary, writing, and spelling. College provides many opportunities for expanding your reading horizons and areas of basic knowledge.

Relax While Studying

The brain works much better when it is relaxed. As you become more confident in your study techniques, you can become more relaxed. Here are some suggestions to help you relax during study time.

- Use distributed practice to take away some of the pressure of learning; take breaks between periods of learning. Give yourself time to absorb the material.
- Plan ahead so that you do not have to cram. Waiting until the last minute to study produces anxiety that is counterproductive.
- If you are anxious, try a physical activity or relaxation exercise before study sessions. For example, imagine a warm, relaxing light beginning at the feet and moving slowly up the body to the top of the head. Feel each part of the body relax as the light makes contact with it. You will find other relaxation techniques in Chapter 12.
- If you are feeling frustrated, it is often a good idea to stop and come back to your studies later. You may gain insight into your studies while you are more relaxed and doing something else. You can often benefit from a fresh perspective.

Using Mnemonics and Other Memory Tricks

Memory tricks can be used to enhance your memory. These memory tricks include acrostics, acronyms, peg systems, and loci systems. These systems are called *mnemonics*, from the Greek word *mneme* which means "to remember."

Mnemonic devices are very effective. A research study by Gerald R. Miller found that students who used mnemonic devices improved their test scores by up to 77 percent.[7] Mnemonics are effective because they help to organize material. They have been used throughout history, in part as a way to entertain people with amazing memory feats.

Mnemonics are best used for memorizing facts. They are not helpful for understanding or thinking critically about the information. Be sure to memorize your mnemonics carefully and review them right before exam time. Forgetting the mnemonic or a part of it can cause major problems.

© 2014, Lightspring. Used under license with Shutterstock, Inc.

Acrostics

Acrostics are creative rhymes, songs, poems, or sentences that help us to remember. Maybe you previously learned some of these in school.

- Continents: Eat an Aspirin after a Nighttime Snack (Europe, Antarctica, Asia, Africa, Australia, North America, South America)
- Directions of the compass: Never Eat Sour Watermelons (North, East, South, West)
- Geological ages: Practically Every Old Man Plays Poker Regularly (Paleocene, Eocene, Oligocene, Miocene, Pliocene, Pleistocene, Recent)
- Guitar Strings: Eat All Dead Gophers Before Easter (E, A, D, G, B, E)
- Oceans: I Am a Person (Indian, Arctic, Atlantic, Pacific)
- Metric system in order: King Henry Drinks Much Dark Chocolate Milk (Kilometer, hectometer, decameter, meter, decimeter, centimeter, millimeter
- Notes on the treble clef in music: Every Good Boy Does Fine (E, G, B, D, F)
- Classification in biology: Kings Play Cards on Fairly Good Soft Velvet (Kingdom, Phylum, Class, Order, Family, Genus, Species, Variety)

Memorization Tricks
• Acrostics
• Acronyms
• Peg systems
• Loci systems
• Visual clues
• Say it aloud
• Have a routine
• Write it down

An effective way to invent your own acrostics is to first identify key ideas you need to remember, underline these key words or write them down as a list, and think of a word that starts with the first letter of each idea you want to remember. Rearrange the words if necessary to form a sentence. The more unusual the sentence, the easier it is to remember.

In addition to acrostics, there are many other creative memory aids:

- Days in each month: Thirty days hath September, April, June, and November. All the rest have 31, except February which has 28 until leap year gives it 29.
- Spelling rules: *i* before *e* except after *c*, or when sounding like *a* as in neighbor and weigh.
- Numbers: Can I remember the reciprocal? To remember the reciprocal of pi, count the letters in each word of the question above. The reciprocal of pi = .3 1 8 3 10

Mnemonics become more powerful when used with visualization. For example, if you are trying to remember the planets, use a mnemonic and then visualize Saturn as a hula-hoop dancer to remember that it has rings. Jupiter could be a king with a number of maids to represent its moons.

Acronyms

Acronyms are commonly used as shortcuts in our language. The military is especially fond of using acronyms. For example, NASA is the acronym for the National Aeronautics and Space Administration. You can invent your own acronyms as a memory trick. Here are some common ones that students have used:

- The colors of the spectrum: Roy G. Biv (red, orange, yellow, green, blue, indigo, violet)
- The Great Lakes: HOMES (Huron, Ontario, Michigan, Erie, Superior)
- The stages of cell division in biology: IPMAT (interphase, prophase, metaphase, and telophase)

To make your own acronym, list the items you wish to remember. Use the first letter of each word to make a new word. The word you make can be an actual word or an invented word.

Peg Systems

Peg systems start with numbers, typically 1 to 100. Each number is associated with an object. The object chosen to represent each number can be based on rhyme or on a logical association. The objects are memorized and used with a mental picture to recall a list. There are entertainers who can have the audience call out a list of 100 objects and then repeat all of the objects through use of a peg system. Here is an example of a commonly used peg system based on rhyme:

One	Bun	Six	Sticks
Two	Shoe	Seven	Heaven
Three	Tree	Eight	Gate
Four	Door	Nine	Wine
Five	Hive	Ten	Hen

For example, if I want to remember a grocery list consisting of milk, eggs, carrots, and butter, I would make associations between the peg and the item I want to remember. The more unusual the association is, the better. I would start by making a visual connection between *bun*, my peg word, and *milk*, the first item on the list. I could picture dipping a bun into a glass of milk for a snack. Next I would make a connection between *shoe* and *eggs*. I could picture eggs being broken into my shoe as a joke. Next I would picture a *tree* with orange *carrots* hanging from it and then a *door* with *butter* dripping from the doorknob. The technique works because of the organization provided by the pegs and the power of visualization.

There are many variations of the peg system. One variation is using the letters of the alphabet instead of numbers. Another variation is to visualize objects and put them in a stack, one on top of the other, until you have a great tottering tower, like a totem pole telling a story. Still another variation is to use your body or your car as a peg system. Using our example of the grocery list above, visualize balancing the milk on your head, carrying eggs in your hands, having carrots tied around your waist and smearing butter on your feet. Remember that the more unusual the pictures, the easier they are to remember.

Loci Systems

Loci or location systems use a series of familiar places to aid the memory. The Roman orators often used this system to remember the outline of a speech. For example, the speaker might connect the entry of a house with the introduction, the living room with the first main point, and each part of the speech with a different room. Again, this technique works through organization and visualization.

Another example of using a loci system to remember a speech or dramatic production is to imagine a long hallway. Mentally draw a picture of each topic or section you need to remember, and then hang each picture on the wall. As you are giving your speech or acting out your part in the play, visualize walking down the hallway and looking at the pictures on the wall to remind yourself of the next topic. For multiple topics, you can place signs over several hallway entrances labeling the contents of each hallway.

Visual Clues

Visual clues are helpful memory devices. To remember your books, place them in front of the door so you will see them on your way to school. To remember to take your finished homework to school, put it in your car when you are done. To remember to fill a prescription, put the empty bottle on the front seat of your car. Tie a bright ribbon on your backpack to remind you to attend a meeting with your study group. When parking your car in the mall, look around and notice landmarks such as nearby stores or row numbers. When you enter a large department store, notice the items that are near the door you entered. Are you worried that you left the iron on? Tie a ribbon around the handle of the iron each time you turn it off or unplug it. To find out if you have all the items you need to go skiing, visualize yourself on the ski slope wearing all those items.

Say It Aloud

Some people are auditory learners and can remember items by repeating them out loud. For example, if you want to remember where you hid your diamond ring; say it out loud a few times. Then reinforce the memory by making a visual picture of where you have hidden the ring. You can also use your auditory memory by making a rhyme or song to remember something. Commercials use this technique all the time to try to get you to remember a product and purchase it.

Have a Routine

Do you have a difficult time trying to remember where you left your keys, wallet, or purse? Having a routine can greatly simplify your life and help you to remember. As you enter your house, hang your keys on a hook each time. Decide where you will place your wallet or purse and put it in the same place each time. When I leave for work, I have a mental checklist with four items: keys, purse, glasses, and cell phone.

Write It Down

One of the easiest and most effective memory techniques is to simply write something down. Make a grocery list or to-do list, send yourself an email, or tape a note to your bathroom mirror or the dashboard of your car.

Remembering Names

Many people have difficulty remembering names of other people in social or business situations. The reason we have difficulty in remembering names is that we do not take the time to store the name properly in our memories. When we first meet someone, we are often distracted or thinking about ourselves. We are trying to remember our own names or wondering what impression we are making on the other person.

To remember a name, first make sure you have heard the name correctly. If you have not heard the name, there is no way you can remember it. Ask the person to repeat his or her name or check to see if you have heard it correctly. Immediately use the name. For example, say "It is nice to meet you, *Nancy*." If you can mentally repeat the name about five times, you have a good chance of remembering it. You can improve the chances of remembering the name if you can make an association. For example, you might think, "She looks like my daughter's friend Nancy." Some people remember names by making a rhyme such as "fancy Nancy."

> ## Journal Entry #2
>
> Review the memory tricks explained in this chapter: acrostics, acronyms, peg systems, loci systems, visual clues, say it aloud, have a routine, write it down, and remembering names. List and briefly explain at least three memory tricks you are willing to try, and give examples of how you would use each of the three memory tricks you select.

Optimize Your Brain Power

The mind can be strengthened and remain healthy throughout life. Scientists have studied a group of nuns from Mankato, Minnesota, who have lived long lives and suffer less from dementia and brain diseases than the general population. These nuns have lived a long time because they do not drink to excess or smoke. They have kept their minds healthy into old age by staying mentally active. They keep active by discussing current events, playing cards, practicing math problems, and doing crossword puzzles. Arnold Scheibel, head of the UCLA Brain Institute, gives the following suggestions for strengthening your mind.

© 2014, Hubis. Used under license with Shutterstock, Inc.

- Do jigsaw and crossword puzzles.
- Play a musical instrument.
- Fix something. The mental challenge stimulates the brain.
- Participate in the arts. Draw or paint something.
- Dance. Exercise and rhythm are good for the brain.
- Do aerobic exercise. This promotes blood flow to the brain.
- Meet and interact with interesting people.
- Read challenging books.
- Take a college class.[8]

Doing these kinds of activities can actually stimulate the development of neurons and nerve connections in the brain so that the brain functions more efficiently. The good news is that you can do this at any age.

Besides doing mental exercises to strengthen your brain, you can take other actions to keep your brain healthy. Here are some ideas:

1. **Do aerobic exercise.** Exercise improves the flow of oxygen to the brain. The brain needs oxygen to function. Researchers have just found that the human brain can grow new nerve cells by putting subjects on a three-month aerobic workout regimen. It was interesting to note that these new nerve cells could be generated at any age and are important in reversing the aging process and delaying the onset of Alzheimer's disease or other cognitive disorders.[9] For optimum health and learning, it is important to exercise the body as well as the mind.

2. **Get enough rest.** Nobel laureate Francis Crick, who studies the brain at the Salk Institute, proposes that the purpose of sleep is to allow the brain to "take out the trash." Sleep provides time for the brain to review the events of the day and to store what is needed and discard what is not worth remembering. During sleep, the brain sorts memories and stores significant ones in long-term memory. Studies have shown that when humans and lab animals are taught a new task and deprived of sleep, they do not perform the task the next day as well as non-sleep-deprived subjects.[10]

3. **Eat a balanced, low-fat diet.** The brain needs nutrients, vitamins, and minerals to be healthy. Low-fat diets have been shown to improve mental performance.[11]

4. **Eat proteins and carbohydrates.** Proteins are the building blocks of neurotransmitters that increase mental activity. Carbohydrates provide energy and are the building blocks of neurotransmitters that have a calming effect.[12]

5. **Drink caffeine in moderation.** Caffeine can make you feel stressed, making it difficult to think.

6. **Don't abuse drugs or alcohol.** These substances kill brain cells and change brain chemistry.

7. **Use safety gear.** Wear a seat belt when driving and a helmet when biking or skating to reduce head injuries.

Journal Entry #3

What is your plan for keeping your brain healthy throughout life? Include some of these ideas: diet, exercise, music, art, games, fixing something, challenging your brain, social contacts, and continued learning.

Improving Your Reading

Myths about Reading

Effective reading techniques are crucial to college success. The level and quantity of reading expected in college may be greatly increased over what you have experienced in the past. The following are some myths about reading that cause problems for many college students.

1. **"If I read a chapter, I should remember what I read."** Many students say that they read the chapter, but "it goes in one ear and out the other." After such a frustrating experience, students often conclude that they cannot read well or are not intelligent

© 2014, Vitchanan Photography. Used under license with Shutterstock, Inc.

enough to succeed in college. If you just read the chapter, you have stored it in short-term memory, which lasts about 30 seconds. Reading a chapter takes a lot of effort. You want to make sure the effort you have invested pays off by storing the material in long-term memory. You can then retrieve the information in the future, as well as pass exams. Material is stored in long-term memory through rehearsal or review. Without review, you will not remember.

2. **"I do not need to read if I go to class."** The role of the college professor is to supplement material in the text and increase student understanding of the material. Some professors do not even cover topics contained in the text and consider it the student's responsibility to learn textbook material. If you do not read the text, you may miss out on important material that is not presented during class. Reading the text also helps you understand the material that the professor presents.

3. **"Practice makes perfect."** Students think that if they keep reading the way they are reading, their reading will get better. The truth is that "perfect practice makes perfect." If you are reading in a way that enhances memory, you will get better and better. Success in college reading may mean learning some new reading habits. You will learn about effective reading habits in this chapter.

4. **"Learn the facts that will be on the test."** Focusing on details without looking at the big picture can slow down learning and lead to frustration. If you start with the big picture or outline, then it is easier to learn the details.

A Study System for Reading a College Text: SQ4R

There are many systems for reading a college textbook. All successful systems involve ways to store information in long-term memory: recognizing major points, organizing material to be learned, reviewing, intending to remember, and critical thinking about reading. The crucial step in transferring information to long-term memory is rehearsal, reviewing, or reciting. You need to keep information in your mind for five to 5 seconds in order for it to be stored in long-term memory. The **SQ4R system (Survey, Question, Read, Recite, Review, Reflect)** is a simple and effective way to store information in long-term memory. This system was derived from an information-processing theory developed by Francis P. Robinson in 1941 for use by military personnel attending college during World War II. Since that time, the system has been used by many colleges to teach students effective study skills. The system can be broken down into three steps.

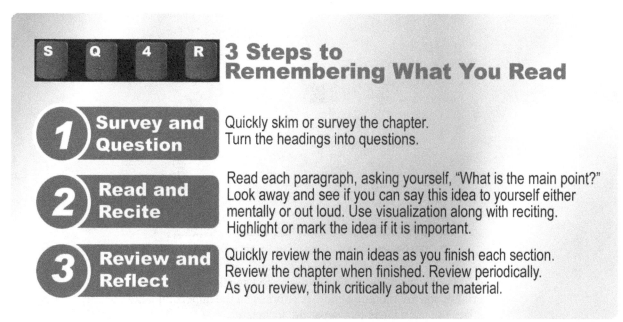

S Q 4 R 3 Steps to Remembering What You Read

1 Survey and Question — Quickly skim or survey the chapter. Turn the headings into questions.

2 Read and Recite — Read each paragraph, asking yourself, "What is the main point?" Look away and see if you can say this idea to yourself either mentally or out loud. Use visualization along with reciting. Highlight or mark the idea if it is important.

3 Review and Reflect — Quickly review the main ideas as you finish each section. Review the chapter when finished. Review periodically. As you review, think critically about the material.

Figure 7.2 The SQ4R System for reading a college textbook.

Step 1: Survey and Question. The first step is to survey and question the chapter before you begin reading. Read the title and first paragraph or introduction to the chapter and then look quickly through the chapter, letting your eyes glide across bold headings, diagrams, illustrations, and photos. Read the last paragraph or summary of the chapter. This process should take five minutes or less for a typical chapter in a college textbook.

While you are surveying the chapter, ask yourself questions. Take each major heading in the chapter and turn it into a question. For example, in this section of the book you might ask: What is a system for reading a college text? Why do I need a system? What is SQ4R? What is the first step of SQ4R? You can also ask some general questions as you survey the chapter: What is the main point? What will I learn? Do I know something about this? Can I find something that interests me? How can I use this? Does this relate to something said in class? What does this mean? Is this a possible test question? Asking questions will help you to become an active reader and to find some personal meaning in the content that will help you remember it. If you at least survey and question the relevant textbook material before you go to class, you will have the advantage of being familiar with some of the key ideas to be discussed.

There are several benefits to taking this first step:

- This is the first step in rehearsal for storage of information into long-term memory.
- The quick survey is a warmup for the brain, similar to an athlete's warmup before exercise.
- A survey step is also good practice for improving your reading speed.
- Reading to answer questions increases comprehension, sparks interest, and has the added bonus of keeping you awake while reading.

If you want to be able to read faster, improve your reading comprehension, and increase retention of your reading material, practice the survey and question step before you begin your detailed reading.

> "The important thing is to not stop questioning."
> Albert Einstein

Step 2: Read and recite. The second step in reading a text is to read and recite. Read each paragraph and look for the most important point or topic sentence. If the point is important, highlight or underline it. You might use different colors to organize the ideas. You can also make a notation or outline in the margin of the text if the point is especially significant, meaningful, useful, or likely to appear on an exam. A picture, diagram, or

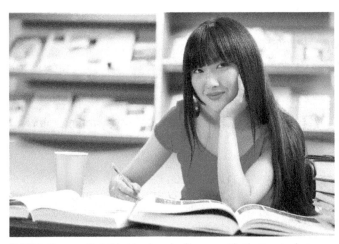

© 2014, George Dolgikh. Used under license with Shutterstock, Inc.

chart drawn in the margin is a great way to use visualization to improve retention of the material. If you are reading online, take notes on the important points or use cut and paste to collect the main ideas in a separate document.

Next, look away and see if you can say the main point to yourself either silently or out loud. Reciting is even more powerful if you combine it with visualization. Make a video in your head to illustrate what you are learning. Include color, movement, and sound if possible. Reciting is crucial to long-term memory storage. It will also keep you awake. Beginning college students will find this step a challenge, but practice makes it a habit that becomes easier and easier.

If you read a paragraph or section and do not understand the main point, try these techniques:

1. **Notice any vocabulary or technical terms that are unfamiliar.** Look up these words in a dictionary or in the glossary at the back of the book. Use index cards; write the words on one side and the definition on the other side. Use the SAFMEDS technique (Say All Fast in one Minute Each Day Shuffle) discussed earlier in this chapter. You are likely to see these vocabulary words on quizzes and exams.

2. **Read the paragraph again.** Until you get into the habit of searching for the main point, you may need to reread a paragraph until you understand. If this does not work, reread the paragraphs before and after the one you do not understand.

3. **Write a question in the margin and ask your instructor or tutor to explain.** College instructors have office hours set aside to assist students with questions, and faculty are generally favorably impressed with students who care enough to ask questions. Most colleges offer tutoring free of charge.

4. **If you are really frustrated, put your reading away and come back to it later.** You may be able to relax and gain some insight about the material.

5. **Make sure you have the proper background for the course.** Take the introductory course first.

6. **Assess your reading skills.** Colleges offer reading assessments, and counselors can help you understand your skill level and suggest appropriate courses. Most colleges offer reading courses that can help you to be successful in college.

7. **If you have always had a problem with reading, you may have a learning disability.** A person with a learning disability is of average or higher-than-average intelligence, but has a problem that interferes with learning. Most colleges offer assessment that can help you understand your learning disability and tutoring that is designed to help you to compensate for the disability.

Step 3: Review and reflect. The last step in reading is to review and reflect. After each section, quickly review what you have highlighted or underlined. Again, ask questions. How can I use this information? How does it relate to what I already know? What is most important? What is likely to be on the exam? Is it true? Learn to think critically about the material you have learned.

When you finish the chapter, quickly (in a couple of minutes) look over the highlights again. This last step, review and reflect, is another opportunity for rehearsal. At this point, you have stored the information in long-term memory and want to make sure that you can access the information again in the future. Think of this last step as a creative step in which you put the pieces together, gain an understanding, and begin to think of how you can apply your new knowledge to your personal life. This is the true reward of studying.

Review is faster, easier, and more effective if done immediately. As discussed previously in this chapter, most forgetting occurs in the first 20 minutes after exposure to new information. If you wait 24 hours to review, you will probably have forgotten 80 percent of the material and will have to spend a longer time in review. Review periodically to make sure that you can access the material easily in the future, and review again right before the test.

As you read about the above steps, you may think that this process takes a lot of time. Remember that it is not how much you read, but how you read that is important. In reality, the SQ4R technique is a time-saver in that you do not have to reread all the material before the test. You just need to quickly review information that is stored in long-term memory. Rereading can be purely mechanical and consume your time with little payoff. Rather than rereading, spend your time reciting the important points. With proper review, you can remember 80 to 90 percent of the material.

In his book *Accelerated Learning*, Colin Rose states that you can retain 88 percent of the material you study using the following review schedule.[13] He also notes that the rate of retention using this schedule is four times better than the expected curve of forgetting.

1. Review immediately within 30 seconds.

2. Review after a few minutes.

3. Review after one hour.

4. Review a day later after an overnight rest.

5. Review after a week.

6. Review after one month.

Suggestions for review schedules vary, but the key point is that review is most effective when it is done in short sessions spaced out over time.

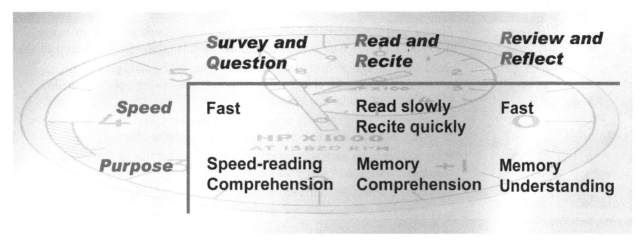

Figure 7.3 This chart summarizes the speed and purpose of each SQ4R step.

Online Reading Strategies

To read efficiently, you will need some reading strategies for the vast amount of online material you will use in college and in everyday life. First, determine your purpose for reading. If you are reading for entertainment, to interact with others, or to find needed information, quickly scan the material to see if it meets your needs. Look for bulleted lists, menu bars, highlighted words, and headers; read only what suits your purpose. Avoid getting lost on your search by using browser tools such as favorites/bookmarks or the history, which is a list of the pages you have visited before. Use multiple browser windows to compare or synthesize information. To avoid eyestrain while reading online, be sure to take breaks and look away from the screen. It is important to get up and stretch periodically.

If you are study reading for an online course, first scan the material for key words. Then carefully read each section and summarize what you have learned. If you cannot do this, reread the section. If you are an auditory learner, you can repeat to yourself what you have learned, either silently or aloud. If you are a kinesthetic learner who learns by the hands-on approach, take notes on the important points. You can save time by opening a separate document in a new window and cutting and pasting the important points into your notes. Be sure to include the source of the material, so that you can use it in writing papers or find the material again. As in reading print material, use some techniques to assure good comprehension: as you read each section, visualize what you are reading, ask questions, and think critically about the material.

Journal Entry #4

Describe a system for college reading. Include these ideas: survey, question, read, recite, review, and reflect.

Guidelines for Marking Your Textbook

Marking your textbook can help you pick out what is important, save time, and review the material. It is a great way to reinforce your memory and help you access the material you have learned. In high school, you were given the command, "Thou shalt not mark in thy book!" College is different. You have paid for the book and need to use it as a tool. Even if you plan to sell your book, you can still mark it up. Here are some guidelines for marking your book:

- Underline or mark the key ideas in your text. You don't have to underline complete sentences; just underline enough to make sense when you review your markings. This technique works especially well for kinesthetics or tactile learners. If reading online, use the highlighter tool to mark the main points and then cut and paste the main points into a separate document.

  - Aim for marking or highlighting about 20 percent of the most important material. If you mark too much of your reading, it will be difficult to review the main points.

  - Read each paragraph first. Ask yourself, "What is the main point?" Highlight or mark the main point if it is important. Not every paragraph has a main point that needs to be marked.

  - Use other marks to help you organize what you have read. Write in numbers or letters and use different colors to help you organize ideas.

  - Most college texts have wide margins. Use these margins to write down questions, outlines, or key points to remember.

  - Learn to be brief, fast, and neat in your marking or highlighting.

  - If you are tempted to mark too much, use the double system of first underlining with a pencil as much as you want and then using a highlighter to pick out the most important 20 percent of the material in the chapter.

© 2014, SnowWhiteimages. Used under license with Shutterstock, Inc.

- Use different kinds of marks and symbols, such as the following:
  - Single or double underlines
  - Brackets around an important paragraph
  - Numbers or letters to organize points
  - Circles or squares to make important words stand out
  - An asterisk or star in the margin for a very important idea
  - A question mark next to something you do not understand
  - "DEF" in the margin to point out a definition
  - Use your imagination to come up with your own symbols
- Learn to recognize organizing patterns in your reading. These patterns will help you to pick out and mark the important ideas.
  - **The listing pattern.** Identify and mark the items in the list. Use numbers and letters to identify the parts of a list.
  - **The sequence pattern.** This pattern presents a list in a certain order. Note the items in the list and the order by using numbers or letters.
  - **The definition pattern.** Circle the word being defined. Underline the definition.
  - **The comparison/contrast pattern.** This pattern explains similarities or differences. Underline or mark these.
  - **The cause/effect pattern.** This pattern describes the reasons things happen. Underline or mark the cause and the effect.
- Quickly review the important points after you have marked each section. Quickly review again when you have finished the chapter. If you review within 20 minutes, the review will be faster and easier.

Reading for Speed and Comprehension

In *How to Read for Speed and Comprehension,* Gordon Wainwright suggests using different gears, or speeds, when reading for different purposes.[14] Understanding these four gears can be helpful for college students.

1. **Studying.** In this gear, the maximum reading speed is about 200 words per minute. It is used for material that is difficult or unfamiliar, such as a college textbook. For this material, a high quality of retention is required. It involves the steps described in SQ4R.

2. **Slow reading.** In this gear, reading speed ranges from 150 to 300 wpm. It is used for material that is fairly difficult when a good quality of retention is desired.

3. **Rapid reading.** In rapid reading, speeds range from 300 to 800 wpm. It is used for average or easy material. Use this gear for review of familiar material.

4. **Skimming.** Skimming is a type of very fast reading, done at 800 to 1000 wpm. With practice, it is possible to skim at 2000 to 3000 wpm. Using this technique, the eyes glide quickly down the page looking for specific information. Not every group of words or line is read. The eyes focus quickly on key ideas, bold headings, and titles. The purpose is to get a quick overview of the important ideas in the material.

Different reading speeds are used for different purposes. In college reading, it is more important to have good comprehension and retention than speed. However, we all live busy lives, and many college students today try to combine study, work, family, and social life. Learning to read faster is important to survival. You can learn to read faster by practicing skimming as a first step in reading. The next step is to slow down, look for the major points, and rehearse them so that they are stored in long-term memory. Using the SQ4R study technique described above will guide you through the process so that you can remember what you read.

Improving Reading

Test what you have learned by circling the letters of the correct answers to the following questions.

1. If you have read the chapter and can't remember what you have read,

   a. read the chapter again.
   b. remember to select important points and review them.
   c. the material is stored in long-term memory.

2. When you start reading a new textbook,

   a. begin with chapter one.
   b. focus on the details you will need to remember.
   c. skim over the text to get a general idea of what you will be reading.

3. The first step in reading a chapter in a college textbook is to

   a. survey and question.
   b. read and recite.
   c. review and reflect.

4. As you are reading each paragraph in a college textbook, it is most important to

   a. read quickly.
   b. identify the main point and recite it.
   c. focus on the details first.

5. When marking a college textbook, it is recommended to mark about

   a. 50%.
   b. 30%.
   c. 20%.

How did you do on the quiz? Check your answers: 1. b, 2. c, 3. a, 4. b, 5. c

What to Do If Your Reading Goes in One Ear and Out the Other

1. **Silence your inner critic.**
   If you have always told yourself that you are a poor reader or hate reading, these thoughts make it difficult to read. Think positively and tell yourself that with some effort, you can read and understand. Focus on what you can do, rather than what you can't do.

2. Look for the key ideas and underline them.

3. **Try visualization.**
   Make a mental picture or video with the material you are reading.

4. **Look for personal meaning.**
   Can you relate the material to your life in any way?

5. Do a quick scan of the material to find some major points and then reread the material closely.

6. Try talking to the text as you read it. Ask questions. Why is this important? Do you know anything about this? Do you agree or disagree? Do you think it is a good or bad idea? Can you use this information in the future? Can you find something interesting in the text? Challenge the material and think critically about it. Make humorous remarks. Imagine yourself in the situation. What would it be like and what would you do? You can write your comments in the text or do this silently in your head.

© 2014, wavebreakmedia. Used under license with Shutterstock, Inc.

Improving Reading Concentration

Hank Aaron said that what separates the superstar from the average ballplayer is that the superstar concentrates just a little longer. Athletes are very aware of the power of concentration in improving athletic performance. Coaches remind athletes to focus on the ball and to develop good powers of concentration and visualization. Being able to concentrate on your reading helps you to study more efficiently.

It is important to have a regular place for studying that has all the needed materials. You will need a table or desk with space for a computer, space for writing, and a comfortable chair. Keep a good supply of writing materials, computer supplies, and reference materials. To minimize fatigue and eyestrain, good lighting is essential. It is best to have an overhead light and a lamp. Place the lamp to your left if you are right-handed. In this way, you will not be writing in a shadow. Do the reverse if you are left-handed. If you have space, use two lamps with one placed on each side. Eliminate glare by using a lampshade. Study lamps often come with a deflector on the bottom of the lampshade that further eliminates glare. Lighter colors on your desk and wall also help to eliminate glare and fatigue.

In setting up your regular place for studying, keep in mind your environmental preferences as identified by your PEPS learning style inventory. Consider these factors:

- Do you need a quiet environment to focus on your studies?
- Do you prefer bright or dim light?
- Do you prefer a warm or cool environment?
- Do you prefer learning by yourself or with others?
- Do you study best in the morning or the afternoon?

Having and using a well-equipped and comfortable study place reduces external distractions. Internal distractions are many and varied and may be more difficult to manage. Internal distractions include being hungry, tired, or ill. It is a good idea to eat and be well rested before reading any course material. If you are ill, rest and get well. Study when you feel better. Many internal distractions are mental, such as personal problems, worrying about grades, lack of interest or motivation, frustration, or just daydreaming.

Here are some ideas for dealing with internal mental distractions while reading.

1. **Become an active reader.** Read to answer questions. Search for the main idea. Recite or re-say the main idea in your mind. Reflect and think critically about the material you are reading. Mark or highlight the text. Visualize what you are reading.

2. **Remind yourself of your purpose for reading.** Think of your future college and career goals.

> **Improving Reading Concentration**
>
> 1. Become an active reader
> 2. Remember your purpose
> 3. Use daydreaming to relax
> 5. Plan to deal with worry
> 6. Break tasks into small parts

3. **Give yourself permission to daydream.** If you like to daydream, give yourself permission to daydream as a break from your studies. Come back to your studies with a more relaxed attitude.

4. **Plan to deal with worry.** Worry is not a very good motivator and it interferes with memory. Take some positive action to deal with problems that cause you to worry. If you are worried about your grades, what can you do right now to improve your chances of making better grades? See a college counselor if worrying about personal problems interferes with studying.

5. **Break the task into small parts.** If the task seems overwhelming, break it into small parts and do the first part. If you have 400 pages to read in 10 days, read 40 pages each day. Make a schedule that allows time to read each day until you have accomplished your goal. Use distributed practice in your studies. Study for a short time each day rather than holding a marathon study session before the test.

Reading Strategies for Different Subjects

While the SQ4R technique is a good general strategy for reading textbook material, there are steps that you will need to add depending on the subject area you are studying.

Math

1. Make sure you have the proper prerequisites or background courses before you begin your math class.

2. When skimming a math book, keep in mind that many of the topics will be unfamiliar to you. You should be able to understand the first few pages and build your knowledge from there. If all the concepts are familiar to you, you may be taking a class that you do not need.

3. It is not enough to read and understand mathematical concepts. Make sure that you add practice to your study system when studying math. Practice gives you the self-confidence to relax when working with math.

4. It is helpful to read over your math book before you go to class so that you will know what areas need special attention.

5. Focus on understanding the math problems and concepts rather than on memorizing problems.

6. Do not get behind in your math studies. You need to understand the first step before you can go on to the next.

7. Ask for help as soon as you have difficulties.

Science

1. In science classes, the scientific method is used to describe the world. The scientific method relies on questioning, observing, hypothesizing, researching, and analyzing. You will learn about theories and scientific principles. Highlight or mark theories, names of scientists, definitions, concepts, and procedures.

2. Understand the scientific principles and use flash cards to remember details and formulas.

3. Study the charts, diagrams, tables, and graphs. Draw your own pictures and graphs to get a visual picture of the material.

4. Use lab time as an opportunity to practice the theories and principles that you have learned.

Social and Behavioral Sciences

1. Social and behavioral scientists focus on principles of behavior, theories, and research. Notice that there are different theories that explain the same phenomena. Highlight, underline, and summarize these theories in your own words.

2. When looking at the research, ask yourself what the point of the research was, who conducted the research, when the research was completed, what data was collected, and what conclusions were drawn.

3. Think of practical applications of theories.

4. Use flash cards to remember details.

Literature Courses

When taking a course in literature, you will be asked to understand, appreciate, interpret, evaluate, and write about the literature.

1. Underline the names of characters and write plot summaries.

2. Write notes about your evaluation of literary works.

3. Make flash cards to remember literary terms.

4. Write down important quotes or note page numbers on a separate piece of paper so that you don't have to go back and find them later when you are writing about a work.

Foreign Language Courses

Foreign language courses require memorization and practice.

1. Distribute the practice. Practice a small amount each day. It is not possible to learn everything at once.

2. Complete the exercises as a way to practice and remember.

3. Study out loud.

4. Practice speaking the language with others.

5. Use flash cards to remember vocabulary.

6. Make charts to practice verb conjugations.

7. Ask for help if you do not understand.

8. Learn to think in the foreign language. Translating from English causes confusion because the structures of languages are different.

> "Whatever the mind of man can conceive and believe, it can achieve."
> Napoleon Hill

KEYS TO SUCCESS

Positive Thinking

You can improve your memory and your reading (as well as your life) by using positive thinking. Positive thinking involves two aspects: thinking about yourself and thinking about the world around you. When you think positively about yourself, you develop confidence in your abilities and become more capable of whatever you are attempting to do. When you think positively about the world around you, you look for possibilities and find interest in what you are doing.

Golfer Arnold Palmer has won many trophies, but places high value on a plaque on his wall with a poem by C.W. Longenecker:

If you think you are beaten, you are.
If you think you dare not, you don't.
If you like to win but think you can't,
It's almost certain that you won't.

(continued)

Life's battles don't always go
To the stronger woman or man,
But sooner or later, those who win
Are those who think they can.[15]

Success in athletics, school, or any other endeavor begins with positive thinking. To remember anything, you first have to believe that you can remember. Trust in your abilities. Then apply memory techniques to help you to remember. If you think that you cannot remember, you will not even try. To be a good reader, you need to think that you can become a good reader and then work toward learning, applying, and practicing good reading techniques.

The second part of positive thinking involves thinking about the world around you. If you can convince yourself that the world and your college studies are full of interesting possibilities, you can start on a journey of adventure to discover new ideas. It is easier to remember and to read if you can find the subject interesting. If the topic is interesting, you will learn more about it. The more you learn about a topic, the more interesting it becomes, and you are well on your way in your journey of discovery. If you tell yourself that the task is boring, you will struggle and find the task difficult. You will also find it difficult to continue.

You can improve your reading through positive thinking. Read with the intent to remember and use reading techniques that work for you. We remember what interests us, and having a positive attitude helps us to find something interesting. To find something interesting, look for personal meaning. How can I use this information? Does it relate to something I know? Will this information be useful in my future career? Why is this information important? Write down your personal goals and remind yourself of your purpose for attending college. You are not just completing an assignment: you are on a path to discovery.

To be successful in college and to remember what you read, start with the belief that you can be successful. Anticipate that the journey will be interesting and full of possibilities. Enjoy the journey!

Journal Entry #5

How can you use positive thinking to improve memory, reading, and success in college? Use any of these questions to guide your thinking:

- How can you improve your memory or reading with positive thinking?
- How can I think positively about myself?
- How can I think positively about my college experience?
- What is the connection between belief and success?
- How can positive thinking make college more fun?

Improving Memory and Reading

Go to http://www.collegesuccess1.com/JournalEntries.htm for Word files of the Journal Entries

Success over the Internet

Visit the *College Success Website* at http://www.collegesuccess1.com/

The *College Success Website* is continually updated with new topics and links to the material presented in this chapter. Topics include:

- Memory techniques
- Reading strategies
- How to concentrate
- How to highlight a textbook
- Speed reading
- How to study science
- Study groups
- Examples of mnemonics

Contact your instructor if you need assistance in accessing the *College Success Website.*

Notes

1. G. A. Miller, "The Magical Number Seven, Plus or Minus Two: Some Limits on Our Capacity for Processing Information," *Psychological Review* 63 (March 1956): 81–97.

2. Colin Rose, *Accelerated Learning* (New York: Dell Publishing, 1985), 33–36.

3. Ibid., 50–51.

4. Walter Pauk, *How to Study in College* (Boston: Houghton Mifflin, 1989), 96–97.

5. Rose, *Accelerated Learning*, 34.

6. Adapted from Paul Chance, *Learning and Behavior* (Pacific Grove, CA: Brooks/Cole, 1979), 301.

7. Pauk, *How to Study in College,* 108.

8. Daniel Golden, "Building a Better Brain," *Life Magazine,* July 1994, 63–70.

9. Mary Carmichael, "Stronger, Faster, Smarter," *Newsweek,* March 26, 2007, 38–46.

10. Scott LaFee, "A Chronic Lack of Sleep Can Lead to the Big Sleep," *San Diego Union Tribune,* October 8, 1997.

11. Randy Blaun, "How to Eat Smart," *Psychology Today,* May/June 1996, 35.

12. Ibid.

13. Rose, *Accelerated Learning*, 51.

14. Gordon R. Wainwright, *How to Read for Speed and Comprehension* (NJ: Prentice-Hall, 1977), 100–101.

15. Rob Gilbert, ed., *Bits and Pieces* (Fairfield, NJ: The Economics Press, 1998), Vol. R, No. 40, p. 12.

CHAPTER 9

Test Taking

Learning Objectives

Read to answer these key questions:

- What are some test preparation techniques?

- How should I review the material?

- How can I predict the test questions?

- What are some emergency test preparation techniques?

- How can I deal with test anxiety?

- How can I study math and deal with math anxiety?

- What are some tips for taking math tests?

- What are some tips for taking objective tests?

- How can I write a good essay?

An important skill for survival in college is the ability to take tests. Passing tests is also important in careers that require licenses, certificates, or continuing education. Knowing how to prepare for and take tests with confidence will help you to accomplish your educational and career goals while maintaining your good mental health. Once you have learned some basic test-taking and relaxation techniques, you can turn your test anxiety into motivation and good test results.

Preparing for Tests

Attend Every Class

The most significant factor in poor performance in college is lack of attendance. Students who attend the lectures and complete their assignments have the best chance for success in college. Attending the lectures helps you to be involved in learning and to know what to expect on the test. College professors know that students who miss three classes in a row are not likely to return, and some professors drop students after three absences. After three absences, students can fall behind in their schoolwork and become overwhelmed with makeup work.

© 2014, Robert Kneschke. Used under license with Shutterstock, Inc.

Distribute the Practice

The key to successful test preparation is to begin early and do a little at a time. Test preparation begins the first day of class. During the first class, the professor gives an overview of the course content, requirements, tests, and grading. These items are described in writing in the class calendar and syllabus. It is very important to attend the first class to obtain this essential information. If you have to miss the first class, make sure to ask the professor for the syllabus and calendar and read it carefully.

Early test preparation helps you to take advantage of the powerful memory technique called distributed practice. In distributed practice, the material learned is broken up into small parts and reviewed frequently. Using this method can enable you to learn a large quantity of material without becoming overwhelmed. Here are some examples of using distributed practice:

- If you have a test on 50 Spanish vocabulary words in two weeks, don't wait until the day before the test to try to learn all 50 words. Waiting until the day before the test will result in difficulty remembering the words, test anxiety, and a dislike of studying Spanish. If you have 50 Spanish vocabulary words to learn in two weeks, learn five words each day and quickly review the words you learned previously. For example, on Monday you would learn five words, and on Tuesday, you would learn five new words and review the ones learned on Monday. Give yourself the weekends off as a reward for planning ahead.

- If you have to read a history book with 400 pages, divide that number by the number of days in the semester or quarter. If there are 80 days in the semester, you will only have to read five pages per day or 10 pages every other day. This is a much easier and more efficient way to master a long assignment.

- Don't wait until the last minute to study for a midterm or final exam. Keep up with the class each week. As you read each chapter, quickly review a previous chapter. In this way you can comfortably master the material. Just before a major test, you can review the material that you already know and feel confident about your ability to get a good grade on the test.

Schedule a Time and a Place for Studying

To take advantage of distributed practice, you will need to develop a study schedule. Write down your work time and school time and other scheduled activities. Identify times that can be used for studying each day. Get in the habit of using these available times for studying each week. As a general rule, you need two hours of study time for each hour spent in a college classroom. If you cannot find enough time for studying, consider either reducing your course load or reducing work hours.

Use your study schedule or calendar to note the due dates of major projects and all test dates. Schedule enough time to complete projects and to finish major reviews for exams. Look at each due date and write in reminders to begin work or review well in advance of the due date. Give yourself plenty of time to meet the deadlines. It seems that around exam time, students are often ill or have problems that prevent them from being successful. Having some extra time scheduled will help you to cope with the many unexpected events that happen in everyday life.

Try to schedule your study sessions during your prime time, when you are awake and refreshed. For many people, one hour of study during the daylight hours is worth one and a half hours at night. Trying to study late at night may not be the best idea, because it is difficult to motivate yourself to study when you are tired. Save the time at the end of the day for relaxing or doing routine chores.

Find a place to study. This can be an area of your home where you have a desk, computer, and all the necessary supplies for studying. As a general rule, do not study at the kitchen table, in front of the television, or in your bed. These places provide powerful cues for eating, watching television, or sleeping instead of studying. If you cannot find an appropriate place at home, use the college library as a place to study. The library is usually quiet and others are studying, so there are not too many distractions.

© 2014, Alexander Raths. Used under license with Shutterstock, Inc.

Review Tools
• Flash cards
• Summary sheets
• Mind maps
• Study groups

Test Review Tools

There are a variety of tools you can use to review for tests. Choose the tools according to your learning style and what works for you. Learning styles include visual, auditory, kinesthetic, and tactile modes of learning. **Visual learners** find it easy to make mental pictures of the material to be learned. **Auditory learners** prefer listening and reciting material out loud. **Kinesthetic learners** benefit from moving around or acting out material to be learned. **Tactile learners** benefit from physical activities such as writing down items to be remembered.

- **Flash cards.** Flash cards are an effective way to learn facts and details for objective tests such as true-false, multiple-choice, matching, and fill-in-the-blank. For example, if you have 100 vocabulary words to learn in biology, put each word on one side of a card and the definition on the other side. First, look at each definition and see if you can recall the word. If you are a visual learner, look at the word and see if you can recall the definition. If you are an auditory learner, say the words and definitions. If you are a tactile or kinesthetic learner, carry the cards with you and briefly look at them as you are going about your daily activities. Make a game of studying by sorting the cards into stacks of information you know and information you still have to practice. Work with flash cards frequently and review them quickly. Don't worry about learning all the items at once. Each day that you practice, you will recall the items more easily. Check http://www.collegesuccess1.com/Links6Tests.htm for online tools for making flash cards.

- **Summary sheets.** Summary sheets are used to record the key ideas from your lecture notes or textbook. It is important to be selective; write only the most important ideas on the summary sheets. At the end of the semester, you might have approximately 10 pages of summary sheets from the text and 10 pages from your notes. If you are a kinesthetic learner, writing down the items you wish to remember will help you learn them. If you are a visual learner, the summary sheet becomes a picture of the ideas you need to remember. If you are an auditory learner, recite aloud the important ideas on the summary sheets.

- **Mind maps.** A mind map is a visual picture of the items you wish to remember. Start in the center of the page with a key idea and then surround it with related topics. You can use drawings, lines, circles, or colors to link and group the ideas. A mind map will help you to learn material in an organized way that will be useful when writing essay exams.

- **Study groups.** A study group is helpful in motivating yourself to learn through discussions of the material with other people. For the study group, select three to seven people who are motivated to be successful in class and can coordinate schedules. Study groups are often used in math and science classes. Groups of students work problems together and help each other understand the material. The study group is also useful in studying for exams. Give each member a part of the material to be studied. Have each person predict test questions and quiz the study group. Teaching the material to the study group can be the best way to learn it.

Reviewing Effectively

Begin your review early and break it into small parts. Remember that repetition is one of the effective ways to store information in long-term memory. Here are some types of review that help you to store information in long-term memory:

- **Immediate review.** This type of review is fast and powerful and helps to minimize forgetting. It is the first step in storing information in long-term memory. Begin the process by turning each bold-faced heading in the text into a question. Read each section to answer the question you have asked. Read your college texts with a highlighter in hand so that you can mark the key ideas for review. Some students use

© 2014, wavebreakmedia. Used under license with Shutterstock, Inc.

a variety of colors to distinguish main ideas, supporting points, and key examples, for instance. When you are finished using the highlighter, quickly review the items you have marked. As you complete each section, quickly review the main points. When you finish the chapter, immediately review the key points in the entire chapter again. As soon as you finish taking your lecture notes, take a few minutes to review them. To be most effective, immediate review needs to occur as soon as possible or at least within the first 20 minutes of learning something.

- **Intermediate review.** After you have finished reading and reviewing a new chapter in your textbook, spend a few minutes reviewing an earlier one. This step will help you to master the material and to recall it easily for the midterm or final exam. Another way to do intermediate review is to set up time periodically in your study schedule for reviewing previous chapters and classroom notes. Doing intermediate reviews helps to access the materials you have stored in long-term memory.

- **Final review.** Before a major exam, organize your notes, materials, and assignments. Estimate how long it will take you to review the material. Break the material into manageable chunks. For an essay exam, use mind maps or summary sheets to write down the main points that you need to remember and recite these ideas frequently. For objective tests, use flash cards or lists to remember details and concepts that you expect to be on the test. Here is a sample seven-day plan for reviewing 10 chapters for a final exam:

Day 1 Gather materials and study Chapters 1 and 2 by writing key points on summary sheets or mind maps. Make flash cards of details you need to remember. Review and highlight lecture notes and handouts on these chapters.

Day 2 Review Chapters 1 and 2. Study Chapters 3 and 4 and the corresponding lecture notes.

Day 3 Review Chapters 1 to 4. Study Chapters 5 and 6 and the corresponding lecture notes.

Day 4 Review Chapters 1 to 6. Study Chapters 7 and 8 along with the corresponding lecture notes.

Day 5 Review Chapters 1 to 8. Study Chapters 9 and 10 along with corresponding lecture notes.

Day 6 Review notes, summary sheets, mind maps, and flash cards for Chapters 1 to 10. Relax and get a good night's sleep. You are well prepared.

Day 7 Do one last quick review of Chapters 1 to 10 and walk into the test with the confidence that you will be successful on the exam.

Predicting Test Questions

There are many ways to predict the questions that will be on the test. Here are some ideas that might be helpful:

- Look for clues from the professor about what will be on the test. Many times professors put information about the tests on the course syllabus. During lectures, they often give hints about what will be important to know. If a professor repeats something more than once, make note of it as a possible test question. Anything written on the board is likely to be on the test. Sometimes the professor will even say, "This will be on the test." Write these important points in your notes and review them.
- College textbooks are usually written in short sections with bold headings. Turn each bold-faced heading into a question and read to answer the question. Understand and review the main idea in each section. The test questions will generally address the main ideas in the text.
- Don't forget to study and review the handouts that the professor distributes to the class. If the professor has taken the time and effort to provide extra material, it is probably important and may be on the test.
- Form a study group and divide up the material to be reviewed. Have each member of the group write some test questions based on the important points in each main section of the text. When the study group meets, take turns asking likely test questions and providing the answers.
- When the professor announces the test, make sure to ask what material is to be covered on the test and what kind of test it is. If necessary, ask the professor which concepts are most important. Know what kinds of test questions will be asked (essay, true-false, multiple-choice, matching, or short-answer). Some professors may provide sample exams or math problems.
- Use the first test to understand what is expected and how to study for future tests.

"The will to win is not nearly as important as the will to prepare to win."
Bobby Knight

Journal Entry # 1

Write one paragraph about the ideal way to prepare for a major exam such as a midterm or final. Consider these factors while thinking about your answer: attendance, distribute the practice, time management, review tools, predicting test questions and the most efficient way to review.

Preparing for an Open-Book Test

In college, you may have some open-book tests. Open-book tests are often used in very technical subjects where specific material from the book is needed to answer questions. For example, in an engineering course, tables and formulas in the book may be needed to solve engineering problems on an exam. To study for an open-book test, focus on understanding the material and being able to locate key information for the exam. Consider making index tabs for your book so that you can locate needed information quickly. Be sure to bring your book, calculator, and other needed material to the exam.

Emergency Procedures

If it is a day or two before the test and you have not followed the above procedures, it is time for the college practice known as "cramming." There are two main problems that result from this practice. First, you cannot take advantage of distributed practice, so it

© 2014, Mike Elliott. Used under license with Shutterstock, Inc.

will be difficult to remember large amounts of material. Second, it is not fun, and if done often will result in anxiety and a dislike of education. Because of these problems, some students who rely on cramming wrongly conclude that they are not capable of finishing their education.

If you must cram for a test, here are some emergency procedures that may be helpful in getting the best grade possible under difficult circumstances:

- When cramming, *it is most important to be selective.* Try to identify the main points and recite and review them.
- Focus on reviewing and reciting the lecture notes. In this way, you will cover the main ideas the professor thinks are important.
- If you have not read the text, skim and search each chapter looking for the main points. Highlight and review these main points. Read the chapter summaries. In a math textbook, practice sample problems.
- Make summary sheets containing the main ideas from the notes and the text. Recite and review the summary sheets.
- For objective tests, focus on learning new terms and vocabulary related to the subject. These terms are likely to be on the test. Flash cards are helpful.
- For essay tests, develop an outline of major topics and review the outline so you can write an essay.
- Get enough rest. Staying up all night to review for the test can result in confusion, reduced mental ability, and test anxiety.
- Hope for the best.
- Plan ahead next time so that you can get a better grade.

If you have very little time to review for a test, you will probably experience information overload. One strategy for dealing with this problem is based on the work of George Miller of Harvard University. He found that the optimum number of chunks of information we can remember is seven plus or minus two (or five to nine chunks of information).[1] This is also known as the Magical Number Seven Theory. For this last-minute review technique, start with five sheets of paper. Next, identify five key concepts that are likely to be on the test. Write one concept on the top of each sheet of paper. Then check your notes and text to write an explanation, definition, or answer for each of these topics. If you have more time, find two to four more concepts and research them, writing the information on additional sheets. You should have no more than nine sheets of paper. Arrange the sheets in order of importance. Review and recite the key ideas on these sheets. Get a regular night's sleep before the test and do some relaxation exercises right before the test.

© 2014, YanLev. Used under license with Shutterstock, Inc.

Ideas That Don't Work

Some students do poorly on tests for the following reasons.

- Attending a party or social event the evening before a major test rather than doing the final review will adversely affect your test score. Study in advance and reward yourself with the party after the test.
- Skipping the major review before the test may cause you to forget some important material.
- Taking drugs or drinking alcohol before a test may give you the impression that you are relaxed and doing well on the test, but the results are disastrous to your success on the exam and your good health.
- Not knowing the date of the test can cause you to get a low grade because you are not prepared.
- Not checking or knowing about the final exam schedule can cause you to miss the final.
- Missing the final exam can result in a lower grade or failing the class.
- Arriving late for the exam puts you at a disadvantage if you don't have time to finish or have to rush through the test.
- Deciding not to buy or read the textbook will cause low performance or failure.
- Having a fight, disagreement, or argument with parents, friends, or significant others before the test will make it difficult to focus on the exam.
- Sacrificing sleep, exercise, or food to prepare for the exam makes it difficult to do your best.
- Cheating on an exam can cause embarrassment, a lower grade, or failure. It can even lead to expulsion from college.
- Missing the exam because you are not prepared and asking the professor to let you make up the exam later is a tactic that many students try. Most professors will not permit you to take an exam late.
- Inventing a creative excuse for missing an exam is so common that some professors have a collection of these stories that they share with colleagues. Creative excuses don't work with most professors.
- Arriving at the exam without the proper materials such as a pencil, Scantron, paper, calculator, or book (for open-book exams) can cause you to miss the exam or start the exam late.

"Failure is simply the opportunity to begin again more intelligently."
Henry Ford

Test Preparation

Test what you have learned by selecting the correct answers to the following questions.

1. In test preparation, it is important to use this memory technique:

   a. Distribute the practice.
   b. Read every chapter just before the test.
   c. Do most of the review right before the test to minimize forgetting.

2. Schedule your study sessions

   a. late at night.
   b. during your prime time, which is generally earlier in the day.
   c. after all other activities are done.

3. Effective tools to learn facts and details are

   a. mind maps.
   b. summary sheets.
   c. flash cards.

4. The best way to review is

   a. to start early and break it into small parts.
   b. immediately before the test.
   c. in large blocks of time.

5. If you have to cram for an exam, it is most important to

   a. stay up all night studying for the exam
   b. focus on the lecture notes and forget about reading the text
   c. be selective and review and recite the main points

How did you do on the quiz? Check your answers: 1. a, 2. b, 3. c, 4. a, 5. c

Ten Rules for Success

Here are 10 rules for success on any test. Are there any new ideas you can put into practice?

1. **Make sure to set your alarm,** and consider having a backup in case your alarm doesn't go off. Set a second alarm or have someone call to make sure you are awake on time.

2. **Arrive a little early for your exam.** If you are taking a standardized test like the Scholastic Aptitude Test (SAT) or Graduate Record Exam (GRE), familiarize yourself with the location of the exam. If you arrive early, you can take a quick walk around the building to relax or spend a few minutes doing a review so that your brain will be tuned up and ready.

3. **Eat a light breakfast including some carbohydrates and protein.** Be careful about eating sugar and caffeine before a test, because this can contribute to greater anxiety and low blood sugar by the time you take the test. The worst breakfast would be something like a doughnut and coffee or a soda and candy bar. Examples of good breakfasts are eggs, toast, and juice or cereal with milk and fruit.

4. **Think positively about the exam.** Tell yourself that you are well prepared and the exam is an opportunity to show what you know.

5. **Make sure you have the proper materials:** Scantrons, paper, pencil or pen, calculator, books and notes (for open-book exams).

6. **Manage your time.** Know how long you have for the test and then scan the test to make a time management plan. For example, if you have one hour and there are 50 objective questions, you have about a minute for each question. Halfway through the time, you should have completed 25 questions. If there are three essay questions in an hour, you have less than 20 minutes for each question. Save some time to look over the test and make corrections.

7. **Neatness is important.** If your paper looks neat, the professor is more likely to have a positive attitude about the paper before it is even read. If the paper is hard to read, the professor will start reading your paper with a negative attitude, possibly resulting in a lower grade.

8. **Read the test directions carefully.** On essay exams, it is common for the professor to give you a choice of questions to answer. If you do not read the directions, you may try to answer all of the questions and then run out of time or give incomplete answers to them.

9. **If you get stuck on a difficult question, don't worry about it.** Just mark it and find an easier question. You may find clues on the rest of the test that will aid your recall, or you may be more relaxed later on and think of the answer.

10. **Be careful not to give any impression that you might be cheating.** Keep your eyes on your own paper. If you have memory aids or outlines memorized, write them directly on the test paper rather than a separate sheet so that you are not suspected of using cheat notes.

Journal Entry #2

Write one paragraph about the most common mistakes students make while getting ready for an exam.

Dealing with Test Anxiety

Some anxiety is a good thing. It can provide motivation to study and prepare for exams. However, it is common for college students to suffer from test anxiety. Too much anxiety can lower your performance on tests. Some symptoms of test anxiety include:

- Fear of failing a test even though you are well prepared
- Physical symptoms such as perspiring, increased heart rate, shortness of breath, upset stomach, tense muscles, or headache
- Negative thoughts about the test and your grade
- Mental blocking of material you know and remembering it once you leave the exam

You can minimize your test anxiety by being well prepared and by applying the memory strategies described in earlier chapters. Prepare for your exams by attending every class, keeping up with your reading assignments, and reviewing during the semester. These steps will help increase your self-confidence and reduce anxiety. Apply the principles of memory improvement to your studying. As you are reading, find the important points and highlight them. Review these points so that they are stored in your long-term memory. Use distributed practice and spread out learning over time rather than trying to learn it all at once. Visualize and organize what you need to remember. Trust in your abilities and intend to remember what you have studied.

If you find that you are anxious, here are some ideas you can try to cope with the anxiety. Experiment with these techniques to see which ones work best for you.

© 2014, Stuart Miles. Used under license with Shutterstock, Inc.

- **Do some physical exercise.** Physical exercise helps to use up stress hormones. Make physical activity a part of your daily routine. Arrive for your test a little early and walk briskly around campus for about 20 minutes. This exercise will help you to feel relaxed and energized.

- **Get a good night's sleep before the test.** Lack of sleep can interfere with memory and cause irritability, anxiety, and confusion.

- **Take deep breaths.** Immediately before the test, take a few deep breaths; hold them for three to five seconds and let them out slowly. These deep breaths will help you to relax and keep a sufficient supply of oxygen in your blood. Oxygen is needed for proper brain function.

- **Visualize and rehearse your success.** Begin by getting as comfortable and relaxed as possible in your favorite chair or lying down in bed. Visualize yourself walking into the exam room. Try to imagine the room in as much detail as possible. If possible, visit the exam room before the test so that you can get a good picture of it. See yourself taking the exam calmly and confidently. You know most of the answers. If you find a question you do not know, see yourself circling it and coming back to it later. Imagine that you find a clue on the test that triggers your recall of the answers to the difficult questions. Picture yourself handing in the exam with a good feeling about doing well on the test. Then imagine you are getting the test back and you get a good grade on the test. You congratulate yourself for a job well done. If you suffer from test anxiety, you may need to rehearse this scene several times. When you enter the exam room, the visual picture that you have rehearsed will help you to relax.

- **Acknowledge your anxiety.** The first step in dealing with anxiety is to admit that you are anxious rather than trying to fight it or deny it. Say to yourself, "I am feeling anxious." Take a few deep breaths and then focus your attention on the test.

- **Do the easy questions first and mark the ones that may be difficult.** This will help you to relax. Once you are relaxed, the difficult questions become more manageable.

Tips to Minimize Anxiety

- Exercise
- Sleep
- Take deep breaths
- Visualize success
- Acknowledge anxiety
- Easy questions first
- Yell, "Stop!"
- Daydream
- Practice perspective
- Give yourself time
- Get help

- **Yell, "Stop!"** Negative and frightening thoughts can cause anxiety. Here are some examples of negative thoughts:

> I'm going to fail this test.
>
> I don't know the answer to number 10!
>
> I never do well on tests.
>
> Essays! I have a hard time with those.
>
> I'll never make it through college.
>
> I was never any good in math!

These types of thoughts don't help you do better on the test, so stop saying them. They cause you to become anxious and to freeze up during the test. If you find yourself with similar thoughts, yell, "Stop!" to yourself. This will cause you to interrupt your train of thought so that you can think about the task at hand rather than becoming more anxious. Replace negative thoughts with more positive ones such as these:

> I'm doing the best I can.
>
> I am well prepared and know most of the answers.
>
> I don't know the answer to number 10, so I'll just circle it and come back to it later.
>
> I'll make an outline in the margin for the essay question.
>
> College is difficult, but I'll make it!
>
> Math is a challenge, but I can do it!

- **Daydream.** Think about being in your favorite place. Take time to think about the details. Allow yourself to be there for a while until you feel more relaxed.
- **Practice perspective.** Remember, one poor grade is not the end of the world. It does not define who you are. If you do not do well, think about how you can improve your preparation and performance the next time.
- **Give yourself time.** Test anxiety develops over a period of time. It will take some time to get over it. Learn the best ways to prepare for the exam and practice saying positive thoughts to yourself.
- **Get help.** If these techniques do not work for you, seek help from your college health or counseling center.

Journal Entry #3

You have a friend who prepares for exams, but suffers from test anxiety. Review the section on test anxiety and write a one paragraph e-mail to your friend with some ideas on dealing with test anxiety. Consider both physical and mental preparation as well as some relaxation techniques that can be helpful.

I am taking a college success course and the book has some ideas on dealing with test anxiety. The book suggests . . .

Studying Math and Dealing with Math Anxiety

When I mention to students that they need to take math, I often see a look of fear on their faces. Everyone needs to take math. Most colleges require math classes and demonstrated math competency in order to graduate. Math is essential for many high-paying technical and professional occupations. Being afraid of math and avoiding it will limit your career possibilities.

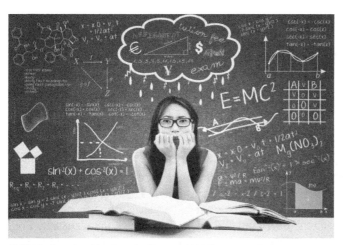

© 2014, Creativa. Used under license with Shutterstock, Inc.

Begin your study of math with some positive thinking. You may have had difficulty with math in the past, but with a positive attitude and the proper study techniques, you can meet the challenge. The first step to success in math is to put in the effort required. Attend class, do your homework, and get help if needed. If you put in the effort and hard work, you will gain experience in math. If you gain experience with math, you will become more confident in your ability to do math. If you have confidence, you will gain satisfaction in doing math. You may even learn to like it! If you like the subject, you can gain competence. The process looks like this:

$$\text{Hard work} \rightarrow \text{Experience} \rightarrow \text{Confidence} \rightarrow \text{Satisfaction} \rightarrow \text{Competence}$$

Although you may have had difficulty with math in the past, you can become successful by following these steps. Your reward is self-satisfaction and increased opportunity in technical and professional careers.

- **Don't delay taking math.** You may need a sequence of math courses in order to graduate. If you delay taking math, you may delay your graduation from college.

- **Think positively about your ability to succeed in math.** You may have had difficulties in math classes before. Think about your educational history. Can you recall having difficulties in the past? These past difficulties cause a fear of math. You may have a picture of failure in your mind. You need to replace it with a picture of success. Acknowledge that you are afraid because of past experiences with math. Acknowledge that the future can be different, and spend the time and effort needed to be successful.

- **Start at the beginning.** Assess where your math skills are at the present time. If you have not taken math classes for some time, you may need to review. Take the college math assessment test, read the college catalog, and speak to a counselor about where you should start.

- **Ask questions in class.** Students are often afraid to ask questions in math classes because they are afraid other students will think they are not smart. It is more likely that other students are wishing that someone would ask a question because they don't understand either. Ask your questions early, as soon as you find something you don't understand.

- **Get help early.** If you are having difficulties, get tutoring right away. If you are confused, you will not understand the next step either.

- **Don't miss your math classes.** It is difficult to catch up if you miss class.

- **Do your math homework regularly.** Math skills depend on practice. Make sure you understand the examples given in the textbook. Practice as many questions as you can until you feel comfortable solving the problems. Assign yourself extra problems if necessary. It is difficult to cram for a math test.

- **Use a study group.** Work with groups of students to study math. Get the phone numbers of other students in the study group. If you do not understand, other students may be able to help.
- **Study for the math test.** Start early so that you will have time to go over each topic in the book and practice doing problems from each section. Check your work against the solutions given in the text.
- **Do the easiest problems first on a math test.** In this way, you can gain confidence and relax. Then focus on the problems that are worth the most points. Don't be distracted by problems that you do not know and that use up test time.
- **Solve problems systematically.** First make sure you understand the problem. Write out the given facts and equations you may need to use before working out the problem. Then make a plan for solving it. What have you learned in class that will help you to solve the problem? Carry out the plan. Then check your answer. Does the answer make sense? Check your calculator work over again at the end of the test.
- **Check for careless errors.** Go over your math test to see if you have made any careless errors. Forgetting a plus or minus sign or adding or subtracting incorrectly can have a big impact on your grade. Save at least five minutes to read over your test.
- **Get enough sleep before the math test.** If you are mentally sharp, the test will be easier.

Math Tests

Taking a math test involves some different strategies:

1. Some instructors will let you write down formulas on an index card or a small crib sheet. Prepare these notes carefully, writing down the key formulas you will need for the exam.

2. If you have to memorize formulas, review them right before the test and write them on the test immediately.

3. As a first step, quickly look over the test. Find a problem you can solve easily and do this problem first.

4. Manage your time. Find out how many problems you have to solve and how much time is available for each problem. Do the problems worth the most points first. Stay on track.

5. Try this four-step process:
   a. Understand the problem.
   b. Devise a plan to solve the problem. Write down the information that is given. Think about the skills and techniques you have learned in class that can help you to solve the problem.
   c. Carry out the plan.
   d. Look back to see if your answer is reasonable.

6. If you cannot work a problem, go on to the next question. Come back later when you are more relaxed. If you spend too much time on a problem you cannot work, you will not have time for the problems that you can work.

7. Even if you think an answer is wrong, turn it in. You may get partial credit.

8. Show all the steps in your work and label your answer. On long and complex problems, it is helpful to use short sentences to explain your steps in solving the problem.

9. Estimate your answer and see if it makes sense or is logical.

"Do not worry about your difficulties in mathematics. I can assure you mine are still greater."

Albert Einstein

Tips for Avoiding Common Math Errors[2]

- Any quantity multiplied by zero is zero
- Any quantity raised to the zero power is one
- Any fraction multiplied by its reciprocal is one
- Only like algebraic terms may be combined
- Break down to the simplest form in algebra
- In algebra, multiply and divide before adding and subtracting
- If an algebraic expression has more than one set of parentheses, get rid of the inner parenthesis first and work outward
- Any operation performed on one side of the equation must be performed on the other side

10. Write your numbers as neatly as possible to avoid mistakes and to make them legible for the professor.

11. Leave space between your answers in case you need to add to them later.

12. If you have time left over at the end, recheck your answers.

© 2014, Ivelin Radkov. Used under license with Shutterstock, Inc.

Taking Tests

True-False Tests

Many professors use objective tests such as true-false and multiple-choice because they are easy to grade. The best way to prepare for these types of tests is to study the key points in the textbook, lecture notes, and class handouts. In the textbook, take each bold-faced topic and turn it into a question. If you can answer the questions, you will be successful on objective tests.

In addition to studying for the test, it is helpful to understand some basic test-taking techniques that will help you to determine the correct answer. Many of the techniques used to determine whether a statement is true or false can also be used to eliminate wrong answers on multiple-choice tests.

To develop strategies for success on true-false exams, it is important to understand how a teacher writes the questions. For a true-false question, the teacher identifies a key point in the book or lecture notes. Then he or she has two choices. For a true statement, the key idea is often written exactly as it appears in the text or notes. For a false statement, the key idea is changed in some way to make it false.

One way to make a statement false is to add a **qualifier** to the statement. Qualifiers that are **absolute** or extreme are generally, but not always, found in false statements. **General** qualifiers are often found in true statements.

Absolute Qualifiers (false)		General Qualifiers (true)	
all	none	usually	frequently
always	never	often	sometimes
only	nobody	some	seldom
invariably	no one	many	much
best	worst	most	generally
everybody	everyone	few	ordinarily
absolutely	absolutely not	probably	a majority
certainly	certainly not	might	a few
no	every	may	apt to

Seven Tips for Success on True-False Tests

1. **Identify the key ideas in the text and class notes and review them.**

2. **Accept the question at face value.** Don't overanalyze or create wild exceptions in your mind.

3. **If you don't know the answer, assume it is true.** There are generally more true statements because we all like the truth (especially teachers) and true questions are easier to write. However, some teachers like to test students by writing all false statements.

4. **If any part of a true-false statement is false, the whole statement is false.** Carefully read each statement to determine if any part of it is false. Students sometimes assume a statement is true if most of it is true. This is not correct.

   Example: Good relaxation techniques include deep breathing, exercise, and visualizing your failure on the exam.

   This statement is false because visualizing failure can lead to test anxiety and failure.

5. **Notice any absolute or general qualifiers.** Remember that absolute qualifiers often make a statement false. General qualifiers often make a statement true.

   Example: The student who crams **always** does poorly on the exam.

   This statement is false because **some** students are successful at cramming for an exam.

   Be careful with this rule. Sometimes the answer can be absolute.

   Example: The grade point average is always calculated by dividing the number of units attempted by the grade points. (true)

6. **Notice words such as *because, therefore, consequently,* and *as a result.*** They may connect two things that are true but result in a false statement.

   Example: Martha does not have test anxiety. (true)

   Martha makes good grades on tests. (true)
   Martha does not have test anxiety and therefore makes good grades on tests.

   This statement is false because she also has to prepare for the exam. Not having test anxiety could even cause her to lack motivation to study and do poorly on a test.

7. **Watch for double negatives.** Two nos equal a yes. If you see two negatives in a sentence, read them as a positive. Be careful with negative prefixes such as un-, im-, mis-, dis-, il-, and ir-. For example, the phrase "not uncommon" actually means "common." Notice that the word "not" and the prefix "un-" when used together form a double negative that equals a positive.

   Example: Not being **un**prepared for the test is the best way to earn good grades.

   The above sentence is confusing. To make it clearer, change both of the negatives into a positive:

   Being prepared for the test is the best way to earn good grades.

Multiple-Choice Tests

College exams often include multiple-choice questions rather than true-false questions because it is more difficult to guess the correct answer. On a true-false question, the student has a 50 percent chance of guessing the correct answer, while on a multiple-choice question, the odds of guessing correctly are only 25 percent. You can think of a multiple-choice question as four true-false questions in a row. First, read the question and try to answer it without looking at the options. This will help you to focus on the question and determine the correct answer. Look at each option and determine if it is true or false. Then choose the **best** answer.

To choose the best option, it is helpful to understand how a teacher writes a multiple-choice question. Here are the steps a teacher uses to write a multiple-choice exam:

© 2014, WilleeCole. Used under license with Shutterstock, Inc.

1. Find an important point in the lecture notes, text, or handouts.

2. Write a **stem**. This is an incomplete statement or a question.

3. Write the correct answer as one of the options.

4. Write three or four plausible but incorrect options that might be chosen by students who are not prepared. These incorrect options are called **decoys**. Here is an example:

   Stem: If you are anxious about taking math tests, it is helpful to:

   a. Stay up the night before the test to review thoroughly. (**decoy**)

   b. Visualize yourself doing poorly on the test so you will be motivated to study. (**decoy**)

   c. Practice math problems regularly during the semester. (**correct answer**)

   d. Do the most difficult problem first. (**decoy**)

Learn to Recognize a Decoy
A Decoy is an Incorrect Answer

1. Decoys are all true or all false
2. Decoys contain absolute qualifiers
3. Decoys can be partly true
4. Decoys have conjunctions that make them false
5. Decoys have double negatives
6. Decoys can be foolish
7. Decoys are high or low numbers
8. Decoys can look like the correct answer
9. Decoys are often the shorter answer
10. Decoys may be grammatically incorrect
11. Decoys may be an opposite
12. Decoys may be the same as another answer

Being well prepared for the test is the most reliable way of recognizing the correct answer and the decoys. In addition, becoming familiar with the following rules for recognizing decoys can help you determine the correct answer or improve your chances of guessing the correct answer on an exam. If you can at least eliminate some of the wrong answers, you will improve your odds of selecting the correct answer.

Rules for recognizing a decoy or wrong answer:

1. **The decoys are all true or all false statements.** Read each option and determine which options are false and which statements are true. This will help you to find the correct answer.

   Example: To manage your time on a test, it is important to:
   a. Skip the directions and work as quickly as possible. (false)
   b. Skim through the test to see how much time you have for each section. (true)
   c. Do the most difficult sections first. (false)
   d. Just start writing as quickly as possible. (false)

   Read the stem carefully, because sometimes you will be asked to identify one false statement in a group of true statements.

2. **The decoy may contain an absolute qualifier.** The option with the absolute qualifier (e.g., always, only, every) is likely to be false because few things in life are absolute. There are generally exceptions to any rule.

3. **The decoy can be partly true.** However, if one part of the statement is false, the whole statement is false and an incorrect answer.

   Example: Memory techniques include visualization, organization, and telling yourself you won't remember.

   In this example, the first two techniques are true and the last part is false, which makes the whole statement false.

4. **The decoy may have a conjunction or other linking words that makes it false.** Watch for words and phrases such as *because, consequently, therefore,* and *as a result.*

5. **The decoy may have a double negative.** Having two negatives in a sentence makes it difficult to understand. Read the two negatives as a positive.

6. **The decoy may be a foolish option.** Writing multiple decoys is difficult, so test writers sometimes throw in foolish or humorous options.

   Example: In a multiple-choice test, a decoy is:
   a. a type of duck.
   b. an incorrect answer.

c. a type of missile used in air defense.

d. a type of fish.

The correct answer is b. Sometimes students are tempted by the foolish answers.

7. **The decoy is often a low or high number.** If you have a multiple-choice question with numbers, and you are not sure of the correct answer, choose the number in the middle range. It is often more likely to be correct.

Example: George Miller of Harvard University theorized that the optimum number of chunks of material that we can remember is:

a. 1–2 (This low number is a decoy.)

b. 5–9 (This is the correct answer.)

c. 10–12 (This is close to the correct answer.)

d. 20–25 (This high number is a decoy.)

There is an exception to this rule when the number is much higher or lower than the average person thinks is possible.

8. **The decoy may look like the correct answer.** When two options look alike, one is incorrect and the other may be the correct answer. Test writers often use words that look alike as decoys.

Example: In false statements, the qualifier is often:

a. absolute.

b. resolute.

c. general.

d. exaggerated.

The correct answer is a. Answer b is an incorrect look-alike option.

9. **Decoys are often shorter than the correct answer.** Longer answers are more likely to be correct because they are more complete. Avoid choosing the first answer that seems to be correct. There may be a better and more complete answer.

Example: Good test preparation involves:

a. doing the proper review for the test.

b. good time management.

c. a positive attitude.

d. having good attendance, studying and reviewing regularly, being able to deal with test anxiety, and having a positive mental attitude.

Option d is correct because it is the most complete and thus the best answer.

10. **Decoys may be grammatically incorrect.** The correct answer will fit the grammar of the stem. A stem ending with "a" will match an answer beginning with a consonant; stems ending with "an" will match a word beginning with a vowel. The answer will agree in gender, number, and person with the stem.

Example: In test taking, a decoy is an:

a. incorrect answer.

b. correct answer.

c. false answer.

d. true answer.

The correct answer is A. It is also the only answer that grammatically fits with the stem. Also note that decoys can be all true or all false. In standardized tests, the grammar is usually correct. On teacher-made tests, the grammar can be a clue to the correct answer.

11. **A decoy is sometimes an opposite.** When two options are opposites, one is incorrect and the other is sometimes, but not always, correct.

Example: A decoy is:

a. a right answer.

b. a wrong answer.

c. a general qualifier.

d. a true statement.

The two opposites are answers a and b. The correct answer is b.

12. **A decoy may be the same as another answer.** If two answers say the same thing in different ways, they are both decoys and incorrect.

Example: A true statement is likely to have this type of qualifier:

a. extreme

b. absolute

c. general

d. factual

Notice that answers a and b are the same and are incorrect. The correct answer is c.

Example: How much does a gallon of water weigh?

a. 8.34 pounds

b. 5.5 pounds

c. 5 pounds 8 ounces

d. 20 pounds

B and c are the same and are therefore incorrect answers. Answer d is a high number. The correct answer is a.

If you are unable to identify any decoys, these suggestions may be helpful:

- Mark the question and come back to it later. You may find the answer elsewhere on the test, or some words that help you remember the answer. After answering some easier questions, you may be able to relax and remember the answer.
- Trust your intuition and choose something that sounds familiar.
- Do not change your first answer unless you have misread the question or are sure that the answer is incorrect. Sometimes students overanalyze a question and then choose the wrong answer.
- The option "All of the above" is often correct because it is easier to write true statements rather than false ones. Options like A and B, B and D, or other combinations are also likely to be correct for the same reason.
- If you have no idea about the correct answer, guess option B or C. Most correct answers are in the middle.

Practice Multiple-Choice Test

Circle the letters of the correct answers. Then check your answers using the key at the end of this section.

1. The correct answer in a multiple-choice question is likely to be
   a. the shortest answer.
   b. the longest and most complete answer.
   c. the answer with an absolute qualifier.
   d. the answer that has some truth in it.

2. When guessing on a question involving numbers, it is generally best to
   a. choose the highest number.
   b. choose the lowest number.
   c. choose the mid-range number.
   d. always choose the first option.

3. If you have test anxiety, what questions should you answer first on the test?
   a. The most difficult questions
   b. The easiest questions
   c. The questions at the beginning
   d. The questions worth the least number of points

4. When taking a multiple-choice test, you should
   a. pick the first choice that is true.
   b. read all the choices and select the best one.
   c. pick the first choice that is false.
   d. choose the extreme answer.

5. A good method for guessing is to
   a. identify which choices are true and false.
   b. use the process of elimination.
   c. notice absolute qualifiers and conjunctions.
   d. all of the above.

6. The key to success when taking a multiple-choice test is
   a. cheating.
   b. good preparation.
   c. knowing how to guess.
   d. being able to recognize a qualifier.

7. The following rule about decoys is correct:
   a. A decoy is always absolute.
   b. A decoy can be partly true.
   c. Every decoy has a qualifier.
   d. Decoys are invariably false statements.

8. An example of an absolute qualifier is
   a. generally.
   b. never.
   c. sometimes.
   d. frequently.

9. Statements with absolute qualifiers are generally
   a. true.
   b. false.
   c. irrelevant.
   d. confusing.

10. If two multiple-choice options are the same or very similar, they are most likely
    a. a decoy and a correct answer.
    b. a correct answer.
    c. a true answer.
    d. a mistake on the test.

11. It is generally not a good idea to change your answer unless
    a. you are very anxious about the test.
    b. you do not have good intuition.
    c. you notice that your intelligent friend has a different answer.
    d. you have misread the question and you are sure that the answer is incorrect.

How did you do on the quiz? Check your answers: 1. b, 2. c, 3. b, 4. b, 5. d, 6. b, 7. b (Notice the absolute qualifiers in the decoys), 8. b, 9. b (Notice the opposites), 10. a (Notice the grammar), 11. d

Matching Tests

A matching test involves two lists of facts or definitions that must be matched together. Here are some tips to help you successfully complete a matching exam:

1. Read through both lists to discover the pattern or relationship between the lists. The lists might give words and definitions, people and accomplishments, or other paired facts.

2. Count the items on the list of answers to see if there is only one match for each item or if there are some extra answer choices.

3. Start with one list and match the items that you know. In this way, you have a better chance of guessing on the items that you do not know.

4. If you have difficulty with some of the items, leave them blank and return later. You may find the answers or clues on the rest of the test.

Practice Matching Test

Match the items in the first column with the items in the second column. Write the letter of the matching item in the blank at the left.

_____	**1.** Meaningful organization	**A.**	Learn small amounts and review frequently.
_____	**2.** Visualization	**B.**	The more you know, the easier it is to remember.
_____	**3.** Recitation	**C.**	Tell yourself you will remember.
_____	**4.** Develop an interest	**D.**	Pretend you like it.
_____	**5.** See the big picture	**E.**	Make a mental picture.
_____	**6.** Intend to remember	**F.**	Rehearse and review.
_____	**7.** Distribute the practice	**G.**	Focus on the main points first.
_____	**8.** Create a basic background	**H.**	Personal organization.

Answers: 1. H,   2. E,   3. F,   4. D,   5. G,   6. C,   7. A,   8. B

Sentence-Completion or Fill-in-the-Blank Tests

Fill-in-the-blank and sentence-completion tests are more difficult than true-false or multiple-choice tests because they require the **recall** of specific information rather than the **recognition** of the correct answer. To prepare for this type of test, focus on facts such as definitions, names, dates, and places. Using flash cards to prepare can be helpful. For example, to memorize names, place each name on one side of a card and some identifying words on the other side. Practice looking at the names on one side of the card and then recalling the identifying words on the other side of the card. Then turn the cards over and look at the identifying words to recall the names.

Sometimes the test has clues that will help you to fill in the blank. Clues can include the length of the blanks and the number of blanks. Find an answer that makes sense in the sentence and matches the grammar of the sentence. If you cannot think of an answer, write a general description and you may get partial credit. Look for clues on the rest of the test that may trigger your recall.

Practice Fill-in-the-Blank Test

Complete each sentence with the appropriate word or words.

1. Fill-in-the-blank tests are more difficult because they depend on the _____ of specific information.

2. On a true-false test, a statement is likely to be false if it contains an _____ qualifier.

3. Test review tools include _____, _____, and _____.

4. When studying for tests, visualize your _____.

Answers: 1. recall, 2. absolute, 3. flash cards, summary sheets, and mind maps (also study groups and highlighters), 4. success

Essay Tests

Many professors choose essay questions because they are the best way to show what you have learned in the class. Essay questions can be challenging because you not only have to know the material, but must be able to organize it and use good writing techniques in your answer.

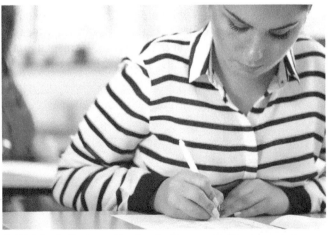

© 2014, Lucky Business. Used under license with Shutterstock, Inc.

Essay questions contain key words that will guide you in writing your answer. One of the keys to success in writing answers to essay questions is to note these key words and then structure your essay accordingly. As you read through an essay question, look for these words:

Analyze	Break into separate parts and discuss, examine, or interpret each part.
Argue	State an opinion and give reasons for the opinion.
Comment	Give your opinion.
Compare	Identify two or more ideas and identify similarities and differences.
Contrast	Show how the components are the same or different.
Criticize	Give your opinion and make judgments.
Defend	State reasons.
Define	Give the meaning of the word or concept as used within the course of study.
Describe	Give a detailed account or provide information.
Demonstrate	Provide evidence.
Diagram	Make a drawing, chart, graph, sketch, or plan.
Differentiate	Tell how the ideas are the same and how they are different.
Describe	Make a picture with words. List the characteristics, qualities, and parts.
Discuss	Describe the pros and cons of the issues. Compare and contrast.
Enumerate	Make a list of ideas, events, qualities, reasons, and so on.
Explain	Make an idea clear. Show how and why.
Evaluate	Describe it and give your opinion about something.
Illustrate	Give concrete examples and explain them. Draw a diagram.
Interpret	Say what something means. Describe and then evaluate.
Justify	Prove a point. Give the reasons why.
Outline	Describe the main ideas.
Prove	Support with facts. Give evidence or reasons.
Relate	Show the connections between ideas or events.
State	Explain precisely. Provide the main points.
Summarize	Give a brief, condensed account. Draw a conclusion.
Trace	Show the order of events.

Here are some tips on writing essays:

1. To prepare for an essay test, use a mind map or summary sheet to summarize the main ideas. Organize the material in the form of an outline or mental pictures that you can use in writing.

2. The first step in writing an essay is to quickly survey the test and read the directions carefully. Many times you are offered a choice of which and how many questions to answer.

3. Manage your time. Note how many questions need to be answered and how many points each question is worth. For example, if you have three questions to answer in one hour, you will have less than 20 minutes for each question. Save some time to check over your work.

   If the questions are worth different numbers of points, divide up your time proportionately. In the above example with three questions, if one question is worth 50 points and the other two are worth 25 points, spend half the time on the 50-point question (less than 30 minutes) and divide the remaining time between the 25-point questions (less than 15 minutes each).

4. If you are anxious about the test, start with an easy question in order to relax and build your confidence. If you are confident in your test-taking abilities, start with the question that is worth the most points.

5. Get organized. Write a brief outline in the margin of your test paper. Do not write your outline on a separate sheet of paper because you may be accused of using cheat notes.

6. In the first sentence of your essay, rephrase the question and provide a direct answer. Rephrasing the question keeps you on track and a direct answer becomes the thesis statement or main idea of the essay.

   Example: (Question:) Describe a system for reading a college textbook.
   (Answer:) A system for reading a college textbook is Survey, Question, Read, Review, Recite, and Reflect (SQ4R). (Then you would go on to expand on each part of the topic.)

7. Use the principles of good composition. Start with a thesis statement or main idea. Provide supporting ideas and examples to support your thesis. Provide a brief summary at the end.

8. Write your answer clearly and neatly so it is easy to grade. Grading an essay involves an element of subjectivity. If your paper looks neat and is easy to read, the professor is likely to read your essay with a positive attitude. If your paper is difficult to read, the professor will probably read your paper with a negative attitude.

9. Determine the length of your essay by the number of points it is worth. For example, a five-point essay might be a paragraph with five key points. A 25-point essay would probably be a five-paragraph essay with at least 25 key points.

10. Save some time at the end to read over your essays. Make corrections, make sure your answers make sense, and add any key information you may have forgotten to include.

What to Do When Your Test Is Returned

When your test is returned, use it as feedback for future test preparation in the course. Look at your errors and try to determine how to prevent these errors in the future.

- Did you study correctly?
- Did you study the proper materials?
- Did you use the proper test-taking techniques?
- Was the test more difficult than you expected?
- Did you run out of time to take the test?
- Was the test focused on details and facts or on general ideas and principles?
- Did you have problems with test anxiety?

Analyzing your test performance can help you to do better in the future.

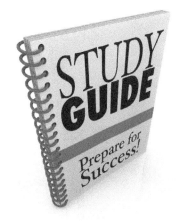

© 2014, iQoncept. Used under license with Shutterstock, Inc.

KEYS TO SUCCESS

Be Prepared

The key idea in this chapter is to be prepared. Good preparation is essential for success in test taking as well as in many other areas of life. Being successful begins with having a vision of the future and then taking steps to achieve your dream.

Sometimes people think of success in terms of good luck. Thomas Jefferson said, "I'm a great believer in luck, and I find the harder I work, the more I have of it." Don't depend on good luck. Work to create your success.

You can reach your dream of attaining a college education through preparation and hard work. Use the ideas in this chapter to ensure your success. Remember that preparation begins on the first day of class: it does not begin when the professor announces a test. On the first day of class, the professor provides an overview, or outline, of what you will learn. Attend every class. The main points covered in the class will be on the test. Read your assignments a little at a time starting from the first day. If you distribute your practice, you will find it easier to learn and to remember.

When it comes time to review for the test, you will already know what to expect on the test, and you will have learned the material by attending the lectures and reading your text. Reviewing for the test is just review; it is not original learning. It is a chance to strengthen what you have learned so that you can relax and do your best on the test. Review is one of the final steps in learning. With review, you will gain a sense of confidence and satisfaction in your studies.

If you are not prepared, you will need to cram for the test and you may not be as successful on the test as you could be. If you are not successful, you may get the mistaken idea that you cannot be successful in college. Cramming for the test produces stress, since you will need to learn a great deal of information in a short time. Stress can interfere with memory and cause you to freeze up on exams. It is also difficult to remember if you have to cram. The memory works best if you do a small amount of learning regularly over a period of time. Cramming is hard work and no fun. The worst problem with cramming is that it causes you to dislike education. It is difficult to continue to do something that you have learned to dislike.

Good preparation is the key to success in many areas of life. Whether you are taking a college course, playing a basketball game, going on vacation, planning a wedding, or building a house, good preparation will help to guarantee your success. Begin with your vision of the future and boldly take the first steps. The best preparation for the future is the good use of your time today.

> "The secret of getting ahead is getting started. The secret of getting started is breaking your complex, overwhelming tasks into small manageable tasks, and then starting on the first one."
>
> Mark Twain

> "The future starts today, not tomorrow."
>
> Pope John Paul II

JOURNAL ENTRIES

Test Taking

Go to http://www.collegesuccess1.com/JournalEntries.htm for Word files
of the Journal Entries

Success over the Internet

Visit the *College Success Website* at http://www.collegesuccess1.com/

The *College Success Website* is continually updated with new topics and
links to the material presented in this chapter. Topics include:

- Tips for taking tests
- Dealing with math anxiety
- How to study for math tests
- How to take math tests
- How to guess on a test
- Test anxiety
- Multiple-choice exams
- Dealing with difficult questions

Contact your instructor if you have any problems accessing the *College
Success Website.*

Notes

1. G. A. Miller, "The Magical Number Seven, Plus or Minus Two: Some Limits on Our
   Capacity for Processing Information," *Psychological Review* 63 (March 1956): 81–97.

2. From Aguilar et al., *The Community College: A New Beginning,* 2nd ed. (Dubuque, IA:
   Kendall Hunt, 1998).

PART III

Career Success

CHAPTER 10

Exploring Interests and Values

Learning Objectives

Read to answer these key questions:

- What are my interests?

- What lifestyle do I prefer?

- How do my interests relate to possible careers?

- What are my values?

- How do I put my values into action?

- How can I make good decisions about my future?

B ecoming aware of your interests and values will increase self-understanding and help you to make good decisions about your college major and future career. Interests and values are also important considerations in thinking about your preferred lifestyle.

Exploring Your Interests

Interests are simply what a person likes to do. Interests are a result of many factors, including personality, family life, values, and the environment. Knowing about your interests is helpful in planning a satisfying career. By studying people who are satisfied with their careers, psychologists have been able to help people choose careers based on their interests.

The U.S. Department of Labor has developed the O*Net Interest Profiler, which helps to identify your career interests.[1] The O*Net Interest Profiler is compatible with Holland's Theory of Vocational Personality. This is one of the most widely accepted approaches to vocational choice. According to the theory, there are six vocational personality types. These six types and their accompanying definitions are presented below.[2] As you read through each description, think about your own interests.

Realistic

People with **realistic** interests like work activities that include practical, hands-on problems and solutions. They enjoy dealing with plants, animals, and real-world materials like wood, tools, and machinery. They enjoy outside work. Often people with realistic interests do not like occupations that mainly involve doing paperwork or working closely with others.

Investigative

People with **investigative** interests like work activities that have to do with ideas and thinking more than with physical activity. They like to search for facts and figure out problems mentally rather than to persuade or lead people.

Artistic

People with **artistic** interests like work activities that deal with the artistic side of things, such as forms, designs, and patterns. They like self-expression in their work. They prefer settings where work can be done without following a clear set of rules.

Social

People with **social** interests like work activities that assist others and promote learning and personal development. They prefer to communicate more than to work with objects, machines, or data. They like to teach, give advice, help, or otherwise be of service to people.

Enterprising

People with **enterprising** interests like work activities that have to do with starting up and carrying out projects, especially business ventures. They like persuading and leading people and making decisions. They like taking risks for profit. These people prefer action rather than thought.

Conventional

People with **conventional** interests like work activities that follow set procedures and routines. They prefer working with data and detail rather than with ideas. They prefer work in which there are precise standards rather than work in which you have to judge things by yourself. These people like working where the lines of authority are clear.

According to Holland, most individuals can be described by one or more of these six personality types, frequently summarized as R-I-A-S-E-C (the first letter of each personality type). Additionally, the theory proposes that there are six corresponding work environments (or occupational groups), and that people seek out work environments that match their personality types. The better the match individuals make, the more satisfied they will be with their jobs.[3]

Holland arranged these interests on a hexagon that shows the relationship of the interests to one another. He notes that most people are not just one type, but rather a combination of types. Types that are close to each other on the hexagon are likely to have interests in common. For example, a person who is social is likely to have some artistic interests and some enterprising interests. Interests on opposite points of the hexagon are very different. For example, artistic and conventional types are opposites. Artistic types prefer freedom to be creative; conventional types prefer structure and order. The figure that follows illustrates the relationship between interest areas.[4]

> "Even if you're on the right track, you'll get run over if you just sit there."
> Will Rogers

> "Real success is finding your life work in work that you love."
> David McCullough

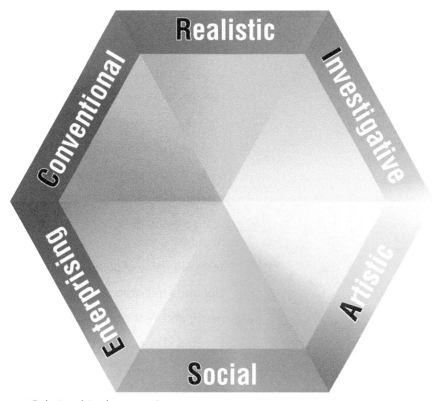

Figure 4.1 Relationships between interest areas.

The Interest Profiler[5]

Place a checkmark next to the items in each list that you might **like to do**. Keep a positive attitude when thinking about your interests. You do not need to know how to do these activities or have the opportunity to do them to select items that you might like to do in the future. Also, be careful not to select an activity just because it is likely to produce higher income. You can earn higher income by increasing your skills and education in these areas. For example, if you would like to build a brick walkway, you could work in construction, or with more education, become a civil engineer. Just indicate what you would enjoy doing. Remember that this is not a test and that there are no right or wrong answers to the questions. The goal is for you to learn more about your personal career interests and related occupations.

When you are finished with each section, tally the number of checkmarks in each area. Sample job titles for each area of interest are included. Underline any jobs that appeal to you. You can also match your interests to over 900 occupations listed at O*Net Online (http://www.onetonline.org/find/descriptor/browse/Interests/). This site includes information on specific occupations, including work tasks; tools and technology; knowledge, skills, and abilities required; work activities and work context; level of education required; work styles; work values; and wages and employment information.

Realistic (R)

I would like to:

_____ Build kitchen cabinets

_____ Guard money in an armored car

_____ Operate a dairy farm

_____ Lay brick or tile

_____ Monitor a machine on an assembly line

_____ Repair household appliances

_____ Drive a taxi cab

_____ Install flooring in houses

_____ Raise fish in a fish hatchery

_____ Build a brick walkway

_____ Assemble electronic parts

_____ Drive a truck to deliver packages to offices and homes

_____ Paint houses

_____ Enforce fish and game laws

_____ Operate a grinding machine in a factory

_____ Work on an offshore oil-drilling rig

_____ Perform lawn care services

_____ Assemble products in a factory

_____ Catch fish as a member of a fishing crew

_____ Refinish furniture

_____ Fix a broken faucet

_____ Do cleaning or maintenance work

_____ Maintain the grounds of a park

_____ Operate a machine on a production line

_____ Spray trees to prevent the spread of harmful insects

_____ Test the quality of parts before shipment

_____ Operate a motorboat to carry passengers

_____ Repair and install locks

_____ Set up and operate machines to make products

_____ Put out forest fires

R =

Matching Job Titles for Realistic Interests[6]

Construction worker, building contractor, cook, landscaper, housekeeper, janitor, firefighter, hazardous materials removal worker, security guard, truck driver, automotive mechanic, cardiovascular technologist, civil engineer, commercial pilot, computer support specialist, plumber, police officer, chemical engineer, fish and game warden, surveyor, archaeologist, athletic trainer, dentist, veterinarian

Investigative (I)

I would like to:

_____ Study space travel

_____ Make a map of the bottom of an ocean

_____ Study the history of past civilizations

_____ Study animal behavior

_____ Develop a new medicine

_____ Plan a research study

_____ Study ways to reduce water pollution

_____ Develop a new medical treatment or procedure

_____ Determine the infection rate of a new disease

_____ Study rocks and minerals

_____ Diagnose and treat sick animals

_____ Study the personalities of world leaders

_____ Conduct chemical experiments

_____ Conduct biological research

_____ Study the population growth of a city

_____ Study whales and other types of marine life

_____ Investigate crimes

_____ Study the movement of planets

_____ Examine blood samples using a microscope

_____ Investigate the cause of a fire

_____ Study the structure of the human body

_____ Develop psychological profiles of criminals

_____ Develop a way to better predict the weather

_____ Work in a biology lab

_____ Invent a replacement for sugar

_____ Study genetics

_____ Study the governments of different countries

_____ Do research on plants or animals

_____ Do laboratory tests to identify diseases

_____ Study weather conditions

I =

Matching Job Titles for Investigative Interests

Electronic engineering technician, emergency medical technician, fire investigator, paralegal, police detective, engineer (aerospace, biomedical, chemical, electrical, computer, environmental, or industrial), chemist, computer systems analyst, geoscientist, market research analyst, anesthesiologist, biochemist, biophysicist, clinical psychologist, dietician, physician, microbiologist, pharmacist, psychiatrist, surgeon, veterinarian, science teacher, college professor

Artistic (A)

I would like to:

_____ Conduct a symphony orchestra

_____ Write stories or articles for magazines

_____ Direct a play

_____ Create dance routines for a show

_____ Write books or plays

_____ Play a musical instrument

(Continued)

_____ Perform comedy routines in front of an audience

_____ Perform as an extra in movies, plays, or television shows

_____ Write reviews of books or plays

_____ Compose or arrange music

_____ Act in a movie

_____ Dance in a Broadway show

_____ Draw pictures

_____ Sing professionally

_____ Perform stunts for a movie or television show

_____ Create special effects for movies

_____ Conduct a musical choir

_____ Act in a play

_____ Paint sets for plays

_____ Audition singers and musicians for a musical show

_____ Design sets for plays

_____ Announce a radio show

_____ Write scripts for movies or television shows

_____ Write a song

_____ Perform jazz or tap dance

_____ Direct a movie

_____ Sing in a band

_____ Design artwork for magazines

_____ Edit movies

_____ Pose for a photographer

A =

Matching Job Titles for Artistic Interests

Model, actor, fine artist, floral designer, singer, tile setter, architectural drafter, architect, dancer, fashion designer, film and video editor, hairdresser, makeup artist, museum technician, music composer, photographer, self-enrichment education teacher, art director, broadcast news analyst, choreographer, editor, graphic designer, landscape architect, creative writer, public relations specialist, teacher (of art, drama, or music)

Social (S)

I would like to:

_____ Teach an individual an exercise routine

_____ Perform nursing duties in a hospital

_____ Give CPR to someone who has stopped breathing

_____ Help people with personal or emotional problems

_____ Teach children how to read

_____ Work with mentally disabled children

_____ Teach an elementary school class

_____ Give career guidance to people

_____ Supervise the activities of children at a camp

_____ Help people with family-related problems

_____ Perform rehabilitation therapy

_____ Do volunteer work at a nonprofit organization

_____ Help elderly people with their daily activities

_____ Teach children how to play sports

_____ Help disabled people improve their daily living skills

_____ Teach sign language to people with hearing disabilities

_____ Help people who have problems with drugs or alcohol

_____ Help conduct a group therapy session

_____ Help families care for ill relatives

_____ Provide massage therapy to people

_____ Plan exercises for disabled patients

_____ Counsel people who have a life-threatening illness

_____ Teach disabled people work and living skills

_____ Organize activities at a recreational facility

_____ Take care of children at a day care center

_____ Organize field trips for disabled people

_____ Assist doctors in treating patients

_____ Work with juveniles on probation

_____ Provide physical therapy to people recovering from injuries

_____ Teach a high school class

S =

Matching Job Titles for Social Interests

Host, hostess, bartender, lifeguard, food server, child care worker, home health aide, occupational therapist, occupational therapist aide, personal and home care aide, physical therapist, physical therapist aide, veterinary assistant, dental hygienist, fitness trainer, medical assistant, nanny, teacher (preschool, kindergarten, elementary, middle, or high school), registered nurse, respiratory therapist, self-enrichment education teacher, tour guide, mediator, educational administrator, health educator, park naturalist, probation officer, recreation worker, chiropractor, clergy, counseling psychologist, social worker, substance abuse counselor, physician assistant, speech and language pathologist

Enterprising (E)

I would like to:

_____ Buy and sell stocks and bonds

_____ Manage a retail store

_____ Sell telephone and other communication equipment

_____ Operate a beauty salon or barber shop

_____ Sell merchandise over the telephone

_____ Run a stand that sells newspapers and magazines

_____ Give a presentation about a product you are selling

_____ Buy and sell land

_____ Sell compact discs at a music store

_____ Run a toy store

_____ Manage the operations of a hotel

_____ Sell houses

_____ Sell candy and popcorn at sports events

_____ Manage a supermarket

_____ Manage a department within a large company

_____ Sell a soft drink product line to stores and restaurants

_____ Sell refreshments at a movie theater

_____ Sell hair-care products to stores and salons

_____ Start your own business

_____ Negotiate business contracts

_____ Represent a client in a lawsuit

_____ Negotiate contracts for professional athletes

_____ Be responsible for the operation of a company

_____ Market a new line of clothing

_____ Sell newspaper advertisements

_____ Sell merchandise at a department store

_____ Sell automobiles

_____ Manage a clothing store

_____ Sell restaurant franchises to individuals

_____ Sell computer equipment to a store

E =

(Continued)

Matching Job Titles for Enterprising Interests

Cashier, food worker, customer service representative, sales worker, supervisor, gaming dealer, inspector, retail sales clerk, chef, food service manager, operations manager, real estate broker, realtor, sheriff, wholesale or retail buyer, advertiser, appraiser, construction manager, criminal investigator, financial manager, insurance sales agent, meeting and convention planner, personal financial advisor, sales engineer, judge, lawyer, business or political science teacher, educational administrator, librarian, medical health manager, treasurer, controller

Conventional (C)

I would like to:

_____ Develop a spreadsheet using computer software

_____ Proofread records or forms

_____ Use a computer program to generate customer bills

_____ Schedule conferences for an organization

_____ Keep accounts payable/receivable for an office

_____ Load computer software into a large computer network

_____ Transfer funds between banks using a computer

_____ Organize and schedule office meetings

_____ Use a word processor to edit and format documents

_____ Operate a calculator

_____ Direct or transfer phone calls for a large organization

_____ Perform office filing tasks

_____ Compute and record statistical and other numerical data

_____ Generate the monthly payroll checks for an office

_____ Take notes during a meeting

_____ Keep shipping and receiving records

_____ Calculate the wages of employees

_____ Assist senior-level accountants in performing bookkeeping tasks

_____ Type labels for envelopes and packages

_____ Inventory supplies using a handheld computer

_____ Develop an office filing system

_____ Keep records of financial transactions for an organization

_____ Record information from customers applying for charge accounts

_____ Photocopy letters and reports

_____ Record rent payments

_____ Enter information into a database

_____ Keep inventory records

_____ Maintain employee records

_____ Stamp, sort, and distribute mail for an organization

_____ Handle customers' bank transactions

C = [   ]

Matching Job Titles for Conventional Interests

Cashier, cook, janitor, landscaping worker, resort desk clerk, medical records technician, medical secretary, bookkeeping and accounting clerk, dental assistant, drafter, loan officer, paralegal, pharmacy technician, purchasing agent, accountant, auditor, budget analyst, city and regional planner, computer security specialist, cost estimator, credit analyst, database administrator, environmental compliance inspector, financial analyst, geophysical data technician, librarian, proofreader, computer science teacher, pharmacist, statistician, treasurer

Summing Up Your Results

Put the number of checkmarks from each section of the Interest Profiler on the lines that follow:

____ **R**ealistic _____ **S**ocial

____ **I**nvestigative _____ **E**nterprising

____ **A**rtistic _____ **C**onventional

What are your top three areas of interest? (Realistic, Investigative, Artistic, Social, Enterprising, Conventional?)

1. _____

2. _____

3. _____

Journal Entry #1

List your top three areas of interest from the Interest Profiler (realistic, investigative, social, enterprising, or conventional). Go to http://www.onetonline.org/find/descriptor/browse/Interests/ and click on your highest interests to find some matching careers. List one career and briefly describe the education required, salary, and projected growth for one of these careers. Here is an easy outline:

My top interests on the Interest Profiler are . . . .

One career that matches my interests is . . .

The education required is . . .

The median annual salary is . . .

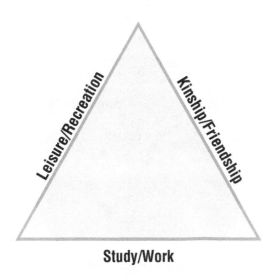

Figure 4.2 Lifestyle Triangle.[7]

Interests and Lifestyle

Our occupational interests determine what we study and the kinds of occupations we choose. While study and work form the basis of our lifestyle, there are other important components. What we choose to do for fun and relaxation helps us to be refreshed and keeps life interesting. Another component of a balanced lifestyle is time spent with friends and family. It is important to choose work that allows you to have the resources and time to lead a balanced lifestyle with all of these components. A balanced lifestyle has been described as a triangle with work and study forming the base, leisure and recreation forming one side, and kinship and friendship forming the other side.

Give some thought to the kind of lifestyle you prefer. Think about balancing your work, leisure, and social activities.

Journal Entry #2

In seeking to accomplish lifetime goals, sometimes people are not successful because they place too much emphasis on work, study, leisure, or social life. How would you balance work, study, leisure, and social life to achieve your lifetime goals?

QUIZ

Interests

Test what you have learned by selecting the correct answers to the following questions.

1. Realistic people are likely to choose a career in
   a. construction or engineering.
   b. accounting or real estate.
   c. financial investments or banking.

2. Investigative people are likely to choose a career in
   a. art or music.
   b. teaching or social work.
   c. science or laboratory work.

3. Enterprising people are likely to choose a career in
   a. computer programming or accounting.
   b. business management or government.
   c. health care or social services.

4. Conventional people are likely to choose a career in
   a. health care or social services.
   b. financial investments or banking.
   c. manufacturing or transportation.

5. Social types generally
   a. enjoy working with tools and machines.
   b. are humanistic and idealistic.
   c. have skills in selling and communication.

How did you do on the quiz? Check your answers: 1. a, 2. c, 3. b, 4. b, 5. b

Using Values to Make Important Life Decisions

Values are what we think is important and what we feel is right and good. Values come from many sources, including our parents, friends, the media, our religious background, our culture, our society, and the historical time in which we live. Our values make us different and unique individuals. Knowing our values helps us to make good decisions about work and life. For example, consider a situation in which a person is offered a high-paying job that involves a high degree of responsibility and a lot of stress. If the person values challenge and excitement and views stress as a motivator, the chances are that it would be a good decision to take the job. If the person values peace of mind and has a difficult time coping with stress, it might be better to forgo the higher income and maintain quality of life. Making decisions consistent with our values is one of the keys to happiness and success.

Values and needs are closely related. Humanistic psychologist Abraham Maslow[8] theorized that we adopt certain values to fulfill psychological or physical needs. He described needs and values in terms of a pyramid organized in a hierarchy arranged from the most basic to the most complex and personal. We cannot move to the next higher level until lower-level needs are met. These needs, listed in order from most basic to most complex, can be defined as follows:

- **Biological needs.** Basic needs for survival, including food, water, air, and clothing.
- **Safety needs.** Basic needs for shelter and a safe and predictable environment.
- **Love and belongingness.** Includes love, respect, and caring from our family and friends.

Figure 4.3 Maslow's Hierarchy of Needs.

- **Self-esteem.** Feeling good about yourself and having confidence in your abilities.
- **Intellectual.** Having the knowledge and understanding needed for survival.
- **Aesthetic.** Having an appreciation of beauty.
- **Self-actualization.** Developing and reaching your fullest potential, enabling you to contribute to society.

An example of a practical application of this theory is finding a solution for homeless people in society. It is easy to say that they should just go get jobs. Applying Maslow's hierarchy of needs, we would say that the first step in helping the homeless is to meet their biological needs. Before they can worry about employment, they need food, water, and clothing. Next, they need shelter so they have a safe and predictable environment. They need to know that people care about them so they can develop self-esteem. Once people have self-esteem and confidence, they can begin to be trained and educated. Once they have skills, they can become employed and enjoy the good life, appreciate beauty, and reach their potential. A person who is employed pays taxes and may do volunteer work to contribute to society.

Self-actualization is another word for success. It means knowing about and using your talents to fulfill your potential. It means being healthy and creative. It is being the best that you can be. Abraham Maslow said, "We may still often (if not always) expect that a new discontent and restlessness will soon develop, unless the individual is doing what he's fitted for. A musician must make music, an artist must paint, a poet must write, if he's to be ultimately at peace. What a person can be, he must be. This need we call self-actualization."[9]

We are all ultimately aiming for self-actualization. Here are some characteristics of the self-actualized person:

- Feels secure, loved, and respected, and makes a connection with others,
- Values self and others,
- Is independent,
- Can make decisions and accept responsibility,
- Appreciates other people and cares for the world,
- Is open to new ideas,
- Resists conformity,
- Has little need for status symbols,
- Is emotionally balanced,
- Is not burdened with anxiety, guilt, or shame,
- Treats others with respect,
- Feels at one with humankind,
- Has deep and caring relationships,
- Can look at life with a sense of humor,
- Is creative, passionate, and enjoys life,
- Takes time for self-renewal and relaxation,
- Has strong values and a philosophy of life.

This sounds great, but may be difficult to achieve. Remember that we are always on the road to self-actualization. Life is about growing and changing. If we do not grow and change, life becomes boring. It all begins with basic needs for survival. Once we have the basic needs for survival, we can focus on wants or desires (the possibilities). We can't have everything, so we determine what is important or what we value the most. Knowing what we value helps us to make good decisions about life goals. In setting our goals, we put values into practice. Meeting the challenges of our lives and accomplishing our goals lead to satisfaction and happiness. The process looks like this:

Figure 4.4 Meeting the challenges of our lives and accomplishing our goals lead to satisfaction and happiness.

Journal Entry #3

Review Maslow's theory of self-actualization. How would you apply Maslow's theory to being successful in life?

> "Try not to be a man of success, but rather to become a man of value."
> Albert Einstein

ACTIVITY

Values Checklist

Assessing Your Personal Values

Use the following checklist to begin to think about what values are important to you.
Place a checkmark next to any value that is important to you. There are no right or wrong answers. If you think of other values that are important to you, add them to the bottom of the list.

_____ Having financial security   _____ Having good family relationships

_____ Making a contributtion to humankind   _____ Preserving the environment

_____ Being a good parent   _____ Having the respect of others

_____ Being honest   _____ Becoming famous

_____ Acquiring wealth   _____ Happiness

(Continued)

———— Being a wise person		———— Freedom and independence	
———— Becoming an educated person		———— Common sense	
———— Believing in a higher power (God)		———— Having pride in my culture	
———— Preserving civil rights		———— Doing community service	
———— Never being bored		———— Achieving my goals in life	
———— Enjoying life and having fun		———— Having adventures	
———— Making something out of my life		———— Having leisure time	
———— Being an ethical person		———— Having good health	
———— Feeling safe and secure		———— Being loyal	
———— Having a good marriage		———— Having a sense of accomplishment	
———— Having good friends		———— Participating in church activities	
———— Having social status		———— Being physically fit	
———— Being patriotic		———— Helping others	
———— Having power		———— Being a good person	
———— Having good morals		———— Having time to myself	
———— Being creative		———— Loving and being loved	
———— Having control over my life		———— Being physically attractive	
———— Growing and developing		———— Achieving something important	
———— Feeling competent		———— Accepting who I am	
———— Feeling relaxed		———— Appreciating natural beauty	
———— Having prestige		———— Using my artistic talents	
———— Improving society		———— Feeling good about myself	
———— Having good mental health		———— Making a difference	
———— Being a good athlete		———— Other: _____	
———— Enjoying the present moment		———— Other: _____	
———— Maintaining peace of mind		———— Other: _____	

Journal Entry #4

What is your most important value? Why is it important to you?

Making Good Decisions

Knowing how to make a good decision about your career and important life events is very important to your future, as this short poem by J. Wooden sums up:

> *There is a choice you have to*
> *make, In everything you do*
>
> *And you must always keep in mind,*
> *The choice you make, makes you.*[10]

© 2014, Anastasia vish. Used under license with Shutterstock, Inc.

Sometimes people end up in a career because they simply seized an opportunity for employment. A good job becomes available and they happen to be in the right place at the right time. Sometimes people end up in a career because it is familiar to them, because it is a job held by a member of the family or a friend in the community. Sometimes people end up in a career because of economic necessity. The job pays well and they need the money. These careers are the result of chance circumstances. Sometimes they turn out well, and sometimes they turn out miserably.

Whether you are male or female, married or single, you will spend a great deal of your life working. By doing some careful thinking and planning about your career, you can improve your chances of success and happiness. Use the following steps to do some careful decision making about your career. Although you are the person who needs to make the decision about a career, you can get help from your college career center or your college counselor or advisor.

Steps in Making a Career Decision

1. **Begin with self-assessment.**
   - What is your personality type?
   - What are your interests?
   - What are your talents, gifts, and strengths?
   - What is your learning style?
   - What are your values?
   - What lifestyle do you prefer?

2. **Explore your options.**
   - What careers match your personal characteristics?

3. **Research your career options.**
   - Read the job description.
   - Investigate the career outlook.
   - What is the salary?
   - What training and education is required?
   - Speak with an advisor, counselor, or person involved in the career that interests you.
   - Choose a career or general career area that matches your personal characteristics.

4. **Plan your education to match your career goal.**
   - Try out courses in your area of interest.
   - Start your general education if you need more time to decide on a major.
   - Try an internship or part-time job in your area of interest.

5. **Make a commitment to take action and follow through with your plan.**

6. **Evaluate.**
   - Do you like the courses you are taking?
   - Are you doing well in the courses?
   - Continue research if necessary.

7. **Refine your plan.**
   - Make your plan more specific to aim for a particular career.
   - Select the college major that is best for you.

8. **Change your plan if it is not working.**
   - Go back to the self-assessment step.

The Decision-Making Process

- **Dependent decisions.** Different kinds of decisions are appropriate in different situations. When you make a dependent decision, you depend on someone else to make the decision for you. The dependent decision was probably the first kind of decision that you ever made. When your parents told you what to do as a child, you were making a dependent decision. As an adult, you make a dependent decision when your doctor tells you what medication to take for an illness or when your stockbroker tells you what stock you should purchase. Dependent decisions are easy to make and require little thought. Making a dependent decision saves time and energy.

  The dependent decision, however, has some disadvantages. You may not like the outcome of the decision. The medication that your doctor prescribes may have unpleasant side effects. The stock that you purchased may go down in value. When students ask a counselor to recommend a major or a career, they are making a dependent decision. When the decision does not work, they blame the counselor. Even if the dependent decision does have good results, you may become dependent on others to continue making decisions for you. Dependent decisions do work in certain situations, but they do not give you as much control over your own life.

- **Intuitive decisions.** Intuitive decisions are based on intuition or a gut feeling about what is the best course of action. Intuitive decisions can be made quickly and are useful in dealing with emergencies. If I see a car heading on a collision path toward me, I have to swerve quickly to the right or left. I do not have time to ask someone else what to do or think much about the alternatives. Another example of an intuitive decision is in gambling. If I am trying to decide whether to bet a dollar on red or black, I rely on my gut feeling to make a choice. Intuitive decisions may work out or they may not. You could make a mistake and swerve the wrong way as the car approaches or you could lose your money in gambling.

- **Planful decisions.** For important decisions, it is advantageous to use what is called a planful decision. The planful decision is made after carefully weighing the consequences and the pros and cons of the different alternatives. The planful decision-making strategy is particularly useful for such decisions as:
  - What will be my major?
  - What career should I choose?
  - Whom should I marry?

Types of Decision

- Dependent
- Intuitive
- Planful

The steps in a planful decision-making process:

1. **State the problem.** When we become aware of a problem, the first step is to state the problem in the simplest way possible. Just stating the problem will help you to clarify the issues.

2. **Consider your values.** What is important to you? What are your hopes and dreams? By keeping your values in mind, you are more likely to make a decision that will make you happy.

3. **What are your talents?** What special skills do you have? How can you make a decision that utilizes these skills?

4. **Gather information.** What information can you find that would be helpful in solving the problem? Look for ideas. Ask other people. Do some research. Gathering information can give you insight into alternatives or possible solutions to the problem.

5. **Generate alternatives.** Based on the information you have gathered, identify some possible solutions to the problem.

6. **Evaluate the pros and cons of each alternative.** List the alternatives and think about the pros and cons of each one. In thinking about the pros and cons, consider your values and talents as well as your future goals.

7. **Select the best alternative.** Choose the alternative that is the best match for your values and helps you to achieve your goals.

8. **Take action.** You put your decision into practice when you take some action on it. Get started!

KEYS TO SUCCESS

Act on Your Values

Values are what are most important to you; they are your highest principles. They provide the road map to your success and happiness. You will face important turning points along life's journey. Should I go to college? What will be my major? What career will I have? Whom should I marry? What job should I take? Where shall I live? You can find good answers to these questions by being aware of your values and using them to make decisions and guide your actions. If your decisions follow your values, you can get what you want out of life.

The first step is knowing your values. You may need some time to think about your values and change them if they are not right for you. What values were you taught as a child? What values do you want to keep as an adult? Look around at people that you admire. What are their values? What values have you learned from your religion? Are these values important to you? Ask your friends about their values and share yours. Revise and rethink your values periodically. Make sure your values are

your own and not necessarily values that someone has told you were important. When you begin to think about values, you can come up with many things that are important. The key is to find out which values are most important. In this way, when you are faced with a choice, you will not be confused. You will know what is most important to you.

> "The great aim of education is not knowledge, but action."
> Herbert Spencer

Knowing about values is not enough. It is important to act consistently with your values and to follow them. For example, if people value health but continue to smoke, they are saying one thing but doing another. If they value family but spend all of their time at work, they are not acting consistently with their values. As a result, they might

(Continued)

find that their family is gone and they have lost something that is really valuable.

Use your actions to question or reaffirm your values. Do you really value your health and family? If so, take action to preserve your good health and spend time with your family. It is necessary to periodically look at your patterns of behavior. Do you act out of habit or do you act according to what is important to you? Habits might need to be changed to get what you value most out of life.

In times of doubt and difficulty, your values can keep you going. If you truly value getting a college education, you can put in the effort to accomplish your goal. When you have doubts about whether you can be successful, examine your values again and remind yourself of why you are doing what you are doing. For example, if you value being an independent business entrepreneur, you will put in the effort to be successful. If you value being a good parent, you will find the patience and develop the skill to succeed. Reminding yourself of your values can help you to continue your commitment to accomplishing your goals.

By knowing your values and following them, you have a powerful tool for making decisions, taking action, and motivating yourself to be successful.

QUIZ

Values

Test what you have learned by selecting the correct answers to the following questions.

1. Values are

   a. what we find interesting.
   b. what we find important.
   c. what we find entertaining.

2. Abraham Maslow described values as a

   a. circle.
   b. pyramid.
   c. square.

3. According to Maslow, our most basic needs are

   a. social.
   b. biological.
   c. intellectual.

4. According to Maslow, we are all aiming for

   a. independence.
   b. wealth.
   c. self-actualization.

5. Knowing what we value helps us to make good

   a. wages.
   b. decisions.
   c. expenditures.

How did you do on the quiz? Check your answers: 1. b, 2. b, 3. b, 4. c, 5. b

Journal Entry #5

Write down your most important value. Write an intention statement about how you plan to act on this value. For example, my most important value is to maintain my good health. I intend to act on this value by eating right and exercising.

Success over the Internet

Visit the *College Success Website* at http://www.collegesuccess1.com/

The *College Success Website* is continually updated with new topics and
links to the material presented in this chapter. Topics include:

- Occupations for realistic, investigative, artistic, social, enterprising,
  and conventional interests
- Holland's self-directed search
- Various self-assessments
- Being a self-actualized person

Contact your instructor if you have any problems in accessing the *College
Success Website*.

Notes

1. U.S. Department of Labor, "O*Net Interest Profiler," available at http://onetcenter.org

2. U.S. Department of Labor, "O*Net Interest Profiler User's Guide," available at http://
   onetcenter.org

3. John L. Holland, *Making Vocational Choices: A Theory of Vocational Personalities and
   Work Environments* (2nd Ed.), (Englewood Cliffs, NJ: Prentice-Hall, 1985).

4. U.S. Department of Labor, "O*Net Interest Profiler User's Guide."

5. Adapted from U.S. Department of Labor, "O*Net Interest Profiler."

6. Job titles in this section from http://www.onetonline.org/find/descriptor/browse/
   Interests/

7. The Lifestyle Triangle adapted with permission from NTL Institute, "Urban Middle-
   Class Lifestyles in Transition," by Paula Jean Miller and Gideon Sjoberg, *Journal of
   Applied Behavioral Science* 9 (1973), nos. 2/3: 149.

8. Abraham Maslow, *Motivation and Personality* (New York: Harper and Row, 1970).

9. Maslow, *Motivation and Personality*, 91.

10. Quoted in Rob Gilbert, ed., Bits and Pieces, 7 October 1999.

Informational Interviewing

The informational interview is an informal conversation useful for finding career information, exploring your career, building your network, or possibly finding future employment. It is not a job interview and the purpose is not to find employment. It is a way to find more personal information about a career you may be considering and to see if you are a good fit for this occupation.

The informational interview differs from the traditional interview in that you are in control and can ask questions about daily job tasks and how they relate to your interests. It is a great way to build your self-confidence and prepare you for an actual job interview. To obtain an informational interview, check your LinkedIn contacts to see if anyone you know is employed in the industry. Ask your friends, family, and employers if they can recommend someone for the interview. You can also work with your college Career Services to see if they have contacts for informational interviews. They often have contacts with college alumni who are willing to speak with students. You can visit websites to identify individuals you would like to interview. Most professionals enjoy helping others who have an interest in their field.

Regard the informational interview as a business appointment and dress the way others dress in this occupation. Make a short appointment (generally 15–30 minutes), state that the purpose of the appointment is to gain career information and advice, and show up on time. You can suggest that the person meet you for coffee (and be sure to pay the bill yourself). Be prepared with a list of questions to ask and to take some brief notes on the information. To begin the interview, give a brief 30 second overview of your career goals and reasons for contacting this person. Remember that the focus of the interview is to find career information. It is best not to ask for a job at this time. If there is a job available and you are a good fit for the job, he or she will likely tell you about it.

It is important to thank the interviewee and then follow up a thank you note or email. Ask the person if he or she is on LinkedIn and if you can request a link online. Bring your resume and hand it to the person at the end of the interview. Do not begin the interview with the resume since you want the focus on career information rather than on yourself.

Here is a sample phone call asking for an informational interview:

Hello. My name is _____ and I am a student at _____ University. I found your name at your company website. (Or _____ gave me your name and suggested that I contact you.) Although I am not currently looking for a job, I am interested in the field of _____ and would like to learn more about this occupation. Would it be possible to schedule 15–30 minutes of your time to ask a few questions and get your advice on how to enter this field?

© 2013, Shutterstock, Inc.

From *Career Success* by Marsha Fralick. Copyright © 2014 by Kendall Hunt Publishing Company. Reprinted by permission.

Following is a list of potential interview questions that you can use to keep the conversation going. You probably won't have time to ask all these questions, so choose the ones most that are most personally relevant.

1. What is your job title? What other job titles are commonly used for this position?

2. How did you get this position? What was your career path from entry-level to the position you now have?

3. What are your key job responsibilities? What is the typical day like for you?

4. What skills and education are needed for this job?

5. What are the most valuable courses that you took to prepare you for this job?

6. What are employers looking for (skills, education, personal qualities)?

7. What certificates or degrees are required for this job?

8. What kinds of internships or work experiences are desirable? Are internships available?

9. How does a person obtain this type of employment? How is the job advertised? Is the job market competitive? How can I meet the competition?

10. What are some entry-level positions in this company?

11. What important words should I include on my resume or cover letter?

12. What are the opportunities for advancement?

13. What are some personal characteristics that lead to success on this job?

14. What do you find most satisfying about your job?

15. What are the best and worst things about working in this job? What do you like about your job? Dislike?

16. What stresses you out about your job? What is the most difficult part of your job?

17. What are some of the most important challenges facing your industry today? How will it change in the next 10 years?

18. What is the salary range? What is the potential for advancement?

19. If you were still a college student, what would it be helpful to know about your current job and how to find employment in your field?

20. Can you suggest other sources or persons who could be valuable sources of information for me?

Journal Entry #6

A friend is looking for a job. What advice would you give him or her about the resume and job interview?

CHAPTER 11

Exploring Your Personality and Major

Learning Objectives

Read to answer these key questions:

- What are the different personality types?

- What is my personality type?

- What are my personal strengths?

- How is personality type related to choice of a major and career?

- What are the characteristics of my ideal career?

- What careers and majors should I consider based on my personality type?

- What are some other factors in choosing a major?

To assure your success in college, it is important to choose the major that is best for you. If you choose a major and career that match your personality, interests, aptitudes, and values, you will enjoy your studies and excel in your work. It was Picasso who said that you know you enjoy your work when you do not notice the time passing by. If you can become interested in your work and studies, you are on your way to developing passion and joy in your life. If you can get up each morning and enjoy the work that you do (at least on most days), you will surely have one of the keys to happiness.

Choose a Major That Matches Your Gifts and Talents

The first step in choosing the major that is right for you is to understand your personality type. Psychologists have developed useful theories of personality that can help you understand how personality type relates to the choice of major and career. The personality theory used in this textbook is derived from the work of Swiss psychologist Carl Jung (1875–1961). Jung believed that we are born with a predisposition for certain personality preferences and that healthy development is based on the lifelong nurturing of inborn preferences rather than trying to change a person to become something different. Each personality type has gifts and talents that can be nurtured over a lifetime.

While assessments are not exact predictors of your future major and career, they provide useful information that will get you started on the path of career exploration and finding the college major that is best suited to you. Knowledge of your personality and the personalities of others is not only valuable in understanding yourself, but also in appreciating how others are different. This understanding of self and others will empower you to communicate and work effectively with others. Complete the Do What You Are personality assessment that is included with this textbook before you begin this chapter. (See the inside front cover for further information.)

© 2014, Andril Kondiuk. Used under license with Shutterstock, Inc.

Understanding Personality Types

Just as no two fingerprints or snowflakes are exactly alike, each person is a different and unique individual. Even with this uniqueness, however, we can make some general statements about personality. When we make generalizations, we are talking about averages. These averages can provide useful information about ourselves and other people, but it is important to remember that no individual is exactly described by the average. As you read through the following descriptions of personality types, keep in mind that we are talking about generalizations or beginning points for discussion and thoughtful analysis.

As you read through your personality description from Do What You Are and the information in this text, **focus on your personal strengths and talents.** Building on these personal strengths has several important benefits. It increases self-esteem and self-confidence, which contribute to your success and enjoyment of life. Building on your strengths provides the energy and motivation required to put in the effort needed to accomplish any worthwhile task. The assessment also identifies some of your possible weaknesses or "blind spots." Just be aware of these blind spots so that they do not interfere with your success. Being aware of your blind spots can even be used to your advantage. For example, some personality types thrive by working with people. A career that involves much public contact is a good match for this personality type, whereas choosing a career where public contact is limited can lead to job dissatisfaction. Knowing about your personality type can help you make the right decisions to maximize your potential.

Personality type has four dimensions:

1. Extraversion or Introversion

2. Sensing or Intuition

3. Thinking or Feeling

4. Judging or Perceiving

These dimensions of personality will be defined and examined in more depth in the sections that follow.

Extraversion or Introversion

The dimension of extraversion or introversion defines how we interact with the world and how our energy flows. In the general school population, 75 percent of students are usually extraverts and 25 percent are introverts.

Extraverts (E) focus their energy on the world outside themselves. They enjoy interaction with others and get to know a lot of different people. They enjoy and are usually good at communication. They are energized by social interaction and prefer being active. These types are often described as talkative and social.

Introverts (I) focus their energy on the world inside of themselves. They enjoy spending time alone to think about the world in order to understand it. Introverts prefer more limited social contacts, choosing smaller groups or one-on-one relationships. These types are often described as quiet or reserved.

We all use the introvert and extravert modes while functioning in our daily lives. Whether a person is an extravert or an introvert is a matter of preference, like being left- or right-handed. We can use our nondominant hand, but it is not as comfortable as using our dominant hand. We are usually more skillful in using the dominant hand. For example, introverts can learn to function well in social situations, but later may need some peace and quiet to recharge. On the other hand, social contact energizes the extravert.

One personality type is not better than the other: it is just different. Being an extravert is not better than being an introvert. Each type has unique gifts and talents that can be used in different occupations. An extravert might enjoy working in an occupation with lots of public contact, such as being a receptionist or handling public relations. An introvert might enjoy being an accountant or writer. However, as with all of the personality dimensions, a person may have traits of both types.

Introverts and Extraverts

The list below describes some qualities of introverts and extraverts. **For each pair of items**, quickly choose the phrase that describes you best and place a checkmark next to it. Remember that one type is not better than another. You may also find that you are a combination type and act like an introvert in some situations and an extravert in others. Each type has gifts and talents that can be used in choosing the best major and career for you. To get an estimate of your preference, notice which column has the most checkmarks.

Introvert (I)

_____ Energized by having quiet time alone

_____ Tend to think first and talk later

_____ Tend to think things through quietly

_____ Tend to respond slowly, after thinking

_____ Avoid being the center of attention

_____ Difficult to get to know, private

_____ Have a few close friends

_____ Prefer quiet for concentration

_____ Listen more than talk

_____ View telephone calls as a distraction

_____ Talk to a few people at parties

_____ Share special occasions with one or a few people

_____ Prefer to study alone

_____ Prefer the library to be quiet

_____ Described as quiet or reserved

_____ Work systematically

Extravert (E)

_____ Energized by social interaction

_____ Tend to talk first and think later

_____ Tend to think out loud

_____ Tend to respond quickly, before thinking

_____ Like to be the center of attention

_____ Easy to get to know, outgoing

_____ Have many friends, know lots of people

_____ Can read or talk with background noise

_____ Talk more than listen

_____ View telephone calls as a welcome break

_____ Talk to many different people at parties

_____ Share special occasions with large groups

_____ Prefer to study with others in a group

_____ Talk with others in the library

_____ Described as talkative or friendly

_____ Work through trial and error

Here are some qualities that describe the ideal work environment. Again, as you **read through each pair of items**, place a checkmark next to the work environment that you prefer.

Introvert (I)

_____ Work alone or with individuals

_____ Quiet for concentration

_____ Communication one-on-one

_____ Work in small groups

_____ Focus on one project until complete

_____ Work without interruption

_____ **Total** (from both charts above)

Extravert (E)

_____ Much public contact

_____ High-energy environment

_____ Present ideas to a group

_____ Work as part of a team

_____ Variety and action

_____ Talk to others

_____ **Total** (from both charts above)

Do these results agree with your personality assessment on the Do What You Are? If your results are the same, this is a good indication that your results are useful and accurate. Are there some differences with the results obtained from your personality assessment? If your results are different, this provides an opportunity for further reflection about your personality type. Here are a couple of reasons why your results may be different.

1. You may be a combination type with varying degrees of preference for each type.

2. You may have chosen your personality type on the Do What You Are based on what you think is best rather than what you truly are. Students sometimes do this because of the myth that there are good and bad personality types. It is important to remember that each personality type has strengths and weaknesses. By identifying strengths, you can build on them by choosing the right major and career. By being aware of weaknesses, you can come up with strategies to compensate for them to be successful.

Look at the total number of checkmarks for extravert and introvert on the two above charts. Do you lean toward being an introvert or an extravert? Remember that one type is not better than the other and each has unique gifts and talents. On the chart below, place an X on the line to indicate how much you prefer introversion or extraversion. If you selected most of the introvert traits, place your X somewhere on the left side. If you selected most of the extravert traits, place your X somewhere on the right side. If you are equally introverted and extraverted, place your X in the middle.

Introvert _____|_____ Extravert

Do you generally prefer introversion or extraversion? In the box below, write **I** for introversion or **E** for extraversion. If there is a tie between **E** and **I**, write **I**.

Notice that it is possible to be a combination type. At times you might prefer to act like an introvert, and at other times you might prefer to act like an extravert. It is beneficial to be able to balance these traits. However, for combination types, it is more difficult to select specific occupations that match this type

Journal Entry #1

Look at the results from Do What You Are and your own self-assessment above. Are you an introvert or an extravert or a combination of these two types? Can you give examples of how it affects your social life, school, or work? Write a paragraph about this preference.

Sensing or Intuition

The dimension of sensing or intuition describes how we take in information. In the general school population, 70 percent of students are usually sensing types and 30 percent are intuitive types.

Sensing (S) persons prefer to use the senses to take in information (what they see, hear, taste, touch, smell). They focus on "what is" and trust information that is concrete and observable. They learn through experience.

Intuitive (N) persons rely on instincts and focus on "what could be." While we all use our five senses to perceive the world, intuitive people are interested in relationships, possibilities, meanings, and implications. They value inspiration and trust their "sixth sense" or hunches. (Intuitive is designated as N so it is not confused with I for Introvert.)

We all use both of these modes in our daily lives, but we usually have a preference for one mode or the other. Again, there is no best preference. Each type has special skills that can be applied to the job market. For example, you would probably want your tax preparer to be a sensing type who focuses on concrete information and fills out your tax form correctly. An inventor or artist would probably be an intuitive type.

ACTIVITY

Sensing and Intuitive

Here are some qualities of sensing and intuitive persons. As you **read through each pair of items**, quickly place a checkmark next to the item that usually describes yourself.

Sensing (S)	INtuitive (N)
_____ Trust what is certain and concrete	_____ Trust inspiration and inference
_____ Prefer specific answers to questions	_____ Prefer general answers that leave room for interpretation
_____ Like new ideas if they have practical applications (if you can use them)	_____ Like new ideas for their own sake (you don't need a practical use for them)
_____ Value realism and common sense	_____ Value imagination and innovation
_____ Think about things one at a time and step by step	_____ Think about many ideas at once as they come to you
_____ Like to improve and use skills learned before	_____ Like to learn new skills and get bored using the same skills
_____ More focused on the present	_____ More focused on the future
_____ Concentrate on what you are doing	_____ Wonder what is next
_____ Do something	_____ Think about doing something
_____ See tangible results	_____ Focus on possibilities
_____ If it isn't broken, don't fix it	_____ There is always a better way to do it

Sensing (S)	INtuitive (N)
_____ Prefer working with facts and figures	_____ Prefer working with ideas and theories
_____ Focus on reality	_____ Use fantasy
_____ Seeing is believing	_____ Anything is possible
_____ Tend to be specific and literal (say what you mean)	_____ Tend to be general and figurative (use comparisons and analogies)
_____ See what is here and now	_____ See the big picture

Here are some qualities that describe the ideal work environment. Again, as you **read through each pair of items**, place a checkmark next to the work environment that you prefer.

Sensing (S)	INtuitive (N)
_____ Use and practice skills	_____ Learn new skills
_____ Work with known facts	_____ Explore new ideas and approaches
_____ See measurable results	_____ Work with theories
_____ Focus on practical benefits	_____ Use imagination and be original
_____ Learn through experience	_____ Freedom to follow your inspiration
_____ Pleasant environment	_____ Challenging environment
_____ Use standard procedures	_____ Invent new products and procedures
_____ Work step-by-step	_____ Work in bursts of energy
_____ Do accurate work	_____ Find creative solutions
_____ **Total** (from both charts above)	_____ **Total** (from both charts above)

Look at the two charts above and see whether you tend to be more sensing or intuitive. One preference is not better than another: it is just different. On the chart below, place an X on the line to indicate your preference for sensing or intuitive. Again, notice that it is possible to be a combination type with both sensing and intuitive preferences.

Sensing _____|_____Intuitive

Do you generally prefer sensing or intuition? In the box below, write **S** for sensing or **N** for intuitive. If there is a tie between **S** and **N**, write **N**.

☐

Journal Entry #2

Look at the results from Do What You Are and your own self-assessment above. Are you a sensing, intuitive, or combination type? Can you give examples of how it affects your social life, school, or work? Write a paragraph about this preference.

Thinking or Feeling

The dimension of thinking or feeling defines how we prefer to make decisions. In the general school population, 60 percent of males are thinking types and 40 percent are feeling types. For females, 60 percent are feeling types and 40 percent are thinking types.

Thinking (T) individuals make decisions based on logic. They are objective and analytical. They look at all the evidence and reach an impersonal conclusion. They are concerned with what they think is right.

Feeling (F) individuals make decisions based on what is important to them and matches their personal values. They are concerned about what they feel is right.

We all use logic and have feelings and emotions that play a part in decision making. However, the thinking person prefers to make decisions based on logic, and the feeling person prefers to make decisions according to what is important to self and others. This is one category in which men and women often differ. Most women are feeling types, and most men are logical types. When men and women are arguing, you might hear the following:

Man: "I think that . . ."

Woman: "I feel that . . ."

By understanding these differences, it is possible to improve communication and understanding. Be careful with generalizations, since 40 percent of men and women would not fit this pattern.

When thinking about careers, a thinking type would make a good judge or computer programmer. A feeling type would probably make a good social worker or kindergarten teacher.

ACTIVITY

Thinking and Feeling

The following chart shows some qualities of thinking and feeling types. As you **read through each pair of items**, quickly place a checkmark next to the items that usually describe yourself.

Thinking (T)	Feeling (F)
_____ Apply impersonal analysis to problems	_____ Consider the effect on others
_____ Value logic and justice	_____ Value empathy and harmony
_____ Fairness is important	_____ There are exceptions to every rule
_____ Truth is more important than tact	_____ Tact is more important than truth
_____ Motivated by achievement and accomplishment	_____ Motivated by being appreciated by others
_____ Feelings are valid if they are logical or not	_____ Feelings are valid whether they make sense
_____ Good decisions are logical	_____ Good decisions take others' feelings into account

Thinking (T)	Feeling (F)
_____ Described as cool, calm, and objective	_____ Described as caring and emotional
_____ Love can be analyzed	_____ Love cannot be analyzed
_____ Firm-minded	_____ Gentle-hearted
_____ More important to be right	_____ More important to be liked
_____ Remember numbers and figures	_____ Remember faces and names
_____ Prefer clarity	_____ Prefer harmony
_____ Find flaws and critique	_____ Look for the good and compliment
_____ Prefer firmness	_____ Prefer persuasion

Here are some qualities that describe the ideal work environment. As you **read through each pair of items**, place a checkmark next to the items that usually describe the work environment that you prefer.

Thinking (T)	Feeling (F)
_____ Maintain business environment	_____ Maintain close personal relationships
_____ Work with people I respect	_____ Work in a friendly, relaxed environment
_____ Be treated fairly	_____ Be able to express personal values
_____ Fair evaluations	_____ Appreciation for good work
_____ Solve problems	_____ Make a personal contribution
_____ Challenging work	_____ Harmonious work situation
_____ Use logic and analysis	_____ Help others
_____ **Total** (from both charts above)	_____ **Total** (from both charts above)

While we all use thinking and feeling, what is your preferred type? Look at the charts above and notice whether you are more the thinking or feeling type. One is not better than the other. On the chart below, place an X on the line to indicate how much you prefer thinking or feeling.

Thinking _____|_____ Feeling

Do you generally prefer thinking or feeling? In the box below, write **T** for thinking or **F** for feeling. If there is a tie between **T** and **F**, write **F**.

```
┌──────┐
│      │
│      │
└──────┘
```

Journal Entry #3

Look at the results from Do What You Are and your own self-assessment above. Are you a thinking, feeling, or combination type? Can you give examples of how it affects your social life, school, or work? Write a paragraph about this preference.

Judging or Perceiving

The dimension of judging or perceiving refers to how we deal with the external world. In other words, do we prefer the world to be structured or unstructured? In the general school population, the percentage of each of these types is approximately equal.

*Judging (J) types like to live in a structured, orderly, and planned way. They are happy when their lives are structured and matters are settled. They like to have control over their lives. **Judging does not mean to judge others.** Think of this type as being orderly and organized.*

*Perceptive (P) types like to live in a spontaneous and flexible way. They are happy when their lives are open to possibilities. They try to understand life rather than control it. **Think of this type as spontaneous and flexible.***

Since these types have very opposite ways of looking at the world, there is a great deal of potential for conflict between them unless there is an appreciation for the gifts and talents of both. In any situation, we can benefit from people who represent these very different points of view. For example, in a business situation, the judging type would be good at managing the money, while the perceptive type would be good at helping the business to adapt to a changing marketplace. It is good to be open to all the possibilities and to be flexible, as well as to have some structure and organization.

ACTIVITY

Judging and Perceptive

As you **read through each pair of items**, quickly place a checkmark next to the items that generally describe yourself.

Judging (J)	Perceptive (P)
_____ Happy when the decisions are made and finished	_____ Happy when the options are left open; something better may come along
_____ Work first, play later	_____ Play first, do the work later
_____ It is important to be on time	_____ Time is relative
_____ Time flies	_____ Time is elastic
_____ Feel comfortable with routine	_____ Dislike routine
_____ Generally keep things in order	_____ Prefer creative disorder
_____ Set goals and work toward them	_____ Change goals as new opportunities arise
_____ Emphasize completing the task	_____ Emphasize how the task is done
_____ Like to finish projects	_____ Like to start projects
_____ Meet deadlines	_____ What deadline?
_____ Like to know what I am getting into	_____ Like new possibilities and situations
_____ Relax when things are organized	_____ Relax when necessary
_____ Follow a routine	_____ Explore the unknown
_____ Focused	_____ Easily distracted
_____ Work steadily	_____ Work in spurts of energy

Here are some qualities that describe the ideal work environment. Again, as you **read through each pair of items**, place a checkmark next to the work environment that you prefer.

Judging (J)		Perceptive (P)	
_____	Follow a schedule	_____	Be spontaneous
_____	Clear directions	_____	Minimal rules and structure
_____	Organized work	_____	Flexibility
_____	Logical order	_____	Many changes
_____	Control my job	_____	Respond to emergencies
_____	Stability and security	_____	Take risks and be adventurous
_____	Work on one project until done	_____	Juggle many projects
_____	Steady work	_____	Variety and action
_____	Satisfying work	_____	Fun and excitement
_____	Like having high responsibility	_____	Like having interesting work
_____	Accomplish goals on time	_____	Work at my own pace
_____	Clear and concrete assignments	_____	Minimal supervision
_____	**Total** (from both charts above)	_____	**Total** (from both charts above)

Look at the charts above and notice whether you are more the judging type (orderly and organized) or the perceptive type (spontaneous and flexible). We need the qualities of both types to be successful and deal with the rapid changes in today's world. On the chart below, place an X on the line to indicate how much you prefer judging or perceiving.

Judging _____|_____Perceptive

Do you generally have judging or perceptive traits? In the box below, write **J** for judging or **P** for perceptive. If there is a tie between **J** and **P**, write **P**.

Journal Entry #4

Look at the results from Do What You Are and your own self-assessment above. Are you a judging, perceptive, or combination type? Can you give examples of how it affects your social life, school, or work? Write a paragraph about this preference.

"Knowing thyself is the height of wisdom."
Socrates

Summarize Your Results

Look at your results above and summarize them on this composite chart. Notice that we are all unique, according to where the Xs fall on the scale.

Extravert (E) _____|_____Introvert (I)

Sensing (S) _____|_____Intuitive (N)

Thinking (T) _____|_____Feeling (F)

Judging (J) _____|_____Perceptive (P)

Write the letters representing each of your preferences.

The above letters represent your estimated personality type based on your understanding and knowledge of self. It is a good idea to confirm that this type is correct for you by completing the online personality assessment, Do What You Are.

© 2014, Pavel L Photo and Video. Used under license with Shutterstock, Inc.

Personality Types

Test what you have learned by selecting the correct answer to the following questions.

1. A person who is energized by social interaction is a/an:

    a. introvert
    b. extravert
    c. feeling type

2. A person who is quiet and reserved is a/an:

    a. introvert
    b. extravert
    c. perceptive type

3. A person who relies on experience and trusts information that is concrete and observable is a/an:

    a. judging type
    b. sensing type
    c. perceptive type

4. A person who focuses on "what could be" is a/an:

    a. perceptive type
    b. thinking type
    c. intuitive type

5. A person who makes decisions based on logic is a/an:

    a. thinker
    b. perceiver
    c. sensor

6. A person who makes decisions based on personal values is a/an:

    a. feeling type
    b. thinking type
    c. judging type

7. The perceptive type:

    a. has extrasensory perception
    b. likes to live life in a spontaneous and flexible way
    c. always considers feelings before making a decision

8. The judging type likes to:

    a. judge others
    b. use logic
    c. live in a structured and orderly way

9. Personality assessments are an exact predictor of your best major and career.

    a. true
    b. false

10. Some personality types are better than others.

    a. true
    b. false

How did you do on the quiz? Check your answers: 1. b, 2. a, 3. b, 4. c, 5. a, 6. a, 7. b, 8. c, 9. b, 10. b

Personality and Preferred Work Environment

Knowing your personality type will help you to understand your preferred work environment and provide some insights into selecting the major and career that you would enjoy. Selecting the work environment that matches your personal preferences helps you to be energized on the job and to minimize stress. Understanding other types will help you to work effectively with co-workers. As you read this section, think about your ideal work environment and how others are different.

Extraverts are career generalists who use their skills in a variety of ways. They like variety and action in a work environment that provides the opportunity for social interaction. Extraverts communicate well and meet people easily. They like to talk while working and are interested in other people and what they are doing. They enjoy variety on the job and like to perform their work in different settings. They learn new tasks by talking with others and trying out new ideas. Extraverts are energized by working as part of a team, leading others in achieving goals, and having opportunities to communicate with others.

Introverts are career specialists who develop in-depth skills. The introvert likes quiet for concentration and likes to focus on a work task until it is completed. They need time to think before taking action. This type often chooses to work alone or with one other person and prefers written communication such as emails to oral communication or presentations. They learn new tasks by reading and reflecting and using mental practice. Introverts are energized when they can work in a quiet environment with few interruptions. They are stressed when they have to work in a noisy environment and do not have time alone to concentrate on a project.

The **sensing** type is realistic and practical and likes to develop standard ways of doing the job and following a routine. They are observant and interested in facts and finding the truth. They keep accurate track of details, make lists, and are good at doing precise work. This type learns from personal experience and the experience of others. They use their experience to move up the job ladder. Sensing types are energized when they are doing practical work with tangible outcomes where they are required to organize facts and details, use common sense, and focus on one project at a time. They are stressed when they have to deal with frequent or unexpected change.

The **intuitive** type likes to work on challenging and complex problems where they can follow their inspirations to find creative solutions. They like change and finding new ways of doing work. This type focuses on the whole picture rather than the details. The intuitive type is an initiator, promoter, and inventor of ideas. They enjoy learning a new skill more than using it. They often change careers to follow their creative inspirations. Intuitive types are energized by working in an environment where they can use creative insight, imagination, originality, and individual initiative. They are stressed when they have to deal with too many details or have little opportunity for creativity.

The **thinking** type likes to use logical analysis in making decisions. They are objective and rational and treat others fairly. They want logical reasons before accepting any new ideas. They follow policy and are often firm-minded and critical, especially when dealing with illogic in others. They easily learn facts, theories, and principles. They are interested in careers with money, prestige, or influence. Thinking types are energized when they are respected for their expertise and recognized for a job well done. They enjoy working with others who are competent and efficient. They become stressed when they work with people they consider to be illogical, unfair, incompetent, or overly emotional.

The **feeling** type likes harmony and the support of co-workers. They are personal, enjoy warm relationships, and relate well to most people. Feeling types know their personal values and apply them consistently. They enjoy doing work that provides a service to people and often do work that requires them to understand and analyze their own emotions and those of others. They prefer a friendly work environment and like to learn with others. They enjoy careers in which they can make a contribution to humanity. Feeling types are energized by working in a friendly, congenial, and supportive work environment. They are stressed when there is conflict in the work environment, especially when working with controlling or demanding people.

The **judging** type likes a work environment that is structured, settled, and organized. They prefer work assignments that are clear and definite. The judging type makes lists and plans to get the job done on time. They make quick decisions and like to have the work finished. They are good at doing purposeful and exacting work. They prefer to learn only the essentials that are necessary to do the job. This type carefully plans their career path. Judging types are energized by working in a predictable and orderly environment with clear responsibilities and deadlines. They become stressed when the work environment becomes disorganized or unpredictable.

The **perceptive** type likes to be spontaneous and go with the flow. They are comfortable in handling the unplanned or unexpected in the work environment. They prefer to be flexible in their work and feel restricted by structures and schedules. They are good at handling work which requires change and adaptation. They are tolerant and have a "live and let live" attitude toward others. Decisions are often postponed because this type wants to know all there is to know and explore all the options before making a decision. This type is often a career changer who takes advantage of new job openings and opportunities for change. Perceptive types are energized when the work environment is flexible and they can relax and control their own time. They are stressed when they have to meet deadlines or work under excessive rules and regulations.

Personality and Decision Making

Your personality type affects how you think and how you make decisions. Knowing your decision-making style will help you make good decisions about your career and personal life as well as work with others in creative problem solving. Each personality type views the decision-making process in a different way. Ideally, a variety of types would be involved in making a decision so that the strengths of each type could be utilized. As you read through the following descriptions, think about your personality type and how you make decisions as well as how others are different.

© 2014, Stephen Coburn. Used under license with Shutterstock, Inc.

The **introvert** thinks up ideas and reflects on the problem before acting. The **extravert** acts as the communicator in the decision-making process. Once the decision is made, they take action and implement the decision. The **intuitive** type develops theories and uses intuition to come up with ingenious solutions to the problem. The **sensing** type applies personal experience to the decision-making process and focuses on solutions that are practical and realistic.

The thinking and feeling dimensions of personality are the most important factors in determining how a decision is made. Of course, people use both thinking and feeling in the decision-making process, but tend to prefer or trust either thinking or feeling. Those who prefer **thinking** use cause-and-effect reasoning and solve problems with logic. They use objective and impersonal criteria and include all the consequences of alternative solutions in the decision-making process. They are interested in finding out what is true and what is false. They use laws and principles to treat everyone fairly. Once a decision is made, they are firm-minded, since the decision was based on logic. This type is often critical of those who do not use logic in the decision-making process. The **feeling** type considers human values and motives in the decision-making process (whether they are logical or not) and values harmony and maintaining good relationships. They consider carefully how much they care about each of the alternatives and how they will affect other people. They are interested in making a decision that is agreeable to all parties. Feeling types are tactful and skillful in dealing with people.

It is often asked if thinking types have feelings. They do have feelings, but use them as a criterion to be factored into the decision-making process. Thinking types are more comfortable when feelings are controlled and often think that feeling types are too emotional. Thinking types may have difficulties when they apply logic in a situation where a feeling response is needed, such as in dealing with a spouse. Thinking types need to know that people are important in making decisions. Feeling types need to know that behavior will have logical consequences and that they may need to keep emotions more controlled to work effectively with thinking types.

Judging and **perceptive** types have opposite decision-making strategies. The judging type is very methodical and cautious in making decisions. Once they have gone through the decision-making steps, they like to make decisions quickly so that they can have closure and finish the project. The perceptive type is an adventurer who wants to look at all the possibilities before making a decision. They are open-minded and curious and often resist closure to look at more options.

If a combination of types collaborates on a decision, it is more likely that the decision will be a good one that takes into account creative possibilities, practicality, logical consequences, and human values.

Personality and Time Management

How we manage our time is not just a result of personal habits: it is also a reflection of our personality type. Probably the dimension of personality type most connected to time management is the judging or perceptive trait. **Judging** types like to have things under control and live in a planned and orderly manner. **Perceptive** types prefer more spontaneity and flexibility. Understanding the differences between these two types will help you to better understand yourself and others.

Judging types are naturally good at time management. They often use schedules as a tool for time management and organization. Judging types plan their time and work steadily to accomplish goals. They are good at meeting deadlines and often put off relaxation, recreation, and fun. They relax after projects are completed. If they have too many projects, they find it difficult to find time for recreation. Since judging types like to have projects under control, there is a danger that projects will be completed too quickly and that quality will suffer. Judging types may need to slow down and take the time to do quality work. They may also need to make relaxation and recreation a priority.

Perceptive types are more open-ended and prefer to be spontaneous. They take time to relax, have fun, and participate in recreation. In working on a project, perceptive types want to brainstorm all the possibilities and are not too concerned about finishing projects. This type procrastinates when the time comes to make a final decision and finish a project. There is always more information to gather and more possibilities to explore. Perceptive types are easily distracted and may move from project to project. They may have several jobs going at once. These types need to try to focus on a few projects at a time in order to complete them. Perceptive types need to work on becoming more organized so that projects can be completed on time.

Research has shown that students who are judging types are more likely to have a higher grade point average in the first semester.[1] It has also been found that the greater the preference for intuition, introversion, and judgment, the better the grade point average.[2] Why is this true? Many college professors are intuitive types that use intuition and creative ideas. The college environment requires quiet time for reading and studying, which is one of the preferences of introverts. Academic environments require structure, organization, and completion of assignments. To be successful in an academic environment requires adaptation by some personality types. Extroverts need to spend more quiet time reading and studying. Sensing types need to gain an understanding of intuitive types. Perceptive types need to use organization to complete assignments on time.

Personality and Money

Does your personality type affect how you deal with money? Otto Kroeger and Janet Thuesen make some interesting observations about how different personality types deal with money.

- **Judging types (orderly and organized).** These types excel at financial planning and money management. They file their tax forms early and pay their bills on time.
- **Perceptive types (spontaneous and flexible).** These types adapt to change and are more creative. Perceivers, especially intuitive perceivers, tend to freak out as the April 15 tax deadline approaches and as bills become due.
- **Feeling types (make decisions based on feelings).** These types are not very money-conscious. They believe that money should be used to serve humanity. They are often attracted to low-paying jobs that serve others.[3]

In studying stockbrokers, these same authors note that ISTJs (introvert, sensing, thinking, and judging types) are the most conservative investors, earning a small but reliable return on investments. The ESTPs (extravert, sensing, thinking, perceptive types) and ENTPs (extravert, intuitive, thinking, perceptive types) take the biggest risks and earn the greatest returns.[4]

Journal Entry #5

Write a paragraph about how being a judging, perceptive, or combination type influences any of the following: how you manage your time, how you budget your money, or your preferred work environment. Remember that judging means orderly and organized, not judging other people; perceptive means spontaneous and flexible. How is this information useful in choosing your career or being successful in college?

Personality and Career Choice

While it is not possible to predict exactly your career and college major by knowing your personality type, it can be helpful in providing opportunities for exploration. Here are some general descriptions of personality types and preferred careers. Included are general occupational fields, frequently chosen occupations, and suggested majors. These suggestions about career selections are based on the general characteristics of each type and research that correlates personality type with choice of a satisfying career.[5] Read the descriptions, careers and majors that match your personality type and then continue your career exploration with the online database in the Do What You Are personality assessment included with your textbook.

> "Choose a job you love, and you will never have to work a day in your life."
> Confucius

ISTJ

ISTJs are responsible, loyal, stable, practical, down-to-earth, hardworking, and reliable. They can be depended upon to follow through with tasks. They value tradition, family, and security. They are natural leaders who prefer to work alone, but can adapt to working with teams if needed. They like to be independent and have time to think things through. They are able to remember and use concrete facts and information. They make decisions by applying logic and rational thinking. They appreciate structured and orderly environments and deliver products and services in an efficient and orderly way.

© 2014, iQoncept. Used under license with Shutterstock, Inc.

General occupations to consider

business	education	health care
service	technical	military
law and law enforcement	engineering	management

Specific job titles

business executive	lawyer	electronic technician
administrator	judge	computer occupations
manager	police officer	dentist
real estate agent	detective	pharmacist
accountant	corrections officer	primary care physician
bank employee	teacher (math, trade,	nursing administrator
stockbroker	technical)	respiratory therapist
auditor	educational administrator	physical therapist
hairdresser	coach	optometrist
cosmetologist	engineer	chemist
legal secretary	electrician	military officer or enlistee

College majors

business	engineering	chemistry
education	computers	biology
mathematics	health occupations	vocational training
law		

ISTP

ISTPs are independent, practical, and easygoing. They prefer to work individually and frequently like to work outdoors. These types like working with objects and often are good at working with their hands and mastering tools. They are interested in how and why things work and are able to apply technical knowledge to solving practical problems. Their logical thinking makes them good troubleshooters and problem solvers. They enjoy variety, new experiences, and taking risks. They prefer environments with little structure and have a talent for managing crises. The ISTP is happy with occupations that involve challenge, change, and variety.

General occupations to consider

sales	technical	business and finance
service	health care	vocational training
corrections		

Specific job titles

sales manager
insurance agent
cook
firefighter
pilot
race car driver
police officer
corrections officer
judge
attorney
intelligence agent
detective

engineer
electronics technician
software developer
computer programmer
radiologic technician
exercise physiologist
coach
athlete
dental assistant/hygienist
physician
optometrist
physical therapist

office manager
small business manager
banker
economist
legal secretary
paralegal
computer repair
airline mechanic
carpenter
construction worker
farmer
military officer or
    enlistee

College majors

business
vocational training
law

computers
biology

health occupations
physical education

ISFJ

ISFJs are quiet, friendly, responsible, hardworking, productive, devoted, accurate, thorough, and careful. They value security, stability, and harmony. They like to focus on one person or project at a time. ISFJs prefer to work with individuals and are very skillful in understanding people and their needs. They often provide service to others in a very structured way. They are careful observers, remember facts, and work on projects requiring accuracy and attention to detail. They have a sense of space and function that leads to artistic endeavors such as interior decorating or landscaping. ISFJs are most comfortable working in environments that are orderly, structured, and traditional. While they often work quietly behind the scenes, they like their contributions to be recognized and appreciated.

General occupations to consider

health care
social service
corrections

education
business
technical

artistic
religious occupations
vocational training

Specific job titles

nurse
physician
medical technologist
dental hygienist
health education
   practitioner
dietician
physical therapist
nursing educator
health administrator
medical secretary
dentist
medical assistant
optometrist
occupational therapist

social worker
social services
   administrator
child care worker
speech pathologist
librarian
curator
genealogist
corrections worker
probation officer
teacher (preschool,
   grades 1–12)
guidance counselor
educational administrator

counselor
secretary
cashier
accountant
personnel administrator
credit counselor
business manager
paralegal
computer occupations
engineer
interior decorator
home economist
religious educator
clergy

College majors

health occupations	education	graphics
biology	business	religious studies
psychology	engineering	vocational training
sociology	art	

ISFP

ISFPs are quiet, reserved, trusting, loyal, committed, sensitive, kind, creative, and artistic. They have an appreciation for life and value serenity and aesthetic beauty. These types are individualistic and generally have no desire to lead or follow; they prefer to work independently. They have a keen awareness of their environment and often have a special bond with children and animals. ISFPs are service-oriented and like to help others. They like to be original and unconventional. They dislike rules and structure and need space and freedom to do things in their own way.

General occupations to consider

artists	technical	business
health care	service	vocational training

Specific job titles

artist	recreation services	forester
designer	physical therapist	botanist
fashion designer	radiologic technician	geologist
jeweler	medical assistant	mechanic
gardener	dental assistant/hygienist	marine biologist
potter	veterinary assistant	teacher (science, art)
painter	veterinarian	police officer
dancer	animal groomer/trainer	beautician
landscape designer	dietician	merchandise planner
carpenter	optician/optometrist	stock clerk
electrician	exercise physiologist	store keeper
engineer	occupational therapist	counselor
chef	art therapist	social worker
nurse	pharmacy technician	legal secretary
counselor	respiratory therapist	paralegal

College majors

art	forestry	psychology
health occupations	geology	counseling
engineering	education	social work
physical education	business	vocational training
biology		

INFJ

INFJs are idealistic, complex, compassionate, authentic, creative, and visionary. They have strong value systems and search for meaning and purpose to life. Because of their strong value systems, INFJs are natural leaders or at least follow those with similar ideas. They intuitively understand people and ideas and come up with new ideas to provide service to others. These types like to organize their time and be in control of their work.

General occupations to consider

counseling	religious occupations	health care
education	creative occupations	social services
science	arts	business

Specific job titles

career counselor	director of religious	dental hygienist
psychologist	education	speech pathologist
teacher (high school or	fine artist	nursing educator
college English, art,	playwright	medical secretary
music, social sciences,	novelist	pharmacist
drama, foreign	poet	occupational therapist
languages, health)	designer	human resources
librarian	architect	manager
home economist	art director	marketer
social worker	health care administrator	employee assistance
clergy	physician	program
	biologist	merchandise planner
		environmental lawyer

College majors

psychology	drama	architecture
counseling	foreign languages	biology
education	English	business
art	health occupations	law
music	social work	science

INFP

INFPs are loyal, devoted, sensitive, creative, inspirational, flexible, easygoing, complex, and authentic. They are original and individualistic and prefer to work alone or with other caring and supportive individuals. These types are service-oriented and interested in personal growth. They develop deep relationships because they understand people and are genuinely interested in them. They dislike dealing with details and routine work. They prefer a flexible working environment with a minimum of rules and regulations.

General occupations to consider

creative arts	counseling	health care
education	religious occupations	organizational
		development

Specific job titles

artist	photographer	dietician
designer	carpenter	psychiatrist
writer	teacher (art, drama,	physical therapist
journalist	music, English, foreign	occupational therapist
entertainer	languages)	speech pathologist
architect	psychologist	laboratory technologist
actor	counselor	public health nurse
editor	social worker	dental hygienist
reporter	librarian	physician
journalist	clergy	human resources
musician	religious educator	specialist
graphic designer	missionary	social scientist
art director	church worker	consultant

College majors

art	foreign languages	medicine
music	architecture	health occupations
graphic design	education	social work
journalism	religious studies	counseling
English	psychology	business

INTJ

INTJs are reserved, detached, analytical, logical, rational, original, independent, creative, ingenious, innovative, and resourceful. They prefer to work alone and work best alone. They can work with others if their ideas and competence are respected. They value knowledge and efficiency. They enjoy creative and intellectual challenges and understand complex theories. They create order and structure. They prefer to work with autonomy and control over their work. They dislike factual and routine kinds of work.

General occupations to consider

business and finance	education	law
technical occupations	health care and medicine	creative occupations
science	architecture	engineering

Specific job titles

management consultant	astronomer	dentist
human resources planner	computer programmer	biomedical engineer
economist	biomedical researcher	attorney
international banker	software developer	manager
financial planner	network integration	judge
investment banker	specialist	electrical engineer
scientist	teacher (university)	writer
scientific researcher	school principal	journalist
chemist	mathematician	artist
biologist	psychiatrist	inventor
computer systems analyst	psychologist	architect
electronic technician	neurologist	actor
design engineer	physician	musician
architect		

College majors

business	physics	journalism
finance	education	art
chemistry	mathematics	architecture
biology	medicine	drama
computers	psychology	music
engineering	law	vocational training
astronomy	English	

INTP

INTPs are logical, analytical, independent, original, creative, and insightful. They are often brilliant and ingenious. They work best alone and need quiet time to concentrate. They focus their attention on ideas and are frequently detached from other people. They love theory and abstract ideas and value knowledge and competency. INTPs are creative thinkers who are not too interested in practical application. They dislike detail and routine and need freedom to develop, analyze, and critique new ideas. These types maintain high standards in their work.

General occupations to consider

planning and development	technical professional	academic creative occupations
health care		

Specific job titles

computer software designer	pharmacist	historian
computer programmer	engineer	philosopher
research and development	electrician	college teacher
systems analyst	dentist	researcher
financial planner	veterinarian	logician
investment banker	lawyer	photographer
physicist	economist	creative writer
plastic surgeon	psychologist	artist
psychiatrist	architect	actor
chemist	psychiatrist	entertainer
biologist	mathematician	musician
pharmaceutical researcher	archaeologist	inventor

College majors

computers	philosophy	mathematics
business	music	archaeology
physics	art	history
chemistry	drama	English
biology	engineering	drama
astronomy	psychology	music
medicine	architecture	vocational training

ESTP

ESTPs have great people skills and are action-oriented, fun, flexible, adaptable, and resourceful. They enjoy new experiences and dealing with people. They remember facts easily and have excellent powers of observation that they use to analyze other people. They are good problem solvers and can react quickly in an emergency. They like adventure and risk and are alert to new opportunities. They start new projects but do not necessarily follow through to completion. They prefer environments without too many rules and restrictions.

General occupations to consider

sales	entertainment	technical
service	sports	trade
active careers	health care	business
finance		

Specific job titles

marketing professional
firefighter
police officer
corrections officer
paramedic
detective
pilot
investigator
real estate agent
exercise physiologist
flight attendant
sports merchandise sales
stockbroker
financial planner
investor

insurance agent
sportscaster
news reporter
journalist
tour agent
dancer
bartender
auctioneer
professional athlete or
    coach
fitness instructor
recreation leader
optometrist
pharmacist
critical care nurse

dentist
carpenter
farmer
construction worker
electrician
teacher (trade, industrial,
    technical)
chef
engineer
surveyor
radiologic technician
entrepreneur
land developer
retail sales
car sales

College majors

business
physical education
health occupations

vocational training
education

English
journalism

ESTJ

ESTJs are loyal, hardworking, dependable, thorough, practical, realistic, and energetic. They value security and tradition. Because they enjoy working with people and are orderly and organized, these types like to take charge and be the leader. This personality type is often found in administrative and management positions. ESTJs work systematically and efficiently to get the job done. These types are fair, logical, and consistent. They prefer a stable and predictable environment filled with action and a variety of people.

General occupations to consider

managerial
sales
business

service
technical
agriculture

professional
military leaders

Specific job titles

retail store manager
fire department manager
small business manager
restaurant manager
financial or bank officer
school principal
sales manager
top-level manager in city/
    county/state
    government
management consultant
corporate executive

military officer or enlistee
office manager
purchasing agent
police officer
factory supervisor
corrections
insurance agent
detective
judge
accountant
nursing administrator
mechanical engineer

physician
chemical engineer
auditor
coach
public relations worker
cook
personnel or labor
    relations worker
teacher (trade, industrial,
    technical)
mortgage banker

College majors

business	small business	law
business management	management	education
accounting	engineering	vocational training
finance	agriculture	

ESFP

ESFPs are practical, realistic, independent, fun, social, spontaneous, and flexible. They have great people skills and enjoy working in environments that are friendly, relaxed, and varied. They know how to have a good time and make an environment fun for others. ESFPs have a strong sense of aesthetics and are sometimes artistic and creative. They often have a special bond with people or animals. They dislike structure and routine. These types can handle many activities or projects at once.

General occupations to consider

education	health care	business and sales
social service	entertainment	service
food preparation	child care	

Specific job titles

child care worker	medical assistant	promoter
teacher (preschool,	critical care nurse	special events coordinator
elementary school,	dentist	editor or reporter
foreign languages,	dental assistant	retail merchandiser
mathematics)	exercise physiologist	fund raiser
athletic coach	dog obedience trainer	receptionist
counselor	veterinary assistant	real estate agent
library assistant	travel or tour agent	insurance agent
police officer	recreation leader or	sporting equipment sales
public health nurse	amusement site worker	retail sales
respiratory therapist	photographer	retail management
physical therapist	designer	waiter or waitress
physician	film producer	cashier
emergency medical	musician	cosmetologist
technician	performer	hairdresser
dental hygienist	actor	religious worker
chef		

College majors

education	health occupations	journalism
psychology	art	drama
foreign languages	design	music
mathematics	photography	business
physical education	English	vocational training
culinary arts	child development	

ESFJ

ESFJs are friendly, organized, hardworking, productive, conscientious, loyal, dependable, and practical. These types value harmony, stability, and security. They enjoy interacting with people and receive satisfaction from giving to others. ESFJs enjoy working in a cooperative environment in which people get along well with each other. They create order, structure, and schedules and can be depended on to complete the task at hand. They prefer to organize and control their work.

General occupations to consider

health care	social service	business
education	counseling	human resources
child care		

Specific job titles

medical or dental assistant	coach	sales representative
nurse	administrator of	hairdresser
radiologic technician	elementary	cosmetologist
dental hygienist	or secondary school	restaurant worker
speech pathologist	administrator of student	recreation or amusement
occupational therapist	personnel	site worker
dentist	child care provider	receptionist
optometrist	home economist	office manager
dietician	social worker	cashier
pharmacist	administrator of social	bank employee
physician	services	bookkeeper
physical therapist	police officer	accountant
health education	counselor	sales
practitioner	community welfare	insurance agent
medical secretary	worker	credit counselor
teacher (grades 1–12,	religious educator	merchandise planner
foreign languages,	clergy	
reading)		

College majors

health occupations	education	religious studies
biology	psychology	business
foreign languages	counseling	vocational training
English	sociology	child development

ENFP

ENFPs are friendly, creative, energetic, enthusiastic, innovative, adventurous, and fun. They have great people skills and enjoy providing service to others. They are intuitive and perceptive about people. ENFPs are good at anything that interests them and can enter a variety of fields. These types dislike routine and detailed tasks and may have difficulty following through and completing tasks. They enjoy occupations in which they can be creative and interact with people. They like a friendly and relaxed environment in which they are free to follow their inspiration and participate in adventures.

General occupations to consider

creative occupations	counseling	social service
marketing	health care	entrepreneurial business
education	religious services	arts
environmental science		

Specific job titles

journalist	public relations	physical therapist
musician	counselor	consultant
actor	clergy	inventor
entertainer	psychologist	sales
fine artist	teacher (health, special	human resources
playwright	education, English, art,	manager
newscaster	drama, music)	conference planner
reporter	social worker	employment development
interior decorator	dental hygienist	specialist
cartoonist	nurse	restaurateur
graphic designer	dietician	merchandise planner
marketing	holistic health practitioner	environmental attorney
advertising	environmentalist	lawyer

College majors

journalism	business (advertising,	religious studies
English	marketing, public	health occupations
drama	relations)	law
art	counseling	vocational training
graphic design	psychology	

ENFJ

ENFJs are friendly, sociable, empathetic, loyal, creative, imaginative, and responsible. They have great people skills and are interested in working with people and providing service to them. They are good at building harmony and cooperation and respect other people's opinions. These types can find creative solutions to problems. They are natural leaders who can make good decisions. They prefer an environment that is organized and structured and enjoy working as part of a team with other creative and caring people.

General occupations to consider

religious occupations	counseling	health care
creative occupations	education	business
communications	human services	administration

Specific job titles

director of religious	newscaster	social worker
education	politician	home economist
minister	editor	nutritionist
clergy	crisis counselor	speech pathologist
public relations	school counselor	occupational therapist
marketing	vocational or career	physical therapist
writer	counselor	optometrist
librarian	psychologist	dental hygienist
journalist	alcohol and drug	family practice physician
fine artist	counselor	psychiatrist

designer
actor
musician or composer
fundraiser
recreational director
TV producer

teacher (health, art,
  drama, English, foreign
  languages)
child care worker
college humanities
  professor

nursing educator
pharmacist
human resources trainer
travel agent
small business executive
sales manager

College majors

religious studies
business (public relations,
  marketing)
art
graphic design
drama

music
journalism
English
foreign languages
humanities
psychology

counseling
sociology
health occupations
business
vocational training

ENTP

ENTPs are creative, ingenious, flexible, diverse, energetic, fun, motivating, logical, and outspoken. They have excellent people skills and are natural leaders, although they dislike controlling other people. They value knowledge and competence. They are lively and energetic and make good debaters and motivational speakers. They are logical and rational thinkers who can grasp complex ideas and theories. They dislike environments that are structured and rigid. These types prefer environments that allow them to engage in creative problem solving and the creation of new ideas.

General occupations to consider

creative occupations
politics
engineering

law
business
science

health care
architecture
education

Specific job titles

photographer
marketing professional
journalist
actor
writer
musician or composer
editor
reporter
advertising director
radio/TV talk show host
producer
art director
new business developer
architect

politician
political manager
political analyst
social scientist
psychiatrist
psychologist
engineer
construction laborer
research worker
electrician
lawyer
judge
corporate executive

computer professional
corrections officer
sales manager
speech pathologist
health education
practitioner
respiratory therapist
dental assistant
medical assistant
critical care nurse
counselor
human resources planner
educator

College majors

art
photography
journalism
drama
English
engineering
science

music
business (advertising,
  marketing,
  management,
  human resources)
architecture

political science
psychology
health occupations
computers
vocational training
education

ENTJ

ENTJs are independent, original, visionary, logical, organized, ambitious, competitive, hardworking, and direct. They are natural leaders and organizers who identify problems and create solutions for organizations. ENTJs are often in management positions. They are good planners and accomplish goals in a timely manner. These types are logical thinkers who enjoy a structured work environment where they have opportunity for advancement. They enjoy a challenging, competitive, and exciting environment in which accomplishments are recognized.

General occupations to consider

business	management	science
finance	health care	law

Specific job titles

executive	manager in city/county/	accountant
manager	state government	auditor
supervisor	management trainer	financial manager
personnel manager	school principal	real estate agent
sales manager	bank officer	lawyer, judge
marketing manager	computer systems analyst	consultant
human resources planner	computer professional	engineer
corporate executive	credit investigator	corrections, probation
college administrator	mortgage broker	officer
health administrator	stockbroker	psychologist
small business owner	investment banker	physician
retail store manager	economist	

College majors

business management	computers	engineering
finance	law	psychology
economics	medicine	vocational training

Other Factors in Choosing a Major

Choosing your college major is one of the most difficult and important decisions you will make during your college years. After assessing their personality types, students often come up with many different options for a major and career. Future chapters will help you to think about your interests, values, and preferred lifestyle. This information will help you to narrow down your choices.

Once you have completed a thorough self-assessment, you may still have several majors to consider. At this point, it is important to do some research on the outlook for a selected career in the future and the pay you would receive. Sometimes students are disappointed after graduation when they find there are few job opportunities in their chosen career field. Sometimes students graduate and cannot find jobs with the salary they had hoped to earn. It is important to think about the opportunities you will have in the future. If you have several options for a career you would enjoy, you may want to consider seriously the career that has the best outlook and pay.

According to the Bureau of Labor Statistics, fields with the best outlook include health care, computers, and new "green jobs" related to preserving the environment. The top-paying careers all require math skills and include the science, engineering, computer science, health care, and business fields. Only four percent of college graduates choose the engineering and computer science fields. Since there are fewer students in these majors, the salaries are higher. If you have a talent or interest in math, you can develop this skill and use it in high-paying careers.

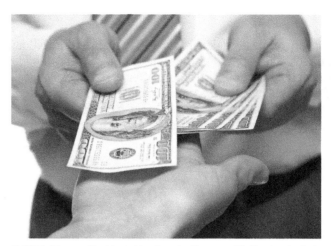

© 2014, Maryna Pleshkun. Used under license with Shutterstock, Inc

Majors with Highest Earnings 2014*[5]

College Major	Beginning Median Salary	Mid-Career Median Salary
Petroleum Engineering	103,000	160,000
Actuarial Mathematics	58,700	120,000
Nuclear Engineering	67,600	117,000
Chemical Engineering	68,200	115,000
Aerospace Engineering	62,800	109,000
Electrical/Computer Engineering	64,300	106,000
Computer Science	59,800	102,000
Physics	53,100	101,000
Mechanical Engineering	60,900	99,700
Materials Science & Engineering	62,700	99,500
Software Engineering	62,500	99,300
Statistics	52,500	98,900
Government	43,200	97,100
Economics	50,100	96,700
Applied Mathematics	52,800	96,200
Industrial Engineering	61,100	94,400
Management Information Systems	53,800	92,200
Biomedical Engineering	59,000	91,700
Civil Engineering	54,300	91,100
Environmental Engineering	49,400	89,800
Construction Management	51,500	88,800
Mathematics	49,400	88,800
Information Systems	51,900	87,200
Finance	49,200	87,100
Chemistry	44,100	84,100

*Includes bachelor's degrees only. Excludes medicine, law, and careers requiring advanced degrees.

Other Common Majors and Earnings 2014[6]

College Major	Beginning Median Salary	Mid-Career Median Salary
Marketing and Communications	40,200	77,600
Political Science	41,700	77,000
Architecture	41,900	75,800
Accounting	45,300	74,900
Business Administration	43,500	71,000
History	39,700	71,000
Biology	40,200	70,800
Health Sciences	38,400	70,500
Forestry	40,000	69,400
Journalism	38,100	67,700
Geography	40,800	67,200
Public Administration	40,600	66,900
English	38,700	65,200
Humanities	37,900	61,800
Psychology	36,300	60,700
Liberal Arts	36,600	60,500
Fashion Merchandising	39,100	59,100
Art History	36,900	59,000
Sociology	37,400	58,800
Criminal Justice	35,300	58,400
Fine Arts	37,400	58,200
Religious Studies	34,900	57,900
Education	37,400	55,200
Music	35,700	51,400

Top 15 Majors That Change the World*[7]

College Major	Beginning Median Salary	Mid-Career Median Salary
Nursing	55,400	71,700
Special Education	33,800	49,600
Medical Technology	48,900	60,500
Sports Medicine	39,300	57,400
Biomedical Engineering	59,000	91,700
Athletic Training	34,800	46,900
Social Work	33,000	46,600
Child and Family Studies	30,300	37,200
Biblical Studies	35,400	50,800
Dietetics	44,200	56,600
Molecular Biology	40,400	76,400
Health Care Administration	39,300	58,600
Elementary Education	32,200	45,300
Exercise Science	32,600	51,000
Public Health	35,900	56,500

*Based on an extensive survey by Payscale.com by asking college graduates, "Does your work make the world a better place to live?"

> "We act as though comfort and luxury were the chief requirements of life, when all that we need to make us really happy is something to be enthusiastic about."
> Charles Kingsley

Every career counselor can tell stories about students who ask, "What is the career that makes the most money? That's the career I want!" However, if you choose a career based on money alone, you might find it difficult and uninteresting for a lifetime of work. You might even find yourself retraining later in life for a job that you really enjoy. Remember that the first step is to figure out who you are and what you like. Then look at career outlook and opportunity. If you find your passion in a career that is in demand and pays well, you will probably be very happy with your career choice. If you find your passion in a career that offers few jobs and does not pay well, you will have to use your ingenuity to find a job and make a living. Many students happily make this informed choice and find a way to make it work.

> "Only passions, great passions, can elevate the soul to great things."
> Denis Diderot

© 2014, iQoncept. Used under license with Shutterstock, Inc.

Mark Twain said, "The secret of success is making your vocation your vacation." Find what you like to do. Better yet, find your passion. If you can find your passion, it is easy to invest the time and effort necessary to be successful. Aviator Charles Lindbergh said, "It is the greatest shot of adrenaline to be doing what you've wanted to do so badly. You almost feel like you could fly without the plane."[8] We may not be as excited about our careers as Charles Lindbergh, but we can find careers that match our personalities and talents and provide meaning to our lives.

How do you know when you have found your passion? You have found your passion when you are doing an activity and you do not notice that the time is passing. The great painter Picasso often talked about how quickly time passed while he was painting. He said, "When I work, I relax; doing nothing or entertaining visitors makes me tired." Whether you are an artist, an athlete, a scientist, or a business entrepreneur, passion provides the energy needed to be successful. It helps you to grow and create. When you are using your talents to grow and create, you can find meaning and happiness in your life.

Psychologist Martin Seligman has written a book entitled *Authentic Happiness,* in which he writes about three types of work orientation: a job, a career, and a calling.[9] A job is what you do for the paycheck at the end of the week. Many college students have jobs to earn money for college. A career has deeper personal meaning. It involves achievement, prestige, and power. A calling is

defined as "a passionate commitment to work for its own sake."[10] When you have found your calling, the job itself is the reward. He notes that people who have found their calling are consistently happier than those who have a job or even a career. One of the ways that you know you have found your calling is when you are in the state of "flow." The state of "flow" is defined as "complete absorption in an activity whose challenges mesh perfectly with your abilities."[11] People who experience "flow" are happier and more productive. They do not spend their days looking forward to Friday. Understanding your personal strengths is the beginning step to finding your calling.

Seligman adds that any job can become a calling if you use your personal strengths to do the best possible job. He cited a study of hospital cleaners. Although some viewed their job as drudgery, others viewed the job as a calling. They believed that they helped patients get better by working efficiently and anticipating the needs of doctors and nurses. They rearranged furniture and decorated walls to help patients feel better. They found their calling by applying their personal talents to their jobs. As a result, their jobs became a calling.

Sometimes we wait around for passion to find us. That probably won't happen. The first step in finding your passion is to know yourself. Then find an occupation in which you can use your talents. You may be able to find your passion by looking at your present job and finding a creative way to do it based on your special talents. It has been said that there are no dead-end jobs, just people who cannot see the possibilities. Begin your search for passion by looking at your personal strengths and how you can apply them in the job market. If the job that you have now is not your passion, see what you can learn from it and then use your skills to find a career where you are more likely to find your passion.

> "Success is not the key to happiness; happiness is the key to success. If you love what you are doing, you will be successful."
>
> Anonymous

JOURNAL ENTRIES

Exploring Your Personality and Major

Go to http://www.collegesuccess1.com/JournalEntries.htm for Word files of the Journal Entries

Success over the Internet

Visit the *College Success Website* at http://www.collegesuccess1.com/

The *College Success Website* is continually updated with new topics and links to the material presented in this chapter. Topics include:

- Personality profiles
- Online personality assessments
- Personality types of famous people in history
- Personality types and relationships
- Personality types and marriage
- Personality and careers
- Personality and communication
- Choosing your major
- Topics just for fun

Contact your instructor if you have any problems in accessing the *College Success Website*.

Notes

1. Judith Provost and Scott Anchors, eds., *Applications of the Myers-Briggs Type Indicator in Higher Education* (Palo Alto, CA: Consulting Psychologists Press, 1991), 51.

2. Ibid., 49.

3. Otto Kroeger and Janet Thuesen, *Type Talk: The 16 Personality Types That Determine How We Live, Love and Work* (New York: Dell, 1989), 204.

4. Ibid.

5. Allen L. Hammer and Gerald P. Macdaid, *MBTI Career Report Manual* (CA: Consulting Psychologist Press, 1998), 57–89.

6. PayScale, "2013–14 College Salary Report," www.payscale.com/college-salary-report-2014/, accessed September 2013.

7. Ibid.

8. Ibid.

9. Ibid.

10. Martin Seligman, *Authentic Happiness* (Free Press, 2002).

11. Martin Seligman, as reported by Geoffrey Cowley, "The Science of Happiness," *Newsweek,* September 16, 2002, 49.

12. Ibid.

CHAPTER 12

Communication and Relationships

Learning Objectives

Read to answer these key questions:

- What is my personal communication style?

- What are some problems in communication?

- What are some techniques for being a good listener?

- What is the best way to communicate in a crisis situation?

- How does language affect behavior?

- What are some conflict management techniques?

- What are the qualities of a good friendship?

- How can I get along with my roommate?

- How can I improve my relationships?

- How is failure an opportunity for learning?

When you look back on your college experience, what you are most likely to remember and value are the personal relationships established while in college. These relationships can be a source of great pleasure or disappointment. What makes a good relationship? The answer to this question is complex and different for each individual. Good relationships begin with an understanding of personality differences and the components of effective communication. These skills can be useful in establishing satisfying friendships, happy marriages, effective parenting skills, and good relationships in the workplace.

Understanding Your Personal Communication Style

Becoming familiar with personality types can help you better understand yourself and others. Personality has a major impact on our style of communication. While we can make some generalizations about personality types, keep in mind that each individual is unique and may be a combination of the various types. For example, some people are a combination of introvert and extravert. The following descriptions will help you begin thinking about your own communication style and understanding others who are different. Remember that each personality type has positive and negative aspects. Knowledge of these differences can help individuals accentuate the positives and keep the negatives in perspective.

© 2014, VLADGRIN. Used under license with Shutterstock, Inc.

Introvert and Extravert Types

Extraverts are very social types who easily start conversations with strangers as well as friends. They know a lot of people and have many friends. They like going to parties and other social events and are energized by talking to people. They like to talk on the telephone and can read while watching TV, listening to music, or carrying on a conversation with someone else. They find talking easy and sometimes dominate the conversation. They find it more difficult to listen. They tend to talk first and think later, and sometimes regret that they have put their foot in their mouths.

In personal relationships, extraverts are fun to know and get along well with others. It is easy for them to make a date and do the talking. When extraverts are in conflict situations, they just talk louder and faster. They believe that the argument can be won if they can say just one more thing or provide more explanation. If there is a problem, extraverts want to talk about it right away. If they cannot talk about it, they become very frustrated.

The **introvert** is the opposite of the extravert. Introverts want to rehearse what they are going to say before they say it. They need quiet for concentration and enjoy peace and quiet. They have great powers of concentration and can focus their attention on projects for a long period of time. Because they tend to be quieter than extraverts, they are perceived as great listeners. Because they need time to think before talking, they often find it difficult to add their ideas to a conversation, especially when talking with extraverts. They often wish they could participate more in conversations. Because they are reserved and reflective, people often label the introvert as shy. In American society, introverts are the minority. There are three extraverts to every introvert. For this reason, the introvert is often pressured to act like an extravert. This can cause the introvert a great deal of anxiety.

The introvert often finds it difficult to start conversations or invite someone on a date. Introverts are often attracted to extraverts because they can relax and let the extravert do the talking. In conflict situations, the introverts are at a disadvantage. They will often withdraw from conflict because they need time to think about the situation and go over in their minds what to say. Introverts become stressed if they are faced with a conflict without advance notice.

Introverts and extraverts can improve their relationship by understanding each other and respecting their differences. The extravert can improve communication with the introvert by pausing to let the introvert have time to speak. He or she has to make a conscious effort to avoid monopolizing the conversation. Introverts can improve communication by making an effort to communicate. Introverts sometimes act like extraverts in social situations. Since this takes effort, they may need quiet time to relax and recharge after social events.

Imagine that two roommates are opposite types, extravert and introvert. The extravert enjoys talking and making noises. She will have guests, take telephone calls, and play music in the background while studying. These actions will cause the introvert to withdraw and leave the room to find a quiet place to study. These two roommates need to talk about their differences and do some compromising to get along with one another.

Sensing and Intuitive Types

Sensing types collect information through the senses. Their motto could be, "Seeing is believing." They are practical and realistic. They like communication to be exact and sequential. They want details and facts. They ask specific questions and want concrete answers. About 70 percent of the population of the United States is the sensing type.

In a dating situation, the sensing type focuses on actual experience. A sensor will describe the date in terms of what his or her companion looked like, how the food tasted, how the music sounded, and the feelings involved. During the date, sensors may talk about concrete events such as people they have known, experiences they have had, and places they have visited. Sensing types are generally on time for the date and get irritated if the other person is late. In conflict situations, sensing types argue the facts. They often don't see the big issues because they are concentrating on the accuracy of the facts.

Intuitive types gather information from the senses and immediately look for possibilities, meanings, and relationships between ideas. They are often ingenious and creative. Sensing types often describe intuitives as dreamers who have their heads in the clouds. They represent about 30 percent of the population.

In social situations such as dating, the intuitive person starts to fantasize and imagine what it is going to be like before it begins. The fantasies are often more exciting than the actual date. Conversations follow many different and creative trains of thought. Intuitive types are more likely to talk about dreams, visions, beliefs, and creative ideas, skipping from one topic to another. Sensing types sometimes have difficulty following the conversation. Intuitive types are less worried about being exactly on time. They believe that time is flexible and may not be on time for the date, much to the annoyance of sensing types. In conflict situations, intuitive types like to make broad generalizations. When sensing types remind them of the facts, they may accuse them of nitpicking.

Having both sensing and intuitive types in a relationship or business environment has many advantages, as long as these types can understand and appreciate one another. Sensing types need intuitive types to bring up new possibilities, deal with changes, and understand different perspectives. Intuitive types need sensing types to deal with facts and details.

Feeling and Thinking Types

Feeling types prefer to make decisions based on what they feel to be right or wrong based on their subjective values. They prefer harmony and are often described as tenderhearted. Other people's feelings are an important consideration in any decision they make. The majority of women (60 percent) are feeling types. In a conflict situation, feeling types take things personally. They prefer to avoid disagreements and will give in to reestablish a harmonious relationship.

Thinking types are logical, detached, analytical, and objective and make decisions based on these characteristics. They like justice and clarity. The majority of men (60 percent) are thinking types. In a conflict situation, thinking types use logical arguments. They often get frustrated with feeling types and think they are too emotional.

In a dating situation, the differences between feelers and thinkers can cause much misunderstanding and conflict. Thinking types strive to understand love and intimacy. Feeling types like to experience emotions. Thinking types process and analyze their feelings. For the thinker, love is to be analyzed. For the feeling types, love just happens.

Remember that while most women are feeling types and most men are thinking types, there are still 40 percent of women who are thinking types and 40 percent of men who are feeling types. Unfortunately, because of gender stereotyping, feeling-type men are often seen as less masculine and thinking-type women are seen as less feminine.

There is much to gain from understanding and appreciating the differences between feeling and thinking types. Feeling types need thinking types to analyze, organize, follow policy, and weigh the evidence. Thinking types need feeling types to understand how others feel and establish harmony in relationships or in a business environment.

Judging and Perceptive Types

Judging types prefer their environment to be structured, scheduled, orderly, planned, and controlled. Judging types even plan and organize their recreation time. They need events to be planned and organized in order to relax. They are quick to make decisions, and once the decisions are made, they find it difficult to change them. In the social scene, judging types schedule and plan the dates. When traveling, judging types carefully pack their suitcases using a list of essential items to make sure that nothing is forgotten. In conflict situations, judging types know that they are right. They tend to see issues in terms of right and wrong, good and bad, or black and white. It is difficult to negotiate with a judging type.

Perceptive types are very much the opposite of the judging types. They prefer the environment to be flexible and spontaneous. Perceptive types find it difficult to make a decision and stick to it because it limits their flexibility. Perceptive types like to collect information and keep the options open. After all, something better might come along and they do not want to be restricted by a plan or schedule. In a social situation, these types are playful and easygoing. They provide the fun and find it easy to relax. They often feel controlled by judging types. In a conflict situation, this type sees many options to resolve the situation. They have trouble resolving conflicts because they keep finding many possible solutions.

The preference for judging or perceiving has the most potential for conflict between individuals. Judging types can drive perceptive types crazy with their need for schedules, planning, and organization. Perceptive types drive the judging types crazy with their spontaneous and easygoing nature. In spite of these differences, judging and perceptive types are often attracted to one another. Judging types need perceptive types to encourage them to relax and have fun. Perceptive types need judging types to help them be more organized and productive. These two types need understanding and appreciation of each other to have a good relationship. They also need excellent communication skills.

It is often asked whether two people should consider personality type in establishing relationships or choosing a marriage partner. There are two theories on this. One theory is that opposites attract. If two people have opposite personality types, they will have the potential for using the strengths of both types. For example, if one marriage partner is a judging type, this person can manage the finances and keep the family organized. The perceptive type can provide the fun and help the other to relax and enjoy life. A disadvantage is that opposite types have great potential for conflict. The conflict can be resolved by understanding the other type and appreciating different strengths the opposite type brings to the relationship. The relationship cannot work if one person tries to change the other. Good communication is essential in maintaining the relationship.

Another theory is that like types attract. If you have a relationship with another person of the same type, your basic preferences are similar. However, even matching types will be different depending on the strength of each preference. Communication is easier when two people have similar views of the world. One disadvantage is that the relationship can become predictable and eventually uninteresting.

QUIZ

Communication Style

Test what you have learned by selecting the correct answers to the following questions.

1. Extraverts can help introverts improve communication by
   a. clearly explaining their point of view.
   b. pausing to give the introvert time to think and respond.
   c. talking louder and faster.

2. In a dating situation, sensing types are likely to talk about
   a. concrete events such as the weather or personal experiences.
   b. dreams and visions.
   c. creative ideas.

3. In a conflict situation, feeling types
   a. use logic to analyze the situation.
   b. engage in debate based on logical arguments.
   c. take things personally.

4. Perceptive types
   a. find it difficult to make a decision and stick to it.
   b. tend to decide quickly in order to finish the project.
   c. find it easy to be on time and meet deadlines.

5. In choosing a marriage partner it is best to
   a. choose a person with the same personality.
   b. choose a person with the opposite personality.
   c. be aware of each other's personality type to appreciate each other.

How did you do on the quiz? Check your answers: 1. b, 2. a, 3. c, 4. a, 5. c

Journal Entry #1

Consider how the following terms describe your communication style: extravert, introvert, sensing, intuitive, feeling, thinking, judging, perceptive. What is your personal communication style?

Communication for Success

To be an effective communicator, it is important to be a good listener and speaker. Practice the techniques of good listening and use language that helps you enhance your success and establish good relationships.

Problems in Communication

Effective communication involves a loop in which a sender sends a message and a receiver receives the message. Communications are disrupted when:

- The receiver doesn't receive the message.
- The receiver hears the wrong message.
- The receiver doesn't care about the message.
- The receiver is more interested in talking than listening.
- The receiver only hears part of the message.
- The receiver only hears what she or he wants to hear.
- The receiver feels threatened by the sender.
- The sender didn't send the message correctly.
- The sender left out part of the message.
- The sender talks so much that nobody listens.
- The sender is not someone you want to hear.
- The sender is annoying.
- The sender was upset and did not mean to send the message.
- The sender assumes that you should know the message already.

© 2014, mast3r. Used under license with Shutterstock, Inc.

There is a joke circulating on the Internet:

A man is driving up a steep, narrow mountain road. A woman is driving down the same road. As they pass each other, the woman leans out the window and yells, "Pig!" The man replies by calling the woman a name. They each continue on their way. As the man rounds the next corner, he crashes into a pig in the middle of the road. If only people would listen!

As you can see, there are many ways to disrupt communication. Just because a message was sent does not mean that it was received. The first step in communication is to be a good listener. Many factors interfere with good listening. Do you recognize some of these reasons for not listening?

Factors That Interfere with Good Listening

- Message overload
- Worries and anxiety
- Rapid thought
- Tired, overloaded, or distracted
- Noise and hearing problems
- Faulty assumptions

- **Message overload.** There is so much communication going on today that it is difficult to keep up with it all. There are stacks of paper, multiple email messages, text messages, television, radio, and people who want to talk to you. Introverts may find this overwhelming, while extraverts may find it exciting. Both find it challenging to keep up with all these communications and to focus on the messages.

- **Worries and anxiety.** It is difficult to listen to other people when you are preoccupied with your own thoughts. You may be thinking about an upcoming test or paper that is due or worried about a personal relationship. While others are talking, you are thinking about something else of more immediate concern to yourself.

- **Rapid thought.** People think faster than they speak. We are capable of understanding speech at about 600 words per minute, but most people talk at 100 to 150 words per minute.[1] People use the spare time to become distracted. They daydream, think about what they will do next, or think about their reply.

- **Listening is hard work.** It takes effort to listen. It requires paying attention and striving to understand. People can't listen effectively if they are tired, overloaded, or distracted.
- **Noise and hearing problems.** Our world is becoming noisier. As people get older, many suffer from hearing loss. Younger persons are suffering hearing loss from listening to loud music. It is more difficult to get your message across when people can't hear everything you are saying.
- **Faulty assumptions.** People often make faulty assumptions. They may assume that other people also know the information, and therefore they do not communicate well. Listeners may assume that they know the information already or that the information is easy, so it is not necessary for them to pay attention. Or they may assume the material is too difficult to understand and block it out.
- **Talking too much.** Since listening involves effort, people consider what they have to gain before they invest the effort in listening. They might think that there is more to gain in speaking than in listening. The speaker often feels that he or she has control. You might feel that in speaking you gain the attention or admiration of others. If you are speaking or telling a joke and everyone is listening, you feel important. Also, through speaking people release their frustration and think about their problems. They need to stop speaking in order to listen.

How to Be a Good Listener

Being a good listener takes practice and effort. Here are some tips on becoming a good listener:

- **Talk less.** It does no good to talk if no one is listening, if no one understands your message, or if your message is irrelevant to the situation. To have a better chance of communicating your message, it is important first to listen to gain an understanding of the other person and then to speak. In marriage counseling, a common technique is to have one person talk and express his or her point of view. Before the other person can talk, he or she has to accurately summarize what the previous person said. Too often people do not really listen; instead they are composing their own messages in their heads. It is a Native American custom that when members of the group assemble to talk about an important issue, a talking stick is used. Persons can only talk when they have the talking stick. When the person holding the talking stick is finished, it is passed to the next person who wants to talk. In this way, only one person can talk at a time, and the others listen.

"We have two ears and one mouth, so we should listen twice as much as we speak."

Epictetus

"Life is an echo: what you send out comes back."

Chinese Proverb

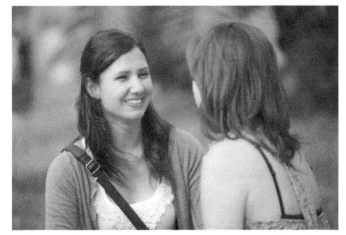

© 2014, William Perugini. Used under license with Shutterstock, Inc.

- **Minimize distractions.** For important conversations, turn off the TV or the music. Find quiet time to focus on the communication. Manage your internal distractions as well. Focus your attention on listening first and then speaking.

- **Don't judge too soon.** Try to understand first and then evaluate. If you judge too soon, you may not have the correct information and might make a mistake. People are especially vulnerable to this problem when their ideas do not agree with those of the speaker. They focus on defending their position without really listening to the other point of view.

- **Look for the main point.** You may become distracted or impatient with people who talk too much. Try to be patient and look for the main points. In a lecture, write these points down.

- **Ask questions.** You will need to ask questions to make sure that you understand. Each person looks at the world in a different way. The picture in my mind will not match the picture in your mind. We will have a better idea of each other's pictures if we ask for more information.

- **Feed back meaning.** This communication technique involves restating the speaker's ideas in your own words to check the meaning. This is important because speakers often:
  - say one thing and mean something else.
  - say something but don't mean it, especially if emotions are involved.
  - speak in a way that causes confusion.

Feeding back meaning has two important benefits. It helps speakers to clarify their thoughts and it helps listeners make sure that they have received the correct message. Here are several ways to feed back meaning:

1. **Restate what has been said.** Sometimes this is called parroting. It is useful for clarifying information, but sometimes it annoys people if you use it too much.

   Statement: Turn right at the light.

   Feedback: Okay. So you want me to turn right at the light?

2. **Ask for clarification.**

   Statement: Take the next exit on the freeway.

   Feedback: Do you mean this exit coming up now or the next one?

   Statement: Pig! (referring to the joke about the man and woman on the mountain road)

   Feedback: What do you mean by "pig"?

   Statement: Be careful. There is a pig in the road ahead.

3. **Reword the message to check your understanding.** First, restate what you have heard and then ask for clarification. This is called active listening.

   Statement: Turn in the draft of your paper next week.

   Feedback: You want the draft next week. Does that include the outline, the draft of the entire paper, and the bibliography? Should it be typed, or is handwritten okay?

   Statement: Don't worry about your grade on this quiz.

   Feedback: You said not to worry about my grade on this quiz. Does that mean that the grade won't count or that I can make up the quiz?

   Statement: I need this project completed by Friday.

   Feedback: So this project needs to be done by Friday. What parts do you want included and how would you like me to do it?

4. **Listen for feelings.** Feelings get in the way of clear thinking. A person may say one thing and mean something else.

   Statement: Just forget about it!

   Feedback: I'm confused. You ask me to forget about it, but you sound angry.

5. **Use your own words to restate what the speaker has said.** In this way, you help the speaker to clarify his or her thoughts and hopefully to come up with some solutions.

   Statement: I wish I didn't have to work so much. I'm getting behind in school, but I have bills to pay. I have to work.

   Feedback: You seem to be caught in a bind between school and work.

   Statement: That's right. I just can't keep working so much. Maybe I should go check out financial aid and scholarships.

- **Be careful about giving advice.** Whenever possible, listen closely and be an active listener. This helps the person speaking to you to clarify his or her thoughts and think about alternatives. When you listen, it is tempting to offer advice because you may have had similar experiences. You can share your experiences and offer suggestions, but beware of giving advice for these reasons:

  - If you give advice and it turns out badly, you may be blamed.
  - If you give advice and it turns out right, the person may become dependent on you.
  - People are unique individuals with unique life situations. Something that works for one person may not work for another person at all.

Journal Entry #2

Review the section on "Communication for Success." What are three ways to improve your communication and listening skills?

I can improve my communication and listening skills by . . . .

Helpful Communication in a Crisis Situation

Most people have been in a situation where their friends or family are in distress and need immediate help. If you become aware of a dangerous or critical situation, seek professional help. Go to your college counseling center, a community service organization, your doctor, or a religious leader for help. Here are some general ideas for being a helpful listener:

- Let the person talk. Talking helps to clarify thinking.
- Paraphrase or feed back meaning.
- Avoid being critical. Comments such as "You asked for it" or "I told you so" do not help. They just make the person angry.
- Help the person analyze the situation and come up with alternatives for solving the problem.
- Share your experiences but resist giving advice.
- Ask questions to clarify the situation.
- Offer to be supportive. Say, "I'm here if you need me" or "I care about you."

© 2014, Monkey Business Images. Used under license with Shutterstock, Inc.

- Let people express their feelings. It is not helpful to say, "Don't feel sad," for example. A person may need to feel sad and deal with the situation. The emotion can be a motivation for change.
- Don't minimize the situation. Saying, "It's only a grade (job, promotion)," minimizes the situation. It might not be important to the listener, but it is causing pain for the speaker. Give him or her time to gain perspective on the problem.
- Replace pity with understanding. It is not helpful to say, "You poor thing."

The following anonymous poem summarizes some ideas on how to be a helpful listener.

When I ask you to listen to me
    and you give me advice
    you have not done what I asked.

When I ask you to listen to me
    and you begin to tell me why I shouldn't feel that way,
    you are trampling on my feelings.

When I ask you to listen to me
    and you feel you have to do something to solve my problem,
    you have failed me, strange as that may seem.

Listen! All I asked was that you listen.
    Not talk or do—just hear me.

Advice is cheap: 50 cents will get you both Dear Abby and
    Billy Graham in the same newspaper.

And I can do for myself; I'm not helpless.
    Maybe discouraged and faltering, but not helpless.

When you do something for me that I can and need to do
    for myself, you contribute to my fear and weakness.

But, when you accept as a simple fact that I do feel what I feel,
    no matter how irrational, then I can quit trying to convince

you and can get about the business of understanding what's
behind this irrational feeling.
And when that's clear, the answers are obvious and I
don't need advice.

Irrational feelings make sense when we understand what's
behind them.

Perhaps that's why prayer works, sometimes, for some people
because God is sometimes mute and doesn't give advice or
try to fix things. He often listens and lets you
work it out for yourself.

So please listen and hear me. And, if you want to
talk, wait a minute for your turn; and I'll listen to you.[2]

The Language of Responsibility

The way we use language reflects our willingness to take responsibility for ourselves and
affects our relationships with others. Knowing about "I" and "you" messages, as well as
how we choose certain words, can help us to improve communications. We can become
aware of how our thoughts influence our behavior and communication. We can choose to
use cooperation in dealing with conflicts.

"I" and "You" Statements

When communicating, watch how you use the pronouns "I" and "you." For example, if you
walk in and find your apartment a mess, you might say to your roommate, "Just look at
this mess! You are a slob!" Your roommate will probably be angry and reply by calling you
an equally offensive name. You have accomplished nothing except becoming angry and
irritating your roommate. Using the pronoun "you" and calling a person a name implies
that you are qualified to make a judgment about another person. Even if this is true, you
will not make any friends or communicate effectively.

"You" statements label and blame. They demand a rebuttal. They cause negative emotions and escalate the situation. How would you react to these statements?

You must be crazy.
You are really a jerk!

You would probably get angry and think of a nasty reply in return. When you use an
"I" message, you accept responsibility for yourself. You might say something like this:

I don't understand.
I feel angry.

There are many ways to make "I" statements. Instead of calling your roommate a
slob, you could:

1. **Make an observation.** Describe the behavior.
   Your things are all over the floor.

2. **State your feelings.** Tell how you feel about the behavior.
   I get angry when I have to step over your things on the floor.

3. **Share your thoughts.** Say what you think about the situation, but beware of disguised "you" messages such as,
   "I think you are a slob."
   I think it is time to clean up.

4. **State what you want.**
   Please pick up your things.

5. **State your intentions.** Say what you are going to do.
   If you do not pick up your things, I will put them in your room.

Here are some examples of "I" statements that can be used to express various feelings:

To express anger	To express sadness
I don't like	I feel disappointed
I feel frustrated	I am sad that
I am angry that	I feel hurt
I feel annoyed	I wanted
I want	I want
To express fear	To say you are sorry
I feel worried	I feel embarrassed
I am afraid	I am sorry
I feel scared	I feel ashamed
I do not want	I didn't want
I need, I want	I want

A complete "I" message describes the other person's behavior, states your feelings, and describes the effect of the other's behavior on you. For example, "When your things are all over the floor (behavior), I feel angry (feeling) because I have to pick up after you (how it affects me)." A variation on the "I" message is the "we" message. The "we" statement assumes that both persons need to work on the problem. For example, "We need to work on this problem so that we don't have to argue."

Journal Entry #3

You are having a disagreement with a roommate, sibling, or spouse about keeping the house clean. Write three "I" statements that could help to improve the situation.

Words Are Powerful

The words that we choose have a powerful influence on behavior. One of the least powerful words is the word "should." This word is heard frequently on college campuses:

I should do my homework.
I should go to class.
I should get started on my term paper.

Figure 10.1 Ladder of Powerful Speaking.

The problem with "should" is that it usually does not lead to action and may cause people to feel guilty. If you say, "I should get started on my term paper," the chances are that you will not start on it.

If you say, "I might get started on my term paper," at least you are starting to think about possibilities. You might actually get started on your term paper. If you say, "I want to get started on my term paper," the chances are getting better that you will get started. You are making a choice. If you say, "I intend to start on my term paper," you have at least expressed good intentions. The best way to get started is to make a promise to yourself that you will get started: "I will start on my term paper." The words "should," "might," "want," and "promise" or "will" represent a powerful ladder of communication. As you move up the ladder, you are more likely to accomplish what you say you will do. This ladder moves from obligation to promise, or a personal choice to act:

Next time you hear yourself saying that you "should" do something, move one more step up the ladder. Move from obligation to making a personal decision to do what is important to you. For example, if a friend wants to borrow money from you, which response is the most powerful?

- I really should pay the money back.
- Well, I might pay the money back.
- I really want to pay the money back.
- I intend to pay the money back.
- I promise to pay the money back.

Negative Self-Talk

Self-talk is what you say to yourself. It is the stream of consciousness or the little voice in your head. This self-talk affects how you communicate with others. If your self-talk is negative, you will have lower self-esteem and find it more difficult to communicate with

Beliefs that Lead to Negative Self-Talk

- I have to be perfect.
- I need everyone's approval.
- That's always the way it is.
- You made me feel that way.
- I'm helpless.
- If something bad can happen, it will.

© 2014, iQoncept. Used under license with Shutterstock, Inc.

others. There are some common irrational beliefs that lead to negative self-talk. Becoming aware of these beliefs can help you to avoid them.

- **I have to be perfect.** If you believe this, you will think that you have to be a perfect communicator and deliver flawless speeches. Since this goal is unattainable, it causes stress and anxiety. If you believe in this idea, you may try to pretend or act as if you were perfect. This takes up a lot of energy and keeps others from liking you. Everyone makes mistakes. When people stop trying to be perfect and accept themselves as they are, they can begin to relax and work on the areas needing improvement. They can write papers and make speeches knowing that they will probably make mistakes, just like the rest of the human population.

- **I need the approval of everyone.** A person who believes this finds it necessary to have the approval of almost everyone. Much energy is spent in gaining approval from others. If approval is not obtained, the person may feel nervous, embarrassed, or apologetic. It is not possible to win the approval of everyone because each individual is unique. Those who constantly seek approval will sacrifice their own values and what they think is right just to please others.

- **That's always the way it is.** People who believe this statement are making a generalization. They take a few events and use them to predict the future or exaggerate their shortcomings. Here are some examples:
  - I'm not a technical person. I can't install my computer.
  - I'm not good at numbers. I'll never to able to pass algebra.
  - Some husband (wife) I am! I forgot our anniversary.
  - You never listen to me.

Notice the absolute nature of these statements. Absolute statements are almost always false and lead to anger and negative thinking. Remember that with a positive attitude, things can change in the future. Just because it was one way in the past does not mean it has to be the same in the future. Beware of "always" and "never" statements.

- **You made me feel that way.** Your own self-talk, rather than the actions of others, is what causes emotions. No one can make you feel sad or happy. You feel sad or happy based what you say to yourself about an event. If someone makes a negative comment about you, you can say to yourself that it is only the other person's opinion and choose how you react. Your reactions and emotions depend on how much importance you decide to attach to the event. People tend to react strongly to a comment if it is from someone they care about.

> It's not who you are that holds you back, it's who you think you're not.
> Denis Waitley

People also do not cause the emotions of others. Some people do not communicate honestly because they are afraid of causing negative emotions in the other person. They may hesitate to tell someone how they really feel. This lack of honesty leads to increasing hostility over time and difficulties in communication.

- **I'm helpless.** If you believe that what happens to you is beyond your control, you will be unlikely to do something to make the situation better. Here are some examples of helpless self-talk:
    - I'm a shy person. It is hard for me to talk to people.
    - I won't consider that career. Women are always discriminated against in that field.
    - It's difficult for me to meet people.

    Believing such statements, shy people don't attempt to talk to others, women limit their career options, and people give up trying to make friends. Believe that there is a way to change, and you can make your life better.

- **If something bad can happen, it will happen.** If you expect the worst, you may take actions that make it happen. If you expect that your speech will be a disaster, you may not prepare or you may forget your notes or props. If you believe that you will not pass the interview and will never get hired, you may not even apply for the job or attempt the interview. If you believe that your personal relationships will not get better, you will not invest the effort to make things better. There will be times when you make a poor speech, get turned down for a job, or have a relationship fail. Learn from these mistakes and do better the next time.

Barriers to Effective Communication

We all want to communicate effectively and get along with people whom we care about. We want to get along with our families, be a good parent, have friends at school, and get along with the boss and our coworkers on the job. Life is just more enjoyable when we have good communication with others. Watch for these barriers to effective communication:

© 2014, ananas. Used under license with Shutterstock, Inc.

- **Criticizing.** Making negative evaluations of others by saying, "It's your fault" or "I told you so" causes anger, which gets in the way of communication.
- **Name-calling and labeling.** If you call someone a name or put a label on them, they will attack you rather than communicate with you in any meaningful way.
- **Giving advice.** Giving advice may be viewed as talking down to a person. The person may resent your advice and you as well.
- **Ordering or commanding.** If you order someone to do something, they are likely to sabotage your request.
- **Threatening.** Trying to control someone by making threats causes resentment.
- **Moralizing.** Preaching about what a person should or should not do doesn't work because it causes resentment.
- **Diverting.** Changing the subject to talk about your own problems tells the person that you do not care about them.
- **Logical arguing.** Trying to use facts to convince without taking feelings into account is a barrier to communication. Present your facts and state your point of view, but respect the other person's feelings and different point of view.[3]

"Who among us does not choose to be a little less right to be a little less lonely?"

Robert Brault

Communication for Success

Test what you have learned by selecting the correct answer to the following questions.

1. One of the biggest problems with communication is that the message sent is not always the message that is

   a. appreciated.
   b. intended.
   c. received.

2. To be a good listener, it is important to remember that

   a. it is important to listen first, so that you can understand before speaking.
   b. it is important to talk first to make sure the other has heard your point of view.
   c. it is important to assume that the other knows what you are talking about.

3. Feeding back meaning is

   a. responding to questions.
   b. restating what has been said to check understanding.
   c. unnecessary because some people find it irritating.

4. "You" statements

   a. put the blame where it needs to be.
   b. results in anger and rebuttal.
   c. are effective communication tools.

5. Which statement is the most powerful?

   a. I should get started on my paper.
   b. I want to get started on my paper.
   c. I will get started on my paper.

How did you do on the quiz? Check your answers: 1. c, 2. a, 3. b, 4. b, 5. c

Dealing with Conflict

There are several ways to approach a conflict. In every conflict, there is the potential to be a winner or a loser.

© 2014, iQoncept. Used under license with Shutterstock, Inc.

- **Win-lose.** With this approach to conflict management, one person wins and the other loses, just as in a game or sport. Competition is part of the win-lose approach. In competition, power is important. In sports, the best and most powerful team wins.

There are many kinds of power, however. Power may be based on authority. Examples might include your boss at work, your teacher, or even your parents. Another kind of power is based on mental ability or cleverness. Sometimes battles are not won by the strongest, but by the cleverest person. Another kind of power is majority rule. In many settings in a democratic society, the person with the most votes wins.

In many situations, we cannot avoid the win-lose approach. Only one team can win, only one person can get the job, and only one person can marry another. In some circumstances the person you are communicating with does not want to cooperate but to compete.

The problem with this approach is that there is only one winner. What happens to the loser? The loser can feel bad, resent the winner, give up, or try again for victory. These are not always the best alternatives in personal relationships.

- **Lose-lose.** Lose-lose is another option for resolving conflicts. Both parties lose. Both parties strive to be winners, but the struggle causes damage to both sides. Wars are often lose-lose situations. In World War II, dropping an atomic bomb caused the surrender of Japan, but it contaminated the environment with radioactive material and set a dangerous precedent for nuclear war. Russia was able to stop a civil war by destroying Grozny, the capital of Chechnya. The city became nearly uninhabitable. Everyone lost. On an interpersonal level, divorce can be a lose-lose situation if the struggle becomes destructive to both parties.

© 2014, Shutterstock, Inc.

- **Compromise.** Another approach to solving conflict is compromise, where both parties to the conflict have some of their needs met. Both make some sacrifice in order to resolve the situation. For example, the buyer and seller of a used car may agree on a price somewhere between what the seller wants to get and the buyer wants to pay. As long as both parties are satisfied with the outcome, the results are satisfactory. Difficulties arise when people are asked to compromise their values. If they must compromise on something that is truly important, they may be dissatisfied with the outcome.

© 2014, Shutterstock, Inc.

- **Win-win.** In a win-win approach, both parties work together to find a solution that meets everyone's needs. There is no loser. To reach a win-win solution, set aside competition and replace it with cooperation. This is often difficult to do because emotions are involved. Put aside emotions to discuss the issue. This may mean waiting until both parties have had the opportunity to calm down. This approach can be impossible, however, when one person wants to cooperate and the other person wants to win.

© 2014, Shutterstock, Inc.

These are the steps in a win-win approach:

1. **Identify the problem.** Identify the problem as your own. If your roommate is having a party and you cannot study, it is your problem. You need to find a quiet place to study.

2. **Set a good time to discuss the issue.** When you are feeling angry is usually not a good time to discuss issues. Set a time when both parties can focus on the problem. A good rule is to wait 24 hours to let the emotions cool down and gain some perspective.

© 2014, iQoncept. Used under license with Shutterstock, Inc.

3. **Describe your problem and needs.** Use "I" messages. Resist the temptation to label and call names. Goodwill is important.

4. **Look at the other point of view.** Understand the other person's needs, and make sure the other person understands your needs.

5. **Look for alternatives that work for both parties.**

6. **Decide on the best alternative.**

7. **Take action to implement the solution.**

The win-win approach is a good tool for effective communication and maintaining good relationships.

- Win-Lose
- Lose-Lose
- Compromise
- Win-Win

Journal Entry #4

Review the section on "Barriers to Effective Communication" and "Dealing with Conflict." What are some common mistakes that people make when trying to resolve problems and communicate effectively?

Friendships

College provides the opportunity to make new friends. These friends can broaden your perspective and make your life richer and more enjoyable. What do you value in a friendship? How can you establish and maintain good friendships?

ACTIVITY

Friendship

Friendship is a relationship that involves trust and support. Beyond this basic definition, we all have different ideas about what is important in a friendship. Here is a list of common qualities of friends. Place a checkmark next to those qualities that are important to you in establishing your personal friendships. A friend is a person who:

_____ can keep information confidential.	_____ spends time with me.
_____ is loyal.	_____ has a sense of humor.
_____ can be trusted.	_____ is independent.
_____ is warm and affectionate.	_____ has good communication skills.
_____ is supportive of who I am.	_____ is an educated person.
_____ is honest.	_____ is an intelligent person.
_____ is a creative person.	_____ knows how to have fun.
_____ encourages me to do my best.	_____ cares about me.

What are the top three qualities you would look for in a friend? List them below.

1. _____

2. _____

3. _____

The friends that you choose can have a big influence on your life, so it is important to choose them wisely. In college and in the workplace, you will have the opportunity to make new friends who can add a new dimension and perspective to your life. For example, if your friends have goals for the future and believe that completing college is important, you will be more likely to finish your own education. If your friends distract you with too many activities outside of school, your college performance may suffer.

Some students naturally make friends easily; others find making new friends more difficult. Here are some ideas for making new friends:

- **Be a good listener.** Spend equal time listening and talking. If you are doing all the talking, the other person is likely to feel left out of the conversation. Show interest in the other person's interests and ideas.

- **Talk about yourself.** Let others get to know you by sharing your interests, where you come from, and what is important to you. In this way, you can find mutual interests to enjoy.

- **Be supportive and caring.** We all have good days and bad ones. Help your friends to celebrate the good days and be supportive through life's challenges. Showing that you care is the basis of developing trust and friendship.

- **Be a friend.** Treat your friends the way you would like to be treated.

- **Spend time with your friends.** It is difficult to maintain relationships if you do not spend time sharing activities. Make spending time with friends a high priority.

- **Accept your friends for who they are.** Everyone has good and bad qualities. Accept the idea that you are not going to be able to change people to match your expectations.

- **Show appreciation.** Say thank you and make honest compliments. Think of something positive to say.

- **Be assertive.** This means that you ask for what you want and that you don't give in to doing something that you don't want to do. Being assertive means that you have the right to your feelings and opinions. There is a fine line, though, between being assertive and being aggressive. Aggressive behavior is domineering, rude, and intimidating. Aggressive individuals act without consideration of other people's rights and feelings.

- **Be selective.** Not everyone makes a good friend. Make friends with people you respect and admire. Stay away from people who are critical or make you feel unhappy. Avoid those who cause you to do things that you do not want to do. Choose friends that make you happy and encourage you to do your best.

> "Lots of people want to ride with you in the limo, but what you want is someone who will take the bus with you when the limo breaks down."
>
> Oprah Winfrey

> "Friendship is born at the moment when one person says to another, 'What! You too! I thought I was the only one.'"
>
> C.S. Lewis

> "When the character of a man is not clear to you, look at his friends."
>
> Japanese Proverb

Roommates

Getting along with a roommate can be a challenge. It can be your best or worst college experience or somewhere in between. The key to getting along with a roommate is to understand differences and to work on compromise or win-win solutions. Making a wise choice of a roommate can make the situation much easier. Below are some areas of possible disagreement for roommates:

- **Neatness.** Some students like to keep their rooms neat and others can tolerate messiness.
- **Smoking.** Some students like to smoke and others are offended by smoking.
- **Noise.** Some students need quiet for study, while others like to study with music and friends.
- **Guests.** Some students like to have guests in the room, and others do not want guests.
- **Temperature.** Some like it warm and some like it cold.
- **Studying.** Is the room a place to study or to have fun?
- **Borrowing.** Some think that borrowing is okay and some do not.
- **Sleeping.** Some go to bed early and some go to bed late. Some need quiet for sleeping.

If you have a choice of roommates, it is a good idea to discuss the above issues in advance. Even best friends can part company over some of these issues. If you are assigned a roommate, discuss the above issues to avoid conflict later on. Aim for a win-win solution or at least a compromise. If there is some conflict, following these guidelines may help.

1. Discuss problems as they arise. If you do not discuss problems, it is likely that anger and resentment will increase, causing a more serious problem at a later date.

2. Ask for what you want. Subtle hints often do not work.

3. Be nice to your roommate and treat him or her as you would want to be treated.

4. Be reasonable and overlook small problems. No one is perfect.

Relationships

A relationship starts as a friendship and then moves a step further. A relationship involves emotional attachment and interdependence. We often get our ideas about good relationships through practice and trial and error. When we make errors, the results are often painful. Although we all have different ideas about what constitutes a good relationship, at a minimum it includes these components:

- Love and caring
- Honesty
- Trust
- Loyalty
- Mutual support
- Acceptance of differences

Relationships between Men and Women

According to John Gray, popular author of *Men Are from Mars, Women Are from Venus,* men and women have such different values and needs in a relationship, it is as if they came from different planets.[4] He states that men generally value power, competency, efficiency, and achievement. He says, "A man's sense of self is defined through his ability to achieve results." While women are fantasizing about romance, a man is fantasizing about "powerful cars, faster computers, gadgets, gizmos, and new and more powerful technology."[5] The worst thing that women can do to men, according to Gray, is to offer unsolicited advice or to try to change them. These actions conflict with men's needs for power and competence and imply that they don't know what to do or can't do it on their own. We can communicate our honest feelings about our partner's behavior and ask for what we want and need. However, we should not use our feelings and requests to manipulate another person to change. Gray identifies the most important needs for men as trust, acceptance, appreciation, admiration, approval, and encouragement.

Gray says that women generally value love, communication, beauty, and relationships. Their sense of self-worth is defined through their feelings and the quality of their relationships. The worst thing that men can do to women is to offer solutions too quickly when women are talking about their feelings, rather than listening and understanding those feelings. When this happens, women get frustrated and feel a lack of intimacy. It is possible to listen carefully and understand these feelings without necessarily agreeing with them. The most important needs for women are caring, understanding, respect, devotion, validation, and reassurance.

Gray's ideas about men and women parallel the thinking and feeling dimensions of personality presented earlier. Men are 60 percent thinking types and women are 60 percent feeling types. His ideas are interesting for discussion and apply in many relationships, but it is important to be aware of gender stereotypes. Remember that 40 percent of women are thinking types and 40 percent of men are feeling types, so not all individuals will fit into the same categories that Gray describes.

Although Gray proposes that men and women generally differ in what they consider most important, he lists the following 12 components of love.[6] Men and women can improve their relationships when they demonstrate the following:

1. **Caring.** Show that you are interested and concerned about each other.

2. **Trust.** Have a positive belief in the intentions and abilities of each other.

3. **Understanding.** Listen without judgment and without presuming that you understand the feelings of the other person. In this way, both men and women can feel free to discuss what is important to them.

4. **Acceptance.** It is probably not a good idea to marry a person if you think you can change him or her into the ideal person you have in mind. Love your partner without trying to change him or her. No one is perfect; we are each a work in progress. The key is to trust the people we love to make their own improvements.

5. **Respect.** Have consideration for the thoughts and feelings of each other.

6. **Appreciation.** Acknowledge the behavior and efforts of your partner. Appreciation can be in the form of a simple "Thank you" or sending cards or flowers.

7. **Devotion.** Give priority to the relationship so that the other person feels important.

8. **Admiration.** Show approval for the unique gifts and talents of your partner.

9. **Validation.** Do not argue with feelings. Each person has a right to his or her own feelings. We can acknowledge, try to understand, and respect the feelings of another without necessarily agreeing with them.

10. **Approval.** Show approval by acknowledging the goodness and satisfaction you have with each other.

11. **Reassurance.** Show reassurance by repeatedly showing that you care, understand, and respect each other.

12. **Encouragement.** Notice the good characteristics of each other and provide encouragement and support.

How to Survive the Loss of a Relationship

Relationships require work and good communication to keep them going strong. Relationships also change over time as people grow and change. As we search for our soul mates, we may need to end some relationships and start new ones. This process can be very painful. Following the breakup of a relationship, people generally go through three predictable stages:

1. Shock or denial

2. Anger or depression

3. Understanding or acceptance[7]

Dealing with pain is a necessary part of life. Whether the pain is a result of the loss of a relationship or the death of someone important to you, there are some positive steps you can take along the road to acceptance and understanding.

- Recognize that a loss has taken place and give yourself time to adjust to this situation. The greater the loss, the more time it will take to feel better. In the meantime, try to keep up with daily routines. It is possible to feel sad and to go to work and to school. Daily routines may even take your mind off your troubles for a while.
- It is healthy to feel sad and cry. You will need to experience the pain to get over it. It is not helpful to deny pain, cover it up, or run away from it, because it will take longer to feel better.
- Talk to a friend or a counselor. Talking about how you feel will help you to understand and accept the loss.
- Don't punish yourself with thoughts that begin "If only I had . . ."
- Realize that there is a beginning and an end to pain.
- Get plenty of rest and eat well.
- Accept understanding and support from friends and family.
- Ask for help if you need it.
- Don't try to get the old relationship going again. It will just prolong the pain.
- Anticipate a positive outcome. You will feel better in the future.
- Beware of the rebound. It is not a good idea to jump into a new relationship right away.
- Beware of addictive activities such as alcohol, drugs, smoking, or overeating.
- Take time to relax and be kind to yourself.
- Use exercise as a way to deal with stress and feel better.
- Keep a journal to help deal with your emotions and learn from the situation.[8]

Failure Is an Opportunity for Learning

Everyone makes mistakes and experiences failure. This is the human condition. There is also a saying that falling down is not failure, but not getting up is. If you can view failure as an opportunity for learning, you can put it into perspective and continue making progress toward your goals. It has been said that the famous inventor Thomas Edison tried 9,999 times to invent the light bulb. When asked if he was going to fail 10,000 times, he answered, "I didn't fail. I just discovered another way not to invent the light bulb." Failure allows you to collect feedback about how you are doing.

Imagine that your life is like a ship heading toward a destination. Sometimes the sailing is smooth, and sometimes the water is choppy and dangerous and knocks you off course. Failure acts like the rudder of the ship. It helps you to make adjustments so that you stay on course. Too often we do not learn from failure because shame and blame get in the way. Gerard Nierenberg, author of *Do It Right the First Time*, advocates the "no shame, no blame" approach to dealing with errors, mistakes, or failure.[9] The first step is to identify the mistake that has been made. What went wrong? Then you look at how much damage has been done. The next step is to take an honest look at what caused the problem. The last step is to figure out a way to fix the problem and see that it does not happen again. There is no shame or blame in the process. Following this approach results in fewer errors and failures.

Harold Kushner has another view about failure:

Life is not a spelling bee, where no matter how many words you have gotten right, if you make one mistake you are disqualified. Life is more like a baseball season, where even the best team loses one-third of its games and even the worst team has its days of brilliance. Our goal is not to go all year without ever losing a game. Our goal is to win more than we lose, and if we can do that consistently enough, then when the end comes, we will have won it all.[10]

Like a baseball player, if you lose a game, analyze what went wrong and keep on practicing. Remember that you will eventually be a winner. Everyone remembers that Babe Ruth was a great baseball player and that he had 714 home runs. People do not remember that he also struck out 1,330 times. If you can look honestly at your mistakes and learn from them, you can have many winning seasons.

Journal Entry #5

Describe a situation in which you have been disappointed, such as a poor grade or the loss of a job or a relationship. Was there an opportunity to learn from the situation?

"Work as hard as you ask others to. Strive for what you believe is right, no matter the odds. Learn that mistakes can be the best teacher."
George Steinbrenner

JOURNAL ENTRIES

Communication and Relationships

Go to http://www.collegesuccess1.com/JournalEntries.htm for Word files of the Journal Entries

Success over the Internet

Visit the *College Success Website* at http://www.collegesuccess1.com/

The *College Success Website* is continually updated with new topics and links to the material presented in this chapter. Topics include:

- Expectations in relationships
- Common mistakes in relationships
- Beginning, enhancing, and ending relationships
- Dealing with anger
- Personality and relationships

Contact your instructor if you have any problems accessing the *College Success Website.*

Notes

1. A. Wolvin and C. G. Coakley, *Listening*, 3rd ed. (Dubuque, IA: W. C. Brown, 1988), 208.

2. *Care of the Mentally Ill* (F.A. Davis, 1977).

3. T. Gordon, *Parent Effectiveness Training* (New York: McGraw-Hill, 1970).

4. John Gray, *Men Are from Mars, Women Are from Venus* (New York: HarperCollins, 1992).

5. Ibid., 16.

6. Ibid., 133–37.

7. Melba Colgrove, Harold Bloomfield, and Peter McWilliams, *How to Survive the Loss of a Love* (New York: Bantam Books, 1988).

8. Adapted from Colgrove, Bloomfield, and McWilliams, *How to Survive the Loss of a Love.*

9. Gerard Nierenberg, *Doing It Right the First Time* (New York: John Wiley and Sons, 1996).

10. Harold Kushner, *Becoming Aware* (Dubuque, IA: Kendall Hunt).

CHAPTER 13

Planning Your Career and Education

Learning Objectives

Read to answer these key questions:

- What are some employment trends for the future?

- What are work skills necessary for success in the twenty-first century?

- How do I research a career?

- How do I plan my education?

- What are some new job search strategies?

- What is a dangerous opportunity?

It is always easier to get where you are going if you have a road map or a plan. To start the journey, it is helpful to know about yourself, including your personality, interests, talents, and values. Once you have this picture, you will need to know about the world of work and job trends that will affect your future employment opportunities. Next, you will need to make decisions about which road to follow. Then, you will need to plan your education to reach your destination. Finally, you will need some job-seeking skills such a writing a resume and cover letter, using social media to market yourself online, and preparing for a successful interview.

© 2014, Kiselev Andrey Valerevich. Used under license with Shutterstock, Inc.

Employment Trends

The world is changing quickly, and these changes will affect your future career. To assure your future career success, you will need to become aware of career trends and observe how they change over time so that you can adjust your career plans accordingly. For example, recently a school was established for training bank tellers. The school quickly went out of business and the students demanded their money back because they were not able to get jobs. A careful observer of career trends would have noticed that bank tellers are being replaced by automatic teller machines (ATMs) and would not have started a school for training bank tellers. Students observant of career trends would not have paid money for the training. It is probably a good idea for bank tellers to look ahead and plan a new career direction.

How can you find out about career trends that may affect you in the future? Become a careful observer by reading about current events. Good sources of information include:

- Your local newspaper, especially the business section
- News programs
- Current magazines
- Government statistics and publications
- The Internet

When thinking about future trends, use your critical thinking skills. Sometimes trends change quickly or interact in different ways. For example, since we are using email to a great extent today, it might seem that mail carriers would not be as much in demand in the future. However, since people are buying more goods over the Internet, there has been an increased demand for mail carriers and other delivery services. Develop the habit of looking at what is happening to see if you can identify trends that may affect your future.

Usually trends get started as a way to meet the following needs:[1]

- To save money
- To reduce cost

- To do things faster
- To make things easier to use
- To improve safety and reliability
- To lessen the impact on the environment

The following are some trends to watch that may affect your future career. As you read about each trend, think about how it could affect you.

Baby Boomers, Generation X, the Millennials and the New Generation Z

About every 20 years, sociologists begin to describe a new generation with similar characteristics based on shared historical experiences. Each generation has different opportunities and challenges in the workplace.

The Baby Boomers were born following World War II between 1946 and 1964. Four out of every 10 adults today are in this Baby Boom Generation.[2] Because there are so many aging Baby Boomers, the average age of Americans is increasing. Life expectancy is also increasing. By 2015 the projected life expectancy will be 76.4 for men and 81.4 for women.[3] In the new millennium, many more people will live to be 100 years old or more! Think about the implications of an older population. Older people need such things as health care, recreation, travel, and financial planning. Occupations related to these needs are likely to be in demand now and in the future.

Those born between 1965 and 1977 are often referred to as Generation X. They are sometimes called the "baby bust" generation because fewer babies were born during this period than in the previous generations. There is much in the media about this generation having to pay higher taxes and Social Security payments to support the large number of aging Baby Boomers. Some say that this generation will not enjoy the prosperity of the Baby Boomers. Those who left college in the early nineties faced a recession and the worst job market since World War II.[4] Many left college in debt and returned home to live with their parents. Because of a lack of employment opportunities, many in this generation became entrepreneurs, starting new companies at a faster rate than previous generations.

Jane Bryant Quinn notes that in spite of economic challenges, Generation Xers have a lot going for them:[5]

- They have record-high levels of education, which correlate with higher income and lower unemployment.
- There is a demand for more skilled workers, so employers are more willing to train employees. Anthony Carnevale, chairman of the National Commission for Employment Policy, "sees a big demand for 'high-school plus'—a high school diploma plus technical school or junior college."
- Generation Xers are computer literate, and those who use computers on the job earn 10 to 15 percent more than those who don't.
- This group often has a good work ethic valued by employers. However, they value a balanced lifestyle with time for outside interests and family.
- As Baby Boomers retire, more job opportunities are created for this group.
- Unlike the Baby Boomers, this generation was born into a more integrated and more diverse society. They are better able than previous generations to adapt to diversity in society and the workplace.

Many of today's college students are part of the Millennial Generation, born between 1977 and 1995. This generation is sometimes called Generation Y or the Echo Boomers, since they are the children of the Baby Boomers.[6] This new generation of approximately 60 million is three times larger than Generation X and will eventually exceed the number of Baby Boomers. In this decade, they will become the largest teen population in U.S. history. As the Millennials reach college age, they will attend college in increasing numbers. In the next 10 years, college enrollments will increase by approximately 300,000 students per year. Colleges will find it difficult to accommodate rapidly increasing numbers of students, and as a result, the Millennial Generation will face increasingly competitive college admissions criteria.

Millennials are more ethnically diverse than previous generations with 34 percent ethnic minorities. One in four lives with a single parent; three in four have working mothers. Most of them started using computers before they were five years old. Marketing researchers describe this new generation as "technologically adept, info-savvy, a cyber-generation, the clickeratti."[7] They are the connected generation, accustomed to cell phones, chatting on the Internet, and listening to downloaded music.

Young people in the Millennial Generation share a different historical perspective from the Baby Boom Generation. Baby Boomers remember the Vietnam War and the assassinations of President John F. Kennedy and Martin Luther King. For Millennials, school shootings such as Columbine and acts of terrorism such as the Oklahoma City bombing and the 9–11 attack on New York City stand out as important events. The Millennial Generation will see their main problems as dealing with violence, easy access to weapons, and the threat of terrorism.

Neil Howe and William Strauss paint a very positive picture of this new generation in their book *Millennials Rising: The Next Great Generation*:

- Millennials will rebel by tearing down old institutions that do not work and building new and better institutions. The authors predict that this will be the can-do generation filled with technology planners, community shapers, institution builders, and world leaders.
- Surveys show that this generation describes themselves as happy, confident, and positive.
- They are cooperative team players.
- They generally accept authority and respect their parents' values.
- They follow rules. The rates of homicides, violent crime, abortion, and teen pregnancy are decreasing rapidly.
- The use of alcohol, drugs, and tobacco is decreasing.
- Millennials have a fascination with and mastery of new technology.
- Their most important values are individuality and uniqueness.[8]

© 2014, Vaju Ariel. Used under license with Shutterstock, Inc.

In the past, new generations emerged about every twenty years. However, because of rapid social change, generations are now being defined in shorter time periods. A new generation born since 1995 is currently emerging. Various names for this generation have been proposed such as Generation Z, Generation Wii, the iGeneration, Gen Tech, Digital Natives, Net Gen, and the Plurals.[9] These names reflect this generation's fascination and ease of using technology as well as their increasing diversity. This is a large generation with one in four Americans under 18 years old.[10]

This generation has been affected by historical events such as the election of President Obama (the first biracial president), events surrounding 9/11, wars in Iraq and Afghanistan, the tsunami and nuclear meltdown in Japan, school violence, and economic recession. They are referred to as digital natives since they have always lived in a world with the Internet, cell phones and iPods, and other devices.

Some characteristic of this new generation include:[11]

- This is the last generation with a Caucasian majority. Only 55% of this generation is Caucasian as compared to 72% of Baby Boomers. In 2019, less than 50% of births will be Caucasian.

- They are more positive than older Americans about becoming an ethnically diverse society and more likely to have friends from different racial, ethnic, and religious groups.

- There is a continuing decline in two-parent households with only two out of three people from two parent households. Increased same sex marriage is changing the definition of family.

- Because of the extended recession, they are less likely to believe in the "American Dream" and to be hopeful for the future. They tend to be more realistic.

- Women are more likely to get a college degree and hold 51% of managerial and professional jobs. As a result, gender roles are blending with men assuming more familial responsibilities.

- It is an age of "girl power." Girls ages 8–15 care more about their grades than boys and have more expectations of receiving a college degree and having work that changes the world.

- Technology will continue to influence this group as in the New Millennial Generation. Use of technology will transform the way that people communicate and purchase goods. People will communicate with shorter and more immediate communications such as texting and Twitter. More purchases will be made on the Internet.

- This generation hopes use technology as a tool to change the world.

It is predicted that the world of work for both the Millennials and Generation Z will be dramatically different. Previous generations anticipated having a lifetime career. By the year 2020, many jobs will probably be short-term contracts. This arrangement will provide cost savings and efficiency for employers and flexibility for employees to start or stop work to take vacations, train for new jobs, or meet family responsibilities. One in five people will be self-employed. Retirement will be postponed as people look forward to living longer and healthier lives.[12]

Journal Entry #1

Describe your generation (Baby Boomer, Generation X, New Millennial or Generation Z.) What are your best qualities and challenges?

Moving from Goods to Services and Technology

Human society has moved through several stages. The first stage, about 20,000 years ago, was the hunting and gathering stage. During this time, society depended on the natural environment for food and other resources. When natural resources were depleted, the community moved to another area. The second stage, some 10,000 years ago, was the agricultural stage. Human beings learned to domesticate animals and cultivate crops. This allowed people to stay in one place and develop more permanent villages. About 200 years ago, industrial societies came into being by harnessing power sources to produce goods on a large scale.

Today in the United States, we are evolving into a service, technology, and information society. Fewer people are working in agriculture and manufacturing. Futurists John Naisbitt et al. note that we are moving toward a service economy based on high technology, rapid communications, biotechnology for use in agriculture and medicine, health care, and sales of merchandise.[13] Service areas with increasing numbers of jobs include health care and social assistance; professional, scientific, and technical services; educational services; administrative and support services; waste management and remediation services; accommodation and food services; government; retail trade; transportation and warehousing, finance and insurance; arts, entertainment, and recreation; wholesale trade; real estate, rental, and leasing; and information and management.

Increased Opportunities in Health Care

If you are interested in science and technology along with helping other people, there are many career opportunities in health care. It is estimated that by 2018, there will be an increase of four million new jobs in health care, which will account for 26 percent of all new jobs.[14] This trend is being driven by an aging population, increased longevity, health care reform, and new developments in the pharmaceutical and medical fields. Because of increased health care costs, many of the jobs done by doctors, nurses, dentists, or physical therapists are now being done by physician's assistants, medical assistants, dental assistants, physical therapy aides, and home health aides. Health care workers will increasingly use technology to do their work. For example, a new occupation is nursing informatics, which combines traditional nursing skills with computer and information science.

Increased Need for Education

In the past, the life pattern for many people was to graduate from school, go to work, and eventually retire. Because of the rapid changes in technology and society today, workers will need additional training and education over a lifetime. Education will take place in a variety of forms: community college courses, training on the job, private training sessions, and learning on your own. Those who do not keep up with the new technology will find that their skills quickly become obsolete. Those who do keep up will find their skills in demand.

As we transition from manufacturing to service and technical careers, education beyond high school will become increasingly important. According to the Bureau of Labor Statistics,

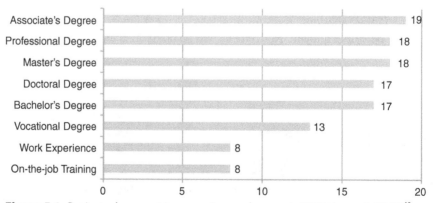

Figure 5.1 Projected percent increase in employment, 2008 through 2018.[15]

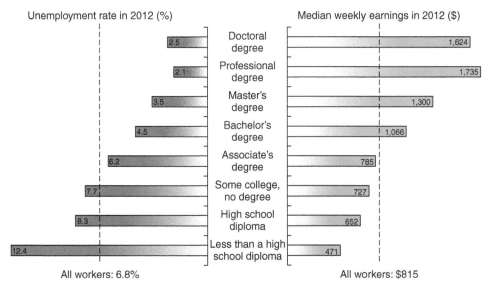

Unemployment rate in 2012 (%)		Median weekly earnings in 2012 ($)
2.5	Doctoral degree	1,624
2.1	Professional degree	1,735
3.5	Master's degree	1,300
4.5	Bachelor's degree	1,066
6.2	Associate's degree	785
7.7	Some college, no degree	727
8.3	High school diploma	652
12.4	Less than a high school diploma	471
All workers: 6.8%		All workers: $815

Figure 5.2 Education pays, unemployment rate and median weekly earnings, 2009.[16]
Source: Bureau of Labor Statistics, Current Population Survey

occupations that require a postsecondary degree will account for nearly half of all new jobs from 2008 to 2018, with the fastest growth in jobs requiring an associate's degree or higher. In addition, higher education will result in higher earnings and lower unemployment.[17]

Young people who do not continue their education are likely to be stuck in lower-paying jobs, while those who continue their education will have higher-paying jobs. Author Joyce Lain Kennedy believes that the middle class is becoming an endangered species.[18] She states that many jobs traditionally held by the middle class have been "dumbed down," making them so simple that anyone can do them. These jobs pay very little and offer no benefits, no employment stability, and little opportunity for advancement. Young people often hold these jobs in their teens and twenties.

At the other end of the job continuum are jobs requiring a college education or training beyond high school. These high-end jobs often require technical or computer skills.

These are the jobs that pay better and offer benefits. It seems that we are becoming a nation of haves and have-nots who are separated by their education and technical skills.

Going Green!

Have you purchased organic products or an energy-efficient light bulb, appliance, or car? If so, you are part of a new environmental movement that is gaining impetus in the U.S., the rise of social responsibility and the citizen consumer. Businesses that are seen as green attract consumers who are concerned about using energy efficiently, new sources of energy, and preserving the environment. In addition to profit, businesses are now concerned about the planet and working conditions for people.

© 2014, zhang kan. Used under license with Shutterstock, Inc.

As fossil fuels are depleted, the world is facing a major transformation in how energy is generated and used. Sustainability, wind turbines, solar panels, farmer's markets, biofuels, and wind energy are just some of the ways to transition to a post-fossil-fuel world. Jobs in this field will include engineers who design new technology, consultants to audit energy needs, and installers who install and maintain systems. Here are some titles of green jobs: environmental lawyer, environmental technician, sustainability consultant, sustainability project director, green architect, green building project manager, marine biologist, environmental technician, energy efficiency specialist, organic farmer, compliance manager, product engineer, wind energy engineer, and solar engineer.

A Diverse Workforce

The workforce in the United States is becoming increasingly more diverse. Diversity includes many demographic variables such as ethnicity, religion, gender, national origin, disability, sexual orientation, age, education, geographic origin, and skill characteristics. Having an appreciation for diversity is important in maintaining a work environment that is open and allows for individual differences. Increasing diversity provides opportunities for many different kinds of individuals and makes it important to be able to have good working relationships with all kinds of people.

The U.S. Bureau of Labor Statistics has described some trends that will affect the workplace by 2018.[19]

- Caucasians are expected to make up a decreasing share of the labor force, while African Americans, Asians, and all other groups will increase their share. Hispanics will increase their share of the labor force from 14.3 to 17.6 percent, reflecting a 33.1 percent growth.

- The number of women in the labor force will grow at a slightly faster rate than the number of men. The male labor force is projected to grow by 7.5 percent, as compared with 9.0 percent for the female labor force.

- The number of workers in younger age groups will decline, while workers in the 55 years and older group will increase, reflecting the increase of aging Baby Boomers.

- Total employment is expected to increase by 10 percent from 2008 to 2018. Changes in consumer demand and advances in technology will continue to change the structure of the economy, with decreasing jobs in manufacturing and increasing numbers of jobs in service and technology.

E-Commerce Is Changing the Way We Do Business

E-commerce, the purchasing of goods, services, and information over the Internet, is a new technology that has revolutionized the way business is done in the 21st century. More people are using e-commerce because of convenience, selection, and the ease of shopping for goods at the best price. Online sales are a growing part of the market, increasing 10 to 20 percent a year for the last several years. By 2017, the web will account for 10% of retail sales. Approximately 43% of sales are influenced by online research.[20] This growth in e-commerce will have implications for education and business. More colleges are offering courses in e-commerce and incorporating e-commerce topics into traditional business offerings. There are more career opportunities in e-commerce and related fields such as computer graphics, web design, online marketing, and package delivery services.

The Microprocessor

The microprocessor is a silicon chip containing transistors that determine the capability of a computer. In the past 20 years, the power of the microprocessor has increased more than one million times. In the next 20 years, the power will increase a million times again.[21] Because of the increased power of the microprocessor, it will be used in new ways and with new devices. Consider the "smart home" of the future:

As you reach the front door, you are welcomed by a flat screen, rather than a doorbell. You can use this screen to ring the doorbell, talk to the person inside the home or leave a message, which can be accessed by telephone or e-mail.

If you're the homeowner, walk through the door and the curtains go up, letting light in, and the entire house is soon subtly illuminated. The hi-fi will access its database to play your favorite music, and the air-conditioning will be preset to the temperature you prefer.

As you move to the kitchen, you take the ingredients for your lunch—say, flour, a piece of fish and a few stalks of broccoli—to a networked table. This will activate a system that will immediately offer you a range of appropriate recipes. Your smart microwave will fix the dish for you, consulting the recipe you prefer, via the Internet.[22]

The microprocessor is increasingly available to all and for less cost. The personal computer would have occupied an entire building 35 years ago. Today we have access to powerful computers and mobile devices that will play an ever greater role in our daily lives.

It's remarkable how we now take all that power for granted. Using a basic home PC costing less than $1,000, you can balance your household budget, do your taxes, write letters to friends and fax or e-mail them over the Internet, listen to CDs or the radio, watch the news, consult a doctor, play games, book a vacation, view a house, buy a book or a car. The list is endless.[23]

New Advances in Technology and Communication

There has been a recent rapid increase in the development of cell phones and other mobile devices, as well as the use of social media, which will continue to have a major impact on career opportunities. Those who can keep up with the current technology will find increasing career and business opportunities. Graduates will become more marketable if they combine traditional career areas with technology such as social media. For example, students in a marketing degree program will be more in demand if they can use Facebook, LinkedIn, or Twitter to market products.

The Bureau of Labor Statistics reports that two million technology-related jobs will be created by 2018. Jobs in computer systems design and related services are expected to increase by 34 percent by 2018. Jobs that will grow faster than the average include computer-network administrators, data-communications analysts, and Web developers. Some new fields include data-loss prevention, online security, and risk management. Computer science degrees are especially marketable when combined with traditional majors such as finance, accounting, or marketing.[24]

Because we are living in the Information Age, information and technology workers are now the largest group of workers in the United States. Careers in information technology include the design, development, and support of computer software, hardware, and networks. Some newer jobs in this area include animation for video games, films, and videos as well as setting up websites and Internet security. There are also good opportunities for network programmers who can program a group of computers to work together. Because computer use has increased greatly, it is expected that computer-related jobs will expand by 40 percent or more in the next decade.[25]

In the future, computers will continue to become more powerful, mobile, and connected. It is predicted that by 2018, microprocessors will be replaced by optical computers that function at the speed of light. Technology will be embedded in products used for entertainment as well as for home and business use. It is predicted that in the future, the desktop computer as we know it will cease to exist. Instead of a home computer, we will have computerized homes with sensors that monitor energy use and smart appliances with computer chips. Gestures, touch, and voice communication will rapidly replace computer keyboards. The Nintendo Wii™ and the iPhone are current examples. Computers will move from homes and offices into human bodies. Microchips may be embedded in human bodies to monitor health conditions and to deliver medical care. Some futurists forecast a time when computer chips will be embedded in the brain and connected to the Internet. Of course, computer security will become increasingly important with these new advances.[26]

Radiation and laser technologies will provide new technical careers in the future. It has been said that lasers will be as important to the 21st century as electricity was for the 20th century. New uses for lasers are being found in medicine, energy, industry, computers, communications, entertainment, and outer space. The use of lasers is creating new jobs and causing others to become obsolete. For example, many welders are being replaced by laser technicians, who have significantly higher earnings. New jobs will open for people who purchase, install, and maintain lasers.

Careers in fiber optics and telecommunications are among the top new emerging fields in the 21st century. Fiber optics are thin glass fibers that transmit light. This new technology may soon make copper wire obsolete. One of the most important uses of fiber optics is to speed up delivery of data over the Internet and to improve telecommunications. It is also widely used in medical instruments, including laser surgery.

Another interesting development to watch is artificial intelligence software, which enables computers to recognize patterns, improve from experience, make inferences, and approximate human thought. Scientists at the MIT Artificial Intelligence Lab have developed a robot named Cog. Here is a description of Cog and its capabilities:

We have given it a multitude of sensors to "feel" and learn what it is like to be touched and spoken to. Cog's ability to make eye contact and reach out to moving objects is also meant to motivate people to interact with it. These features have taught Cog, among other things, to distinguish a human face from inanimate objects (this puts its development at about a 3-month-old's). It can also listen to music and keep rhythm by tapping on a drum (something a 5-year-old can do). One of the most startling moments in Cog's development came when it was learning to touch things. At one point, Cog began to touch and discover its own body. It looked so eerie and human, I was stunned.[27]

Beware of Outsourcing

To reduce costs and improve profits, many jobs in technology, manufacturing, and service are being outsourced to countries such as India, China, and Taiwan, where well-educated, English-speaking workers are being used to do these jobs. For example, programmers in India can produce software at only 10 percent of the cost of these services in the United States. Jobs that are currently being outsourced include accounting, payroll clerks, customer service, data entry, assembly line workers, industrial and production engineers, machine operators, computer-assisted design (CAD) technicians, purchasing managers, textile workers, software developers, and technical support. It is a good idea to consider this trend in choosing your future career and major. Jobs that are most likely to be outsourced are:[28]

- Repetitive jobs, such as accounting,
- Well-defined jobs, such as customer service,
- Small manageable projects, such as software development,
- Jobs in which proximity to the customer is not important, such as technical support.

Jobs that are least likely to be outsourced include:

- Jobs with ambiguity, such as top management jobs,
- Unpredictable jobs, such as troubleshooters,
- Jobs that require understanding of the culture, such as marketing,
- Jobs that require close proximity to the customer, such as auto repair,
- Jobs requiring a high degree of innovation and creativity, such as product design,
- Jobs in entertainment, music, art, and design.

To protect yourself from outsourcing:

- Strive to be the best in the field.
- Be creative and innovative.
- Avoid repetitive jobs that do not require proximity to the customer.
- Choose a career where the demand is so high that it won't matter if some are outsourced.
- Consider a job in the skilled trades; carpenters, plumbers, electricians, hair stylists, construction workers, auto mechanics, and dental hygienists will always be in demand.

New Advances in Biology

Future historians may describe the 21st century as the biology century because of all the developments in this area. If you are interested in biology, it can lead to good careers in the future. One of the most important developments is the Human Genome Project, which has identified the genes in human DNA, the carrier of genetic material. The research done on the human genome has been an impetus for development in some new careers in biotechnology and biomedical technology. Watch the news for future developments that will affect how we all live and work.

Biotechnology will become increasingly important as a way to combat disease, develop new surgical procedures and devices, increase food production, reduce pollution, improve recycling, and provide new tools for law enforcement. Biotechnology includes genomic profiling, biomedical engineering, new pharmaceuticals, genetic engineering, and DNA identification. One of the most promising outcomes of biotechnology will be the production of new pharmaceuticals. About 90 percent of all drugs ever invented have been developed since 1975, and about 6,000 new drugs are waiting for regulatory approval.[29] In the future, biotechnology may be used to find cures for diabetes, arthritis, Alzheimer's disease, and heart disease.

The field of biomedical engineering, which involves developing and testing health care innovations, is expected to grow by 72 percent by 2018.[30] Biomedical technology is the field in which bionic implants are being developed for the human body. Scientists are working on the development of artificial limbs and organs including eyes, ears, hearts, and kidneys. A promising new development in this field is brain and computer interfaces. Scientists recently implanted a computer chip into the brain of a quadriplegic, enabling him to control a computer and television with his mind.[31] Biotechnology also develops new diagnostic test equipment and surgical tools.

Increase in Entrepreneurship

An important trend for the new millennium is the increase in entrepreneurship, which means starting your own business. For the Baby Boom Generation, it was expected that one would have a job for life. Because of rapid changes in society and the world of work, Millennials can expect to have as many as 10 different jobs over a lifetime.[32] A growing number of entrepreneurs operate their small businesses from home, taking advantage of telecommuting and the Internet to communicate with customers. While being an entrepreneur has some risks involved, there are many benefits, such as flexible scheduling, being your own boss, taking charge of your own destiny, and greater potential for future income if your company is successful. You won't have to worry about being outsourced, either.

© 2014, Kheng Guan Toh. Used under license with Shutterstock, Inc.

The Effect of Terrorism and Need for Security

Fear of terrorism has changed attitudes that will affect career trends for years to come. Terrorist attacks have created an atmosphere of uncertainty that has had a negative effect on the economy and has increased unemployment. For example, the airline industry is struggling financially as people hesitate to fly to their vacation destinations. People are choosing to stay in the safety of their homes, offices, cars, and gated communities. Since people are spending more time at home, they spend more money making their homes comfortable. Faith Popcorn, who is famous for predicting future trends, has called this phenomenon "cocooning," which is "our desire to build ourselves strong and cozy nests where we can retreat from the world, enjoying ourselves in safety and comfort."[33] As a result, construction, home remodeling, and sales of entertainment systems are increasing.

Another result of terrorism is the shift toward occupations that provide value to society and in which people can search for personal satisfaction.[31] More people volunteer their time to help others, and are considering careers in education, social work, and medical occupations. When people are forced to relocate because of unemployment, they are considering moving to smaller towns that have a sense of community and a feeling of safety.

As the world population continues to grow, there is continued conflict over resources and ideologies and an increased need for security and safety. Law enforcement, intelligence, forensics, international relations, foreign affairs, and security administration careers will be in demand.

Nontraditional Workers

Unlike traditional workers, nontraditional workers do not have full-time, year-round jobs with health and retirement benefits. Employers are moving toward using nontraditional workers, including multiple job holders, contingent and part-time workers, independent contractors, and temporary workers. Nearly four out of five employers use nontraditional workers to help them become more efficient, prevent layoffs, and access workers with special skills. There are advantages and disadvantages to this arrangement. Nontraditional workers have no benefits and risk unemployment. However, this arrangement can provide workers with a flexible work schedule in which they work during some periods and pursue other interests or gain new skills when not working.

Journal Entry #2

Do a quick review of the career trends presented in this chapter:

- Moving from the production of goods to service and technology
- Increased opportunities in health care occupations
- Increased need for education
- New green careers
- Increasing diversity in the workplace
- Increased e-commerce and entrepreneurship
- New developments in technology, communication, and biology
- The effect of terrorism and the need for security
- Nontraditional workers

Write one paragraph about how any of these trends might affect your future.

Top Jobs for the Future[32]

Based on current career trends, here are some jobs that should be in high demand for the next 10 years.

Field of Employment	Job Titles
Business	Marketing Manager, Security and Financial Service, Internet Marketing Specialist, Advertising Executive, Buyer, Sales Person, Real Estate Agent, Business Development Manager, Marketing Researcher, Recruiter
Education	Teacher, Teacher's Aide, Adult Education Instructor, Math and Science Teacher
Entertainment	Dancer, Producer, Director, Actor, Content Creator, Musician, Artist, Commercial Artist, Writer, Technical Writer, Newspaper Reporter, News Anchor Person
Health	Emergency Medical Technician, Surgeon, Chiropractor, Dental Hygienist, Registered Nurse, Medical Assistant, Therapist, Respiratory Therapist, Home Health Aide, Primary Care Physician, Medical Lab Technician, Radiology Technician, Physical Therapist, Dental Assistant, Nurse's Aide
Information Technology	Computer Systems Analyst, Computer Engineer, Web Specialist, Network Support Technician, Java Programmer, Information Technology Manager, Web Developer, Database Administrator, Network Engineer
Law/Law Enforcement	Correction Officer, Law Officer, Anti-Terrorist Specialist, Security Guard, Tax/Estate Attorney, Intellectual Property Attorney
Services	Veterinarian, Social Worker, Hair Stylist, Telephone Repair Technician, Aircraft Mechanic, Guidance Counselor, Occupational Therapist, Child Care Assistant, Baker, Landscape Architect, Pest Controller, Chef, Caterer, Food Server
Sports	Athlete, Coach, Umpire, Physical Trainer
Technology	Electrical Engineer, Biological Scientist, Electronic Technician, CAD Operator, Product Designer, Sales Engineer, Applications Engineer, Product Marketing Engineer, Technical Support Manager, Product Development Manager
Trades	Carpenter, Plumber, Electrician
Travel/Transportation	Package Delivery Person, Flight Attendant, Hotel/Restaurant Manager, Taxi Driver, Chauffeur, Driver

QUIZ

Career Trends of the Future

Test what you have learned by selecting the correct answers to the following questions:

1. Students in Generation Z are
   a. more optimistic about the future.
   b. fewer in number than previous generations.
   c. increasingly diverse.

2. Use of the Internet will result in
   a. increased e-commerce.
   b. increased use of conventional stores.
   c. decreased mail delivery.

3. The largest group of workers in the United States is in
   a. manufacturing.
   b. information technology.
   c. agriculture.

4. Jobs unlikely to be outsourced include
   a. jobs that require close proximity to the customer.
   b. computer programming jobs.
   c. customer service jobs.

5. Future historians will describe the 21st century as the
   a. art and entertainment century.
   b. biology century.
   c. industrial development century.

How did you do on the quiz? Check your answers: 1. c, 2. a, 3. b, 4. a, 5. b

Work Skills for the 21st Century

Because of rapid changes in technology, college students of today may be preparing for jobs that do not exist right now. After graduation, many college students find employment that is not even related to their college majors. One researcher found that 48 percent of college graduates find employment in fields not related to their college majors.[33] More important than one's college major are the general skills learned in college that prepare students for the future.

To define skills needed in the future workplace, the U.S. Secretary of Labor created the Secretary's Commission on Achieving Necessary Skills (SCANS). Based on interviews with employers and educators, the members of the commission outlined foundation skills and workplace competencies needed to succeed in the workplace in the 21st century.[34] The following skills apply to all occupations in all fields and will help you to become a successful employee, regardless of your major. As you read through these skills, think about your competency in these areas.

Foundation Skills

Basic Skills

- Reading
- Writing
- Basic arithmetic
- Higher-level mathematics
- Listening
- Speaking

© 2014, iQoncept. Used under license with Shutterstock, Inc.

Thinking Skills

- Creative thinking
- Decision making
- Problem solving
- Mental visualization
- Knowing how to learn
- Reasoning

© 2014, VLADGRIN. Used under license with Shutterstock, Inc.

Personal Qualities

- Responsibility
- Self-esteem
- Sociability
- Self-management
- Integrity/honesty

Workplace Competencies

Resources

- **Time.** Selects relevant goals, sets priorities, and follows schedules.
- **Money.** Uses budgets, keeps records, and makes adjustments.
- **Materials and facilities.** Acquires, stores, and distributes materials, supplies, parts, equipment, space, or final products.
- **Human resources.** Assesses knowledge and skills, distributes work, evaluates performance, and provides feedback.

Interpersonal

- **Participates as a member of a team.** Works cooperatively with others and contributes to group efforts.
- **Teaches others.** Helps others learn needed skills.
- **Serves clients/customers.** Works and communicates with clients and customers to satisfy their expectations.
- **Exercises leadership.** Communicates, encourages, persuades, and convinces others; responsibly challenges procedures, policies, or authority.
- **Negotiates to arrive at a decision.** Works toward an agreement involving resources or diverging interests.
- **Works with cultural diversity.** Works well with men and women and with people from a variety of ethnic, social, or educational backgrounds.

Information

- **Acquires and evaluates information.** Identifies the need for information, obtains information, and evaluates it.
- **Organizes and maintains information.** Organizes, processes, and maintains written or computerized records.
- **Uses computers to process information.** Employs computers to acquire, organize, analyze, and communicate information.

Systems

- **Understands systems.** Knows how social, organizational, and technological systems work and operates efficiently within them.
- **Monitors and corrects performance.** Distinguishes trends, predicts impacts of actions on systems operations, and takes action to correct performance.
- **Improves and designs systems.** Develops new systems to improve products or services.

Technology

- **Selects technology.** Judges which procedures, tools, or machines, including computers, will produce the desired results.
- **Applies technology to tasks.** Understands the proper procedures for using machines and computers.
- **Maintains and troubleshoots technology.** Prevents, identifies, or solves problems with machines, computers, and other technologies.

Because the workplace is changing, these skills may be more important than the background acquired through a college major. Work to develop these skills and you will be prepared for whatever lies ahead.

How to Research Your Career

After you have assessed your personality, interests, values, and talents, the next step is to learn about the world of work. If you can match your personal strengths to the world of work, you can find work that is interesting and you can excel in it. To learn about the world of work, you will need to research possible careers. This includes reading career descriptions and investigating career outlooks, salaries, and educational requirements.

> "The supreme accomplishment is to blur the line between work and play."
> Arnold Toynbee

Career Descriptions

The career description tells you about the nature of the work, working conditions, employment, training, qualifications, advancement, job outlook, earnings, and related occupations. The two best sources of job descriptions are the *Occupational Outlook Handbook* and *Occupational Outlook Quarterly*. The *Handbook*, published by the Bureau of Labor Statistics, is like an encyclopedia of careers. You can search alphabetically by career or by career cluster.

The *Occupational Outlook Quarterly* is a periodical with up-to-date articles on new and emerging occupations, training opportunities, salary trends, and new studies from the Bureau of Labor Statistics. You can find these resources in a public or school library, at a college career center, or on the *College Success Website* at http://www.collegesuccess1.com/Links9Career.htm.

> "Starting out to make money is the greatest mistake in life. Do what you feel you have a flair for doing, and if you are good enough at it, the money will come."
> Greer Garson

Career Outlook

It is especially important to know about the career outlook of an occupation you are considering. Career outlook includes salary and availability of employment. How much does the occupation pay? Will the occupation exist in the future, and will there be employment opportunities? Of course, you will want to prepare yourself for careers that pay well and have future employment opportunities.

You can find information about career outlooks in the sources listed above, current periodicals, and materials from the Bureau of Labor Statistics. The following table, for example, lists the fastest-growing occupations, occupations with the highest salaries, and occupations with the largest job growth. Information from the Bureau of Labor Statistics is also available online.

10 Fastest-Growing Occupations	10 Industries with the Largest Wage and Salary Employment Growth	10 Occupations with the Largest Numerical Job Growth
Biomedical engineers	Management, scientific, technical	Registered nurses
Network systems and data communications analysts	Physicians	Home health aides
Home health aides	Computer systems design and related	Customer service representatives
Personal and home care aides	General merchandise stores	Food preparation workers
Financial examiners	Employment services	Personal and home care aides
Medical scientists	Local government	Retail salespersons
Physician assistants	Home health care services	Office clerks
Skin care specialists	Services for elderly and disabled	Accountants and auditors
Biochemists and biophysicists	Nursing care facilities	Nursing aides, orderlies
Athletic trainers	Full-service restaurants	Postsecondary teachers

© 2014, iQoncept. Used under license with Shutterstock, Inc.

Planning Your Education

Once you have assessed your personal characteristics and researched your career options, it is important to plan your education. If you have a plan, you will be able to finish your education more quickly and avoid taking unnecessary classes. You can begin work on your educational plan by following the steps below. After you have done some work on your plan, visit your college counselor or advisor to make sure that your plan is appropriate.

Finding Employment

After investing your time in achieving a college education, you will need some additional skills to get a job. Having a good resume and cover letter, marketing yourself online and know how to successfully interview for a job will help you to obtain your dream job.

> "Think not of yourself as the architect of your career but as the sculptor. Expect to have a lot of hard hammering, chiseling, scraping and polishing."
>
> B.C. Forbes

Get Started with a Resume and Cover Letter

Your resume is important in establishing a good first impression and provides the basic content for job seeking social media sites such as LinkedIn and Facebook. A resume is a snapshot of your education and experience. It is generally one page in length. You will need a resume to apply for scholarships, part-time jobs, or find a position after you graduate. Start with a file of information you can use to create your resume. Keep your resume on file in your computer or on your flash drive so that you can revise it or post it online as needed.

A resume includes the following basic components:

> "The nearest to perfection that most people come is when filling out an employment application."
>
> Source unknown

- Contact information: your name, address, telephone number, and e-mail address
- A brief statement of your career objective
- A summary of your education:
  - Names and locations of schools
  - Dates of attendance
  - Diplomas or degrees received

Steps in Planning Your Education

_____ 1. **Take your college entrance or assessment tests before you apply to colleges.** Most colleges require the Scholastic Aptitude Test (SAT) or their own local placement tests in order for you to be admitted. You can find information about these tests at your high school or college counseling center or online at http://www.ets.org/ or http://cbweb1.collegeboard.org/index.html. If you are attending a community college, check the college website, admissions office, or counseling office to see what placement exams are required.

_____ 2. **Take English the first semester, and continue each semester until your English requirement is complete.** English courses provide the foundation for further college study. Your SAT or college placement test will determine what level of English you need to take. As a general rule, community colleges require one semester of college-level English. Four-year colleges and universities generally require two semesters or three quarters of college-level English. If your placement scores are low, you may be required to take review courses first.

_____ 3. **Start your math classes early, preferably in the first semester or quarter.** Many high-paying careers require a long series of math classes, particularly those in the sciences, engineering, and business. If you delay taking math courses until later, you may limit your career options and extend your time in college.

_____ 4. **Take the required general education courses.** Find out what your college requires for general education and put these classes on your plan. You will find this information in the college catalog. Be careful to select the correct general education plan. At community colleges, there are different plans for transfer and associate's degree students. At a university, there may be different plans for different colleges within the university. Check with a college counselor or advisor to make sure you have the correct plan.

_____ 5. **Prepare for your major.** Consult your college catalog to see what courses are required for your major. If you are undecided on a major, take the general education courses and start working on a decision about your major. If you are interested in the sciences or engineering, start work on math in the first semester. Start on your major requirements as soon as possible so that you do not delay your graduation.

_____ 6. **Check prerequisites.** A prerequisite is a course that is required before taking a higher-level course. The college catalog lists courses offered and includes prerequisites. Most colleges will not let you register for a course for which you do not have the prerequisite. It is also difficult to succeed in an advanced course without taking the prerequisite first.

_____ 7. **Make an educational plan.** The educational plan includes all the courses you will need to graduate. Again, use the college catalog as your guide.

_____ 8. **Check your plan.** See your college counselor or advisor to check your plan. He or she can save you from taking classes that you do not need and help you to graduate in the minimum amount of time.

© 2014, NAN728. Used under license with Shutterstock, Inc.

- A summary of your work and/or volunteer experience
- If you have little directly related work experience, a list of courses you have taken that would help the employer understand your skills for employment
- Special skills, honors, awards, or achievements
- References (people who can recommend you for a job or scholarship)

There is no one best way to write a resume, but here are some helpful tips:

- Begin your resume with your contact information. Make sure that your email is professional. Consider creating a new email for job seeking purposes. Your email should include your first and last name.
- In the job history section, include brief statements about job tasks including what you did to make your company better. It is helpful to look for key words in the job announcement and make sure these key words are in your resume.
- List your present or most recent job first and work back chronologically.
- If you are just graduating from college and have little work experience, put the education section first along with related coursework.
- Keep in mind that the average resume gets read in 10 seconds. Make sure your resume is organized and brief. Bold those ideas that you want to highlight.
- Do not include personal information or photos.
- Carefully proofread your resume to make sure it has no errors. It is a good idea to have someone else review it also.
- Store your resume on your computer so that you can update it regularly and have it available to post online.

It is easy to upload your content to resume templates online. Here are some resume template sites:

Choose your template from a variety of examples and then create or upload your content. http://www.myperfectresume.com/

This site has 114 templates depending on your experience and career. You can upload your current resume into a suggested template and add thezir suggested improvements. http://www.resume-now.com/

Create a resume and set up a resume webpage. http://www.jobwinningresume.com/

View sample resume templates and create your resume. http://www.everymanbusiness.com/human-resources/resume-template/

Ask for a letter of reference from your current supervisor at work or someone in a position to recommend you, such as a college professor or community member. Ask the person to address the letter "To Whom It May Concern" so that you can use the letter many times. If the person is on LinkedIn, ask him or her for an endorsement. The person recommending you should comment on your work habits, skills, and personal qualities. If appropriate, offer to write the letter yourself and then the person can edit it or send it as is. This often helps for people who would like to recommend you, but are very busy. If you wait until you graduate to obtain letters of reference, potential recommenders may no longer be there or may not remember who you are. Always ask if you can use a person's name as a reference. When you are applying for a job and references are requested, phone the persons who have agreed to recommend you and let them know to expect a call.

While most resumes are shared online, if you need a printed copy, print your resume so that it looks professional. Use a good-quality white, tan, or gray paper. It is a good idea to take a printed copy of your resume to an interview.

© 2014, Alexandar Iotzov. Used under license with Shutterstock, Inc.

When you respond to job announcements, you may be asked to send a cover letter with your resume attached. Address your letter to a specific person at the company or organization and spell the name correctly. You can call the personnel office to obtain this information. The purpose of the cover letter is to state your interest in the job, highlight your qualifications, and get the employer to read your resume and call you for an interview. The cover letter should be brief and to the point. Include the following items:

- State the job you are interested in and how you heard about the opening.
- Briefly state how your education and experience would be assets to the company.
- Ask for an interview and tell the employer how you can be contacted.
- Attach your resume.
- Your cover letter is the first contact you have with the employer. Make it neat and free from errors. Use spell check and grammar check, read it over again, and have someone else check it for you.

Select templates and view samples of cover letters online at http://www.cover-letter-now.com/

> "A major reason many Americans still struggle to find meaningful work is because they are using tactics from the 1990s and early 2000s. The future for employment is now here . . . and it's online."
> Matt Keener

Establishing Your Personal Brand Online

Personal branding is the process by which we market ourselves to others. It is an important concept that has been used to sell products and services. Through the use of social media, you can use this concept to market your strengths to potential employers and to find a satisfying career. Throughout this textbook you have been challenged to become more aware of these personal strengths which can be used to create your own personal brand. Here are the steps for establishing your personal brand and marketing yourself:

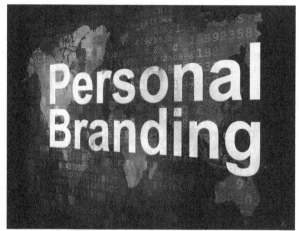

© 2014, Maksim Kabakou. Used under license with Shutterstock, Inc.

Define Your Brand

The first step in marketing yourself is to define your personal brand. What are your passions, goals, and personal strengths and how can they be used in the job market? Review the assessments in this textbook and write a brief description of your personal brand along with a brief job title. A few examples of a personal brand include financial expert, entrepreneur, educator, consultant, engineer, and personal trainer.

Manage Your Online Presence

Most employers do online searches to find employees and to find information on job candidates before the interview. Make sure that your online presence is a professional one that you would want an employer to see. Make sure that your email address is a professional one or consider setting up an account for job seeking. Google your name and see what information a potential employer can find about you. Take a look at your online sites and make sure that the content is appropriate. Some online content may make it difficult to be hired including:

- photos or references to drug or alcohol use or abuse.
- discriminatory comments on race, religion, or gender.
- negative comments about previous employers.
- poor communication skills.

When using Facebook, manage your privacy settings so that no one can see your list of friends since you can be judged by the company you keep and you have no control over what your friends post. To keep your friends private, specify that no one can tag you in a Facebook photo without your authorization. Be careful about what you put on your front page, since it is the most visible page.

Set Up a Nameplate Website

Take control of your online presence by setting up a nameplate website which defines who you are and directs potential employers to your media sites. Good sites for setting up this nameplate include about.me and vizify.com. Both of these sites are free and provide samples that can be helpful in setting up your own site. On these sites, you can upload your photo, include your biography, list your education, describe your work experience, and provide links to LinkedIn or Facebook.

Using Online Tools

At the present time, LinkedIn and Facebook are the most commonly used sites used by employers to research job candidates. Invest some of your time setting up accounts at these sites.

LinkedIn

LinkedIn is a directory of professionals and companies used for job searching, networking, and hiring. Many employers use LinkedIn profiles to search for potential employees. This profile is similar to a resume and includes your education and job experience. Make sure that your profile is complete and well written since it represents who you are online. Since recruiting software is used to search through profiles, use key words in your resume that relate to your desired job. Key words include job requirements, experience, software competencies, education, and previous employers. To find key words, take a look at job listings in your area of interest and expertise and include the words in your profile. It is helpful to include recommendations and endorsements which you can request from other contacts on LinkedIn. Personalize your profile by uploading a photo. Use a current photo and dress appropriately for the type of job you are seeking.

LinkedIn is also a job search tool in which you can search for and apply for jobs within the site. The job listings page allows you to search for jobs by location, industry, company, job function, level or position, employer, or key words. The site can also be used for networking. As you link to others, they can refer you to jobs open at their site. Maintaining a large network is job security because you can use it for job advancement or to find a new job in the future. You can join groups of other professionals in your area of expertise to receive notices about job openings in your area of interest. Use the status update function to let your contacts know that you are looking for a job.

When you find a specific job listing in which you are interested, you will have the option to apply within LinkedIn or you will be directed to the company website where you will need to create an account. The site also provides company profiles to help you to find the job that best matches your qualifications and help you with information useful for interviewing.

Facebook

Facebook is a social network that can be useful in finding a job. The first step in using your Facebook account to find a job is to clean up your profile to make sure that it does not contain any detrimental content. You can delete any questionable material or even use a software package such as Reppler which scans your profile for embarrassing content and suggests items you might want to remove. The next step is to post a status update letting your friends know that you are looking for a job and ask if they know about any job openings.

Use Facebook as a marketing tool. Post samples or links to your work online. If you are a photographer, post some of your photos online. If you are a writer, post links to material you have written. Keep your materials up to date so that prospective employers can see your best and most recent work. If your chosen company has a public Facebook page, you can show your passion, knowledge, and interest for your dream job by participating in discussion boards that can showcase your expertise. You can "like" the company on Facebook and receive news, information, and job openings from them. You can join or create groups on Facebook to discuss your area of interest. In this way, you may be considered for a job before it is posted.

Use Facebook's Marketplace app to search for jobs. Just click on Jobs in Marketplace and enter the job in which you are interested. It contains information about job openings and links to sites with job applications. Facebook also has an app called Social Jobs that allows you to search for jobs.

> "We do not go to work only to earn an income, but to find meaning in our lives. What we do is a large part of what we are."
> Alan Ryan

> "Many of life's failures are people who do not realize how close they were to success when they gave up."
> Thomas Edison

Journal Entry #3

What steps can you take to establish or improve your personal brand?

Notes

1. Michael T. Robinson, "Top Jobs for the Future," from www.careerplanner.com, 2004.

2. Gail Sheehy, *New Passages* (New York: Random House, 1995), 34.

3. U.S. National Center for Health Statistics, National Vital Statistics Reports (NVSR), *Deaths: Final Data for 2006,* Vol. 57, No. 14, April 17, 2009.

4. Jeff Giles, "Generalization X," *Newsweek,* June 6, 1994.

5. Jane Bryant Quinn, "The Luck of the Xers, Comeback Kids: Young People Will Live Better Than They Think," *Newsweek,* 6 June 1994, 66–67.

6. Ellen Neuborne, http://www.businessweek.com, 1999.

7. Claudia Smith Brison, http://www.thestate.com, 14 July 2002.

8. Neil Howe and William Strauss, *Millennials Rising: The Next Great Generation* (New York: Vintage Books, 2000).

9. *USA Today*, "After Gen X, Millennials, What Should Next Generation Be?" by Bruce Horovitz, May 24, 2012.

10. US Census Bureau, "State and County QuickFacts 2012", http://quickfacts.census. gov/qfd/states/00000.html

11. "The First Generation of the Twenty First Century, an Introduction to the Pluralist Generation" by Magid Generational Strategies, April 30, 2012 from http://magid.com/ sites/default/files/pdf/MagidPluralistGenerationWhitepaper.pdf

12. Neuborne, www.businessweek.com, 1999.

13. John Naisbitt, Patricia Aburdeen, and Walter Kiechel III, "How We Will Work in the Year 2000," *Fortune,* 17 May 1993, 41–52.

14. U.S. Bureau of Labor Statistics, *Occupational Outlook Handbook*, 2010–11 Edition, "Overview of the 2008–18 Projections," accessed from http://data.bls.gov

15. Ibid.

16. Ibid.

17. U.S. Bureau of Labor Statistics, "Employment Projections," May 22, 2013 accessed from http://www.bls.gov/emp/ep_chart_001.htm)

18. U.S. Bureau of Labor Statistics, "Overview of the 2008–18 Projections."

19. "US Online Sales to Reach $370 Billion by 2017" by Forrester Research, March 13, 2013 accessed from www.forrester.com

20. Bill Gates, "Microprocessors Upgraded the Way We Live," *USA Today,* 22 June 1999.

21. From "The Microsoft Future According to Bill Gates," accessed from http://www .ameinfo.com/33384.html, 2004.

22. Bill Gates, *Business @ the Speed of Thought: Using a Digital Nervous System* (Warner, 1999). Excerpts available at www.speed-of-thought.com.

23. U.S. Bureau of Labor Statistics, "Overview of the 2008–18 Projections."

24. "Tomorrow's Best Careers," from http://www.future-trends.com, 2004.

25. Dan Tynan, "The Next 25 Years in Tech," www.pcworld.com, January 30, 2008.

26. Anne Foerst, "A New Breed of 'Replicants' Is Redefining What It Means to Be Human," *Forbes ASAP,* 1999.

27. Michael T. Robinson, "Offshoring of America's Top Jobs," from http://www .careerplanner.com, 2004.

28. "Tomorrow's Best Careers," from http://www.future-trends.com, 2004.

29. U.S. Bureau of Labor Statistics, "Overview of the 2008–18 Projections."

30. Roxanne Khamsi, "Paralyzed Man Sends E-Mail by Thought," *News @ Nature.Com*, October 13, 2004.

31. Judith Kautz, "Entrepreneurship Beyond 2000," from www.smallbusinessnotes.com, 2004.

32. Faith Popcorn and Lys Marigold, *Clicking: 16 Trends to Future Fit Your Life, Your Work, and Your Business* (New York: HarperCollins, 1996).

33. James E. Challenger, "Career Pros: Terrorism's Legacy," from www.jobjournal.com, 2003.

34. Michael T. Robinson, "Top Jobs for the Future," CareerPlanner.com, 2008.

35. T. J. Grites, "Being 'Undecided' Could Be the Best Decision They Could Make," *School Counselor* 29 (1981): 41–46.

36. Secretary's Commission on Achieving Necessary Skills (SCANS), *Learning a Living: A Blueprint for High Performance* (Washington, DC: U.S. Department of Labor, 1991).

37. U.S. Bureau of Labor Statistics, "Overview of the 2008–18 Projections."

38. Quoted in Rob Gilbert, ed., *Bits and Pieces,* 7 October 1999.

Rate Your Skills for Success in the Workplace

Name _____ Date _____

Read each statement relating to skills needed for success in the workplace. Use the following scale to rate your competencies:

5 = Excellent **4** = Very good **3** = Average **2** = Needs improvement **1** = Need to develop

_____ 1. I have good reading skills. I can locate information I need to read and understand and interpret it. I can pick out the main idea and judge the accuracy of the information.

_____ 2. I have good writing skills. I can communicate thoughts, ideas, and information in writing. I know how to edit and revise my writing and use correct spelling, punctuation, and grammar.

_____ 3. I am good at arithmetic. I can perform basic computations using whole numbers and percentages. I can make reasonable estimates without a calculator and can read tables, graphs, and charts.

_____ 4. I am good at mathematics. I can use a variety of mathematical techniques including statistics to predict the occurrence of events.

_____ 5. I am good at speaking. I can organize my ideas and participate in discussions and group presentations. I speak clearly and am a good listener. I ask questions to obtain feedback when needed.

_____ 6. I am a creative thinker. I can come up with new ideas and unusual connections. I can imagine new possibilities and combine ideas in new ways.

_____ 7. I make good decisions. I can specify goals and constraints, generate alternatives, consider risks, and evaluate alternatives.

_____ 8. I am good at solving problems. I can see when a problem exists, identify the reasons for the problem, and devise a plan of action for solving the problem.

_____ 9. I am good at mental visualization. I can see things in my mind's eye. Examples include building a project from a blueprint or imagining the taste of a recipe from reading it.

_____ 10. I know how to learn. I am aware of my learning style and can use learning strategies to obtain new knowledge.

_____ 11. I am good at reasoning. I can use logic to draw conclusions and apply rules and principles to new situations.

_____ 12. I am a responsible person. I work toward accomplishing goals, set high standards, and pay attention to details. I usually accomplish tasks on time.

_____ 13. I have high self-esteem. I believe in my self-worth and maintain a positive view of myself.

_____ 14. I am sociable, understanding, friendly, adaptable, polite, and relate well to others.

_____ 15. I am good at self-management. I know my background, skills, and abilities and set realistic goals for myself. I monitor my progress toward completing my goals and complete them.

_____ 16. I practice integrity and honesty. I recognize when I am faced with a decision that involves ethics and choose ethical behavior.

_____ 17. I am good at managing my time. I set goals, prioritize, and follow schedules to complete tasks on time.

_____ 18. I manage money well. I know how to use and prepare a budget and keep records, making adjustments when necessary.

_____ 19. I can manage material and resources. I can store and distribute materials, supplies, parts, equipment, space, or products.

_____ 20. I can participate as a member of a team. I can work cooperatively with others and contribute to group efforts.

_____ 21. I can teach others. I can help others to learn needed knowledge and skills.

_____ 22. I can exercise leadership. I know how to communicate, encourage, persuade, and motivate individuals.

_____ 23. I am a good negotiator. I can work toward an agreement and resolve divergent interests.

_____ 24. I can work with men and women from a variety of ethnic, social, or educational backgrounds.

_____ 25. I can acquire and evaluate information. I can identify a need for information and find the information I need.

_____ 26. I can organize and maintain information. I can find written or computerized information.

_____ 27. I can use computers to process information.

_____ 28. I have an understanding of social, organizational, and technological systems and can operate effectively in these systems.

_____ 29. I can improve the design of a system to improve the quality of products and services.

_____ 30. I can use machines and computers to accomplish the desired task.

_____ Total

Score your skills for success in the workplace.

150–121	Excellent
120–91	Very good
90–61	Average
Below 60	Need improvement

From the previous list of workplace skills, make a list of five of your strong points. What do you do well?

From the list of workplace skills, make a list of areas you need to improve.

CHAPTER 14

Thinking Positively about the Future

Learning Objectives

Read to answer these key questions:

- What is my life stage?

- How does positive thinking affect my future success?

- What are some beliefs of successful people?

- What are some secrets to achieving happiness?

Psychologists have identified life stages that we all go through. Knowing about life stages can help you to understand where you are now and where you might be in the future. Positive thinking is also a powerful tool for achieving life goals. Learn to use your attitudes and beliefs to enhance your future success. Many of you have happiness as one of your lifetime goals. This chapter ends with some useful ideas about how to achieve happiness in your life.

Life Stages

A number of researchers believe that adults progress through a series of orderly and predictable stages in which success or failure at each stage has an influence on later stages. Understanding these stages can help you to understand where you are now and where you are headed in the future. Life stage theorists include Erik Erikson and Daniel Levinson. Gail Sheehy, author of *Passages* and *New Passages*, is a journalist who has summarized and popularized current research on life stages.[1] As you read through these theories, think about how they apply to you at the present and in your future life.

© 2014, arbit. Used under license with Shutterstock, Inc.

Erik Erikson

Erik Erikson proposes that human beings progress through eight stages of psychosocial development in a fixed order.[2] These stages are turning points, or crises, and the outcome of each turning point will determine future personality development. Each crisis has two possible outcomes: one is negative and the other positive. For example, the first turning point happens during the first year of life. He titles this stage trust vs. mistrust. If the infant's parents and caregivers provide consistent, caring, and adequate treatment, the infant learns to trust the world as a safe place. If the infant is abused or not cared for adequately, he or she will learn that the world is an unsafe place. The sense of trust or mistrust is carried with the individual throughout life. Erickson identifies eight stages, which range from birth to age 65 and beyond.

1. **Basic trust vs. mistrust (age 0–1).** Based on the parents' care, the infant learns to trust others and feel comfortable in the world or learns to distrust a world that is perceived to be unsafe.

2. **Autonomy vs. shame and doubt (age 1–3).** Between the ages of one and three, children learn to feel competent by feeding themselves, learning to use the toilet, and

playing alone. If they do not accomplish these tasks successfully, children learn to doubt their own abilities.

3. **Initiative vs. guilt (age 3–5).** During this stage, children learn to plan their own activities within the parents' guidelines. If the children do not learn these tasks, they develop guilt over their misbehavior.

4. **Industry vs. inferiority (age 5–11).** In this stage children learn to meet the demands of parents, teachers, and peers. They learn to clean their rooms, do their homework, and ride a bike, for example. If they accomplish these tasks successfully, they learn that their effort (industry) leads to success. If they do not learn these tasks, Erikson believes that they develop a lifelong feeling of inferiority.

5. **Identity vs. role confusion (age 11–18).** During this stage, the child develops his or her identity. It is also during this stage that the child starts to prepare for work by gaining insights into personality, interests, and values as well as learning about the world of work. If these tasks are not successfully accomplished, the result is confusion over his or her role in life.

6. **Intimacy vs. isolation (age 18–40).** This is an adult stage of development in which relationships are formed with a partner. The task is to develop loving and committed relationships with others that partially replace the bonds with parents. If this task is not completed, the adult remains isolated from others and has difficulty establishing meaningful relationships. He or she is less capable of full emotional development.

7. **Generativity vs. stagnation (age 40–65).** During this adult stage, the person contributes to future generations through raising children, helping others, developing products, or coming up with creative new ideas. At this time, the person continues to grow and produce, but puts unfulfilled dreams aside and finds meaning in work and family. If this task is not accomplished, growth is stopped and the person becomes stagnant and self-centered.

8. **Integrity vs. despair (age 65-plus).** At this stage, people reap the benefits of all that they have done during their lives and accept the fact that life is temporary. If this task is not accomplished, the individual is in despair and struggles to find meaning in life.

Daniel Levinson

The research and writing by Daniel Levinson has been very useful in understanding adult development and career development.[3] Levinson proposes four stages in adult development:

1. Pre-adulthood

2. Early adulthood (age 17–45)

3. Middle adulthood (age 40–60)

4. Late adulthood (age 60–65)

Each of these stages of adulthood alternates between stable and transitional periods. Stable periods last six to seven years, during which people pursue their goals and create a desired structure in their lives. Transitional periods last four to five years, during which people question and reappraise the structure and consider making changes. These transitional periods provide the opportunity for growth and reflection.

These stable and transitional periods are related to age. Levinson's research showed that people do vary a little on the onset or termination of each stage, but generally by not more than two years. He also believes that people go through these stages in a fixed sequence during which certain developmental tasks present themselves in a fixed order. How a person deals with these developmental tasks has a big impact on later life.

Transitional and stable periods, including developmental tasks, are summarized below. As you read each description, think about your life stage and where you may be headed in the future.

- **Age 17–22 Transitional Period.** The task here is to move from adolescence to young adulthood and to separate from parents.

- **Age 22–28 Stable Period.** This is a period of settling down and creating life structure, while still keeping the options open to explore jobs and relationships.

- **Age 28–33 Transitional Period.** During this period, adults reappraise their current life structure. There is the feeling that if a change is to be made, it must be made before it is too late.

- **Age 33–40 Stable Period.** During this time, adults build clear work, family, and leisure roles. The need to attain one's dream is powerful and intense. Levinson says that this stage ends with BOOP (Becoming One's Own Person). Women often have the challenge of balancing work and family roles at this time.

- **Age 40–45 Transitional Period.** This is a time of turmoil. Up to 80 percent of men and 85 percent of women experience a moderate to severe crisis at this time.[4] At this point there is an awareness of human mortality and the feeling that half of life is now over. There is often a generational shift at this point; adults may have teenage children, and their parents are getting old or have passed away. At this point adults assess their progress toward accomplishing their dream. If the dream has not been accomplished, there is a sense of failure. If the dream has been accomplished, the person considers whether it was worth the effort and wonders, "Is this all there is?" Women are often juggling three roles: career, marriage, and motherhood. Only 4 percent of women manage to have it all: marriage, motherhood, and a full-time career.[5] Efforts to combine these roles often do not provide the satisfaction that women expect.

- **Age 45–50 Stable Period.** During this period, adults work on stable life structures for the middle years. They often have more autonomy and flexibility in choosing roles.

- **Age 50–55 Transitional Period.** Adults continue to work on questions raised during the midlife crisis.

- **Age 55–60 Stable Period.** Adults work on stable life structures.

- **Age 60–65 Transitional Period.** Adults deal with retirement transitions.

Gail Sheehy

Journalist Gail Sheehy, author of *New Passages*, notes that because of increasing life spans, earlier theories of life stages need to be updated. Previous theories of life development covered a life span to age 65. Sheehy notes that women today who reach 50 (without developing cancer or heart disease) can expect to live to be 92 years old. Men who are healthy and live to age 65 can expect to live until the age of 81.[6] She quotes the president of a nursing home: "Twenty years ago I'd see 40-year-olds bringing in their 60-year-old parents. Now I'm seeing 72-year-olds bringing in their 90-year-old parents."[7]

The good news is that we will all be living longer and healthier lives in the years to come. In terms of life stages, Sheehy states that "the territory of the mid-forties, fifties and sixties and beyond is changing so fundamentally it now opens up whole new passages and stages of life." She asks us to "stop and recalculate. Imagine the day you turn 45 as the infancy of another life . . . a second adulthood in middle life."[8] She divides adult life stages into the stages:

- Provisional adulthood (18–30)
- First adulthood (30–45)
- Second adulthood (45–85)

Provisional Adulthood and the Try-Out 20s (age 18–30)

This stage is traditionally characterized by two opposing goals: (1) a desire for exploration and (2) a desire for stability. Historically, this was a time to finish one's education and move away from the parents' home to start a career and family. Young people are now living at home longer, and the period of adolescence has been extended. The author notes that of unmarried American men between 25 and 34, more than one third are still living at home.[9] She describes a dramatic shift that occurs around the age of 30. "Before the shift men and women feel unable to make clear choices or cope with life's vicissitudes without expecting some help from parents. After the shift they feel confident enough in their own values to make their own choices and competent enough in life skills to set a course."[10]

Some challenges for the Try-Out 20s include coping with a rapidly changing world:

- Views on marriage are changing. Young women have seen their mothers struggling to balance career, marriage, and children. Many young people are delaying marriage into the 20s or 30s or are deciding not to get married at all.
- Sheehy notes that in previous generations the enemies were external: wars, communism, and the nuclear bomb. Today for many young people, the enemies are internal: drugs, guns, and violence.
- The world has become more unpredictable and violent. Many teenagers do not feel safe in their schools or communities.
- There is a growing gap between the rich and poor.
- There is increased competition for jobs.
- Young people have to reassess their morals, as they become full of fear and anxiety about sex outside of marriage.
- Many worry that they are being educated for jobs that no longer exist.

Some positives include the following:

- This group is becoming more educated: by age 20 to 24, 58 percent of women and 53 percent of men have some college education or have graduated from college.
- Because of increased education, this group will be better able to adapt to change and to do freelance or free-agent work.
- This generation is becoming more ethnically diverse and is more receptive to multiculturalism.
- They will participate in great advances in technology and biotechnology.
- This group will use the Internet to conduct business in a more efficient way than ever before.
- Since young people are waiting longer to marry, they may have fewer divorces.[11]

First Adulthood: The Turbulent 30s and the Flourishing 40s

Thirty-year-olds step into first adulthood with questions about who they are and what life is all about. They pay the rent or mortgage, make the car payment, and take care of the children. Maybe they used to say that someone over 30 could not be trusted. Now they are 30 themselves and become conscious that they are getting older. At age 35, they take inventory and ask, "Is half of my life over? Is this what it is all about?" These questions are the beginning of a midlife crisis. Since people are living longer, half of their life is not over at age 35. The midlife crisis used to happen around age 38 to 43. Gail Sheehy suggests that the midlife crisis is now often delayed until the mid-40s.

A **midlife crisis** is a major transition in life in which we question what we did during the first half of our life. The central issue in midlife is dealing with growing older and our own mortality. During this time, adults make major changes in their lives. They may start a new hobby, change careers, go back to school, start a new business, get a divorce, or buy a new sports car. During this transition adults often go through what Gail Sheehy calls middlescence, which she defines as adolescence the second time around. She gives this example:

> "'At forty-eight I lost 40 pounds, looked younger than I did at 40 and took up a long-repressed passion—music,' says a typical homemaker. Jeannie enrolled in music school to study electric bass and drums. She now plays in a garage rock band with 18-year-old boys. She already has planned her antidote to 'hardening of the attitudes.' After 65 she plans to launch a heavy metal band called Guns and Geezers."[12]

© 2014, Paul Vasarhelyi. Used under license with Shutterstock, Inc.

While the midlife crisis can be dangerous, it can have some positive outcomes. Adults look at their lives and make changes that lead to continued growth and enjoyment of life. The midlife crisis is a gateway to a new beginning or second adulthood. Half of life is not over; half of life lies ahead, and adults can take advantage of their experiences in the first half of life to find exciting new opportunities in the second half.

Second Adulthood: The Ages of Mastery and Integrity

The second adulthood begins with the resolution of the midlife crisis at around age 45 and goes to age 85 or longer. We expect that people will be living into their 80s and 90s and leading healthy and productive lives. Sheehy divides the second adulthood into two stages: the Age of Mastery (45–65) and the Age of Integrity (65–85 or beyond).[13]

The Age of Mastery (45–65) marks the apex of life, in which people have a stable psychological sense of mastery. People face the second half of life with 50 years of experience in living. Sheehy states that "45 represents the old age of youth, while 50 initiates the youth of Second Adulthood." She compares life to watching a play:

> "It's as though when we are young, we have seen only the first act of the play. By our forties we have reached the climactic second-act curtain. Only as we approach fifty does the shape and meaning of the whole play become clear."[14]

People in their 50s are more serene about their mortality. At age 35, our mortality becomes a realization and at age 40, it becomes a terrifying idea. We try to turn back the clock. At age 50, we are better able to accept the aging process. We have had experience with life and have successfully dealt with many challenges. At this age, many may even feel physically fit and devote time to exercise and better health. The question is, "How long do I want to live and how can I invest my time in my mental and physical health?"

Successful aging does not happen automatically. To age successfully, people need to look at their priorities and determine what is most important in life. Successful aging means taking an active part in life rather than being sedentary and inactive. The central question of this age is a search for the meaning of life. People find meaning by searching for their passion. They need to find what they really enjoy and do it.

The Age of Integrity (65–85 and beyond) is a new life stage resulting from the extended average life span. In the "serene 60s," only 10 percent of Americans 65 and older have a chronic health problem that restricts them from carrying on a major activity. Those who do have chronic health problems are often suffering as a result of neglecting their health at earlier ages.[15] In the sixties, most people are healthy and looking forward to using their experience with life to make contributions to their families and communities. People who have lived to the Age of Integrity have learned to deal with life. They have passed through many stages and dealt with many crises. They have learned how to put life into perspective. It takes about 65 years for human beings to finally figure it all out and to be happy with their lives!

An example of a woman in the "serene 60s" is Deborah Szekely, a pioneer in creating fitness spas. She says that life can be divided into three parts:

> *"The first third of life is devoted to being a child, learning in school and at home. The next third is spent working as hard as you're able and being rewarded for it. The final third is perhaps the most important: taking a role in making the world better for the next generation."[16]*

Retirement is one of the most difficult transitions in the Age of Integrity. It used to be that people worked for about 30 years and then retired. However, if a person retires at age 65, there are still 20 to 30 years of life to live. A new idea is serial retirement. A person retires from one career and enters a new career and retires again. This happens because of the need to stay active and involved as well as the need to extend financial resources over a longer life span. It is difficult to predict how much money will be needed to retire 20 or 30 years into the future. To successfully move through the retirement transition, people need to continue to grow and learn how to play after a life of work.

Gail Sheehy summarizes some of the research on factors contributing to health and well-being in the 60s and beyond.[17]

© 2014, Julie Campbell. Used under license with Shutterstock, Inc.

- Having mature love (a wife, husband, partner) is more important than money or power.
- Continued growth experiences and feeling an excitement about life help people to feel happy.
- It is important to find your passion and pursue it.
- Exercise is the most important factor in retarding the aging process. It was found that men and women who walk a half-hour a day cut their mortality rates in half.[18]

Many people are living to the age of 90 to 100. Gail Sheehy describes the **characteristics of successful centenarians:**

> *"Characteristics of healthy centenarians, garnered from a number of studies, are these: most have high native intelligence, a keen interest in current events, a good memory, and few illnesses. They tend to be early risers, sleeping on average between six and seven hours. Most drink coffee, follow no special diets, but generally prefer diets high in protein, low in fat. There is no uniformity in their drinking habits, but they use less medication in their lifetimes than many old people use in a week. They prefer living in the present, with changes, and are usually religious in the broad sense. All have a degree of optimism and a marked sense of humor. Life seems to have been a great adventure."[19]*

Writer F. Scott Fitzgerald said that we need to learn "to accept life not as a series of random events but as path of awakening."[20] We learn and grow and develop over a lifetime. Knowing about the stages of our lives helps us to realize that as long as we continue to grow and develop, we can awaken to each new day with the prospect of continued satisfaction and enjoyment of life.

> "Learn from yesterday, live for today, hope for tomorrow. The important thing is not to stop questioning."
> Albert Einstein

QUIZ

Understanding Life Stages

Test what you have learned by selecting the correct answers to the following questions.

1. Erik Erikson believes that all human beings pass through eight stages of development

   a. that last 10 years for each stage.
   b. in a random pattern.
   c. in a fixed order.

2. According to Erikson, the main task of the identity vs. role confusion stage (age 11–18) is

   a. learning to follow the rules of society.
   b. discovering personality and interests in preparation for work.
   c. forming intimate relationships.

3. Daniel Levinson says that stages of adult development alternate between

   a. stable and transitional periods.
   b. calm and stressful periods.
   c. integrity and despair.

4. The midlife crisis is defined as

   a. a brief period of insanity.
   b. a major transition in which we question what we did in the first half of life.
   c. the realization that half of life is over.

5. Factors contributing to successful aging include

   a. increasing time for relaxation.
   b. continuing exercise throughout life.
   c. reflecting on past accomplishments.

How did you do on the quiz? Check your answers: 1. c, 2. b, 3. a, 4. b, 5. b

Thinking Positively about Your Life

Thinking positively about yourself and your life is one of the most important skills you can learn for your future success. Following are some ways to practice positive thinking.

© 2014, kentoh. Used under license with Shutterstock, Inc.

Optimism, Hope, and Future-Mindedness

You can increase your chances of success by using three powerful tools: optimism, hope, and future-mindedness. These character traits lead to achievement in athletics, academics, careers, and even politics. They also have positive mental and physical effects. They reduce anxiety and depression as well as contributing to physical well-being. In addition, they aid in problem solving and searching out resources to solve problems. A simple definition of optimism is expecting good events to happen in the future and working to make them happen. Optimism leads to continued efforts to accomplish goals, whereas pessimism leads to giving up on accomplishing goals. A person who sets no goals for the future cannot be optimistic or hopeful. Here are some ideas about optimism from Optimist International.[21]

Promise yourself:

- To talk health, happiness, and prosperity to every person you meet.
- To make all your friends feel that there is something important in them.
- To look at the sunny side of everything and make your optimism come true.
- To be just as enthusiastic about the success of others as you are about your own.
- To forget the mistakes of the past and press on to the greater achievements of the future.
- To give so much time to the improvement of yourself that you have no time to criticize others.
- To wear a cheerful countenance at all times and give every living creature you meet a smile.

Being hopeful is another way of thinking positively about the future. One research study showed for entering college freshmen, level of hope was a better predictor of college grades than standardized tests or high school grade point average.[22] Students who have a high level of hope set higher goals and work to attain these goals. If they are not successful, they change goals and move in a new direction with a renewed sense of hope for a positive future.

Future-mindedness is thinking about the future, expecting that desired events and outcomes will occur, and then acting in a way that makes the positive outcomes come true. It involves setting goals for the future and taking action to accomplish these goals as well as being confident in accomplishing these goals. Individuals with future-mindedness are conscientious and hardworking and can delay gratification. They make to-do lists and use schedules and day planners. Individuals who are future-minded would agree with these statements: [23]

- Despite challenges, I always remain hopeful about the future.
- I always look on the bright side.
- I believe that good will always triumph over evil.
- I expect the best.
- I have a clear picture in mind about what I want to happen in the future.
- I have a plan for what I want to be doing five years from now.
- If I get a bad grade or evaluation, I focus on the next opportunity and plan to do better.

Believe in Yourself

Anthony Robbins defines belief as "any guiding principle, dictum, faith, or passion that can provide meaning and direction in life . . . Beliefs are the compass and maps that guide us toward our goals and give us the surety to know we'll get there."[24] The beliefs that we have about ourselves determine how much of our potential we will use and how successful we will be in the future. If we have positive beliefs about ourselves, we will feel confident and accomplish our goals in life. Negative beliefs get in the way of our success. Robbins reminds us that we can change our beliefs and choose new ones if necessary.

"The birth of excellence begins with our awareness that our beliefs are a choice. We usually do not think of it that way, but belief can be a conscious choice. You can choose beliefs that limit you, or you can choose beliefs that support you. The trick is to choose the beliefs that are conducive to success and the results you want and to discard the ones that hold you back."[25]

The Self-Fulfilling Prophecy

The first step in thinking positively is to examine your beliefs about yourself, your life, and the world around you. Personal beliefs are influenced by our environment, significant events that have happened in life, what we have learned in the past, and our picture of the future. Beliefs cause us to have certain expectations about the world and ourselves. These expectations are such a powerful influence on behavior that psychologists use the term "self-fulfilling prophecy" to describe what happens when our expectations come true.

For example, if I believe that I am not good in math (my expectation), I may not try to do the assignment or may avoid taking a math class (my behavior). As a result, I am not good in math. My expectations have been fulfilled. Expectations can also have a positive effect. If I believe that I am a good student, I will take steps to enroll in college and complete my assignments. I will then become a good student. The prophecy will again come true.

To think positively, it is necessary to recognize your negative beliefs and turn them into positive beliefs. Some negative beliefs commonly heard from college students include the following:

I don't have the money for college.
English was never my best subject.
I was never any good at math.

When you hear yourself saying these negative thoughts, remember that these thoughts can become self-fulfilling prophecies. First of all, notice the thought. Then see if you can change the statement into a positive statement such as:

I can find the money for college.
English has been a challenge for me in the past, but I will do better this time.
I can learn to be good at math.

If you believe that you can find money for college, you can go to the financial aid office and the scholarship office to begin your search for money to attend school. You can look for a better job or improve your money management. If you believe that you will do better in English, you will keep up with your assignments and go to the tutoring center or ask the professor for help. If you believe that you can learn to be good at math, you will attend every math class and seek tutoring when you do not understand. Your positive thoughts will help you to be successful.

Positive Self-Talk and Affirmations

Self-talk refers to the silent inner voice in our heads. This voice is often negative, especially when we are frustrated or trying to learn something new. Have you ever had thoughts about yourself that are similar to these:

How could you be so stupid!
That was dumb!
You idiot!

ACTIVITY

What do you say to yourself when you are angry or frustrated? Write several examples of your negative self-talk.

Negative thoughts can actually be toxic to your body. They can cause biochemical changes that can lead to depression and negatively affect the immune system.[26] Negative self-talk causes anxiety and poor performance and is damaging to self-esteem. It can also lead to a negative self-fulfilling prophecy. Positive thoughts can help us build self-esteem, become confident in our abilities, and achieve our goals. These positive thoughts are called affirmations.

If we make the world with our thoughts, it is important to become aware of the thoughts about ourselves that are continuously running through our heads. Are your thoughts positive or negative? Negative thoughts lead to failure. What we hear over and over again shapes our beliefs. If you say over and over to yourself such things

"We are what we think.
All that we are arises
With our thoughts.
With our thoughts
we make the world."
                    Buddha

as, "I am stupid," "I am ugly," or "I am fat," you will start to believe these things and act in a way that supports your beliefs. Positive thoughts help to build success. If you say to yourself, "I'm a good person," "I'm doing my best," or "I'm doing fine," you will begin to believe these things about yourself and act in a way that supports these beliefs. Here are some guidelines for increasing your positive self-talk and making affirmations:

1. Monitor your thoughts about yourself and become aware of them. Are they positive or negative?

2. When you notice a negative thought about yourself, imagine rewinding a tape and recording a new positive message.

3. Start the positive message with "I" and use the present tense. Using an "I" statement shows you are in charge. Using the present tense shows you are ready for action now.

4. Focus on the positive. Think about what you want to achieve and what you can do rather than what you do not want to do. For example, instead of saying, "I will not eat junk food," say, "I will eat a healthy diet."

5. Make your affirmation stronger by adding an emotion to it.

6. Form a mental picture of what it is that you want to achieve. See yourself doing it successfully.

7. You may need to say the positive thoughts over and over again until you believe them and they become a habit. You can also write them down and put them in a place where you will see them often.

Here are some examples of negative self-talk and contrasting positive affirmations:

Negative: I'm always broke.

Affirmation: I feel really good when I manage my finances. See yourself taking steps to manage finances. For example, a budget or savings plan.

Negative: I'm too fat. It just runs in the family.

Affirmation: I feel good about myself when I exercise and eat a healthy diet. See yourself exercising and eating a healthy diet.

Negative: I can't do this. I must be stupid.

Affirmation: I can do this. I am capable. I feel a sense of accomplishment when I accomplish something challenging. See yourself making your best attempt and taking the first step to accomplish the project.

ACTIVITY

Select one example of negative self-talk that you wrote earlier. Use the examples above to turn your negative message into a positive one and write it here.

Visualize Your Success

Visualization is a powerful tool for using your brain to improve memory, deal with stress, and think positively. Coaches and athletes study sports psychology to learn how to use visualization along with physical practice to improve athletic performance. College students can use the same techniques to enhance college success.

© 2014, Sergey Nivens. Used under license with Shutterstock, Inc.

If you are familiar with sports or are an athlete, you can probably think of times when your coach asked you to use visualization to improve your performance. In baseball, the coach reminds players to keep their eye on the ball and visualize hitting it. In swimming, the coach asks swimmers to visualize reaching their arms out to touch the edge of the pool at the end of the race. Pole-vaulters visualize clearing the pole and sometimes even go through the motions before making the jump. Using imagery lets you practice for future events and pre-experience achieving your goals. Athletes imagine winning the race or completing the perfect jump in figure skating. In this way they prepare mentally and physically and develop confidence in their abilities. It still takes practice to excel.

Just as the athlete visualizes and then performs, the college student can do the same. It is said that we create all things twice. First we make a mental picture, and then we create the physical reality by taking action. For example, if we are building a house, first we get the idea; then we begin to design the house we want. We start with a blueprint and then build the house. The blueprint determines what kind of house we construct. The same thing happens in any project we undertake. First we have a mental picture, and then we complete the project. Visualize what you would like to accomplish in your life as if you were creating a blueprint. Then take the steps to accomplish what you want.

As a college student, you might visualize yourself in your graduation robe walking across the stage to receive your diploma. You might visualize yourself in the exam room confidently taking the exam. You might see yourself on the job enjoying your future career. You can make a mental picture of what you would like your life to be and then work toward accomplishing your goal.

> "The future first exists in imagination, then planning, then reality."
> R.A. Wilson

Successful Beliefs

Stephen Covey's book *The 7 Habits of Highly Effective People* has been described as one of the most influential books of the 20th century.[27] In 2004, he released a new book called *The 8th Habit: From Effectiveness to Greatness.*[28] These habits are based on beliefs that lead to success.

1. **Be proactive.** Being proactive means accepting responsibility for your life. Covey uses the word "response-ability" for the ability to choose responses. The quality of your life is based on the decisions and responses that you make. Proactive people make things happen through responsibility and initiative. They do not blame circumstances or conditions for their behavior.

2. **Begin with the end in mind.** Know what is important and what you wish to accomplish in your life. To be able to do this, you will need to know your values and goals in life. You will need a clear vision of what you want your life to be and where you are headed.

3. **Put first things first.** Once you have established your goals and vision for the future, you will need to manage yourself to do what is important first. Set priorities so that you can accomplish the tasks that are important to you.

4. **Think win-win.** In human interactions, seek solutions that benefit everyone. Focus on cooperation rather than competition. If everyone feels good about the decision, there is cooperation and harmony. If one person wins and the other loses, the loser becomes angry and resentful and sabotages the outcome.

5. **First seek to understand, then to be understood.** Too often in our personal communications, we try to talk first and listen later. Often we don't really listen: we use this time to think of our reply. It is best to listen and understand before speaking. Effective communication is one of the most important skills in life.

6. **Synergize.** A simple definition of synergy is that the whole is greater than the sum of its parts. If people can cooperate and have good communication, they can work together as a team to accomplish more than each individual could do separately. Synergy is also part of the creative process.

7. **Sharpen the saw.** Covey shares the story of a man who was trying to cut down a tree with a dull saw. As he struggled to cut the tree, someone suggested that he stop and sharpen the saw. The man said that he did not have time to sharpen the saw, so he continued to struggle. Covey suggests that we need to take time to stop and sharpen the saw. We need to stop working and invest some time in ourselves by staying healthy physically, mentally, spiritually, and socially. We need to take time for self-renewal.

8. **Find your voice, and inspire others to find theirs.** Believe that you can make a positive difference in the world and inspire others to do the same. Covey says that leaders "deal with people in a way that will communicate to them their worth and potential so clearly that they will come to see it in themselves." Accomplishing this ideal begins with developing one's own voice or "unique personal significance."[29]

QUIZ

Positive Thinking

Test what you have learned by selecting the correct answers to the following questions.

1. The self-fulfilling prophecy refers to

   a. the power of belief in determining your future.
   b. good fortune in the future.
   c. being able to foretell the future.

2. Positive self-talk results in

   a. lower self-esteem.
   b. overconfidence.
   c. higher self-esteem.

3. The statement "We create all things twice" refers to

   a. doing the task twice to make sure it is done right.
   b. creating and refining.
   c. first making a mental picture and then taking action.

4. A win-win solution means

   a. winning at any cost.
   b. seeking a solution that benefits everyone.
   c. focusing on competition.

5. The statement by Stephen Covey, "Sharpen the saw," refers to

   a. proper tool maintenance.
   b. studying hard to sharpen thinking skills.
   c. investing time to maintain physical and mental health.

How did you do on the quiz? Check your answers: 1. a, 2. c, 3. c, 4. b, 5. c

Secrets to Happiness

Many of you probably have happiness on your list of lifetime goals. It sounds easy, right? But what is happiness, anyway?

Psychologist Martin Seligman says that real happiness comes from identifying, cultivating, and using your personal strengths in work, love, play, and parenting.[30] You have identified these strengths by learning about your personality type, learning style, interests, and values.

Seligman contrasts authentic happiness with hedonism. He states that a hedonist "wants as many good moments and as few bad moments as possible in life."[31] Hedonism is a shortcut to happiness that leaves us feeling empty. For example, we often assume that more material possessions will make us happy. However, the more material possessions we have, the greater the expectations, and we no longer appreciate what we have.

> "Suppose you could be hooked up to a hypothetical 'experience machine' that, for the rest of your life, would stimulate your brain and give you any positive feelings you desire. Most people to whom I offer this imaginary choice refuse the machine. It is not just positive feelings we want, we want to be entitled to our positive feelings. Yet we have invented myriad shortcuts to feeling good: drugs, chocolate, loveless sex, shopping, masturbation, and television are all examples. (I am not, however, suggesting that you should drop these shortcuts altogether.) The belief that we can rely on shortcuts to happiness, joy, rapture, comfort, and ecstasy, rather than be entitled to these feelings by the exercise of personal strengths and virtues, leads to the legions of people who in the middle of great wealth are starving spiritually. Positive emotion alienated from the exercise of character leads to emptiness, to inauthenticity, to depression, and as we age, to the gnawing realization that we are fidgeting until we die."[32]

Most people assume that happiness is increased by having more money to buy that new car or HDTV. However, a process called hedonistic adaptation occurs that makes this type of happiness short-lived. Once you have purchased the new car or TV, you get used to it quickly. Soon you will start to think about a better car and a bigger TV to continue to feel happy. Seligman provides a formula for happiness:[33]

$$\text{Happiness} = S + C + V$$

In the formula S stands for set range. Psychologists believe that 50 percent of happiness is determined by heredity. In other words, half of your level of happiness is determined by the genes inherited from your ancestors. In good times or bad times, people generally return to their set range of happiness. Six months after receiving a piece of good fortune such as a raise or promotion or winning the lottery, unhappy people are still unhappy. Six months after a tragedy, naturally happy people return to being happy.

The letter C in the equation stands for circumstances such as money, marriage, social life, health, education, climate, race, gender, and religion. These circumstances account for 8 to 15 percent of happiness. Here is what psychologists know about how these circumstances affect happiness:

- Once basic needs are met, greater wealth does not increase happiness.
- Having a good marriage is related to increased happiness.

"Most folks are about as happy as they make up their minds to be."
Abraham Lincoln

Success is getting what you want; happiness is wanting what you get.
Dale Carnegie

- Happy people are more social.
- Moderate ill health does not bring unhappiness, but severe illness does.
- Educated people are slightly happier.
- Climate, race, and gender do not affect level of happiness.
- Religious people are somewhat happier than nonreligious people.

The letter V in the equation stands for factors under your voluntary control. These factors account for approximately 40 percent of happiness. Factors under voluntary control include positive emotions and optimism about the future. Positive emotions include hope, faith, trust, joy, ecstasy, calm, zest, ebullience, pleasure, flow, satisfaction, contentment, fulfillment, pride, and serenity. Seligman suggests the following ideas to increase your positive emotions:

- Realize that the past does not determine your future. The future is open to new possibilities.
- Be grateful for the good events of the past and place less emphasis on the bad events.
- Build positive emotions through forgiving and forgetting.
- Work on increasing optimism and hope for the future.
- Find out what activities make you happy and engage in them. Spread these activities out over time so that you will not get tired of them.
- Take the time to savor the happy times. Make mental photographs of happy times so that you can think of them later.
- Take time to enjoy the present moment.
- Build more flow into your life. Flow is the state of gratification we feel when totally absorbed in an activity that matches our strengths.

Are you interested in taking steps to increase your happiness? Here are some activities proposed by Sonya Lyubomirsky, a leading researcher on happiness and author of *The How of Happiness*.[34] Choose the ones that seem like a natural fit for you and vary them so that they do not become routine or boring. After putting in some effort to practice these activities, they can become a habit.

1. **Express gratitude.** Expressing gratitude is a way of thinking positively and appreciating good circumstances rather than focusing on the bad ones. It is about appreciating and thanking the people who have made positive contributions to your life. It is feeling grateful for the good things you have in life. Create a gratitude journal and at the end of each day write down things for which you are grateful or thankful. Regularly tell those around you how grateful you are to have them in your life. You can do this in person, by phone, in a letter, or by email. Being grateful helps us to savor positive life experiences.

2. **Cultivate optimism.** Make a habit of looking at the bright side of life. If you think positively about the future, you are more likely to take the effort to reach your goals in life. Spend some time thinking or writing about your best possible future. Make a mental picture of your future goals as a first step toward achieving them. Thinking positively boosts your mood and promotes high morale. Most importantly, thinking positively can become a self-fulfilling prophecy. If you see your positive goals as attainable, you are more likely to work toward accomplishing them and invest the energy needed to deal with obstacles and setbacks along the way.

3. **Avoid overthinking and social comparison.** Overthinking is focusing on yourself and your problems endlessly, needlessly, and excessively. Examples of overthinking include "Why am I so unhappy?" "Why is life so unfair?" and "Why did he/she say that?" Overthinking increases sadness, fosters biased thinking, decreases motivation, and makes it difficult to solve problems and take action to make life better.

Social comparison is a type of overthinking. In our daily lives, we encounter people who are more intelligent, beautiful, richer, healthier, or happier. The media fosters images of people with impossibly perfect lives. Making social comparisons can lead to feelings of inferiority and loss of self-esteem.

Notice when your are overthinking or making comparisons with others and stop doing it. Use the "Yell, 'Stop!'" technique to refocus your attention. This technique involves yelling, "Stop!" to yourself or out loud to change your thinking. Another way to stop over-thinking is to distract yourself with more positive thoughts or activities. Watch a funny movie, listen to music, or arrange a social activity with a friend. If these activities are not effective, try writing down your worries in a journal. Writing helps to organize thoughts and to make sense of them. Begin to take some small steps to resolve your worries and problems.

4. **Practice acts of kindness.** Doing something kind for others increases your own personal happiness and satisfies your basic need for human connection. Opportunities for helping others surround us each day. How about being courteous on the freeway, helping a child with homework, or helping your elderly neighbor with yard work? A simple act of kindness makes you feel good and often sets off a chain of events in which the person who receives the kindness does something kind for someone else.

5. **Increase flow activities.** Flow is defined as intense involvement in an activity so that you do not notice the passage of time. Musicians are in the flow when they are totally involved in their music. Athletes are in the flow when they are totally focused on their sport. Writers are in the flow when they are totally absorbed in writing down their ideas. The key to achieving flow is balancing skills and challenges. If your skills are not sufficient for the activity, you will become frustrated. If your skills are greater than what is demanded for the activity, you will become bored. Work often provides an opportunity to experience flow if you are in a situation in which your work activities are matched to your skills and talents.

As our skills increase, it becomes more difficult to maintain flow. We must be continually testing ourselves in ever more challenging activities to maintain flow. You can take some action to increase the flow in your life by learning to fully focus your attention on the activity you are doing. It is important to be open to new and different experiences. To maintain the flow in your life, make a commitment to lifelong learning.

6. **Savor life's joys.** Savoring is the repetitive replaying of the positive experiences in life and is one of the most important ingredients of happiness. Savoring happens in the past, present, and future. Think often about the good things that have happened in the past. Savor the present by relishing the present moment. Savor the future by anticipating and visualizing positive events or outcomes in the future.

There are many ways to savor life's joys. Replay in your mind happy days or events from the past. Create a photo album of your favorite people, places, and events and look at it often. This prolongs the happiness. Take a few minutes each day to appreciate ordinary activities such as taking a shower or walking to work. Engage the senses to notice your environment. Is it a sunny day? Take some time to look at the sky, the trees, and the plants. Landscape architects incorporate artwork, trees, and flowers along the freeways to help drivers to relax on the road. Notice art and objects of beauty. Be attentive to the present moment and be aware of your surroundings. Picture in your mind positive events you anticipate in the future. All of these activities will increase your "psychological bank account" of happy times and will help deal with times that are not so happy.

7. **Commit to accomplishing your goals.** Working toward a meaningful life goal is one of the most important things that you can do to have a happy life. Goals provide structure and meaning to our lives and improve self-esteem. Working on goals provides something to look forward to in the future.

> "Finish each day and be done with it. You have done what you could; some blunders and absurdities have crept in; forget them as soon as you can. Tomorrow is a new day; you shall begin it serenely and with too high a spirit to be encumbered with your old nonsense."
> Ralph Waldo Emerson

> "Happiness consists more in small conveniences or pleasures that occur every day, than in great pieces of good fortune that happen but seldom."
> Benjamin Franklin

The types of goals that you pursue have an impact on your happiness. The goals that have the most potential for long-term happiness involve changing your activities rather than changing your circumstances. Examples of goals that change your circumstances are moving to the beach or buying a new stereo. These goals make you happy for a short time. Then you get used to your new circumstances and no longer feel as happy as when you made the initial change. Examples of goals that change your activities are returning to school or taking up a new sport or hobby. These activities allow you to take on new challenges that keep life interesting for a longer period of time. Choose intrinsic goals that help you to develop your competence and autonomy. These goals should match your most important values and interests.

> "An aim in life is the only fortune worth finding."
> Robert Louis Stevenson

8. **Take care of your body.** Engaging in physical activity provides many opportunities for increasing happiness. Physical activity helps to:

- Increase longevity and improve the quality of life.
- Improve sleep and protect the body from disease.

© 2014, Efired. Used under license with Shutterstock, Inc.

- Keep brains healthy and avoid cognitive impairments.
- Increase self-esteem.
- Increase the opportunity to engage in flow.
- Provide a distraction from worries and overthinking.

Journal Entry #3

Psychologists Martin Seligman and Sonya Lyubomirsky write about the secrets to happiness. Write about four of their ideas with which you agree or disagree.

David Myers, a professor of psychology at Hope College in Michigan, is a leading researcher on happiness. He says that 90 percent of us are naturally happy. He adds that if most of us "were characteristically unhappy, the emotional pain would lose its ability to alert us to an unusual and possibly harmful condition."[35]

Just as you have made a decision to get a college degree, make a decision to be happy. Make a decision to be happy by altering your internal outlook and choosing to change your behavior. Here are some suggestions for consciously choosing happiness.

1. Find small things that make you happy and sprinkle your life with them. A glorious sunset, a pat on the back, a well-manicured yard, an unexpected gift, a round of tennis, a favorite sandwich, a fishing line cast on a quiet lake, the wagging tail of the family dog, or your child finally taking some responsibility—these are things that will help to create a continual climate of happiness.

2. Smile and stand up straight. Michael Mercer and Maryann Troiani, authors of *Spontaneous Optimism: Proven Strategies for Health, Prosperity and Happiness,* say that "unhappy people tend to slouch, happy people don't. . . . Happy people even take bigger steps when they walk."[36]

3. Learn to think like an optimist. "Pessimists tend to complain; optimists focus on solving their problems."[37] Never use the word "try"; this word is for pessimists. Assume you will succeed.

4. Replace negative thoughts with positive ones.

5. Fill your life with things you like to do.

6. Get enough rest. If you do not get enough sleep, you will feel tired and gloomy. Sleep deprivation can lead to depression.

7. Learn from your elders. Psychologist Daniel Mroczek says that "people in their sixties and seventies who are in good health are among the happiest people in our society. . . . They may be better able to regulate their emotions, they've developed perspective, they don't get so worried about little things, and they've often achieved their goals and aren't trying to prove themselves."[38]

8. Reduce stress.

9. Take charge of your time by doing first things first.

10. Close relationships are important. Myers and Mroczek report higher levels of happiness among married men and women.[39]

11. Keep things in perspective. Will it matter in six months to a year?

12. Laugh more. Laughter produces a relaxation response.

Journal Entry # 4

Write five intention statements about increasing your future happiness.
I intend to . . .

You Are What You Think

"Whether you think you can, or think you can't . . . you're right." Henry Ford

© 2014, iQoncept. Used under license with Shutterstock, Inc.

Sometimes students enter college with the fear of failure. This belief leads to anxiety and behavior that leads to failure. If you have doubts about your ability to succeed in college, you might not go to class or attempt the challenging work required in college. It is difficult to make the effort if you cannot see positive results ahead. Unfortunately, failure in college can lead to a loss of confidence and lack of success in other areas of life as well.

Henry Ford said, "What we believe is true, comes true. What we believe is possible, becomes possible." If you believe that you will succeed, you will be more likely to take actions that lead to your success. Once you have experienced some small part of success, you will have confidence in your abilities and will continue on the road to success. Success leads to more success. It becomes a habit. You will be motivated to make the effort necessary to accomplish your goals. You might even become excited and energized along the way. You will use your gifts and talents to reach your potential and achieve happiness. It all begins with the thoughts you choose.

"Watch your thoughts; they become words.
Watch your words; they become actions.
Watch your actions; they become habits.
Watch your habits; they become character.
Watch your character; it becomes your destiny."[10]

—*Frank Outlaw*

To help you choose positive beliefs, picture in your mind how you want your life to be. Imagine it is here now. See all the details and experience the feelings associated with this picture. Pretend it is true until you believe it. Then take action to make your dreams come true.

Journal Entry #5

Henry Ford said, "Whether you think you can, or think you can't . . . you're right." Based on this quote, how can your thoughts help you to be successful in college and in your career?

JOURNAL ENTRIES

Thinking Positively about the Future

Go to http://www.collegesuccess1.com/JournalEntries.htm for Word files of the Journal Entries

Success over the Internet

Visit the *College Success Website* at http://www.collegesuccess1.com/

The *College Success Website* is continually updated with new topics and links to the material presented in this chapter. Topics include:

- Adult development
- Happiness
- Self-improvement
- Self-esteem
- Sports psychology
- How to be successful

Contact your instructor if you have any problems in accessing the *College Success Website*.

Notes

1. Gail Sheehy, *Passages* (New York: E.P. Dutton, 1976) and *New Passages* (New York: Random House, 1995).

2. Erik H. Erikson, *Childhood and Society* (New York: W.W. Norton, 1963).

3. D. J. Levinson and J. D. Levinson, *Seasons of a Woman's Life* (New York: Knopf, 1996). D. J. Levinson, C. N. Darrow, E. B. Klein, M. H. Levinson, and B. McKee, *Seasons of a Man's Life* (New York: Knopf, 1978).

4. D. J. Levinson, "A Conception of Adult Development," *American Psychologist* 41 (1986): 107.

5. Levinson and Levinson, *Seasons of a Woman's Life*, 372.

6. Sheehy, *New Passages*, 5–6.

7. Ibid., 7.

8. Ibid., 6.

9. Ibid., 49.

10. Ibid., 52.

11. Ibid., 43–53.

12. Ibid., 140.

13. Ibid., 145.

14. Ibid., 150.

15. Ibid., 351.

16. Ibid., 395.

17. Ibid., 384.

18. Ibid., 426.

19. Ibid., 427.

20. Sheehy, *New Passages*, 429.

21. Christopher Peterson and Martin Seligman, *Character Strengths and Virtues: A Handbook and Classification* (Oxford: University Press, 2004), 583–584.

22. Daniel Goleman, "Hope Emerges a Key to Success in Life," *New York Times*, December 24, 1991.

23. Peterson and Seligman, *Character Strengths and Virtues,* 570. Goleman, "Hope Emerges a Key to Success in Life."

24. Anthony Robbins, *Unlimited Power* (New York: Fawcett Columbine, 1986), 54–55.

25. Ibid., 54–55.

26. Joan Smith, "Nineteen Habits of Happy Women," *Redbook Magazine,* August 1999, 68.

27. Stephen R. Covey, *The 7 Habits of Highly Effective People* (New York: Simon and Schuster, 1989).

28. Stephen R. Covey, *The 8th Habit: From Effectiveness to Greatness* (New York: Free Press, 2004).

29. Ibid.

30. Martin Seligman, *Authentic Happiness: Using the New Positive Psychology to Realize Your Potential for Lasting Fulfillment* (New York: Free Press), xiii.

31. Ibid., 6.

32. Ibid., 8.

33. Ibid., 45.

34. Sonya Lyubomirsky, *The How of Happiness* (New York: The Penguin Press, 2008).

35. Quoted in Joan Smith, "Nineteen Habits of Happy Women," *Redbook Magazine,* August 1999, 66.

36. Quoted in Smith, "Nineteen Habits of Happy Women."

37. Ibid.

38. Ibid.

39. Ibid.

40. Rob Gilbert, ed., *Bits and Pieces* (Fairfield, NJ: The Economics Press), Vol. R, No. 40, p. 7, copyright 1998.

CHAPTER 15

Job Search Strategies

Learning Objectives

Read to answer these key questions:

- What are some tips for writing my resume and cover letter?

- How do I establish my own personal brand for marketing myself online?

- What are some online tools that can help me find a job?

- How can I prepare for the job interview?

- What is an informational interview?

- What are some options for starting my own business?

- How do I set up a job search plan and begin taking action?

While in college, you can increase your chances of obtaining employment after graduation by using Career Services at your college, volunteering, doing internships, and working part time. Get started by writing your resume and cover letter. Establish your personal brand by assessing your personal strengths and using social media to market yourself to potential employers. Learn about some online tools for searching for that ideal job as well as how to be successful on the interview. Alternatively you may want to consider starting your own business. The most important last step is taking action on your job search plan.

Increasing Your Chances for Employment

Using Your College Career Services

Your College Career Services can assist you in your career planning as well as finding employment, internships, and volunteer opportunities while in college and after graduation. Here are some typical career services:

- Career assessment and counseling
- Career fairs
- Career library
- Employment information
- Job postings
- Job search resources
- Majors and related careers
- Resume assistance
- Interview assistance
- Reference service
- Opportunities for volunteering, internships, and work or study abroad

Volunteering

Volunteering not only helps your community, but it can help your job search in many ways:

- Volunteering improves your confidence and self-worth and gives you a sense of accomplishment. It helps you to develop leadership skills.
- You can add contacts to your network. Most people find jobs through personal and professional contacts.
- If you have little job experience, volunteering looks good on your resume.
- You can learn new skills by volunteering.
- Volunteering is a way to try out a career to see if you like it. For example, if you are thinking about becoming a teacher, volunteer at a school to gain some first-hand experience and to see if teaching is really the career for you.
- Learn about job opportunities while volunteering.
- Ask for recommendations or endorsements after you have finished your volunteer position.

To find a volunteer position, start with Career Services at your college. This office often has volunteer positions related to the majors at their college. You can also research volunteer positions online at volunteermatch.com, which matches your interests to positions available in your community.

© 2013, Shutterstock, Inc.

Internships

The purpose of an internship is to learn job skills and increase your networking possibilities while you are in college. Internships are often low paid or unpaid positions in a company or organization that is in your area of career interest. Some internships can lead to jobs when you finish college or at least look good on your resume. Colleges set up internships with local companies and may even offer you college credit for them. Begin by contacting Career Services at your college. This office often sets up internships to match the majors at the college. You can also use internmatch.com to begin an Internet search, or join LinkedIn and click on Jobs for Students and Recent Graduates to find opportunities in your area. Another possibility is contacting companies matching your interests and asking them if they have any internship possibilities.

A good internship is one in which you have the opportunity to experience hands-on learning and gain knowledge in the field, which can be valuable in your future career. Often interns shadow employees to learn about their jobs. Internships vary in quality, with the least valuable ones having interns doing busy work with little opportunity to learn valuable skills for the future. It is best to start by figuring out the careers you would like to explore and then carefully investigating what you will be doing as an intern to make sure it is worth your time.

Working While in College

About 80 percent of students work while in college and this employment provides many advantages. It can provide needed income and valuable job experience as well as increased social contacts that can be useful in the future. This work looks good on your resume and can be used for future references. It is also a way of limiting debt by reducing the money you have to borrow for college. Research has shown that students who work 10–15 hours a week are more likely to persist and finish their college degrees. Working while in colleges requires time management skills that can be useful in future employment. Having to plan your study time and work can even result in higher grades, since you will have to schedule your study time and will be more focused on getting your school work done.[1]

However, students are often tempted to work more than the recommended amount, which results in increased stress as they try to balance the demands of employment, study, and social life. This is likely to result in longer time for degree completion or may even interfere with attaining a degree. If you find it necessary to work more than the recommended amount, consider going to college part time.

Journal Entry #1

What are some ways you can increase your chances of employment while in college? Consider volunteering, internships, or work opportunities.

Resume and Cover Letters

Your resume is important in establishing a good first impression and provides the basic content for job seeking social media sites such as LinkedIn and Facebook. A resume is a snapshot of your education and experience. It is generally one page in length. You will need a resume to apply for scholarships, part-time jobs, or find a position after you graduate. Start with a file of information you can use to create your resume. Keep your resume on file in your computer or on your flash drive so that you can revise it or post it online as needed.

© 2013, Shutterstock, Inc.

A resume includes the following basic components:

- Contact information: your name, address, telephone number, and email address
- A brief statement of your career objective
- A summary of your education:
  - Names and locations of schools
  - Dates of attendance
  - Diplomas or degrees received

- A summary of your work and/or volunteer experience
- If you have little directly related work experience, a list of courses you have taken that would help the employer understand your skills for employment
- Special skills, honors, awards, or achievements
- References (people who can recommend you for a job or scholarship)

There is no one best way to write a resume, but here are some helpful tips:

- Begin your resume with your contact information. Make sure that your email is professional. Consider creating a new email for job seeking purposes. Your email should include your first and last name.
- In the job history section, include brief statements about job tasks, including what you did to make your company better. It is helpful to look for key words in the job announcement and make sure these key words are in your resume.
- List your present or most recent job first and work back chronologically.
- If you are just graduating from college and have little work experience, put the education section first along with related coursework.
- Keep in mind that the average resume gets read in 10 seconds. Make sure your resume is organized and brief. Bold those ideas that you want to highlight.
- Do not include personal information or photos.
- Carefully proofread your resume to make sure it has no errors. It is a good idea to have someone else review it also.
- Store your resume on your computer so that you can update it regularly and have it available to post online.

It is easy to upload your content to resume templates online. Here are some resume template sites:

Choose your template from a variety of examples and then create or upload your content.
http://www.myperfectresume.com/

This site has 114 templates depending on your experience and career. You can upload your current resume into a suggested template and add their suggested improvements.
http://www.resume-now.com/

Create a resume and set up a resume webpage.
http://www.jobwinningresume.com/

View sample resume templates and create your resume.
http://www.everymanbusiness.com/human-resources/resume-template/

Ask for a letter of reference from your current supervisor at work or someone in a position to recommend you, such as a college professor or community member. Ask the person to address the letter "To Whom It May Concern" so that you can use the letter many times. If the person is on LinkedIn, ask him or her for an endorsement. The person recommending you should comment on your work habits, skills, and personal qualities. If appropriate, offer to write the letter yourself and then the person can edit it or send it as is. This often helps for people who would like to recommend you, but are very busy. If you wait until you graduate to obtain letters of reference, potential recommenders may no longer be there or may not remember who you are. Always ask if you can use a person's name as a reference. When you are applying for a job and references are requested, phone the persons who have agreed to recommend you and let them know to expect a call.

© 2013, Shutterstock, Inc.

While most resumes are shared online, if you need a printed copy, print your resume so that it looks professional. Use a good quality white, tan, or gray paper. It is a good idea to take a printed copy of your resume to an interview.

When you respond to job announcements, you may be asked to send a cover letter with your resume attached. Address your letter to a specific person at the company or organization and spell the name correctly. You can call the personnel office to obtain this information. The purpose of the cover letter is to state your interest in the job, highlight your qualifications, and get the employer to read your resume and call you for an interview. The cover letter should be brief and to the point. Include the following items:

- State the job you are interested in and how you heard about the opening.
- Briefly state how your education and experience would be assets to the company.
- Ask for an interview and tell the employer how you can be contacted.
- Attach your resume.
- Your cover letter is the first contact you have with the employer. Make it neat and free from errors. Use spell check and grammar check, read it over again, and have someone else check it for you.

Select templates and view samples of cover letters online at http://www.cover-letter-now.com/

Getting Started

1. While attending college, you can gain valuable experience by working, but it is recommended that if you are a full-time student, you work no more than ___ hours per week.

   a. 30–35
   b. 10–15
   c. 5–10

2. A resume is generally _____ page(s) in length.

   a. four
   b. one
   c. two

3. Begin your resume with your

   a. job objective.
   b. educational history.
   c. contact information.

4. To format your resume, use

   a. an online template.
   b. an outline.
   c. bold headings.

5. The cover letter

   a. contains a brief statement of how your qualifications would be an asset to the company.
   b. includes a detailed list of your education and experience.
   c. does not include a request for an interview.

How did you do on the quiz? Check your answers: 1. b, 2. b, 3. c, 4. a, 5. a

Establishing Your Personal Brand Online

Personal branding is the process by which we market ourselves to others. It is an important concept that has been used to sell products and services. Through the use of social media, you can use this concept to market your strengths to potential employers and to find a satisfying career. Throughout this textbook you have been challenged to become more aware of these personal strengths that can be used to create your own personal brand. Here are the steps for establishing your personal brand and marketing yourself:

> "Everyone should find something they love doing. Then work isn't work. It's a part of themselves. Of who they are."
> Paul McAuley

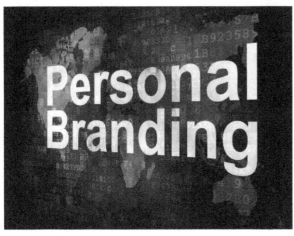

Define Your Brand

The first step in marketing yourself is to define your personal brand. What are your passions, goals, and personal strengths and how can they be used in the job market? Review the assessments in this textbook and write a brief description of your personal brand along with a brief job title. A few examples of a personal brand include financial expert, entrepreneur, educator, consultant, engineer, and personal trainer.

Manage Your Online Presence

Most employers do online searches to find employees and to find information on job candidates before the interview. Make sure that your online presence is a professional one that you would want an employer to see. Make sure that your email address is a professional one or consider setting up an account for job seeking. Google your name and see what information a potential employer can find about you. Take a look at your online sites and make sure that the content is appropriate. Some online content may make it difficult to be hired, including:

- Photos or references to drug or alcohol use or abuse.
- Discriminatory comments on race, religion, or gender.
- Negative comments about previous employers.
- Poor communication skills.

When using Facebook, manage your privacy settings so that no one can see your list of friends, since you can be judged by the company you keep and you have no control over what your friends post. To keep your friends private, specify that no one can tag you in a Facebook photo without your authorization. Be careful about what you put on your front page, since it is the most visible page.

Set up a Nameplate Website

Take control of your online presence by setting up a nameplate website that defines who you are and directs potential employers to your media sites. Good sites for setting up this nameplate include about.me and vizify.com. Both of these sites are free and provide samples that can be helpful in setting up your own site. On these sites, you can upload your photo, include your biography, list your education, describe your work experience, and provide links to LinkedIn or Facebook.

© 2013, Shutterstock, Inc.

Using Online Tools

At the present time, LinkedIn and Facebook are the most common sites used by employers to research job candidates. Invest some of your time setting up accounts at these sites.

LinkedIn

LinkedIn is a directory of professionals and companies used for job searching, networking, and hiring. Many employers use LinkedIn profiles to search for potential employees. This profile is similar to a resume and includes your education and job experience. Make sure that your profile is complete and well written since it represents who you are online. Since recruiting software is used to search through profiles, use key words in your resume that relate to your desired job. Key words include job requirements, experience, software competencies, education, and previous employers. To find key words, take a look at job listings in your area of interest and expertise and include the words in your profile. It is helpful to include recommendations and endorsements that you can request from other contacts on LinkedIn. Personalize your profile by uploading a photo. Use a current photo and dress appropriately for the type of job you are seeking.

LinkedIn is also a job search tool in which you can search for and apply for jobs within the site. The job listings page allows you to search for jobs by location, industry, company, job function, level or position, employer, or key words. The site can also be used for networking. As you link to others, they can refer you to jobs open at their site. Maintaining a large network is job security, because you can use it for job advancement or to find a new job in the future. You can join groups of other professionals in your area of expertise to receive notices about job openings in your area of interest. Use the status update function to let your contacts know that you are looking for a job.

When you find a specific job listing in which you are interested, you will have the option to apply within LinkedIn or you will be directed to the company website where you will need to create an account. The site also provides company profiles to help you to find the job that best matches your qualifications and help you with information useful for interviewing.

Facebook

Facebook is a social network that can be useful in finding a job. The first step in using your Facebook account to find a job is to clean up your profile to make sure that it does not contain any detrimental content. You can delete any questionable material or even use a software package such as Reppler, which scans your profile for embarrassing content and suggests items you might want to remove. The next step is to post a status update to let your friends know that you are looking for a job and to ask if they know about any job openings.

Use Facebook as a marketing tool. Post samples or links to your work online. If you are a photographer, post some of your photos online. If you are a writer, post links to material you have

© 2013, Shutterstock, Inc.

written. Keep your materials up to date so that prospective employers can see your best and most recent work. If your chosen company has a public Facebook page, you can show your passion, knowledge, and interest for your dream job by participating in discussion boards that can showcase your expertise. You can "like" the company on Facebook and receive news, information, and job openings from them. You can join or create groups on Facebook to discuss your area of interest. In this way, you may be considered for a job before it is posted.

Use Facebook's Marketplace app to search for jobs. Just click on Jobs in Marketplace and enter the job in which you are interested. It contains information about job openings and links to sites with job applications. Facebook also has an app called Social Jobs that allows you to search for jobs.

> "We do not go to work only to earn an income, but to find meaning in our lives. What we do is a large part of what we are."
>
> Alan Ryan

Classified Ads

One of the most traditional ways to find a job is by looking at classified ads in your local newspaper. These ads are available in online editions of newspapers and are searchable by date, category, keyword, and location. CareerBuilder.com, one of the leading job search sites, contains classified ads from many local and national newspapers as well as employer websites. You can search this site by key word, date, location, or zip code and create an alert to have matching job openings emailed to you. With the Advanced Search option, you can search jobs by radius of a certain location, required degree, salary range, and type of employment. Use the Career Builder Job Machine to upload your resume and cover letter.

Job Search Engines

The Do What You Are personality assessment and the MI Advantage career assessment are linked to the SimplyHired job search engine (www.simplyhired.com/), which sorts jobs by location and category. This search engine also contains information on job trends and salaries. There are numerous Internet sites with job listings including:

* www.indeed.com
* www.linkup.com/
* http://us.jobs/

© 2013, Shutterstock, Inc.

Employment Agencies

An employment agency is a firm hired by the employer to help with finding the right employees for both temporary and permanent jobs. Employers are motivated to use employment agencies because they do the initial screening and interviewing and save the employer time and money. The cost is usually paid by the employer, but it is a good idea to find out up front if there is any cost to you. Generally the agency works on a contingency basis and does not get paid until they find suitable employees for the job listings. Some private employment agencies do charge for finding you a job and the payment can be a percentage of your first year salary.

The employment agency acts as your advocate and looks for jobs for you. The process begins by submitting a resume and having an interview with the employment agency. The agency will help you with your resume and prepare you for the interview.

Using Email to Find a Job

You can use email as a tool for finding a job by letting people in your network know that you are looking for a position. You can also target potential employers and ask about job openings. Here are some ideas for using email in your job search:

- Use a separate email account for your job search. The account name should be professional and include your first and last name. Gmail and Yahoo offer free email accounts.
- Write your email like a business letter with complete sentences, good grammar, and clear writing. Check your message for accuracy.
- It is important to include the position for which you are applying in the subject line.
- Copy and paste your cover letter into the email and attach your resume.
- Include an email signature with your contact information that includes your full name, email address, and phone number.
- You can include a link to your LinkedIn profile or nameplate website, such as about.me.

Journal Entry #3

List some tools that you can use to find a job.

The Job Interview

Knowing how to be successful in an interview will help you to get the job that you want. Here are some ideas for being prepared and making a good impression.

- **Learn about the job.** Before the interview, it is important to research both the company and the job. This research will help you in two ways: you will know if the job is really the one you want and you will have information that will help you to succeed at the interview. If you have taken the time to learn about the company before the interview, you will make a good impression and show that you are really interested in the job. Here are some ways that you can find this information:
  - Visit the company website on the Internet and find out about the company mission and services or products provided. You can find many company profiles on LinkedIn and Facebook.

Tips for a Successful Job Interview

- Learn about the job
- Understand the criteria used in the interview
- Make a good impression
- Anticipate interview questions
- Send a thank you note

- Do any of your friends on Facebook or contacts on LinkedIn work for the company? You can ask for their advice on how to apply for a job. Do any of your family, friends, or teachers know someone who works for the company? If so, you can find out valuable information about the company.

- The personnel office often has informational brochures that describe the employer.

- **Understand the criteria used in an interview.** The interviewer represents the company and is looking for the best person to fill the job. It is your job to show the interviewer that you will do a good job. Of course you are interested in salary and benefits, but in order to get hired you must first convince the interviewer that you have something to offer the company. Focus on what you can offer the company based on your education and experience and what you have learned about the company. You may be able to obtain information on salary and benefits from the personnel office before the interview.

Interviewers look for candidates who show the enthusiasm and commitment necessary to do a good job. They are interested in hiring someone who can work as part of a team. Think about your education and experience and be prepared to describe your skills and give examples of how you have been successful on the job. Give a realistic and honest description of your work.

- **Make a good impression.** Here are some suggestions for making a good impression:

  - Dress appropriately for the interview. Look at how the employees of the company dress and then dress a little better. Of course, your attire will vary with the type of job you are seeking. You will dress differently if you are interviewing for a position as manager of a surf shop or an entry-level job in an engineering firm. Wear a conservative, dark colored or neutral suit for most professional positions. Do not wear too much jewelry and remove excess body piercings (unless you are working at a piercing shop). Cover any tattoos if they are not appropriate for the workplace.

  - Relax during the interview. You can relax by preparing in advance. Research the company so you have some familiarity with it. Visualize yourself in the interview room feeling confident about the interview.

  - When you enter the interview room, smile, introduce yourself, and shake hands with the interviewer. If your hands are cold and clammy, go to the restroom before the interview and run warm water over your hands or rub them together.

Making a Good Impression

- Dress appropriately
- Relax
- Prepare in advance
- Smile
- Shake hands
- Introduce yourself
- Maintain eye contact
- Sit up straight

"Was the interview too early for you?"

- Maintain eye contact with the interviewer and sit up straight. Poor posture or leaning back in your chair could be seen as a lack of confidence or interest in the job.
- **Anticipate the interview questions.** Listen carefully to the interview questions. Ask for clarification of any question you do not understand. Answer the questions concisely and honestly. It helps to anticipate the questions that are likely to be asked and to think about your answers in advance. Generally, be prepared to talk about yourself, your goals, and your reasons for applying for the job. Have a friend ask you the following interview questions and practice answering them. Here are some questions that are typically asked in interviews and some suggestions for answering them:

1. **What can you tell us about yourself?**
   Think about the job requirements and remember that the interviewer is looking for someone who will do a good job for the company. Talk about your education and experience as it relates to the job. You can put in interesting facts about your life and your hobbies, but keep your answers brief. This question is generally an ice breaker that helps the interviewer get a general picture of you and help you relax.

2. **Why do you want this job? Why should I hire you?**
   Think about the research you did on this company and several ways that you could benefit the company. A good answer might be, "I have always been good at technical skills and engineering. I am interested in putting these technical skills into practice in your company." A not-so-good answer would be, "I'm interested in making a lot of money and need health insurance."

3. **Why are you leaving your present job?**
   Instead of saying that the boss was horrible and the working conditions were intolerable (even if this was the case), think of some positive reasons for leaving such as:
   - I am looking for a job that provides challenge and an opportunity for growth.
   - I received my degree and am looking for a job where I can use my education.
   - I had a part-time job to help me through school. I have graduated and am looking for a career.
   - I moved (or the company downsized or went out of business).

   Be careful about discussing problems on your previous job. The interviewers might assume that you were the cause of the problems or that you could not get along with other people.

4. **What are your strengths and weaknesses?**
   Think about your strengths in relation to the job requirements and be prepared to talk about them during the interview. When asked about your weaknesses, smile and try to turn them into strengths. For example, if you are an introvert, you might say that you are quiet and like to concentrate on your work, but you make an effort to communicate with others on the job. If you are an extrovert, say that you enjoy talking and working with others, but you are good at time management and get the job done on time. If you are a perfectionist, say that you like to do an excellent job, but you know the importance of meeting deadlines, so you do the best you can in the time available.

5. **Tell us about a difficulty or problem that you solved on the job.**
   Think about some problem that you successfully solved on the job and describe how you did it. Focus on what you accomplished. If the problem was one that dealt with other people, do not focus on blaming or complaining. Focus on your desire to work things out and work well with everyone.

> **Tips for Answering Questions**
>
> - Research the company
> - Anticipate interview questions
> - Listen carefully
> - Ask for clarification
> - Answer concisely and honestly
> - Write a thank you note

6. **Tell us about one of your achievements on the job.**
Give examples of projects you have done on the job that have turned out well and projects that gave you a sense of pride and accomplishment.

7. **What do you like best about your work? What do you like least?**
Think about these questions in advance and use the question about what you like best to highlight your skills for the job. For the question about what you like the least, be honest but express your willingness to do the job that is required.

8. **Are there any questions that you would like to ask?**
Based on your research on the company, think of some specific questions that show your interest in the company. A good question might be, "Tell me about your company's plans for the future." A not-so-good question would be, "How much vacation do I get?"

9. **Write a thank you note.**
Express your interest in the job and thank the interviewer. It makes a good impression and causes the interviewer to think about you again.

> "All our dreams can come true, if we have the courage to pursue them."
> Walt Disney

Informational Interviewing

The informational interview is an informal conversation useful for finding career information, exploring your career, building your network, or possibly finding future employment. It is not a job interview and the purpose is not to find employment. It is a way to find more personal information about a career you may be considering and to see if you are a good fit for this occupation.

The informational interview differs from the traditional interview in that you are in control and can ask questions about daily job tasks and how they relate to your interests. It is a great way to build your self-confidence and prepare you for an actual job interview. To obtain an informational interview, check your LinkedIn contacts to see if anyone you know is employed in the industry. Ask your friends, family, and employers if they can recommend someone for the interview. You can also work with your college Career Services to see if they have contacts for informational interviews. They often have contacts with college alumni who are willing to speak with students. You can visit websites to identify individuals you would like to interview. Most professionals enjoy helping others who have an interest in their field.

Regard the informational interview as a business appointment and dress the way others dress in this occupation. Make a short appointment (generally 15–30 minutes), state that the purpose of the appointment is to gain career information and advice, and show up on time. You can suggest that the person meet you for coffee (and be sure to pay the bill yourself). Be prepared with a list of questions to ask and to take some brief notes on the information. To begin the interview, give a brief 30 second overview of your career goals and reasons for contacting this person. Remember that the focus of the interview is to find career information. It is best not to ask for a job at this time. If there is a job available and you are a good fit for the job, he or she will likely tell you about it.

It is important to thank the interviewee and then follow up a thank you note or email. Ask the person if he or she is on LinkedIn and if you can request a link online. Bring your resume and hand it to the person at the end of the interview. Do not begin the interview with the resume since you want the focus on career information rather than on yourself.

Here is a sample phone call asking for an informational interview:

Hello. My name is _____ and I am a student at _____University. I found your name at your company website. (Or _____ gave me your name and suggested that I contact you.) Although I am not currently looking for a job, I am interested in the field of _____ and would like to learn more about this occupation. Would it be possible to schedule 15–30 minutes of your time to ask a few questions and get your advice on how to enter this field?

© 2013, Shutterstock, Inc.

Following is a list of potential interview questions that you can use to keep the conversation going. You probably won't have time to ask all these questions, so choose the ones most that are most personally relevant.

1. What is your job title? What other job titles are commonly used for this position?

2. How did you get this position? What was your career path from entry-level to the position you now have?

3. What are your key job responsibilities? What is the typical day like for you?

4. What skills and education are needed for this job?

5. What are the most valuable courses that you took to prepare you for this job?

6. What are employers looking for (skills, education, personal qualities)?

7. What certificates or degrees are required for this job?

8. What kinds of internships or work experiences are desirable? Are internships available?

9. How does a person obtain this type of employment? How is the job advertised? Is the job market competitive? How can I meet the competition?

10. What are some entry-level positions in this company?

11. What important words should I include on my resume or cover letter?

12. What are the opportunities for advancement?

13. What are some personal characteristics that lead to success on this job?

14. What do you find most satisfying about your job?

15. What are the best and worst things about working in this job? What do you like about your job? Dislike?

16. What stresses you out about your job? What is the most difficult part of your job?

17. What are some of the most important challenges facing your industry today? How will it change in the next 10 years?

18. What is the salary range? What is the potential for advancement?

19. If you were still a college student, what would it be helpful to know about your current job and how to find employment in your field?

20. Can you suggest other sources or persons who could be valuable sources of information for me?

Journal Entry #4

A friend is looking for a job. What advise would you give him or her about the resume and job interview?

Starting Your Own Business

One solution to the problem of limited job opportunities is to start your own business. The New Millennial and Generation Z are more than twice as likely as past generations to start their own businesses. They are inspired by Mark Zuckerberg who founded Facebook while he was a sophomore at Harvard University. This new trend is powered by the opportunities provided by Facebook and other social media and the availability of support and funding for entrepreneurs. Companies such as RoughDraft.vc and the Experiment Fund are some examples of companies providing investment funds for students who start businesses in college. Websites like Kickstarter help you obtain funds from friends, family, and contacts. Many colleges offer business plan competitions with startup money for new businesses.[2]

If you are considering the option of starting your own business, here are some steps you may want to consider:

- Use time management to take advantage of some of the flexible time between classes and studying to make plans for your own business.
- Realize that starting your own business requires motivation, hard work, and focus. You will need discipline to balance going to class, studying, and starting your own business.
- Building on a central theme in this textbook, "find your passion," build your skills and find ways you can make money doing something that you enjoy. You can also research small business ideas for college students on the Internet.[3]
- Find an entry-level job or internship in the area of your interest so that you can see how the industry works. Look around and see how things can be improved or how you can help the company make more money.
- Find other motivated students who want to start a business and work with them as a group.
- Become familiar with social media. Most new businesses started by college students are promoted through Facebook, Twitter, and Instagram.
- Look around for common problems and find solutions. For example, Daniel Vitiello of Texas Tech University had a friend who dropped his iPhone and Daniel was able to fix it. He started an Internet-based iPhone repair business that earned $25,000 a month.[4]
- Take some summer courses in business, marketing, finance, and entrepreneurship.
- Create a business plan with a description, mission, values statement, pricing, financial projections, start-up capital required, and operations timeline.

You can search the Internet for examples of successful student businesses. Here are just a few examples that show how students look for problems and find solutions using their own personal experience:[5]

- Fei Xiao and Anna Sergeeva of the University of Southern California created trueRSVP, which compares the number of people who RSVP to an event to the number who actually attend. This app is useful for event planners.
- Todd Medema of Carnegie Mellon University created AutoRef, which he hopes will make automobile salespersons obsolete. He site has three million cars from 5,000 dealers.
- Brian Silverman of Duke University created Star Toilet Paper, which features ads from local businesses.
- Wesley Zhao of the University of Pennsylvania created FamilyLeaf, a social media site that allows family members to exchange photos.
- Gabrielle Palermo of Arizona State University created G3Box to create cost-effective medical clinics out of recycled shipping containers.
- Kenny Nguyen of Louisiana State University observed that his professors needed help in making their lectures better. He founded Big Fish Presentations, which does design, consultation, and production of commercial video.
- Karina Pikhart of the Massachusetts Institute of Technology created 6Dot, a label maker for blind people.
- Jack McDermott of Tufts University used his own experience with speech therapy to create an app, Speech4Good, which helps stutterers improve speech.
- Eric and Matt Lowe of Emerson College are the co-founders of Quiyk, a company that makes athletic apparel for Quidditch, a fictional sport from the Harry Potter novels.

> "When you create more small businesses, you create small entrepreneurship. Out of that comes self-determination and employment."
> Jesse Jackson

> "Pessimism is an excuse for not trying and a guarantee to a personal failure."
> Bill Clinton

Online Resources and Interviewing

1. Personal branding involves

    a. using brand name products.
    b. avoiding name brand products to save money.
    c. using social media to market yourself.

2. One step in managing your online presence is to

    a. limit your use of online tools.
    b. remove inappropriate content.
    c. turn off all privacy controls.

3. At the present time, the most common social media used by employers to research job candidates are

    a. Twitter and Facebook
    b. Tumblr and Instagram
    c. LinkedIn and Facebook

4. The first step in the interview process is

    a. to research information about the company and the job.
    b. ask the interviewer about salary and vacation time.
    c. prepare casual and comfortable clothes.

5. The informational interview is

    a. a good way to find career information and build your network.
    b. a good way to ask for a job.
    c. controlled by the employer.

How did you do on the quiz? Check your answers: 1. c, 2. b, 3. c, 4. a, 5. a

Taking Action

The most important and challenging part of your job search is taking action. Realize that finding a job requires time management and hard work, but it will all pay off when you find a good job. Also realize that you will do many job searches over a lifetime, so keep your resume tuned up, do the best at your current job so that you can get good references, and maintain your professional network.

© 2013, Shutterstock, Inc.

There will be times when you do not receive a response to a job application, do not get an interview, or do not get the job you consider to be your dream job. It is essential to realize that these are all part of the job search process and to maintain a positive attitude.

Here is a checklist for beginning your job search action plan:

_____ Find out what resources your college Career Services office provides.

_____ Attend job fairs and career conferences.

_____ Assess your skills (multiple intelligences), interests, and personal strengths.

_____ Complete career research on your areas of interest. What are the job activities, skills required, and career outlook?

_____ Investigate opportunities for volunteering and internships.

_____ Identify your goals. Where do you want to be in six months? A year? Five years?

_____ Create your personal brand based on your personal strengths and how they match the job market, including potential job titles.

_____ Set up a Facebook and LinkedIn account if you have not already done so. If you have an existing account check to make sure it is appropriate for a prospective employer to view.

_____ Complete your resume and cover letter.

_____ Do some informational interviews.

_____ Compile reference letters.

_____ Practice interview questions.

_____ Prepare your interview clothes.

_____ Search online career databases for current job openings.

_____ Write thank you letters to anyone helping you in your search.

_____ Use time management. Make a To Do list for each day and set goals for the week and month.

_____ Organize a job search system to keep track of resumes sent, employers contacted, and any other actions taken on your job search. Keep a simple diary that includes these items.

_____ Keep a positive attitude. Stay physically, emotionally, and mentally healthy during your job search.

As you are conducting your job search, ask these questions to evaluate how you are doing:

- What is working well? What is not working?
- How can I improve?
- What resources are available? Where can I go or who can I ask for help?
- How can I stay motivated?

"Many of life's failures a
people who do not rea
how close they were to
success when they gave
up."

Thomas Edi

Journal Entry #5

How can you keep yourself motivated during the job search process?

Act on Your Values

> "Whether you think you can, or
> think you can't . . . you're right."
> Henry Ford

Sometimes students enter college with the fear of failure and worry about college success or transitioning to a satisfying career. This belief leads to anxiety and behavior that leads to failure. If you have doubts about your ability to succeed, you might not go to class, attempt the challenging work, or work on your career action plan. It is difficult to make the effort if you cannot see positive results ahead. Unfortunately, failure can lead to a loss of confidence and lack of success in other areas of life as well.

Henry Ford said that "what we believe is true, comes true. What we believe is possible, becomes possible." If you believe that you will succeed, you will be more likely to take actions that lead to your success. Once you have experienced some small part of success, you will have confidence in your abilities and will continue on the road to success. Success leads to more success. It becomes a habit. You will be motivated to make the effort necessary to accomplish your goals. You might even become excited and energized along the way. You will use your gifts and talents to reach your potential and achieve happiness. It all begins with the thoughts you choose.

> Watch your thoughts; they become words.
> Watch your words; they become actions.
> Watch your actions; they become habits.
> Watch your habits; they become character.
> Watch your character; it becomes your destiny.[6]
> Frank Outlaw

To help you choose positive beliefs, picture in your mind how you want your life to be. Imagine it is here now. See all the details and experience the feelings associated with this picture. Pretend it is true until you believe it. Then take action to make your dreams come true.

© 2013, Shutterstock, Inc.

JOURNAL ENTRIES

Updated Job Search Strategies

Go to http://www.collegesuccess1.com/JournalEntries.htm for Word files of the Journal Entries

Success over the Internet

Visit the College Success Website at http://www.collegesuccess1.com/

The *College Success Website* is continually updated with new topics and links to the material presented in this chapter. Topics include

- Information about internships and volunteering
- Resume templates
- Sample resumes and cover letters
- Examples of personal brands
- Information on interviewing
- Tips for starting your own business

Contact your instructor if you have any problems in accessing the *College Success Website..*

Notes

1. Kelsey Lucier, "Consider Pros and Cons of Working in College," www.usnews.com, September 13, 2012.

2. Scott Kirsner, "Some Graduates Diving Right into Business," www.bostonglobe.com, April 28, 2013.

3. Felicia Joy, "College Entrepreneurs: 25 Business Ideas That Students Can Launch for $200 or Less," feliciajoyonline.wordpress.com, August 6, 2011.

4. Courtney Rubin, "Create Your Own College Job," www.usnews.com, September 27, 2012.

5. Mariana Simoes and Max Nisen, "16 Great Startups College Students are Working on Right Now," www.businessinsider.com, February 11, 2013.

6. Rob Gilbert, ed., *Bits and Pieces* (Fairfield, NJ: The Economics Press), Vol. R, No. 40, p. 7, copyright 1998.

CHAPTER 16

Exploring Multiple Intelligences

Learning Objectives

Read to answer these key questions:

- What are multiple intelligences?

- What kinds of intelligence do I have?

- What are my personal strengths?

- What is emotional intelligence?

- What are my goals for the future?

- How can I create the future I want for myself?

What Are Multiple Intelligences?

In 1904, the French psychologist Alfred Binet developed the IQ test, which provided a single score to measure intelligence. This once widely used and accepted test came into question because it measured the intelligence of individuals in schools in a particular culture. In different cultures and different situations, the test was less valid. As an alternative to traditional IQ tests, Harvard professor Howard Gardner developed the theory of multiple intelligences.[1] He looked at intelligence in a broader and more inclusive way than people had done in the past.

Howard Gardner observed famous musicians, artists, athletes, scientists, inventors, naturalists, and others who were recognized contributors to society to formulate a more meaningful definition of intelligence. He defined intelligence as **the human ability to solve problems or design or compose something valued in at least one culture**. His definition broadens the scope of human potential. He identified nine different intelligences: musical, interpersonal, logical-mathematical, spatial, bodily-kinesthetic, linguistic, intrapersonal, naturalist, and existential. He selected these intelligences because they are all represented by an area in the brain and are valued in different cultures. His theory can help us to understand and appreciate many different kinds of talents.

These intelligences are measured by looking at performance in activities associated with each intelligence. A key idea in this theory is that most people can develop all of their intelligences and become relatively competent in each area. Another key idea is that these intelligences work together in complex ways to make us unique. For example, an athlete uses bodily-kinesthetic intelligence to run, kick, or jump. They use spatial intelligence to keep their eye on the ball and hit it. They also need linguistic and interpersonal skills to be good members of a team.

Developing intelligences is a product of three factors:

1. Biological endowment based on heredity and genetics
2. Personal life history
3. Cultural and historical background[2]

For example, Wolfgang Amadeus Mozart was born with musical talent (biological endowment). Members of his family were musicians who encouraged Mozart in music (personal life history). Mozart lived in Europe during a time when music flourished and wealthy patrons were willing to pay composers (cultural and historical background).

Each individual's life history contains **crystallizers** that promote the development of the intelligences and **paralyzers** that inhibit the development of the intelligences. These crystallizers and paralyzers often take place in early childhood. For example, Einstein was given a magnetic compass when he was four years old. He became so interested in the compass that he started on his journey of exploring the universe. An example of a paralyzer is being embarrassed or feeling humiliated about your math skills in elementary school so that you begin to lose confidence in your ability to do math. Paralyzers involve shame, guilt, fear, and anger and prevent intelligence from being developed.

This textbook includes an access code for taking the MI Advantage, which assesses multiple intelligences, provides a profile of your individual strengths, and matches your results to careers with links to online career information. As you take this assessment, think positively about your skills. The following information and activities help to gain a deeper understanding of your multiple intelligences and related skills along with matching careers.

> "I have no special talent. I am only passionately curious."
>
> Albert Einstein

Journal Entry #1

Look at your results from the MI Advantage multiple intelligences assessment. According to this assessment, what are your highest multiple intelligences? List any suggested careers in which you are interested.

ACTIVITY

Describing Your Multiple Intelligences

Below are some definitions and examples of the different intelligences. As you read each section, think positively about your intelligence in this area. Place a checkmark in front of each item that is true for you.

Musical

Musical intelligence involves hearing and remembering musical patterns and manipulating patterns in music. Some occupations connected with this intelligence include musician, performer, composer, and music critic. Place a checkmark next to each skill that you possess in this area.

_____ I enjoy singing, humming, or whistling.

_____ One of my interests is playing recorded music.

_____ I have collections of recorded music.

_____ I play or used to play a musical instrument.

_____ I can play the drums or tap out rhythms.

_____ I appreciate music.

_____ Music affects how I feel.

_____ I enjoy having music on while working or studying.

_____ I can clap my hands and keep time to music.

_____ I can tell when a musical note is off key.

_____ I remember melodies and the words to songs.

_____ I have participated in a band, chorus, or other musical group.

Look at the items you have checked above and summarize your musical intelligence.

_____

_____

_____

Interpersonal

Interpersonal intelligence is defined as understanding people. Occupations connected with this intelligence involve working with people and helping them, as in education or health care. Place a checkmark next to each skill that you possess in this area.

_____ I enjoy being around people.

_____ I am sensitive to other people's feelings.

_____ I am a good listener.

_____ I understand how others feel.

_____ I have many friends.

_____ I enjoy parties and social gatherings.

_____ I enjoy participating in groups.

_____ I can get people to cooperate and work together.

_____ I am involved in clubs or community activities.

_____ People come to me for advice.

_____ I am a peacemaker.

_____ I enjoy helping others.

Look at the items you have checked above and summarize your interpersonal intelligence.

_____

_____

_____

Logical-Mathematical

Logical-mathematical intelligence involves understanding abstract principles and manipulating numbers, quantities, and operations. Some examples of occupations associated with logical-mathematical intelligence are mathematician, tax accountant, scientist, and computer programmer. Place a checkmark next to each skill that you possess. Keep an open mind. People usually either love or hate this area.

_____ I can do arithmetic problems quickly.

_____ I enjoy math.

_____ I enjoy doing puzzles.

_____ I enjoy working with computers.

_____ I am interested in computer programming.

_____ I enjoy science classes.

_____ I enjoy doing the experiments in lab science courses.

_____ I can look at information and outline it easily.

_____ I understand charts and diagrams.

_____ I enjoy playing chess or checkers.

_____ I use logic to solve problems.

_____ I can organize things and keep them in order.

Look at the items you have checked above and summarize your logical-mathematical intelligence.

_____

_____

_____

Spatial

Spatial intelligence involves the ability to manipulate objects in space. For example, a baseball player uses spatial intelligence to hit a ball. Occupations associated with spatial intelligence include pilot, painter, sculptor, architect, inventor, and surgeon. This intelligence is often used in athletics, the arts, or the sciences. Place a checkmark next to each skill that you possess in this area.

_____ I can appreciate a good photograph or piece of art.

_____ I think in pictures and images.

_____ I can use visualization to remember.

_____ I can easily read maps, charts, and diagrams.

_____ I participate in artistic activities (art, drawing, painting, photography).

_____ I know which way is north, south, east, and west.

_____ I can put things together.

_____ I enjoy jigsaw puzzles or mazes.

_____ I enjoy seeing movies, slides, or photographs.

_____ I can appreciate good design.

_____ I enjoy using telescopes, microscopes, or binoculars.

_____ I understand color, line, shape, and form.

Look at the items you have checked above and summarize your spatial intelligence.

_____

_____

_____

Bodily-Kinesthetic

Spatial intelligence involves the ability to manipulate objects in space. For example, a baseball player uses spatial intelligence to hit a ball. Occupations associated with spatial intelligence include pilot, painter, sculptor, architect, inventor, and surgeon. This intelligence is often used in athletics, the arts, or the sciences. Place a checkmark next to each skill that you possess in this area.

_____ I am good at using my hands.

_____ I have good coordination and balance.

_____ I learn best by moving around and touching things.

_____ I participate in physical activities or sports.

_____ I learn new sports easily.

_____ I enjoy watching sports events.

_____ I am skilled in a craft such as woodworking, sewing, art, or fixing machines.

_____ I have good manual dexterity.

_____ I find it difficult to sit still for a long time.

_____ I prefer to be up and moving.

_____ I am good at dancing and remember dance steps easily.

_____ It was easy for me to learn to ride a bike or skateboard.

Look at the items you have checked above and summarize your spatial intelligence.

_____

_____

_____

Linguistic

People with linguistic intelligence are good with language and words. They have good reading, writing, and speaking skills. Linguistic intelligence is an asset in any occupation. Specific related careers include writing, education, and politics. Place a checkmark next to each skill that you possess in this area.

_____ I am a good writer.

_____ I am a good reader.

_____ I enjoy word games and crossword puzzles.

_____ I can tell jokes and stories.

_____ I am good at explaining.

_____ I can remember names, places, facts, and trivia.

_____ I'm generally good at spelling.

_____ I have a good vocabulary.

_____ I read for fun and relaxation.

_____ I am good at memorizing.

_____ I enjoy group discussions.

_____ I have a journal or diary.

Look at the items you have checked above and summarize your linguistic intelligence.

_____

_____

_____

Intrapersonal

Intrapersonal intelligence is the ability to understand yourself and how to best use your natural talents and abilities. Examples of careers associated with this intelligence include novelist, psychologist, or being self-employed. Place a checkmark next to each skill that you possess in this area.

_____ I understand and accept my strengths and weaknesses.

_____ I am very independent.

_____ I am self-motivated.

_____ I have definite opinions on controversial issues.

_____ I enjoy quiet time alone to pursue a hobby or work on a project.

_____ I am self-confident.

_____ I can work independently.

_____ I can help others with self-understanding.

_____ I appreciate quiet time for concentration.

_____ I am aware of my own feelings and sensitive to others.

_____ I am self-directed.

_____ I enjoy reflecting on ideas and concepts.

Look at the items you have checked above and summarize your intrapersonal intelligence.

_____

_____

_____

Naturalist

The naturalist is able to recognize, classify, and analyze plants, animals, and cultural artifacts. Occupations associated with this intelligence include botanist, horticulturist, biologist, archeologist, and environmental occupations. Place a checkmark next to each skill you possess in this area.

_____ I know the names of minerals, plants, trees, and animals.

_____ I think it is important to preserve our natural environment.

_____ I enjoy taking classes in the natural sciences such as biology.

_____ I enjoy the outdoors.

_____ I take care of flowers, plants, trees, or animals.

_____ I am interested in archeology or geology.

_____ I would enjoy a career involved in protecting the environment.

_____ I have or used to have a collection of rocks, shells, or insects.

_____ I belong to organizations interested in protecting the environment.

_____ I think it is important to protect endangered species.

_____ I enjoy camping or hiking.

_____ I appreciate natural beauty.

Look at the items you have checked above and describe your naturalist intelligence.

_____

_____

_____

Existential

Existential intelligence is the capacity to ask profound questions about the meaning of life and death. This intelligence is the cornerstone of art, religion, and philosophy. Related occupations include minister, philosopher, psychologist, and artist. Place a checkmark next to each skill that you possess in this area.

_____ I often think about the meaning and purpose of life.

_____ I have strong personal beliefs and convictions.

_____ I enjoy thinking about abstract theories.

_____ I have considered being a philosopher, scientist, theologian, or artist.

_____ I often read books that are philosophical or imaginative.

_____ I enjoy reading science fiction.

_____ I like to work independently.

_____ I like to search for meaning in my studies.

_____ I wonder if there are other intelligent life forms in the universe.

Look at the items you have checked above and describe your existential intelligence.

_____

_____

_____

Journal Entry #2

Look at the above charts and see where you have the most checkmarks. What do you think are your highest intelligences? Do your opinions match the results on the MI Advantage multiple intelligences assessment?

Build on Your Strengths

Consider your personal strengths when deciding on a career. People in each of the multiple intelligence areas have different strengths:

- Musical strengths include listening to music, singing, playing a musical instrument, keeping a beat, and recognizing musical patterns. People with this intelligence are "musical smart."

- Interpersonal strengths include communication skills, social skills, helping others, understanding others' feelings, and the ability to resolve conflicts. People with this intelligence are "people smart."

- Logical-mathematical strengths include math aptitude, interest in science, problem solving skills, and logical thinking. People with this intelligence are "number/reasoning smart."

© 2013, Shutterstock, Inc.

- Spatial strengths include visualization, understanding puzzles, navigation, visual arts, reading, and writing. People with this intelligence are "picture smart."
- Bodily-kinesthetic strengths include hand and eye coordination, athletics, dance, drama, cooking, sculpting, and learning by doing. People with this intelligence are "body smart."
- Linguistic strengths include good reading, writing, vocabulary, and spelling skills; good communication skills; being a good listener; having a good memory, and learning new languages easily. People with this intelligence are "word smart."
- Intrapersonal strengths include good self-awareness. They are aware of their feelings and emotions and are often independent and self-motivated to achieve. People with this intelligence are "self-smart."
- Naturalist strengths include exploring and preserving the environment and are very aware of natural surroundings. People with this intelligence are "nature smart."
- Existential strengths include reflecting on important questions about the universe, the purpose of life, and religious beliefs. People with this intelligence are "curiosity smart."

ACTIVITY

In what areas are you "smart?"

_____

_____

_____

_____

_____

Some Careers and Multiple Intelligences

Circle any careers that seem interesting to you.

Musical	Interpersonal	Logical-Mathematical
Disc Jockey	Cruise Director	Engineer
Music Teacher	Mediator	Accountant
Music Retailer	Human Resources	Computer Analyst
Music Therapist	Dental Hygienist	Physician
Recording Engineer	Nurse	Detective
Singer	Psychologist	Researcher
Song Writer	Social Worker	Scientist
Speech Pathologist	Administrator	Computer Programmer
Music Librarian	Marketer	Database Designer
Choir Director	Religious Leader	Physicist
Music Critic	Teacher	Auditor
Music Lawyer	Counselor	Economist

Spatial	Bodily-Kinesthetic	Linguistic
Architect	Athlete	Journalist
Artist	Carpenter	Writer
Film Animator	Craftsperson	Editor
Mechanic	Mechanic	Attorney
Pilot	Jeweler	Curator
Webmaster	Computer Game Designer	Newscaster
Interior Decorator	Firefighter	Politician
Graphic Artist	Forest Ranger	Speech Pathologist
Sculptor	Physical Therapist	Translator
Surveyor	Personal Trainer	Comedian
Urban Planner	Surgeon	Historian
Photographer	Recreation Specialist	Librarian
		Marketing Consultant

Intrapersonal	Naturalist	Existential
Career Counselor	Park Ranger	Counselor
Wellness Counselor	Dog Trainer	Psychologist
Therapist	Landscaper	Psychiatrist
Criminologist	Meteorologist	Social Worker
intelligence Officer	Veterinarian	Ministry
Entrepreneur	Animal Health Technician	Philosopher
Psychologist	Ecologist	Artist
Researcher	Nature Photographer	Scientist
Actor	Wilderness Guide	Researcher
Artist	Anthropologist	Motivational Speaker
Philosopher	Environmental Lawyer	Human Resources
Writer	Water Conservationist	Writer

> "The best years of your life are the ones in which you decide your problems are your own. You do not blame them on your mother, the ecology, or the president. You realize that you control your own destiny."
>
> Albert Ellis

Multiple Intelligences

Test what you have learned by selecting the correct answers to the following questions.

1. Multiple intelligences are defined as

   a. the many parts of intelligence as measured by an IQ test.
   b. the ability to design something valued in at least one culture.
   c. the ability to read, write, and do mathematical computations.

2. The concept of multiple intelligences is significant because

   a. it measures the intelligence of students in schools.
   b. it does not use culture in measuring intelligence.
   c. it broadens the scope of human potential and includes all cultures.

3. Intelligences are measured by

   a. IQ tests.
   b. performance in activities related to the intelligence.
   c. performance in the classroom.

4. Each individual's life history contains crystallizers that

   a. promote the development of the intelligences.
   b. inhibit the development of the intelligences.
   c. cause the individual to be set in their ways.

5. Multiple intelligences include

   a. getting good grades in college.
   b. bodily kinesthetic skills.
   c. good test-taking skills.

How did you do on the quiz? Check your answers: 1. b, 2. c, 3. b, 4. a, 5. b

Using Emotional Intelligence

Emotional intelligence is related to interpersonal and intrapersonal intelligences. It is the ability to recognize, control, and evaluate your own emotions while realizing how they affect people around you. Emotional intelligence affects career success, because it is related to our ability to express ourselves, work as part of a team, concentrate, remember, make decisions, deal with stress, overcome challenges, deal with conflict, and empathize with others. Research has shown emotional intelligence can predict career success and that workers with high emotional intelligence are more likely to end up in leadership positions in which they are happy with their jobs.[3]

The premise of emotional intelligence is that you can be more successful if you are aware of your own emotions as well as the emotions of others. There are two aspects of emotional intelligence:

- Understanding yourself, your goals, intentions, responses, and behavior.
- Understanding others and their feelings.

Daniel Goleman has identified the five most important characteristics of emotional intelligence:[4]

1. **Self-Awareness.** People with high emotional intelligence are aware of their emotions, including strengths and weaknesses.

2. **Self-Regulation.** This involves the ability to control emotions and impulses. Being impulsive can lead to careless decisions like attending a party the night before a final exam. Characteristics of self-regulation include comfort with change, integrity, and the ability to say no.

3. **Motivation.** People with high emotional intelligence can defer immediate results for long-term success. For example, investing your time in education can lead to future career opportunities and income.

4. **Empathy.** Empathy is the ability to understand the needs and viewpoints of others around you and avoiding stereotypes. It involves good listening skills that enhance personal relationships.

5. **Social Skills.** People with good social skills are good team players and willing to help others to be successful.

You can enhance your career success by developing your emotional intelligence. Here are some tips for improving your emotional intelligence and managing personal relationships on the job.

- Be empathetic when working with others by trying to put yourself in their place to understand different perspectives and points of view. Don't be quick to jump to conclusions or stereotype others.

- Think about how your actions affect others. Always treat others as you would like to be treated.

- Be open-minded and intellectually curious. Consider the opinions of others in a positive manner. Be willing to examine and change your mindset.

- Give others credit for their accomplishments in the workplace. When speaking about your own accomplishments, confidently state what you did without trying to seek too much attention.

- Evaluate your own strengths and weaknesses. Focus on your strengths, but be aware of the weaknesses and work to improve them. The personality assessment in Chapter 2 helps you to understand your personal strengths and weaknesses.

- Work on stress management by finding some stress reduction techniques that work for you. In stressful situations, it is helpful to remain calm and in control. Seek workable solutions without blaming others. Your college health services office often provides workshops on stress management.

- Take a college course to improve verbal as well as nonverbal communication. When talking with others, focus on what they are saying rather than what you are going to say next. Learn how to make "I statements" that effectively communicate your thoughts without blaming others. Become aware of nonverbal communication, which adds a significant dimension to communication.

- Use humor to help you deal with challenges. Humor helps you to keep things in perspective, deal with differences, relax, and come up with creative solutions.

- Deal with conflicts in a way that builds trust. Focus on win-win solutions that allow both parties to have their needs met.

- Take responsibility for your actions. Admit when you make mistakes and work to improve the situation in the future.

- Use critical thinking to analyze the pros and cons of the situation.

- Be goal oriented and focus on the task and the steps needed to achieve your goals.
- Be optimistic. Optimism leads to greater opportunities and results in better personal relationships.

© 2013, Shutterstock, Inc.

Journal Entry #3

Comment on your emotional intelligence and how you can use it to be successful in your career.

What Are My Lifetime Goals?

You have now completed the assessment part of the course and have a greater awareness of your personal strengths, vocational interests, values, and multiple intelligences. Use this knowledge to begin thinking about some goals for the future.

Setting goals helps you to establish what is important and provides direction for your life. Goals help you to focus your energy on what you want to accomplish. Goals are a promise to yourself to improve your life. Setting goals can help you turn your dreams into reality. Steven Scott in his book, *A Millionaire's Notebook*, lays out five steps in this process:

1. Dream or visualize.

2. Convert the dream into goals.

3. Convert your goals into tasks.

4. Convert your task into steps.

5. Take your first step and then the next.[5]

GOAL SETTING

Specific
Measurable
Achievable
Realistic
Timely

> "A goal is a dream with a deadline."
>
> Napoleon Hill

As you begin to think about your personal goals in life, make your goals specific and concrete. Rather than saying, "I want to be rich," make your goal something that you can break into specific steps. You might want to start learning about money management or begin a savings plan. Rather than setting a goal for happiness, think about what brings you happiness. If you want to live a long and healthy life, think about the health habits that will help you to accomplish your goal. You will need to break your goals down into specific tasks to be able to accomplish them.

Here are some criteria for successful goal setting:

1. **Is it achievable?** Do I have the skills, abilities, and resources to accomplish this goal? If not, am I willing to spend the time to develop the skills, abilities, and resources needed to achieve this goal?

2. **Is it realistic?** Do I believe I can achieve it? Am I positive and optimistic about this goal?

3. **Is it specific and measurable?** Can it be counted or observed? The most common goal mentioned by students is happiness in life. What is happiness, and how will you know when you have achieved it? Is happiness a career you enjoy, owning your own home, or a travel destination?

4. **Do you want to do it?** Is this a goal you are choosing because it gives you personal satisfaction rather than meeting a requirement or an expectation of someone else?

5. **Are you motivated to achieve it?** What are your rewards for achieving it?

6. **Does the goal match your values?** Is it important to you?

7. **What steps do you need to take to begin?** Am I willing to take action to start working on it?

8. **When will you finish this goal?** Set a date to accomplish your goal.

Journal Entry #4

Write a paragraph about your lifetime goals. Use any of these questions to guide your thinking:

What is your career goal? If you do not know what your career goal is, describe your preferred work environment. Would your ideal career require a college degree?

What are your family goals? Are you interested in marriage and family? What would be your important family values?

What are your social goals (friends, community, and recreation)?

When you are older and look back on your life, what are the three most important life goals that you would want to make sure to accomplish?

A Goal or a Fantasy?

One of the best questions ever asked in my class was, "What is the difference between a goal and a fantasy?" As you look at your list of lifetime goals, are some of these items goals or fantasies? Think about this question as you read the following scenario:

© 2013, Shutterstock, Inc.

> When Linda was a college student, she was walking through the parking lot and noticed a beautiful red sports car and decided that it would become a lifetime goal to own a similar car one day. However, with college expenses and her part-time job, it was not possible to buy the car. She would have to be content with the used car that her dad had given her so that she could drive to college. Years passed by, and Linda now has a good job, a home, and a family. She is reading a magazine and sees a picture of a similar red sports car. She cuts out this picture and tapes it to the refrigerator. After it has been on the refrigerator for several months, her children ask her why the picture is on the refrigerator. Linda replies, "I just like to dream about owning this car." One day as Linda is driving past a car dealership, she sees the red sports car on display and stops in for a test drive. To her surprise, she decides that she does not like driving the car. It doesn't fit her lifestyle either. She enjoys outdoor activities that would require a larger car. Buying a second car would be costly and reduce the amount of money that the family could spend on vacations. She decides that vacations are more important than owning the sports car. Linda goes home and removes the picture of the red sports car from the refrigerator.

There are many differences between a goal and a fantasy. A fantasy is a dream that may or may not become a reality. A goal is something that we actually plan to achieve. Sometimes we begin with a fantasy and later it becomes a goal. A fantasy can become a goal if steps are taken to achieve it. In the preceding example, the sports car is a fantasy until Linda actually takes the car for a test drive. After driving the car, she decides that she really does not want it. The fantasy is sometimes better than the reality. Goals and fantasies change over a lifetime. We set goals, try them out, and change them as we grow and mature and find out what is most important in life. Knowing what we think is important, and what we value most, helps us make good decisions about lifetime goals.

> "Vision without action is a daydream. Action without vision is a nightmare."
> Japanese Proverb

> "In life, as in football, you won't go far unless you know where the goalposts are."
> Arnold Glasgow

What is the difference between a goal and a fantasy? A goal is something that requires action. Ask yourself if you are willing to take action on the goals you have set for yourself. Begin to take action by thinking about the steps needed to accomplish the goal. Then take the first step and continue. Change your goals if they are no longer important to you.

Emotional Intelligence and Goal Setting

Test what you have learned by selecting the correct answers to the following questions.

1. Emotional intelligence involves

   a. self-criticism.
   b. self-awareness.
   c. self-doubt.

2. A criteria for successful goal setting includes

   a. is it achievable?
   b. can you postpone it?
   c. is it worth your time?

3. An important step in goal setting is

   a. getting started when you feel like it.
   b. asking others what is important.
   c. identifying the steps needed to get started.

4. An example of a measurable goal is:

   a. I will be rich.
   b. I will be financially secure.
   c. I will open a savings account.

5. The difference between a goal and a fantasy is

   _____.

   a. action
   b. money
   c. luck

How did you do on the quiz? Check your answers: 1. b, 2. a, 3. c, 4. c, 5. a

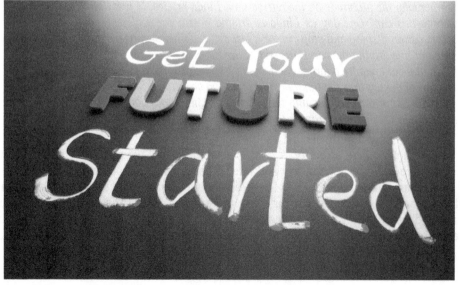

© 2013, Shutterstock, Inc.

Create Your Future

We are responsible for what happens in our lives. We make decisions and choices that create the future. Our behavior leads to success or failure. Too often we believe that we are victims of circumstance. When looking at our lives, we often look for others to blame for how our life is going:

- My grandparents did it to me. I inherited these genes.
- My parents did it to me. My childhood experiences shaped who I am.
- My teacher did it to me. He gave me a poor grade.
- My boss did it to me. She gave me a poor evaluation.
- The government did it to me. All my money goes to taxes.
- Society did it to me. I have no opportunity.

These factors are powerful influences in our lives, but we are still left with choices. Concentration camp survivor Viktor Frankl wrote a book, Man's Search for Meaning, in which he describes his experiences and how he survived his ordeal. His parents, brother, and wife died in the camps. He suffered starvation and torture. Through all of his sufferings and imprisonment, he still maintained that he was a free man because he could make choices.

We who lived in concentration camps can remember the men who walked through the huts comforting others, giving away their last piece of bread. They may have been few in number, but they offer sufficient proof that everything can be taken from a man but one thing: the last of the human freedoms—to choose one's attitude in any given set of circumstances, to choose one's own way. . . . Fundamentally, therefore, any man can, even under such circumstances, decide what shall become of him—mentally and spiritually. He may retain his human dignity even in a concentration camp.[6]

Viktor Frankl could not choose his circumstances at that time, but he did choose his attitude. He decided how he would respond to the situation. He realized that he still had the freedom to make choices. He used his memory and imagination to exercise his freedom. When times were the most difficult, he would imagine that he was in the classroom lecturing to his students about psychology.

He eventually did get out of the concentration camp and became a famous psychiatrist.

Hopefully none of you will ever have to experience the circumstances faced by Viktor Frankl, but we all face challenging situations. It is empowering to think that our behavior is more a function of our decisions rather than our circumstances. It is not productive to look around and find someone to blame for your problems. Psychologist Abraham Maslow says that instead of blaming we should see how we can make the best of the situation.

One can spend a lifetime assigning blame, finding a cause, "out there" for all the troubles that exist. Contrast this with the responsible attitude of confronting the situation, bad or good, and instead of asking, "What caused the trouble? Who was to blame?", asking, "How can I handle the present situation to make the best of it?"[7]

Author Stephen Covey suggests that we look at the word responsibility as "response-ability."[8] It is the ability to choose responses and make decisions about the future. When you are dealing with a problem, it is useful to ask yourself what decisions you made that led to the problem. How did you create the situation? If you created the problem, you can create a solution.

At times, you may ask, "How did I create this?", and find that the answer is that you did not create the situation. We certainly do not create earthquakes or hurricanes, for example. But we do create or at least contribute to many of the things that happen to us. Even if you did not create your circumstances, you can create your reaction to the situation. In the case of an earthquake, you can decide to panic or find the best course of action at the moment.

Stephen Covey believes that we can use our resourcefulness and initiative in dealing with most problems. When his children were growing up and they asked him how to solve a certain problem, he would say, "Use your R and I!". He meant resourcefulness and initiative. He notes that adults can use this R and I to get a good job.

But the people who end up with the good jobs are the proactive ones who are solutions to problems, not problems themselves, who seize the initiative to do whatever is necessary, consistent with correct principles, to get the job done.[9]

Use your resourcefulness and initiative to create the future that you want.

Journal Entry #5

How can you create the future you want for yourself?

JOURNAL ENTRIES

Exploring Your Multiple Intelligences

Go to http://www.collegesuccess1.com/JournalEntries.htm for Word files of the Journal Entries.

Success over the Internet

Visit the College Success Website at http://www.collegesuccess1.com/

The *College Success Website* is continually updated with new topics and links to the material presented in this chapter. Topics include

- Multiple intelligences
- Emotional intelligence
- Goal setting

Contact your instructor if you have any problems in accessing the *College Success Website.*.

Notes

1. Howard Gardner, *Intelligence Reframed: Multiple Intelligences for the Twenty-First Century* (Boulder, CO: Basic Books, 1999).

2. Thomas Armstrong, *Multiple Intelligences in the Classroom* (Alexandria, VA: Association for Curriculum Development, 1994).

3. "Emotional Intelligence in Career Planning," accessed August 2013, https://www1.cfnc.org/

4. "Emotional Intelligence, Developing Strong People Skills," accessed August 2013, http://www.mindtools.com/pages/article/newCDV_59.htm

5. Steven K. Scott, *A Millionaire's Notebook*, quoted in Rob Gilbert, Editor, *Bits & Pieces*, November 4, 1999, p. 15.

6. Viktor Frankl, *Man's Search for Meaning* (New York: Pocket Books, 1963), 104–105.

7. Quoted in Rob Gilbert, ed., *Bits and Pieces*, November 4, 1999.

8. Stephen Covey, *The 7 Habits of Highly Effective People* (New York: Simon and Schuster, 1989), 71.

9. Ibid., 75.

Name _____

Time Management Grid

	Monday	Tuesday	Wednesday	Thursday	Friday	Saturday	Sunday
7:30am							
8:00am							
8:30am							
9:00am							
9:30am							
10:00am							
10:30am							
11:00am							
11:30am							
12:00pm							
12:30pm							
1:00pm							
1:30pm							
2:00pm							
2:30pm							
3:00pm							
3:30pm							
4:00pm							
4:30pm							
5:00pm							
5:30pm							
6:00pm							
6:30pm							
7:00pm							
7:30pm							
8:00pm							
8:30pm							
9:00pm							
9:30pm							
10:00pm							
10:30pm							
11:00pm							
11:30pm							
12:00am							

Time Management Grid

	Monday	Tuesday	Wednesday	Thursday	Friday	Saturday	Sunday
7:30am							
8:00am							
8:30am							
9:00am							
9:30am							
10:00am							
10:30am							
11:00am							
11:30am							
12:00pm							
12:30pm							
1:00pm							
1:30pm							
2:00pm							
2:30pm							
3:00pm							
3:30pm							
4:00pm							
4:30pm							
5:00pm							
5:30pm							
6:00pm							
6:30pm							
7:00pm							
7:30pm							
8:00pm							
8:30pm							
9:00pm							
9:30pm							
10:00pm							
10:30pm							
11:00pm							
11:30pm							
12:00am							

Name _____

Time Management Grid

	Monday	Tuesday	Wednesday	Thursday	Friday	Saturday	Sunday
7:30am							
8:00am							
8:30am							
9:00am							
9:30am							
10:00am							
10:30am							
11:00am							
11:30am							
12:00pm							
12:30pm							
1:00pm							
1:30pm							
2:00pm							
2:30pm							
3:00pm							
3:30pm							
4:00pm							
4:30pm							
5:00pm							
5:30pm							
6:00pm							
6:30pm							
7:00pm							
7:30pm							
8:00pm							
8:30pm							
9:00pm							
9:30pm							
10:00pm							
10:30pm							
11:00pm							
11:30pm							
12:00am							

Sun	Mon	Tue	Wed	Thu	Fri	Sat
						1
2	3	4	5	6	7	8
9	10	11	12	13	14	15
16	17	18	19	20	21	22
23	24	25	26	27	28	29
30	31					

Notes:

September 2015

Sun	Mon	Tue	Wed	Thu	Fri	Sat
		1	2	3	4	5
6	7	8	9	10	11	12
13	14	15	16	17	18	19
20	21	22	23	24	25	26
27	28	29	30	Notes:		

Sun	Mon	Tue	Wed	Thu	Fri	Sat
				1	2	3
4	5	6	7	8	9	10
11	12	13	14	15	16	17
18	19	20	21	22	23	24
25	26	27	28	29	30	31

November 2015

Sun	Mon	Tue	Wed	Thu	Fri	Sat
1	2	3	4	5	6	7
8	9	10	11	12	13	14
15	16	17	18	19	20	21
22	23	24	25	26	27	28
29	30	Notes:				

Sun	Mon	Tue	Wed	Thu	Fri	Sat
		1	2	3	4	5
6	7	8	9	10	11	12
13	14	15	16	17	18	19
20	21	22	23	24	25	26
27	28	29	30	31	Notes:	

2 Constructing a Master List of Campus Resources

Construct a master list of all support services that are available to you on your campus. Your final product should be a list that includes the following:

- The names of different support services your campus offers
- The types of support each service provides
- A short statement indicating whether you think you would benefit from each particular type of support
- The name of a person whom you could contact for support from each service

Use each of the following sources to gain more in-depth knowledge about the support services available on your campus:

- Information published in your college catalog and student handbook
- Information posted on your college's Web site
- Information gathered by speaking with professionals in different offices or centers on your campus

3 Support Services

Learning Center

How will I benefit?   Whom should I contact?

_____

Writing Center

How will I benefit?   Whom should I contact?

_____

Disability Services

How will I benefit?   Whom should I contact?

_____

College Library

How will I benefit?   Whom should I contact?

_____

Academic Advising Center

How will I benefit?   Whom should I contact?

_____

Office of Student Life

How will I benefit?   Whom should I contact?

_____

Financial Aid Office

How will I benefit?   Whom should I contact?

_____

From *Thriving in College and Beyond: Research-Based Strategies for Academic Success and Personal Development, 3rd Edition* by Joseph Cuseo, Aaron Thompson, Michele Campagna, and Viki S. Fecas. Copyright © 2013 by Kendall Hunt Publishing Company. Reprinted by permission.

Counseling Center

How will I benefit?   Whom should I contact?

_____

Health Center

How will I benefit?   Whom should I contact?

_____

Career Development Center

How will I benefit?   Whom should I contact?

_____

Experiential Learning Resources

How will I benefit?   Whom should I contact?

_____

Other Types of Support Available on Campus

How will I benefit?   Whom should I contact?

_____

1 Term at a Glance

Term _____, Year _____

Review the syllabus (course outline) for all classes you're enrolled in this term, and complete the following information for each course

Course	Professor Exams	Projects & Papers	Other Assignments	Attendance Policy	Late & Makeup Assignment Policy

Self-Assesment Questions

1. Is the overall workload what you expected? Are you surprised by the amount of work required in any particular course or courses?

2. At this point in the term, what do you see as your most challenging or demanding course or courses? Why?

3. Do you think you can handle the total workload required by the full set of courses you're enrolled in this term?

4. What adjustments or changes could you make to your personal schedule that would make it easier to accommodate your academic workload this term?

Time Management Reflection

What activities do you engage in for fun or recreation?

What do you do to relax or relieve stress?

Do you build these activities into your daily or weekly schedule?

Do you have a calendar for the current academic term that you carry with you? What about and up-to-date to-do list?

If yes to either, why? If no to either, why not?

If you carry neither a calendar nor a to-do list, why do you think you don't?

List your two most common sources of distraction while working. Next to each distraction, identify a strategy that you might use to reduce or eliminate it.

Source of Distraction   Strategy for Reducing This Distraction

1.

2.

1 Self-Assessment of Higher-Level Thinking Characteristics

Listed here are four general characteristics of higher-level thinkers accompanied by a set of traits related to each characteristic. When you read the traits listed beneath each of the general characteristics, place a checkmark next to any trait that you think is true of you.

Characteristics of Higher-Level Thinkers

1. **Tolerant and Accepting**
   - Keep emotions under control when someone criticizes their viewpoint
   - Do not tune out ideas that conflict with their own
   - Feel comfortable with disagreement
   - Are receptive to hearing different points of view

2. **Inquisitive and Open-Minded**
   - Are eager to continue learning new things from different people and different experiences
   - Have an inquiring mind that's genuinely curious, inquisitive, and ready to explore new ideas
   - Find differences of opinion and opposing viewpoints interesting and stimulating
   - Attempt to understand why people hold different viewpoints and try to find common ground between them

3. **Reflective and Tentative**
   - Suspend judgment until all the evidence is in, rather than making snap judgments before knowing the whole story
   - Acknowledge the complexity, ambiguity, and uncertainty associated with certain issues, and are willing to perhaps say, "I need to give this more thought," or "I need more evidence before I can draw a conclusion"
   - Take time to think things through before drawing conclusions, making choices, and reaching decisions
   - Periodically reexamine personal viewpoints to see whether they should be maintained or changed as a result of new experiences and evidence

4. **Honest and Courageous**
   - Give fair consideration to ideas that others may instantly disapprove of or find distasteful
   - Are willing to express personal viewpoints that may not conform to those of the majority
   - Are willing to change old opinions or beliefs when they are contradicted by new evidence
   - Are willing to acknowledge the limitations or weaknesses of their attitudes and beliefs

Look back at the list and count the number of checkmarks you placed in each of the four general areas:

1. Tolerant and Accepting = _____

2. Inquisitive and Open-Minded = _____

3. Relfective and Tentative = _____

4. Honest and Courageous = _____

For which characteristic did you have (a) the *most* checkmarks, (b) the *least* check? What do you think accounts for this difference?

1 Midterm Self-Evaluation

Since you are near the midpoint of this textbook, you may be near the midpoint of your first term in college. At this time of the term, you are likely to experience the midterm crunch—a wave of midterm exams and due dates for certain papers and projects. This may be a good time to step back and assess your academic progress thus far.

Use the form that follows to list the courses you're taking this term and the grades you are currently receiving in each of these courses. If you do not know what your grade is, take a few minutes to check your syllabus for your instructor's grading policy and add up your scores on completed tests and assignments; this should give you at least a rough idea of where you stand in your courses. If you're having difficulty determining your grade in any course, even after checking your course syllabus and returned tests or assignments, then ask your instructor how you could estimate your current grade.

	Course No.	Course Title	Instructor	Grade
1.				
2.				
3.				
4.				
5.				

Self-Assesment Questions

1. Were these the grades you were hoping for? Are you pleased or disappointed by them?

2. Were these the grades you expected to get? If not, were they better or worse than expected?

3. Do you see any patterns in your performance that suggest things you are doing well or things that you need to improve?

4. If you had to pinpoint one action you could immediately take to improve your lowest course grades, what would it be?

1 Wellness Self-Assessment and Self-Improvement

For each aspect of wellness listed here, rate yourself in terms of how close you are to doing what you should be doing.

	Nowhere Close to What I Should be Doing	Not Bad but Should Be Better	Right Where I Should Be
Nutrition			
Exercise			
Sleep			
Alcohol and Drugs			

For each area where there's a gap between where you are now and where you should be, identify the best action you could take to reduce or eliminate this gap.

Health and Wellness Reflection

What would you say are the three most important things that college students could do to maintain reserve their health and promote peak performance?

1.

2.

3.

1 Self-Assesment of Financial Attitudes and Habits

Answer the following questions as accurately and honestly as possible

		Agree	Disagree
1.	I pay my rent or mortgage on time each month.	————	————
2.	I avoid maxing out or going over the limit on my credit cards.	————	————
3.	I balance my checkbook each month.	————	————
4.	I set aside money each month for savings.	————	————
5.	I pay my phone and utility bills on time each month.	————	————
6.	I pay my credit card bills in full each month to avoid interest charges.	————	————
7.	I believe it's important to buy the things I want when I want them.	————	————
8.	Borrowing money to pay for college is a smart thing to do.	————	————
9.	I have a monthly or weekly budget that I follow.	————	————
10.	The thing I enjoy most about making money is spending money.	————	————
11.	I limit myself to one credit card.	————	————
12.	Getting a degree will get me a good job and good income.	————	————

Sources: Cude et al. (2006); Niederjohn (2008).

Give yourself a point for each item that you marked "agree"—except for item 7, 9, and 10. For these items, give yourself a point if you marked "disagree."

A perfect score on this short survey would be 12.

Self-Assesment Questions

1. What was your total score?

2. Which items lowered your score?

3. Do you detect any pattern across the items that lowered your score?

4. Do you see any realistic way(s) for improving your score on this test?

1 Gaining Awareness of Multi-Group Identities

We can be members of multiple groups at the same time, and our membership in these overlapping groups can influence our personal development and self-identity. In the figure that follows, consider the shaded center circle to be yourself and the six non-shaded circles to be six groups you belong to that you think have influenced your personal development or personal identity.

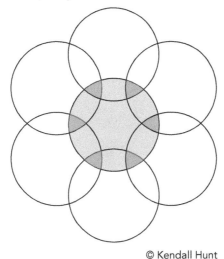

© Kendall Hunt

Fill in the non-shaded circles with the names of groups to which you belong that have had the most influence on your personal development. You can use the diversity spectrum that appears on the second page of this chapter to help you identify different groups. You don't have to come up with six groups and fill all six circles. What's important is to identify those groups that have had a major influence on your development and identity.

Self-Assesment Questions

1. Which one of the groups you identified has had the greatest influence on your personal identity? Why?

2. Have you ever felt limited or disadvantaged by being a member of any particular group or groups?

3. Have you ever felt that you experienced advantages or privileges because of your membership in any group or groups?

Educational Planning and Academic Decision Making Reflection

In addition to taking formal tests to assess your learning style, you can gain awareness of your learning style through some simple self-reflection. Take a moment to reflect on your learning style by completing the following statements:

I learn best if …

I learn most from …

I enjoy learning when …

Consider the following statement: "Choosing a major is a life-changing decision because it will determine what you do for the rest of your life."

Would you agree or disagree with this statement?

Why?

At this point in your college experience, are you decided or undecided about your major?

If you're undecided, what subjects might be possibilities?

If you're decided:

1. What is your choice?

2. How sure are you about your choice? (Circle one.)

    absolutely sure   fairly sure   not too sure   likely to change

Answer the following questions about a career you're considering or have chosen:

1. What attracted you to this career? (What led or caused you to become interested in it?)

2. Would you say that your interest in this career is characterized primarily by *intrinsic* motivation—something "inside" of you, such as your personal abilities, interests, needs, and values? Or, would you say that your interest in the career is driven by *extrinsic* motivation—something "outside" of you, such as starting salary, pleasing parents, or meeting expectations of your gender (i.e., an expected career role for a male or female)?

3. If money wasn't an issue and you could earn a comfortable living working in any career, would you choose the same career that you're currently considering?

Have you done volunteer work? If you have, did you learn anything about yourself or anything from your volunteer work that might help you identify careers that best match your interests, talents, and values?

Project yourself 10 years into the future and visualize your ideal career and your ideal life.

1. What are you spending most of your time doing during your typical workday?

2. Where and with whom are you working?

3. How many hours are you working per week?

4. Where are you living?

5. Are you married or in a committed relationship? Do you have children?

6. How does your work influence your home life?

From *Thriving in College and Beyond: Research-Based Strategies for Academic Success and Personal Development, 3rd Edition* by Joseph Cuseo, Aaron Thompson, Michele Campagna, and Viki S. Fecas.